The Apocalypse of the Birds

Edinburgh Studies in Religion in Antiquity

Series editors: Matthew V. Novenson, James B. Rives, Paula Fredriksen

Edinburgh Studies in Religion in Antiquity publishes cutting-edge research in religion in the ancient world. It provides a platform for creative studies spanning time periods (classical antiquity and late antiquity), geographical regions (the Mediterranean and West Asia), religious traditions (Greek, Roman, Jewish, Christian and more), disciplines (comparative literature, archaeology, anthropology, and more) and theoretical questions (historical, philological, comparative, redescriptive, and more). Deconstructing literary canons and confessional boundaries, the series considers and questions what we moderns call "religion" as a prominent feature of the human past and a worthy object of historical enquiry.

Advisory Board
Helen Bond, University of Edinburgh
Kimberley Czajkowski, University of Edinburgh
Benedikt Eckhardt, University of Edinburgh
Martin Goodman, University of Oxford
Oded Irshai, Hebrew University of Jerusalem
Timothy Lim, University of Edinburgh
Yii-Jan Lin, Yale University
Candida Moss, University of Birmingham
Paul Parvis, University of Edinburgh
Matthew Thiessen, McMaster University
Philippa Townsend, University of Edinburgh
Greg Woolf, University of California-Los Angeles

Books published in the series
Elena L. Dugan, *The Apocalypse of the Birds: 1 Enoch and the Jewish Revolt against Rome*
Megan S. Nutzman, *Contested Cures: Identity and Ritual Healing in Roman and Late Antique Palestine*
Matthew T. Sharp, *Divination and Philosophy in the Letters of Paul*

Visit the series webpage: https://edinburghuniversitypress.com/series-edinburgh-studies-in-religion-in-antiquity

The Apocalypse of the Birds
1 Enoch and the Jewish Revolt against Rome

Elena L. Dugan

Edinburgh University Press is one of the leading university presses in the UK. We publish academic books and journals in our selected subject areas across the humanities and social sciences, combining cutting-edge scholarship with high editorial and production values to produce academic works of lasting importance. For more information visit our website: edinburghuniversitypress.com

© Elena Dugan, 2023, 2024

Edinburgh University Press Ltd
13 Infirmary Street
Edinburgh, EH1 1LT
First published in hardback by Edinburgh University Press 2023

Typeset in 11/13 Bembo Std by
IDSUK (DataConnection) Ltd

A CIP record for this book is available from the British Library

ISBN 978 1 3995 0865 0 (hardback)
ISBN 978 1 3995 0866 7 (paperback)
ISBN 978 1 3995 0867 4 (webready PDF)
ISBN 978 1 3995 0868 1 (epub)

The right of Elena Dugan to be identified as the author of this work has been asserted in accordance with the Copyright, Designs and Patents Act 1988, and the Copyright and Related Rights Regulations 2003 (SI No. 2498).

Contents

List of Illustrations   vi
Acknowledgements   viii

Introduction: Absence of Evidence or Evidence of Absence?   1
1. On Subsidiary Works, Absent and Present from our Documents   16
2. The Nature of the Beast: Literary Evidence for Animal Apocalypse(s) of Enoch   39
3. Material Evidence for Animal Apocalypse(s) of Enoch   68
4. Dating the Animal Apocalypses   83
5. The Early Christian Readers of the Apocalypse of the Birds   105
6. The Apocalypse of the Birds and the First Jewish Revolt   139
7. On Animal Apocalypses in the First Century and Beyond   216

Appendix: An Annotated Apocalypse of the Birds (1 Enoch 89.59–90.42)   236
Bibliography   243
Index   263

Illustrations

Figures

3.1	Overlaps Between Qumran MSS of Vision of the Beasts	70
6.1	Eagle on Silver Tetradrachm of Galba. Antioch, 68–69 CE., American Numismatic Society	159
6.2	Eagle on Silver Denarius of Vespasian. Ephesus, 76 CE., American Numismatic Society	159
6.3	Aquila between Two Standards on Silver Denarius of Nero. Rome, AD 67–68. American Numismatic Society	166
6.4	Ibis [left] next to Reclining "Aegyptos." Silver Denarius of Hadrian. 134–38 CE., American Numismatic Society	184
6.5	Bronze Coin Countermarked by XII Fulminata with Thunderbolt and Eagle. Neopolis, Samaria. Domitian, 82–83 CE. BnF 1968/227	187
6.6	Legionaries with Feathered Crests, Bronze Sestertius of Gaius/Caligula. Rome, 39–40 CE. American Numismatic Society	192
6.7	Soldier with Helmet Feathers, Silver Denarius. Rome, 100 BCE. American Numismatic Society	194
6.8	"Jerusalem the Holy," Silver Shekel, Jerusalem, "Year 3." American Numismatic Society	206

Tables

1.1	Levels of Organization within 1 Enoch: 1 Enoch, Books and Subsections	11
1.2	Sections of the Book of the Watchers, Book of Dreams and Epistle of Enoch	18
1.3	Sections of 1 Enoch Attested at Qumran	19

1.4	Subsidiary Works of the Book of the Watchers in Ancient Documents	22
1.5	Subsidiary Works of the Epistle of Enoch in Ancient Documents	24
1.6	Subsidiary Works of the Book of Dreams in Ancient Documents	27
2.1	Summary, Protagonists and Antagonists of the Animal Apocalypse	46
2.2	Summary of Contents of Animal Apocalypse	52
2.3	Two Allegories within the Animal Apocalypse	53
2.4	Destruction of Jerusalem in Vision of the Beasts and Apocalypse of the Birds	57
3.1	Contents of the Animal Apocalypse Present and Absent at Qumran	68
3.2	Qumran Manuscripts of the Vision of the Beasts	69
4.1	Chronological Information in Apocalypse of the Birds	98
5.1	1 Enoch 89 and Barnabas 16	109
5.2	Common Elements in Passages Attributed to Enoch in the Testaments of the Twelve Patriarchs	115
5.3	Testament of Benjamin 9 and the Apocalypse of the Birds	122
5.4	"Corruptions" of 1 Enoch 90.37–8	126
5.5	Updated: Subsidiary Works of the Book of Dreams in Ancient Documents	136
6.1	The Babylonian and Persian–Hellenistic Period	146
6.2	The Beginning of the Roman Period	156
6.3	A *terminus ante quem* at 70 CE?	170
6.4	The Massacres of 66 CE	180
6.5	Resistance and the Calamity of Cestius	185
6.6	The Apocalypse of the Birds: A First Century Reading	209
6.7	The Apocalypse of the Birds: A Comparison of Approaches	210

Acknowledgements

This book is a revised version of my dissertation, defended at Princeton University in January of 2021. I gather that it is customary for young scholars to try and hide that fact a bit, so that the reader doesn't reflexively start reaching for their red grading pen. But in this case, it would be unfair to the reader, as the project was shaped by both the intellectual climate of Princeton, and the reality that it primarily developed during the extraordinary years of 2020 and 2021. Given my focus in the monograph on knowing the times and circumstances through which texts travel, I thought I would share my own, and express gratitude accordingly.

I want to thank my mentors at Princeton: Martha Himmelfarb, AnneMarie Luijendijk, Elaine Pagels, Moulie Vidas, and Ra'anan Boustan. From 2014–21, it was my great fortune to take their classes, read texts and talk shop in their offices, and learn from their wisdom and example. They were kind enough to read versions upon versions of the present work and this project was shaped immeasurably by their input and guidance. And my advisor, Martha Himmelfarb, went above and beyond to support me and encourage this project to develop in (to me) fun ways that it might not otherwise have done.

I am grateful to Patricia Bogdziewicz, Mary Kay Bodnar, and Kerry Smith for their magnificent stewardship of the Religion Department and the warm and supportive environment they create for every student who enters 1879 Hall.

I am grateful to the scholars who took time out of their lives to engage and read my work, and whose keen questions and generous welcome have grown this project. I would thank, in particular, Daniel Assefa, Wendy Belcher, Beth Berkowitz, Aaron Butts, John J. Collins, Ted Erho, Matthew Larsen, Liv Ingeborg Lied, Daniel Machiela, James Nati, Laura Quick, Madadh Richey, Annette Yoshiko Reed, Seth Sanders, Sarah Schwarz, Jillian Stinchcomb, Loren Stuckenbruck, Jack Tannous, and James VanderKam. I also had the opportunity to present and discuss pieces of this project with the participants of the

Yale University Hebrew Bible workshop, the Harvard University Workshop on Scribes, Texts, and Libraries in the Ancient World, and the Ancient Judaism Regional Seminar, and I am grateful for the feedback of all the participants.

Each one of my fellow graduate students in the Department of Religion, and the Religions of Mediterranean Antiquity subfield, at Princeton University impacted this project in their own way and contributed to creating a lovely and collegial community in which I worked among friends. I am grateful to A. J. Berkovitz, Madeleine Brown, Alyssa Cady, Djair Dias Filho, Nyle Fort, Adina Goldman, Eliav Grossman, Amit Gvaryahu, Rebekah Haigh, Jon Henry, Yedidah Koren, John LaDoeuceur, Ari Lamm, Yitz Landes, Mark Letteney, and Andrea Peecher.

Moreover, I must express deep gratitude to Raissa von Doetinchem de Rande, with whom I was so lucky to share a fearsome trio of experiences: new motherhood, motherhood during a pandemic, and the composition and defense of a dissertation. The book you are now holding could not have existed without her friendship and support.

I am grateful to my current research community at Harvard University's Department of Classics and the Center for Jewish Studies. And I am especially grateful to Paul Kosmin and David Stern, for helping me on board, and for asking careful and probing questions about the greater significance of my project.

I am grateful to my current department at Phillips Academy Andover. I have learned more from teaching with my colleagues in the Department of Philosophy and Religious Studies – Kiran Bhardwaj, Andrew Housiaux, Joshua Kissel, and Michael Legaspi – than I had ever thought possible. I am immeasurably lucky to work with these kind, funny, thoughtful colleagues and friends, and the imprint of our happy and supportive office should show in the fact that I somehow got this book to publication during my first year of teaching.

I am grateful to the wonderful editors, readers, and production managers of Edinburgh University Press, for helping bring this book into the material world. I am especially grateful to Matthew Novenson, who has been an encouraging and generous editor throughout.

I am grateful to Katrina Tosh, Maria Corinne Meara-Bainbridge, and Calandra Guasti, who have honored me with their friendship, and humbled me with their clear memories of middle school, for eighteen years. I am grateful to my sister and constant companion, Avra Dugan, who joined our quarantine and watched my daughter so that I could write, then picked me up off the floor when I was tired of writing. I am grateful to my grandmother, Patricia Dugan, who taught me to love reading and solving puzzles.

This project would not be the same without the help of all of the people whose names appear above, and more. Any errors or infelicities that remain in this work, of course, entirely belong to my partner, Michael Reed, who was supposed to check this over.

I am (nevertheless) grateful to Michael Reed, brilliant and kind, and the half that is my very own. In the extraordinary years of 2020 and 2021, he practiced sacrifice and joy on my behalf. And I am grateful to my daughter, Fia, who never let me float too far off the ground. I could not have done this without them.

I have dedicated this book to my mother, Maria Dugan, and my father, Douglas Dugan. Maria Dugan is a lifelong activist, joyful and accomplished nurse and counselor, and tireless advocate for all that is good and new in the world. Douglas Dugan is a famously determined question-asker, and a curious and thoughtful aide to voices that would otherwise go unheard. If there is much of value in this project, itself a quest for once-lost voices seeking to articulate hope in the most fragile of times, I credit it to them.

On that note, I would like to provide a reflection on the meaning of my work in the wake of the events of 2020. The Apocalypse of the Birds inhabits a strange kind of optimism. I will argue that this work reflects a time in which a revolution against Rome seemed to be going quite well. Within a few years, the tide turned, and what looked like it might be a successful revolution, wound up committed to the history-books (such as Josephus saw to inform them) as a failed revolt.

But there is something to be said for how lovely I have found it to discover voices of hope in the annals of a period I was used to viewing as a dismal and bloody fiasco. I do not mean to identify myself with one party in this now-two-millenia-old dispute or another. Nor do I mean to reclaim soon-to-be-crushed hopes as if they were a cheerful balm, instead of a sobering bummer.

Rather, I think we can all agree that we have recently lived through historical times in which a great many things have not gone as planned. The Animal Apocalypse does not teach us that everything is going to work out in the end, as sometimes it very much does not, but rather that hope can always be found, if you look a little closer.

This book features a few nods to J. R. R. Tolkien's *The Lord of the Rings*. In the third and final installment, Tolkien (in the personage of the elf Legolas) remarks that "oft hope is born when all is forlorn." With the benefit of hindsight, we know that the cause of the revolutionaries in Judaea was forlorn. And yet, as my work has helped to uncover, hope was born. I find that to be worthy of recognition, as an illustration of the very human capacity for hope, regardless of what is to come.

Elena Dugan
Andover, Massachusetts
August 2022

INTRODUCTION

Absence of Evidence or Evidence of Absence?

There are a few starting points for this project, but perhaps the most important comes from puzzling over the scholarly maxim that "absence of evidence is not evidence of absence." This is true, but an absence of evidence is also not evidence of presence.

The Dead Sea Scrolls represent an unexpected cache for the historian, offering new windows onto Second Temple Judaism and Early Christianity. But we often have tattered fragments of manuscripts, when we would prefer pristine productions, and what we might see by way of our new data-set is necessarily limited by our material remains. We can easily understand the draw of a "full" work, or even the possibility thereof. Even the way we articulate the remains, as "fragments," leaves conceptual room for the existence of a whole. However, some works attested at Qumran, where the Scrolls were found, are found nowhere else. Since Second Temple fragments are all we have, we quickly reach a limit on our reconstructions of literary wholes.[1]

Nevertheless, some works found at Qumran seem to be textually related to works found in other manuscript traditions; that is, the same text is found on leather scraps at Qumran, as is also found in late ancient or medieval parchment leaves or papyrus codices. The non-Qumran witnesses are often, materially, better preserved: less tattered and fragmentary, more continuous and perceptibly whole-looking. It is therefore easy to correlate superior material preservation with the hypothesis of better *textual* preservation, and assume that fuller documents best model the literary whole to which all our material remains attest.

---

[1] Some extensive but still demonstrably materially incomplete examples include: the War Scroll (esp. 1QM), the Genesis Apocryphon, and 4QInstruction.

1 Enoch, as I understand it, succinctly demonstrates the flaws of this logic in practice. 1 Enoch is the modern scholarly name for an Ethiopic work known as *Henok* (ሄኖክ).[2] 1 Enoch was likely translated into Gəʿəz between the fourth and sixth centuries CE.[3] But the text of 1 Enoch is not attested in manuscripts until the fourteenth century CE.[4] 1 Enoch contains a great deal of textual material that corresponds to that found in a set of Qumran fragments. Therefore, the Ethiopic is sometimes called the "fullest" or "complete" version of the work or works represented by our Qumran fragments.[5] The pressing question becomes how, and whether, to correlate earlier fragments to later documents, or to fill in the blanks of the earlier with the later. One of the perils of treating our earlier documents as if they were de facto fragmentary remains of the work known as 1 Enoch is that it might falsely enable the importation of text and textual expectations from later traditions to earlier contexts in which these never existed. That is, one might conceivably import 108 chapters of textual

---

[2] I have called the work Henok, though it is also known in Western scholarship under the title Maṣḥafa Henok Nabiy (መጽሐፈ ሄኖክ ነቢይ), or "the Book of Enoch the Prophet." Ted Erho and Loren T. Stuckenbruck have suggested, however, that the prominence of this title may have to do with its inclusion in the seventeenth century manuscript commissioned by James Bruce and translated by Richard Laurence, with which Europe was re-introduced to 1 Enoch, rather than its applicability to our evidence generally. Erho's recent cataloguing of new manuscript evidence, and analysis of their titles, indicates that the most common title is, more simply, *Henok* (ሄኖክ), though there is some variation among our evidence. See Ted M. Erho and Loren T. Stuckenbruck, "The Gəʿəz Manuscript Tradition and the Study of 1 Enoch: Problems and Prospects" (10th Enoch Seminar: Enoch and Enochic Traditions in the Early Modern period: A Reception History from the 15th to the end of the 19th Centuries, Florence, Italy, 2019).

[3] This date is awarded on analogy with the translation of other Jewish and Christian scriptures into Ethiopic. To my knowledge, there is minimal guidance on the date of the Ethiopic translation of 1 Enoch in particular.

[4] This gap between translation and attestation is not unique to Enoch in Ethiopia, as 99% of our Ethiopian manuscripts hail from the modern period. See Erho and Stuckenbruck, "Gəʿəz Manuscript Tradition." Further on the manuscript history of 1 Enoch, see Ted M. Erho and Loren T. Stuckenbruck, "A Manuscript History of Ethiopic Enoch," *Journal for the Study of the Pseudepigrapha* 23, no. 2 (2013): 87–133.

[5] In the formulation of Ephraim Isaac, "1 Enoch is found complete only in the Ethiopic version." Or, for a more nuanced phrasing by Loren T. Stuckenbruck still using the language of fullness, "This tradition, commonly associated with a document that in modern times has been designated as '1 Enoch' or 'Ethiopic Enoch' is preserved in its fullest form in Ethiopic manuscripts." See E. Isaac, "1 Enoch: A New Translation and Introduction," in *The Old Testament Pseudepigrapha*, ed. James H. Charlesworth, vol. 1 (London: Darton, Longman & Todd, 1983), 6; Loren T. Stuckenbruck, "The Early Traditions Related To 1 Enoch From The Dead Sea Scrolls: An Overview And Assessment," in *The Early Enoch Literature*, ed. Gabriele Boccaccini and John J. Collins, Supplements to the Journal for the Study of Judaism 121 (Leiden: Brill, 2007), 41. See the reasoned discussion of these terms, and cautionary warnings, in Michael A. Knibb, "Christian Adoption and Transmission of Jewish Pseudepigrapha: The Case of 1 Enoch," in *Essays on the Book of Enoch and Other Early Jewish Texts and Traditions* (Leiden: Brill, 2009), 63–5. Ultimately, he concludes "only the Ethiopic provides a *complete* text [emphasis mine]" (p. 64).

material from medieval Ethiopia into a far-distant, ancient context: Judaea in the second century BCE. Against this, the general scholarly opinion is that the work known as 1 Enoch in its 108-chaptered form does not have a Second Temple pedigree.[6] But exactly how this consensus view is applied to concrete historical and textual work varies in practice.

Accordingly, this project moves away from viewing our documents through the lens of the medieval work 1 Enoch, and towards letting our ancient documents guide our (modern) literary histories. In what follows, I demonstrate that a level of organization I call subsidiary works should be the literary wholes to which we correlate our ancient documents, and whose parameters we use to guide *and limit* any practices of textual restoration from the Ethiopic to other textual traditions. Therefore, if we find subsidiary works missing from Qumran, we should not be quick to restore them, either to the Qumran library or to Second Temple Judaea more generally.[7] Absence from the Scrolls is not in itself definitive proof of absence from the literature of the period, given the fragmentary nature of the corpus, but it does alert us to the necessity of mounting an argument for or against the existence of a subsidiary work during the Second Temple period on a case-by-case basis.

This observation of absence proves to be, ironically, quite generative. As I understand it, we are faced with a new and exciting task of reformulating our conception of where, exactly, the works absent from Qumran *were* present, and where we might newly spot sites of composition and transmission. These reconstructions might lead us back into Second Temple Judaea, but they also might not. Instead, attention to absence of subsidiary works from our documents at Qumran opens the way to compositional histories of works belonging to 1 Enoch that stretch past Qumran, perhaps even beyond Judaism, and into the common era. Subsidiary works absent from Qumran effectively lose their *terminus ante quem* – and this means they require new ones.

---

[6] E.g., the 2020 summary statement by Kelley Coblenz Bautch in the Textual History of the Bible's treatment of 1 Enoch (though note the designation of the Ethiopic collection as 'late antique,' in light of the hypothetical date of its purported translation and assembly, rather than 'medieval' in light of its documentary evidence): "Because we do not have evidence for the collection we call 1 Enoch prior to late antiquity a cautious approach is to refer only to individual booklets and to the form in which each circulated initially or alternatively to refer more generally to the Books of Enoch." In Kelley Coblentz Bautch, "5.1.1 Textual History of 1 Enoch," in *Textual History of the Bible*, ed. Armin Lange (Brill, February 19, 2020).

[7] The Scrolls were called a "library" in a more casual sense in the early years of their study. So, in Józef T. Milik's early monograph, there is a chapter called "The Qumrân Library." See Józef T. Milik, *Ten Years of Discovery in the Wilderness of Judaea*, Studies in Biblical Theology 26 (Naperville, IL: Alec R. Allenson Inc., 1959). Recently, this has received more extensive scholarly attention: see, for instance, the many articles in Sidnie White Crawford and Cecilia Wassen, eds., *The Dead Sea Scrolls at Qumran and the Concept of a Library*, Studies on the Texts of the Desert of Judah 116 (Boston: Brill, 2016).

This opening chapter will build on preceding scholarship to make such a case in the abstract, and demonstrate the pressing nature of this line of inquiry. In the process, I will set out and test the theoretical mettle of this kind of project. This chapter situates my research question – how to rediscover the missing subsidiary works – at the intersection of two evolving scholarly discourses: new/material philology, on the one hand, and the study of Jewish works in Christian transmission, on the other. These two avenues of research into ancient literature ask, in different ways, about how to correlate material documents with literary works, and how best to pursue and reconstruct compositional histories that precede our documents. Both encourage the prioritization of documents in our analysis and inspire my subsequent attention to the presence and absence of subsidiary works at Qumran. Moreover, both can be levied against ancient works as the grounds by which we disqualify their usage in earlier periods, as both emphasize the inextricability of text from documents. If our documents are relatively late, it becomes difficult to use the text found therein to speak to earlier contexts.

It is here, at this nexus, that my study will make a particular and fundamental contribution. The remainder of my study will set one work in its sights, the Animal Apocalypse, which is uniquely amenable to dating, thanks to its unusual attention to historical detail. Future chapters will propose a new provenance for this work in the environs of the first Jewish Revolt, a conclusion which should interest students of ancient Judaism and Christianity alike. But it is also my hope to introduce the Animal Apocalypse to a broader community of philologists, as a work whose proper setting and function has been obscured for many years by a confusion of philological categories. The Animal Apocalypse has been fundamentally misunderstood due to our privileging of modern scholarly imaginations of work over our ancient documents. When we begin with our manuscripts, the story unfolds rather differently.

Text, work, and document

I have called 1 Enoch a work, and spoken also of its text and documents. These nouns – work, text, and document – are often used interchangeably in the secondary literature.[8] I am going to be quite strict in the following exposition, because I think there is something coded within these distinctions that represents a tremendous advance for scholars of ancient Judaism and Christianity. It has to do with what we actually have (documents), and what we theorize (work and text). Let me define my terms, which I have borrowed

---

[8] The most common crossover is calling the entities that we have called "works" (e.g. 1 Enoch, 4 Ezra, Deuteronomy) "texts."

primarily from Liv Ingeborg Lied's pioneering work on text-criticism of "Old Testament Pseudepigrapha," such as 1 Enoch.[9]

I will use J. R. R. Tolkien's *The Lord of the Rings* as an example. I have chosen a modern example because it illustrates the operative function of these categories, especially that of "work," but also the ways that these terms can and should be invested with meaning outside of an author's intentions. In so doing, I want to debunk the hypothetical that there is one single correct way in which we might philologically parse 1 Enoch, if only we knew more about its composition or the intentions of its various writers and redactors.[10] In the case of *The Lord of the Rings*, we have substantial information about the author – himself a thoughtful philologist – his process of writing, and his reflections on his work. And yet, even if Tolkien had one singular vision of a work, and text belonging to that work, and the shape of documents attesting that text (which he likely did not, as the ongoing editing of the work over many decades indicates), this is not the only or even the best way that his readers have found to think about or enter into his literary vision of Middle Earth. So, I will introduce this tripartite schematic – work, text, and documents – but also the idea that this process of boundary-making is flexible and responsive to the vision of writer(s) and reader(s) alike. These categories are helpful heuristics that serve as a starting point – not a resting place – for further inquiry.

The Lord of the Rings is a work. Works are conceptual constructs that readers agree have enough in common with each other, and enough not-in-common with other entities, to be separated into their own category.[11] A work is at once

---

[9] Liv Ingeborg Lied, "Text–Work–Manuscript: What Is an 'Old Testament Pseudepigraphon'?," *Journal for the Study of the Pseudepigrapha* 25, no. 2 (2015): 150–65. Lied notes that her terms come from Matthew J. Driscoll, "The Words on the Page: Thoughts on Philology, Old and New," in *Creating the Medieval Saga: Versions, Variability, and Editorial Interpretations of Old Norse Saga Literature*, ed. Judy Quinn and Emily Lethbridge (Odense: University Press of Southern Denmark, 2010), 85–102. See also the use of these terms in the dissertation of Lied's student, Matthew Monger, on Jubilees, a project closely related to my own: Matthew Monger, "4Q216: Rethinking Jubilees in the First Century BCE" (PhD diss., MF Norwegian School of Theology, 2018), https://mfopen.mf.no/mf-xmlui/handle/11250/2491963

[10] Against, for instance, the intentionalism most recently and influentially defended by George Thomas Tanselle, who maintains a work is what the author had in mind, or intended to create. For an influential articulation of this intentionalist definition, see George Thomas Tanselle, *A Rationale of Textual Criticism* (Philadelphia: University of Pennsylvania Press, 1992), esp. 18–22. Note Lied's stated concern that it is this definition of work that is exclusively operative in modern studies of the pseudepigrapha, in Lied, "Text–Work–Manuscript," 153n5.

[11] Lied, "Text–Work–Manuscript," 5; Driscoll, "Words on the Page," 92–3. Note also the similar definition laid out by John Bryant, with the subsuming of intentions under the heading of a larger conception: "Work is a conceptualized notion of an intended literary creation, and as a conception it denotes a thing in its full and independent form. Of course, our only concrete sense of this concept is derived from the sum total of extant physical and inferred versions." In John Bryant, *The Fluid Text: A Theory of Revision and Editing for Book and Screen*, Editorial Theory and Literary Criticism (Ann Arbor: University of Michigan Press, 2002), 86.

the additive sum of all the documents existing, and the reduction of all those documents to a (subjective) core. For *The Lord of the Rings*, we might say it is the sum of all the printings ever published.

Work is, however, a nebulous enough category that it can be operative at multiple levels. Three books make up *The Lord of the Rings*: *The Fellowship of the Ring*, *The Two Towers*, and *The Return of the King*. These three are often recognized as works of their own, and are sometimes printed, bound, and circulated separately. J. R. R. Tolkien, ever the philologist, might not have granted that they were separate works (though the dictates of publishing expenses mandated they be published in three volumes), since he imagined them as one work: *The Lord of the Rings*. So, in August 1952, Tolkien wrote to his publisher: "I am anxious to publish 'The Lord of the Rings' as soon as possible . . . I believe it to be a great (though not flawless) work.'"[12] But the author is not in hegemonic control over the work function, and the three books can now be purchased both separately and bound together. Today we often use book covers to delineate the boundaries of a 'work' – often, for us, work is book, and it's as simple as that, though this mode of categorization does not transfer to antiquity.[13]

Work is ultimately a marker that readers use, more or less subjectively, to demarcate what *we* consider to be a literary unity. In the case of 1 Enoch, the operative "we" is modern scholarship, largely proceeding without reference to native Ethiopian traditions. Another operative "we" for the study of 1 Enoch, not pursued in this project, is the Ethiopic Orthodox tradition, as different understandings of works emerge from different vantage points.[14] Intuitions of coherence, at least theoretically, take no small guidance from the horizons opened up by a writer, but are not entirely dependent upon them. After all, there can be different demarcations. So, I will also use below the category of "subsidiary work," which means roughly what it sounds like – a work within a work. By this, I mean to indicate that scholars have perceived two levels of literary wholeness, something like how *The Two Towers* might be deemed a subsidiary work of *The Lord of the Rings*.[15] In the case of 1 Enoch, subsidiary

---

[12] As quoted in Wayne G. Hammond, *J. R. R. Tolkien: A Descriptive Bibliography*, Winchester Bibliographies of 20th Century Writers (Newcastle, Delaware: Oak Knoll Books, 1993), 87.

[13] For a modern genealogy of the book, see Roger Chartier and Peter Stallybrass, "What Is a Book?," in *The Cambridge Companion to Textual Scholarship*, ed. Neil Fraistat and Julia Flanders (Cambridge: Cambridge University Press, 2013), 188–204.

[14] On the reception of 1 Enoch in the Ethiopian Orthodox tradition, see Bruk Ayele Asale, *1 Enoch as Christian Scripture: A Study in the Reception and Appropriation of 1 Enoch in Jude and the Ethiopian Orthodox Tewahədo Canon* (Eugene, OR: Pickwick Publications, 2020).

[15] Over and against the possible objections of Tolkien himself – remember that we have tied the ability to define a work to the work's readership, rather than assuming the author controls it entirely.

works are sections of 1 Enoch in which scholars have perceived some sort of coherence, and thus track to independent sites of composition.[16]

Then we have "text." Text is a series of words in a particular order. When I was younger, I accessed the work of *The Lord of the Rings* by reading the text of the 1994 HarperCollins edition. Had I read the 1956 Allen & Unwin edition, I would have been completely without the appendix of family trees and other (crucial!) details that Tolkien readied for publication only in 1965. I would never have known, for instance, that the hobbit Merry eventually married Estella Bolger, the sister of his childhood best friend. The force of this textual variation (which may, or may not, be sufficient to convince us that we should call these two printed editions different versions[17]) does not travel up the chain and alter our previous categorization. *The Lord of the Rings* is still the same work, according to most readers. Even if Tolkien tinkered with the text over time, it is generally understood that the "before" and "after" of his editing represent the same work. And so, text is words-in-order (even though the order of the words is subject to change!)

An artifact, or document, or manuscript, is a text-bearing object.[18] My copy of *The Lord of the Rings* has dirt on it from its time traveling with me to Alaska. Note that my travel mishaps have no necessary impact going up the chain to our conceptualization of text. The 1994 HarperCollins edition of *The Lord of the Rings* is, of course, dirt-free. I would also note that my personal copy of *The Lord of the Rings* is an omnibus – all three subsidiary works bound as one. This is an unusual documentary manifestation of the text of *The Lord of the Rings*, as most copies that I have seen bind the three works separately. But these documents are, nevertheless, the only ways that we have of accessing the text. None can enter into Tolkien's mind and find a master-text to supersede that attested in any or all of our documents.

So, we have started at the top and gone down, conceptually. A work is not the same as a text, but a text can attest a work. A text is not the same as a document, but a document can attest a text. These levels should not be collapsed. We should not mistake text for work, or work for text, and so on.

My use of these terms, and the questions which I understand their particular use to open up, is deeply indebted to a movement in the study of texts

---

[16] I am simplifying at this point in order to establish a terminology with which to speak going forwards. I directly engage the methodological difficulties of establishing coherence, and the relationship between "coherence" and the identification of a work or subsidiary work, with specific reference to source criticism of the Hebrew Bible and apocalyptic literature in Chapter 2.

[17] For the definition of versions employed here, see Bryant, *The Fluid Text*, 88–90.

[18] This definition is the most straightforward and widely used of the three. Note that this is not the same use as "document" in contradistinction with "literary," e.g. in discussing documentary papyri from Oxyrhynchus (receipts, legal notices, etc.), vs. literary papyri (Gospel of Thomas etc.).

sometimes called New Philology or Material Philology.[19] New or Material Philology is associated with a variety of interventions, such as a) a suspicion of models of textual development which rest on a single author working at a single moment,[20] b) an expectation that textual fluidity was constitutive of both transmission *and* composition,[21] c) a critique of modern textual editions which house a singular text and in so doing designate and demote "variants,"[22] d) discomfort with the ideological underpinnings of classical philology,[23] and e) a general call to greater focus on materiality and the inextricable embeddedness of all text in documents.[24] These questions can be directed towards all literary products – ancient, medieval and modern alike – but often take particular form depending on the era concerning which a particular scholarly inquiry is directed.

For those engaged in the study of pre-modern works, Lied and Hugo Lundhaug have summarized the intervention succinctly: "at the heart of new philology is a focus on the material artifact constituted by the manuscript."[25] Using the tripartite schema outlined above, the fundamental insistence of New/Material Philology in the study of ancient and medieval literature is that we must begin with our historical documents, rather than (our modern estimation of) works.[26]

A new/material philological analysis of 1 Enoch could prompt a number of avenues of research.[27] From this network of possible queries, I wish to isolate one question which will ground the analysis in this chapter: what do our manuscripts

---

[19] A much-cited summary statement can be found in Stephen G. Nichols, "Introduction: Philology in a Manuscript Culture," *Speculum* 65, no. 1 (1990): 1–10. See also Stephen G. Nichols, "Why Material Philology? Some Thoughts," *Zeitschrift für Deutsche Philologie* 116, no. 13 (1997): 12.

[20] E.g. Jerome J. McGann, *A Critique of Modern Textual Criticism* (Chicago: University of Chicago Press Chicago, 1983).

[21] E.g. Bryant, *The Fluid Text*; John Bryant, "Witness and Access: The Uses of the Fluid Text," *Textual Cultures*, 2007, 16–42.

[22] E.g. Bernard Cerquiglini, *In Praise of the Variant: A Critical History of Philology*, trans. Betsy Wing (Baltimore: Johns Hopkins University Press, 1999).

[23] For some field-specific explorations of the origins and legacy of classical (e.g. Lachmannian) philology, see Yii-Jan Lin, *The Erotic Life of Manuscripts: New Testament Textual Criticism and the Biological Sciences* (New York: Oxford University Press, 2016); Brennan W. Breed, *Nomadic Text: A Theory of Biblical Reception History* (Bloomington: Indiana University Press, 2014), esp. 15–93.

[24] E.g. Richard Trachsler, "How to Do Things with Manuscripts: From Humanist Practice to Recent Textual Criticism," *Textual Cultures*, 2006, 5–28.

[25] Liv Ingeborg Lied and Hugo Lundhaug, eds., *Snapshots of Evolving Traditions: Jewish and Christian Manuscript Culture, Textual Fluidity, and New Philology*, Texte und Untersuchungen zur Geschichte der altchristlichen Literatur 175 (Boston: De Gruyter, 2017), 6.

[26] An introduction to new/material philology as applied to ancient Jewish and Christian works is provided in Lied and Lundhaug, 1–19. See also Monger, "4Q216: Rethinking Jubilees," 1–31; Michaël Langlois, "Les Manuscrits de La Mer Morte à l'aune de La Philologie Matérielle," *Revue d'Histoire et de Philosophie Religieuses* 95, no. 1 (2015): 3–31.

[27] One might pursue things, for instance, on the level of text, interrogating the extent to which our textual attestations of a verse or a chapter can vary from manuscript to manuscript, or documentary tradition to tradition (e.g. Aramaic vs. Greek vs. Gəʿəz).

have to teach us about the literary history of 1 Enoch? Or, said differently: what do our documents have to tell us about the history of (1) Enochic works?

What is (not) 1 Enoch & what is in a name

1 Enoch is a title modern scholars have come up with to designate a work extant only in Gəʿəz. 108 chapters is the usual length stated, though that chapter breakdown is not a consistent feature of the Gəʿəz manuscript tradition.[28] In Gəʿəz this work is called simply, Henok, and it is broken by both our manuscript tradition and modern scholars into five pieces. Materially speaking, five sections of text are often separated from one another in the Gəʿəz tradition that transmitted 1 Enoch with the help of internal rubrications, the use of red text to mark off a new section.[29] This is an unusual happenstance in Ethiopic scribal tradition, and likely reflects a five-booked Greek Vorlage.[30] Modern scholars have titled these five sections the Book of the Watchers, the Book of Parables, the Book of the Luminaries, the Book of Dreams, and the Epistle of Enoch, though they are not necessarily named as such in the Gəʿəz manuscript tradition.[31]

---

[28] For instance, in a private communication from September 14, 2018, Loren T. Stuckenbruck notes that the sixteenth-century Cambridge manuscript 1570 (dated 1588) is the first instance of all 108 chapters being explicitly numbered from beginning to end. Earlier manuscripts (for instance, Lake Tana 9) do not provide this chapter breakdown, though the text transmitted is of the same overall length.

[29] According to a private communication with Ted Erho, June 25, 2019.

[30] Whether this internal divisioning stems from a pre-existent divisioning in a Greek Vorlage cannot be proven with reference to any of our extant Greek documents, each of which preserves only one of the five sections later demarcated in Gəʿəz. It is therefore also possible that the internal rubrications point to the combination of multiple, independently circulating works into one super-work at the time of translation into Gəʿəz, or at some early point in Ethiopic transmission history. But note the comments of Knibb, who regards it as "virtually certain" that a five-booked Enoch had already coalesced in Greek, and became the Vorlage for the Ethiopic, in Michael A. Knibb, "The Book Of Enoch Or Books Of Enoch? The Textual Evidence For 1 Enoch," in *The Early Enoch Literature*, ed. Gabriele Boccaccini and John J. Collins, Supplements to the Journal for the Study of Judaism 121 (Leiden: Brill, 2007), 28.

[31] There are two different ways that modern titles relate to what we know about the history of each of the five books. In two cases, the Book of the Watchers and the Epistle of Enoch, the book is titled by modern scholars in keeping with evidence for a title in Greek sources, even though no corresponding title exists to my knowledge in Gəʿəz tradition. So, the Book of the Watchers is named in keeping with Syncellus' statement on the source of his Enochic extract: ἐκ τοῦ πρώτου βιβλίου (or λόγου) Ἑνώχ περὶ τῶν ἐγρηγόρων, which is taken for a kind of title. The Book of the Watchers is not named as such in the Gəʿəz manuscript tradition. The Epistle of Enoch gets its title from the clear subscription to the Greek Chester Beatty/Michigan manuscript, which reads, "Ἐπιστολή Ἑνώχ." This is also not named as such in the Gəʿəz manuscript tradition.

In the case of the Book of Parables, Book of the Luminaries, and Book of Dreams, scholars have extracted titles from introductory phrases within the book (which are not necessarily

The fact that these sections of text are mostly called "books" points to the conviction of modern scholars that these five represent separate works.[32] The splitting of one textual set, the work of *Henok*, into five "books" is anchored in scholarly suspicions that different authors, or communities, were responsible for each of these five works.[33] For modern scholars of Enoch, the work function is controlled by considerations having to do with probable sites of composition.[34] (Note that, very often, the entity that I am calling a "work" is called a "source" within the study of Enoch.) At the same time, a consensus about multiple sites of composition highlights the anthological character of 1 Enoch. In this way, it could be contrasted with scholarship on similar works such as Jubilees (also a work extant in its longest form in Gəʿəz, with paralleling text found on small Qumran fragments), which some scholars still treat as a unified composition, and proposals for multi-stage compositional models have not been greeted with universal agreement (which is not to say they are impossible).[35] 1 Enoch, however, is an obvious and widely recognized product of historical practices of collection, which should gear us up to expect a more extended process of development for its included text.

scribally marked as titles in the Gəʿəz manuscripts from which the text is extracted.) So, the title "Book of Parables" comes from 1 En 37.5, where the Gəʿəz states that Enoch will expound upon three parables, though a better candidate for a title might be 1 En 37.1, where Enoch introduces his "Second Vision which he saw." The Book of the Luminaries is similarly extracted from the Gəʿəz textual tradition. 1 En 82:1 introduces, as R. H. Charles translates it, "the book of the courses of the luminaries." See R. H. Charles, *The Book of Enoch or, 1 Enoch: Translated from the Editor's Ethiopic Text* (Oxford: Clarendon Press, 1912), 147. (Note that there are such substantial differences between the Gəʿəz Book of the Luminaries, and the Aramaic Astronomical Book, that many scholars use two different titles to denote their recognition of textual variance culminating in understanding two different works.) Finally, the Book of Dreams is a title used by modern scholars with some parallels in the Gəʿəz text, as 1 En 83.1 introduces Enoch's "visions (ራእያት, *raʾəyatä*)." Both visions are later described as dreams (see 1 En 83.7 and 85.1), and thus "Book of Dreams" caught on as a more descriptive title. The "Animal Apocalypse" is not a title known to the Gəʿəz tradition, to my knowledge.

[32] Note that I have included the qualifier that this is the conviction of *modern* scholars. Nineteenth-century scholarship, in particular, dreamed up a panoply of ways of breaking down the purported compositional layers of 1 Enoch. See the literature cited in Chapter 4.

[33] I am simplifying a bit for the purposes of clarity, as most specialists recognize the book to be split into five parts, but with caveats – usually, one or two appendices at the end (1 En 106–7 & 1 En 108). This 5+1 or 5+2 schema is "accepted by almost every scholar who has worked on this text for the last 150 years," as in George W. E. Nickelsburg, *1 Enoch 1*, ed. Klaus Baltzer, Hermeneia – A Critical and Historical Commentary on the Bible (Minneapolis: Fortress Press, 2012), 2.

[34] See the treatment of "Unity as a claim about authorship," which I understand to be the operative function here, alongside "unity as a judgment about textual features," and "unity as a phenomenological postulate about all reading," in Andrew Teeter and William A. Tooman, "Standards of (In) Coherence in Ancient Jewish Literature," *Hebrew Bible and Ancient Israel* 9, no. 2 (2020): 101–3.

[35] See the reflections on scholarship of Jubilees in Hindy Najman and Eibert Tigchelaar, "Unity after Fragmentation," *Revue de Qumran* 26, no. 4 (2014): 495–500.

Table 1.1 Levels of Organization within 1 Enoch: 1 Enoch, Books and Subsections

1 Enoch	"Book"	Subsections[a]
1 Enoch	Book of the Watchers	Oracle of Enoch (1 En 1–5)
		Rebellion of the Watchers (1 En 6–11)
		Enoch's Interaction with the Fallen Watchers (1 En 12–16)
		Enoch's Journey to the Northwest (1 En 17–19)
		Enoch's Journey Eastward (1 En 20–36)
	Book of Parables	Superscription and Introduction (1 En 37)
		The First Parable (1 En 38–44)
		The Second Parable (1 En 45–57)
		The Third Parable (1 En 58–69)
		A Set of Concluding Appendices (1 En 70–1)
	Astronomical Book	The Law of the Sun, Moon, Lunar Year (1 En 72–4)[b]
		The Angelic Leaders, Twelve Winds and Four Quarters (1 En 74–7)
		The Sun and the Moon (1 En 78)
		Enoch and Uriel's Summary (1 En 79–80)
		Enoch views the Heavenly Tablets, Instructs Methuselah (1 En 81–2)
		The Law of the Stars (1 En 82)
	Book of Dreams	Enoch's First Dream Vision: The Flood (1 En 83–4)
		The Animal Apocalypse (1 En 85–90)
	Epistle of Enoch	Introduction (1 En 92)
		Apocalypse of Weeks (1 En 93, 91)
		Body of the Epistle (1 En 94–105)
		Book of Noah (1 En 106–7)
		Eschatological Exhortation (1 En 108)

[a] I discuss below how, in the case of the Book of the Watchers, Book of Dreams, and Epistle, scholars generally accept that these subsections represent some sort of independent compositions. I therefore come to consider these divisions to mark off subsidiary works. This chart exists only to show different levels of organization within 1 Enoch.
[b] I have compressed the multiple sections into groupings of the Astronomical Book solely for the purposes of concise illustration in this chart, an imprecision hopefully justified by the fact that the Astronomical Book will not be addressed further in this study.

Within some of these five books, it is further possible to discern multiple subsidiary textual units that we might call works. These are entities apparently stemming from independent sites of composition before being assembled together within one of the five books. Within the Epistle of Enoch (1 En 91–108), the Book of Noah (1 En 106–7) and Eschatological Exhortation (1 En 108) are generally recognized to be originally independent appendices.

Similarly, the Apocalypse of Weeks (1 En 93, 91) is separable from the longer-form social and ethical ruminations often called the Body of the Epistle (1 En 94–105). The Book of Dreams (1 En 83–90) contains two dreams, which may represent two separate works, meaning (as we have established the function of the term "work" above) that they would represent two separate hypothesized sites of composition.

So, there are at least three conceptual levels at which we might identify a "work" using the text of Ethiopic Henok: the level of the totality (called 1 Enoch by modern scholars), the level of the five books, and the level of the identifiable subsidiaries of the five books.

Not everyone agrees that these textual subsidiaries are to be classed as works. Lied cautions that scholars are prone to excerpt text from certain works, and treat these excerpts as works in and of themselves. She warns that these "works" have insufficient evidence speaking in favor of their autonomy from the larger works in which they are attested, or their historical existence as discrete products.[36] In other words, our documents should provide primary guidance on how to construe works. Over the course of this chapter, I will take Lied's critique gradually on board, as I test scholarly hypotheses about the subsidiaries against the metric of documentary attestation. But it is important to note that much of the history of scholarship on Enoch has proceeded on the hypothesis that the work function is tied to concerns about authorship. The basic definitional problem at hand is how to classify identifiable moments of textual growth. For Lied, identifiable moments of textual growth might not represent works, especially if they do not ever stand alone or circulate separately from the larger works in which they are attested. In some scholarship on Enoch, identifiable moments of textual growth have been treated as if they were works – as "sources" traceable to certain compositional contexts, that might be independently evaluated. Ultimately, the assignation of "work" to a moment of textual growth is case-dependent. We should, then, test some cases, and allow our documents to tell us about identifiable moments of textual growth. In order to begin, however, we need to get a better grasp on what is, and is not, in our documents of Enoch.

With reference to our non-Ethiopian documents, what we should be seeking is the closest possible match between work, text, and document. We should be able to signal in our descriptions of the documents the work that is attested, without speculatively restoring large quantities of text in the naming of the document. It is important to be alert to the challenge posed by Annette Yoshiko Reed (here speaking about "subdocuments," by which she means the five books) that:

---

[36] E.g. the Book of Noah in the *More Old Testament Pseudepigrapha* volume on which her article comments. See Lied, "Text–Work–Manuscript," 153–65.

just because the fragments from Qumran correspond with verses from certain subdocuments that we can delineate in 1 Enoch, scholars typically presume that these fragments attest these very subdocuments in the same form, scope, and order now preserved in the collection 1 Enoch.[37]

What do we find if we do not "presume"? As it turns out, perhaps more than we bargained for.

Summary

In what follows, material philology and the revelation of absence among our documents will disrupt the scholarly consensus that the entirety of the Animal Apocalypse belongs to the Maccabean Revolt. Instead, I will propose that a crucial piece of 1 Enoch belongs in first-century CE Roman Judaea – specifically, to the world of the First Jewish Revolt.

I begin in the first chapter by embarking on a detailed survey of where pieces of 1 Enoch appear in our pre-Ethiopic documentary record – what parts of 1 Enoch do we have before the fourteenth century CE, and where? In providing this textured report, we can notice not only patterns of presence, but also of absence. And the newly discovered absence of pieces of Enoch from our earliest manuscripts is, I argue, an opportunity – an open window to reconsider new possible presences, and new histories of composition for Enoch. Unfortunately, most of the missing subsidiary works of Enoch largely resist dating on internal grounds, making the task of re-presencing difficult. However, there is one subsidiary work within Enoch that is considered to be uniquely datable in accordance with its detailed historical allusions – the Animal Apocalypse. And nobody, up until this point, has noticed that the Animal Apocalypse breaks into two, with only one of those works attested at Qumran.

It is the task of my next two chapters to make this very argument. In Chapter 2, it is proposed that the Animal Apocalypse as extant in Ethiopic manuscripts breaks into two separate works on literary grounds, with particular reference to terminological and thematic differences between the two. But I am cautious about enacting source criticism on purely literary grounds, and therefore embark on a quest to confirm my hypothesis with reference to our material record in Chapter 3. I observe that only one of these works is attested among the Dead Sea Scrolls, and likely belongs to the world of second-century BCE Judaea. The other, comprising the portion of the text that brings the allegorical history into the post-exilic era and leads into the eschaton, is

---

[37] In Annette Yoshiko Reed, "The Textual Identity, Literary History, and Social Setting of 1 Enoch," *Archiv Für Religionsgeschichte* 5, no. 1 (2003): 290.

14　THE APOCALYPSE OF THE BIRDS

not attested at Qumran. With literary indicators that the Apocalypse of Enoch splits into two works, alongside material evidence for absence of one of these works, I arrive at a new description of the Animal Apocalypse of Enoch. One work, the Vision of the Beasts (1 En 84.1–89.58), is present and accounted for by the second century BCE. One work, the Apocalypse of the Birds (1 En 89.59–90.42) is, as yet, missing, and needs to be re-dated.

　The task of the book from Chapter 4 on is the ascertainment of a new provenance for the Apocalypse of the Birds. To begin, I must demonstrate the weakness of the current consensus that the work belongs to the Maccabean period. Previous scholarship, assuming a second-century BCE *terminus ante quem*, read the work as if it were obviously a product of the second century BCE. But in Chapter 4, I note the shortcomings of these approaches, and a lack of consensus within the literature. Everybody has agreed, for decades, that the Animal Apocalypse had to be a Hellenistic-era work because of its Hellenistic-era manuscripts – but there is very little consensus on how, exactly, that conversation between text and context took place. Disagreement on the chronology of the text, the identification of key historical figures, and the importance (or character) of intertextual parallels will all be discussed, with the outcome that the Apocalypse of the Birds will be decoupled from the literature and history of the Hellenistic era.

　It then becomes time to actually find the work itself in historical time, as we must now ask where and when the Apocalypse of the Birds surfaced before fourteenth-century Ethiopia. Chapter 5 finds evidence of a second-century CE readership (Barnabas and the Testaments of the Twelve Patriarchs), and thereby provides an external *terminus ante quem* for the work. I also demonstrate that these early readers interpret the Apocalypse of the Birds as a prophecy of the events of the first century CE. This match of text to events would represent a curious and unexpected reception history to those committed to a Hellenistic-era Animal Apocalypse, but paves the way for my own re-reading of the work as a composition of the first-century.

　Finally, Chapter 6 is the payoff, arguing at length that the historical allusions in the Apocalypse of the Birds most closely match the First Jewish Revolt. I provide a full interpretation of the text as an account of the early Revolt, matching the allegorical characters and narratives to the events of the first century CE. I suggest that the account of the Persian–Hellenistic period is (as is not unusual in Jewish historiography) compressed to make way for Roman events, that the eagles of 1 En 90.2–16 are best interpreted as Romans, that the inciting events of the Apocalypse are the massacres of 66 CE, that the rams are to be equated with the early Judaean resistance, and that the rebuffed siege of the ravens refers to the unexpected and infamous defeat of Cestius Gallus by the rebel forces. This chapter demonstrates that the Apocalypse of the Birds, given the second-century CE *terminus ante quem* established by our early readers, is most readily matched to the early Jewish Revolt. Finally, my work in this chapter brings the argument full circle – the demonstrable functionality of the Apocalypse of the Birds in the first century CE demonstrates that we were right to suspect the absence of this work from the Scrolls. Absence of evidence, in this case, seems to have been real evidence of absence.

In my final chapter, I provide a new summation and contextualization of the Apocalypse of the Birds among first-century CE literature, with particular attention to the implications for the study of Paul, first-century apocalyptic (Revelation, 4 Ezra, 2 Baruch, the Synoptic tradition), and the methodology of dating of the New Testament. I reflect on the Animal Apocalypse as a literary tradition with energy and life, one that effloresced into the Vision of the Beasts and the Apocalypse of the Birds. And I confirm my model of an energetic Animal Apocalypse by identifying a small work I call the "Little Animal Apocalypse", hidden in the Armenian Testaments of the Twelve Patriarchs.

In this way, what seems at first to be a simple methodological move inspired by New Philology – resisting the urge to restore later text around earlier fragments – reveals the lost voices of revolutionaries from the First Jewish Revolt, a dynamic and evolving animal apocalyptic tradition, and a startling new perspective on the history and literature of the first century CE.

CHAPTER 1

On Subsidiary Works, Absent and Present from our Documents

This chapter will test out the hypothesis that subsidiary works, and not 1 Enoch or the five books of Enoch, are the literary wholes to which our documents best attest, and in which ancient readers were most demonstrably invested. Said differently, rather than asking our manuscripts to reveal what parts of 1 Enoch they contain, we should be asking at a slightly lower level of literary organization, and cataloging our evidence accordingly. The purpose of this chapter is to try and find the correct balance between map and territory, and to create a catalog that is usefully (but not excessively!) detailed concerning what we actually do have in our documents, so that we might better realize what we do not.

As noted above, five books make up Ethiopic Henok. The secondary literature is generally cautious when it comes to restoring the text of two of these books to Second Temple Judaea. The first, the Book of Parables, is entirely absent from the remains recovered at Qumran, leading to wild speculation about where and when it might have been written before appearing for the very first time in the material record of fourteenth-century Ethiopia.[1] Since it does not appear in the non-Ethiopic material record, we will leave it aside for now. The second, the Book of the Luminaries, appears in such different forms at Qumran versus its purported Ethiopic "equivalent" that many scholars talk about an Aramaic Astronomical Book as a very different work from that which appears as Book 3 of Ethiopic Henok, though with some textual overlap.[2] This leaves the

---

[1] For one recent survey of research, see Darrell L. Bock, "Dating the Parables of Enoch: A Forschungsbericht," in *Parables of Enoch: A Paradigm Shift*, ed. James H. Charlesworth and Darrell L. Bock (London: Bloomsbury, 2012), 58–113. For a critique of overconfidence in dating of the Parables, see Ted M. Erho, "Historical-Allusional Dating and the Similitudes of Enoch," *Journal of Biblical Literature* 130, no. 3 (2011): 493–511.

[2] So, note the comment of James VanderKam: "It is obvious, in comparing the Aramaic (the Astronomical Book) and the Ethiopic (the Book of the Luminaries), that something drastic happened in the journey from one to the other." In James C. VanderKam, *1 Enoch 2: A Commentary on the Book of 1 Enoch: Chapters 37–82*, Hermeneia – A Critical and Historical Commentary on the Bible (Minneapolis: Fortress Press, 2012), 351.

Book of the Watchers, the Book of Dreams, and the Epistle as the three books whose text is often confidently imagined to belong in the library of Second Temple literature.[3]

Even if we narrow our inquiry to tracking the appearance of three of the five Enochic books in our pre-Ethiopic material record, we are not yet at the simplest level of our textual building blocks [Table 1.2]. These three books have long been recognized to be composite in and of themselves, made up of various textual sections. In keeping with our definitions above, these textual sections stemming back to independent sites of composition would mean they represent works in their own right. As might be expected, the exact delineation of subsidiary works varies from scholar to scholar. But, for the purposes of illustration, I will use the sections adopted for the popular Hermeneia translation of 1 Enoch, by the eminent Enoch scholars George W. E. Nickelsburg and James VanderKam, noting different source-critical breakdowns in the footnotes.

We can now observe that not every subsidiary work identified by scholars is attested at Qumran. Below is a table [Table 1.3] indicating the attestation, or non-attestation, of these three books of 1 Enoch and their subsidiary works at Qumran.[4] I have bolded the sections which are likely **absent**:

The above categorization of data indicates a few things. On the one hand, we have at least three copies apiece of five of the *present* subsidiary works. (Note also that four of these triply attested works belong to the Book of the Watchers.) These manuscripts occasionally overlap in the pieces of text they attest, but more importantly may indicate that the vagaries of transmission

---

[3] The most expedient way to demonstrate this is to summarize the conclusions of Nickelsburg's influential commentary. He suggests that the "compositional and redactional process that led to the compilation of traditions in 4QEn^c [i.e. the Book of the Watchers, Book of Dreams, and Epistle of Enoch] concluded before the turn of the era." Though Nickelsburg does not assume that the Qumran Aramaic is necessarily the direct ancestor of all our later evidence, the assumption is that in the common era, there was no further large-scale modification of these three books of 1 Enoch. From that point forward, a line can be drawn from Second Temple Judaea straight to Ethiopia, as Ethiopic Enoch was "translated from a Greek translation of the Aramaic original." See Nickelsburg, *1 Enoch 1*, 26, 15. Note, however, the critique of this unilinear model of development in Reed, "Textual Identity."

[4] This is a fragment corresponding to 1 En 8.4–9.3, first published by Hanan Eshel and Esther Eshel. In recent years, it has been flagged as a possible forgery by Michael Langlois, in a group publication with other scholars debunking fragments sold since 2002. And in 2018 Årstein Justnes and Torleif Elgvin made a full case for the reclassification of this fragment as a forgery. See Esther Eshel and Hanan Eshel, "New Fragments from Qumran: 4Q226, 8QGen, and XQpapEnoch," *Dead Sea Discoveries* 12, no. 2 (2005): 134–57; Michael Langlois et al., "Nine Dubious 'Dead Sea Scrolls' Fragments from the Twenty-First Century," *Dead Sea Discoveries* 24, no. 2 (2017): 189–228; Årstein Justnes and Torleif Elgvin, "A Private Part of Enoch: A Forged Fragment of 1 Enoch 8:4–9:3," in *Wisdom Poured Out Like Water: Studies on Jewish and Christian Antiquity in Honor of Gabriele Boccaccini*, Deuterocanonical and Cognate Literature Studies 38 (Berlin: De Gruyter, 2018), 195–203. I find Justnes and Elgvin's case convincing, and will not treat XQPapEnoch further.

Table 1.2 Sections of the Book of the Watchers, Book of Dreams and Epistle of Enoch

Book	Chapters	Subsection
Book of the Watchers[a]	1–5	Oracle of Enoch
	6–11	Rebellion of the Watchers
	12–16	Enoch's Interaction with the Fallen Watchers
	17–19	Enoch's Journey to the Northwest
	21–36	Enoch's Journey Eastward
Book of Dreams[b]	83–4	Enoch's First Dream Vision: The Flood
	85–90.42	"The Animal Apocalypse"[c]
Epistle of Enoch[d]	91	A Narrative Bridge
	93, 91	Apocalypse of Weeks
	94–105	Body of the Epistle
	106–7	Book of Noah
	108	Eschatological Exhortation

[a] The hypothesis that the Book of the Watchers breaks into these five subsidiary works is over a century old, tracing back to the pioneering work of R. H. Charles. See Charles, *Enoch or, 1 Enoch*, xlvi–xlvii. Most scholarship agrees on the independence of 1–5, and (at least) the existence of a kind of Watchers cycle (covering something among 6–16), and a kind of Enochic journeys work (covering something among 17–36). For a summary of other delineations of subsidiary works, see the helpful chart in Florentino García Martínez, *Qumran and Apocalyptic: Studies on the Aramaic Texts from Qumran* (Leiden: Brill, 1992), 61.

[b] On the subject of the literary relationship between 1 En 83–4 and 1 En 85–90, see the thorough review of scholarship in Anathea Portier-Young, *Apocalypse Against Empire: Theologies of Resistance in Early Judaism* (Grand Rapids, MI: Eerdmans, 2011), 347–8.

[c] For the purposes of this stage of the argument, I have split the text into subsidiary works which previous scholarship has addressed. I will have more to say about the possibility of works within the Animal Apocalypse, but for now, it will be treated as it is elsewhere, as a singular work.

[d] As above, the chapter delineations of the various works here are approximate, as the exact textual material assigned to one subsidiary work or the other varies depending on the scholar—I have simplified things for clarity's sake. For instance, the "Body" of the Epistle is listed as 1 En 92–105 in Nickelsburg and VanderKam because they attach 1 En 92 as the "Introduction" to the "Body", but as pieces of 93 are excepted from this group, I thought it would be simpler to streamline and begin at 94. See George W. E. Nickelsburg and James C. VanderKam, *1 Enoch: The Hermeneia Translation* (Minneapolis: Fortress Press, 2004). For a more detailed schema, see Stuckenbruck's recent magisterial commentary, which introduces the "Apocalypse of Weeks" (93.1–10; 91.11–17); "Exhortation" [in Nickelsburg and VanderKam "A Narrative Bridge"] 91.1–10, 91.11–17; "Epistle" (92.1–5; 93.11–105.2," "Birth of Noah" (106.1–7.3), and "Eschatological Admonition" (108.1–15)." In his estimation, the Epistle further subdivides into two independent compositions: "Epistle of Enoch A (92.1–5; 93.11–14; 94.1–5; 104.9–5.2)" and "Epistle of Enoch B (94.6–104.8)." In Loren T. Stuckenbruck, *1 Enoch 91–108* (Berlin: De Gruyter, 2007).

have not been so cruel – some subsidiary works might have been quite popular, and that seems to be reflected in our material record. On the other side of things, with reference to some subsidiary works of the Epistle, a single manuscript stands between the possibility of presence and the possibility of absence. If this one manuscript had not survived, we might have drawn unnecessarily skeptical conclusions about the absence of the entire Epistle of Enoch, and all its subsidiary works, at Qumran. So, we see the rationale of both thinking optimistically and pessimistically with our Dead Sea evidence.

Table 1.3 Sections of 1 Enoch attested at Qumran

Book	Chapters	Section	Qumran
Book of the Watchers	1–5	Oracle of Enoch	4Q201, 4Q202, 4Q204
	6–11	Rebellion of the Watchers	4Q201, 4Q202, 4Q204,
	12–16	Enoch's Interaction with the Fallen Watchers	4Q201, 4Q202, 4Q204
	17–19	**Enoch's Journey to the Northwest**	(4Q204?)
	21–36	Enoch's Journey Eastward	4Q204, 4Q205, 4Q206
Book of Dreams	83–4	**Enoch's First Dream Vision: The Flood**	**Absent**
	85–90.42	"The Animal Apocalypse"	4Q204, 4Q205, 4Q206, 4Q207
Epistle of Enoch	91	A Narrative Bridge	4Q212
	93, 91	Apocalypse of Weeks	4Q212
	94–105	**Body of the Epistle**	**Absent**
	106–7	Book of Noah	4Q204
	108	**Eschatological Exhortation**	**Absent**

This impasse should encourage caution in evaluating the second key conclusion: there are three missing subsidiary works: Enoch's First Dream Vision: The Flood (1 En 83–4), the "Body" of the Epistle (1 En 94–105), and the Eschatological Exhortation (1 En 108).[5] A fourth possibly "missing" subsidiary work is "Enoch's Journey to the Northwest (1 En 17–19)," though this is an ambiguous case.[6]

We could assume that the vagaries of transmission have, indeed, been cruel, and these once-present subsidiary works have disintegrated or otherwise

---

[5] 4Q204 f 5 i a (f 16 according to Drawnel's new system) contains text apparently corresponding to 1 En 104.9–105.2 [Body of the Epistle in this chart], then, after a vacat, 1 En 106.1 ["Book of Noah."] It would thus seem to present material belonging to the Body of the Epistle.
 These verses have a complicated textual history in relation to the Body of the Epistle, complicated quite a bit by the fact that 1 En 105 does not appear in the Chester Beatty/Michigan manuscript of the Epistle, which simply proceeds from 1 En 104 into 1 En 106. They are separated by Stuckenbruck into a textual set called "Epistle of Enoch A (92.1–5; 93.11–14; 94.1–5; 104.9–5.2)," a collection of "several somewhat disparate fragments" of textual material, differentiated from "Epistle of Enoch B (94.6–104.8)," whose contents are roughly what is meant by Body of the Epistle in Nickelsburg and VanderKam's schema. And in Stuckenbruck's commentary, the work he calls "Epistle of Enoch B" is affirmed to be "not attested among the Qumran Aramaic manuscripts," a conclusion I follow here. See Stuckenbruck, *1 Enoch 91–108*, 7.

[6] See my forthcoming article "On the Identification of 1 Enoch 17–19 at Qumran," for a presentation of the evidence by which the identification to 1 Enoch 18 in 4Q204 is deemed inconclusive.

disappeared from our documents. So, with reference to Enoch's Dream Vision, Florentino García Martínez opines, "its [1 En 83–4] absence from the fragments recovered in Qumran may, thus, be accounted for – given their shortness – as purely accidental and easily understandable."[7] The fact that they appear together in some form, in most instances in medieval Christian Ethiopic transmission, but sometimes in late antique Greek Christian transmission, is enough to create an understanding of a textual whole from which we can restore subsidiary works to our imagination of the Qumran library.

A second possibility is that these subsidiary works are actually absent from the library at Qumran, either because they were somehow distasteful to the assemblers/producers of the Dead Sea Scrolls, or were written too late to make the cut in the assembly and storage of the Scrolls. To that end, some previous scholarship on Enoch has noted the conspicuous absence of these three subsidiary works – Enoch's First Dream Vision (1 En 83–4),[8] the Body of the Epistle (1 En 92–105),[9] and the Eschatological Exhortation (1 En 108)[10] – from the Qumran library. This precedent within modern scholarship opens the door to a slightly different line of thinking, taking seriously the possibility that the absence of evidence for these subsidiary works is evidence of absence from

---

[7] García Martínez, *Qumran and Apocalyptic*, 76. Note his similar treatment of 4Q204 as if it contained the "Epistle of Enoch," an entity which includes the Body of the Epistle: "The references to the other Enochic works and the fact that, in 4QEn^c, the Epistle was incorporated in them ...." In García Martínez, 90. Cf also Matthew Black's comments that "probably no significance can be attached to the absence of any fragment of the First Dream-Vision in the Aramaic manuscripts." In Matthew Black, *The Book of Enoch or I Enoch: A New English Edition* (Leiden: Brill, 1985), 20.

[8] Józef T. Milik, *The Books of Enoch: Aramaic Fragments of Qumran Cave 4* (Oxford: Clarendon Press, 1976), 41; Philip L. Tite, "Textual and Redactional Aspects of the Book of Dreams (1 Enoch 83–90)," *Biblical Theology Bulletin* 31, no. 3 (2001): 106–7; Nickelsburg, *1 Enoch 1*, 352–3. Note also the comments on absence from Qumran in Andrew B. Perrin, "Dream Visions (1 Enoch 83–84)," in *T&T Clark Encyclopedia of Second Temple Judaism*, ed. Loren T. Stuckenbruck and Daniel Gurtner (London: Bloomsbury Publishing, 2020), 175–6.

[9] See especially Gabriele Boccaccini, *Beyond the Essene Hypothesis: The Parting of the Ways between Qumran and Enochic Judaism* (Grand Rapids, MI: Eerdmans, 1998). A written dialogue between Boccaccini and Nickelsburg is particularly instructive – both recognize that the Epistle is somehow at odds with the "sectarian" Qumran material, though differ as to whether they consider it "pre" or "post" sectarian. See George W. E. Nickelsburg, "The Epistle of Enoch and the Qumran Literature," in *George W. E. Nickelsburg in Perspective: An Ongoing Dialogue of Learning*, vol. 1, ed. Jacob Neusner and Alan J. Avery-Peck (Leiden: Brill, 2003), 105–22; Gabriele Boccaccini, "Response to George Nickelsburg: The Epistle of Enoch and the Qumran Literature," in Neusner and Avery-Peck, *Nickelsburg in Perspective*, 123–33; George W. E. Nickelsburg, "Response to Gabrielle Boccaccini," in Neusner and Avery-Peck, *Nickelsburg in Perspective*, 133–8. Stuckenbruck also affirms the absence of "Epistle of Enoch B" from Qumran in Stuckenbruck, *1 Enoch 91–108*.

[10] Milik, *Books of Enoch*, 106–7; Stuckenbruck, *1 Enoch 91–108*, 692–4; Nickelsburg, *1 Enoch 1*, 554.

Qumran. We should not restore these subsidiary works, then, to documents that attest various other subsidiary works belonging to the same book.

Indeed, by expanding our documentary archive beyond Qumran to include late antique evidence, we see even more clearly the ongoing relevance of subsidiary works. The respective material histories of these three books demonstrate the ongoing independent circulation of their subsidiary works in late antiquity. These subsidiary works were not stripped of their independent identities as works by being folded into longer textual progressions – progressions which then became the primary circulating product in late antiquity. For example, the Body of the Epistle did not necessarily disappear into the Epistle of Enoch by the time the Romans invaded Judaea. For these sections of Enoch, subsidiary works were still identifiable building blocks in late antiquity, rather than being fixed components of completed structures.

This is not a universally applicable statement – it seems, for instance, that the Book of the Watchers' component parts came together relatively early, and we can look to this literary whole as that to which subsequent documents attest. Various pieces of the Book of the Watchers are attested in fragments of the second–first century BCE sorted into five manuscripts from Qumran.[11] A sixth-century Egyptian codex known as the Codex Panopolitanus provides the longest continuous attestation among our non-Ethiopic evidence.[12] As can be seen in the chart below, our ancient documents often witness the text of multiple subsidiary works together.

---

[11] **4Q Aramaic Enoch Fragments:** *Provenance:* I am currently working on the provenance of the Aramaic Enoch fragments, using material from József T. Milik's personal archives, for a forthcoming article.

Text: Initially published in Milik, *Books of Enoch*. The text of the Astronomical Book was revisited in E. J. C. Tigchelaar and Florentino García Martínez, "4QAstronomical Enoch," in *Qumran Cave 4 XVI: Miscellanea, Part I*, Discoveries in the Judaean Desert (Oxford: Clarendon Press, 2000), 95–172. All of the Enoch manuscripts of Cave 4 were revisited in Henryk Drawnel, *Qumran Cave 4: The Aramaic Books of Enoch* (Oxford: Oxford University Press, 2019).

Date: Milik states that "the dates of the 4QEn manuscripts are spread over the second and first centuries B.C," in *Books of Enoch*, 5. These dates are adopted in Drawnel's recent republication.

[12] **Codex Panopolitanus (TM 59976 / LDAB 1088):** *Provenance:* The exact details of the Codex Panopolitanus' discovery story are debatable, though the codex does seem to be linked to some sort of excavation carried out in the ancient Egyptian city of Panopolis, modern-day Akhmim. Note the criticism of Peter van Minnen: "In 1884, the then director of the Egyptian antiquities service G. Maspero started digging there, but he did not exercise the supervision in person. The result is that no reliable information exists on anything that was found there ... Somewhere in this mess the codex ... was found." In Peter van Minnen "The Greek Apocalypse of Peter," in *The Apocalypse of Peter*, ed. J. N. Bremmer and I. Czachesz, Studies on Early Christian Apocrypha 7 (Leuven: Peeters, 2003), 17.

Text: The text was initially published by Bouriant, but is now most commonly accessed in Black. See Urbain Bouriant, "Fragments du texte grec du livre d'Hénoch et de quelques

Table 1.4 Subsidiary Works of the Book of the Watchers in Ancient Documents

	Book of the Watchers				
	Oracle of Enoch (1 En 1–5)	Rebellion of the Watchers (1 En 6–11)	Enoch's Interaction with the Fallen Watchers (1 En 12–16)	Enoch's Journey to the Northwest (1 En 17–19)	Enoch's Journey Eastward (1 En 21–36)
4Q201	X	X			
4Q202	X	X			
4Q204	X	X	X	X (?)	X
4Q205					X
4Q206					X
Codex Panopolitanus	X	X	X	X	X

Some documents, 4Q205 and 4Q206, witness only one subsidiary work – Enoch's Journey Eastward (1 En 21–36). But these documents belong to a library in which the subsidiary work in question is attested alongside others. I consider this kind of intra-archival restoration, from one Qumran manuscript to another, justified for now because of the precedent established by 4Q204. So, even though 4Q201 and 4Q202 contain material only from (what we would now call) the first half of the Book of the Watchers, whereas 4Q205 and 4Q206 contain material only from the second half, the example of 4Q204 in which they are clustered in the same manuscript provides a strong indication that something like the Book of the Watchers was current *at the time*. I think this precedent tilts the balance of probability towards restoring our tattered documents belonging to this library with reference to this literary whole, though this is not a certainty. Similarly, the Codex Panopolitanus

écrits attribués à Saint Pierre," in *Memoires publies par les membres de la Mission archeologique ecrits attribues a Saint Pierre* (Paris: Libraire de la Societe asiatique, 1892), 93–147; Matthew Black, *Apocalypsis Henochi Graece* (Leiden: Brill, 1970), 1–37.

Date: The Codex Panopolitanus (including two hands responsible for scribing 1 Enoch) is the product of at least four scribal hands, three of which Cavallo and Maehler place in the sixth century. Cavallo and Maehler do not assign a date to the fourth and final hand – the final leaf in the codex, comprising an excerpt from a Julianic composition – though this omission is perhaps justified because it is only a single leaf glued to the back cover. See Guglielmo Cavallo and Herwig Maehler, *Greek Bookhands of the Early Byzantine Period, AD 300–800* (JSTOR, 1987), 90, http://www.jstor.org/stable/pdf/43646221.pdf

Contents: The codex contains, in order, extracts from the Gospel of Peter, Apocalypse of Peter, Book of the Watchers, and a leaf from a Julianic composition.

would constitute another surfacing of this kind of Book of the Watchers, one covering material from all of our subsidiary works.

The Book of the Watchers is, on balance, a reasonably apt designator of the length and breadth of the text found in these documents; our expectations are set at a reasonable level by this naming. It is not practically misleading to call 4Q201, 4Q202, 4Q204, 4Q205, 4Q206, as well as the Codex Panopolitanus manuscripts of the Book of the Watchers – they are most probably understood as documents that witness that conceptual whole. But the merits of naming our manuscripts after one of the five Enochic books becomes more problematic when we look at the documents which present text belonging to the entities known to modern scholars as the Book of Dreams and Epistle of Enoch.

The Epistle of Enoch certainly has the most varied documentary set. Text belonging to the Epistle can be found in Aramaic, Greek, Coptic, and Latin documents. In Aramaic, there are two manuscripts assembled from the fragments at Qumran: 4Q204 and 4Q212. In Greek, we have what amounts to our most extensive textual attestation apart from the Gəʿəz, in a fourth-century Egyptian papyrus codex split between the papyrological holdings of the University of Michigan and Chester Beatty Library in Dublin.[13] (It is here, at the end of the final folio of the Enochic text, that we find the subscription, "Epistle of Enoch" [Ἐπιστολή Ἐνώχ], which has given the work its modern title.) In Coptic, we have the remains of a single sixth- or seventh-century parchment leaf ("Antinoë Fragment," below) containing text corresponding to the Epistle of Enoch.[14] And finally, certainly representing the most far-flung

---

[13] **Chester Beatty/Michigan Epistle (TM 61462 / LDAB 2608):** *Provenance:* There are many proposed find-spots for the Chester Beatty Biblical papyri among which the Michigan/Chester Beatty Enoch codex is counted – for our purposes, it suffices to note that all the proposals are in Egypt. For a detailed review of the evidence on their provenance, see Brent Nongbri, *God's Library: The Archaeology of the Earliest Christian Manuscripts* (New Haven: Yale University Press, 2018), 122–30.

Text: The text was initially published by Bonner, but is most commonly accessed in Black. See Campbell Bonner, *The Last Chapters of Enoch in Greek* (London: Christophers, 1937), 32–88; Black, *Apocalypsis Henochi Graece*, 37–44.

Date: The fourth-century dating of the Chester Beatty/Michigan codex was proposed by its earliest students, Bonner and Kenyon, and has been held ever since with little dissent. See Bonner, *Last Chapters of Enoch*, 13; Frederic G Kenyon, *Fasciculus 8: Enoch and Melito*, The Chester Beatty Biblical Papyri Descriptions and Texts of Twelve Manuscripts On Papyrus of the Greek Bible (London: Walker, 1941), 12.

Contents: The codex also contains an excerpt from Melito's paschal sermon, and some fragments which have been labeled as "Pseudo-Ezekiel."

[14] **Antinoë Fragment (TM 109718 / LDAB 109718):** *Provenance:* According to Donadoni's publication, in a 1937 excavation in the northern cemetary of Antinoë, this parchment leaf was found among other manuscript fragments.

Text: Published in Sergio Donadoni, "Un Frammento Della Versione Copta Del «Libro Di Enoch»," *Acta Orientalia* 25 (1960): 197–202.

of our witnesses, is a ninth century Latin extract of text corresponding to the Epistle of Enoch found in a Breton codex of religious miscellanea.[15]

Here is the attestation of the subsidiary works of the Epistle of Enoch:

Table 1.5 Subsidiary Works of the Epistle of Enoch in Ancient Documents

	Epistle of Enoch				
	A Narrative Bridge (1 En 91)	The Apocalypse of Weeks (1 En 93, 91)	"Body" of the Epistle (1 En 94–105)	Book of Noah (1 En 106–7)	Eschatological Exhortation (1 En 108)
4Q204				X	
4Q212	X	X			
Chester Beatty			X	X	
Antinoë fragment		X			
BL Royal MS E XII				X	

Date: One of the fragments, a Homeric codex, was dated to the sixth or seventh century, and Donadoni suggests that the remainder of the fragments, including the Enoch fragment, can be assigned a date "più o meno" on analogy with the Homeric codex. I am unaware of any other work on the dating of this fragment.

[15] **BL Royal MS 5 E XII:** *Provenance:* See the comments on date below. On ownership, the British Library's notes trace the codex as far back as the Benedictine cathedral priory of St Mary in Worcester in 1622. See http://www.bl.uk/manuscripts/FullDisplay.aspx?ref=Royal_MS_5_E_XIII

Text: The text was initially published by M.R. James in 1893. Loren T. Stuckenbruck's recent commentary provides a helpful survey of subsequent treatments of the text. See Montague Rhodes James, *Apocrypha Anecdota* (Cambridge: Cambridge University Press, 1893), 146–50; Stuckenbruck, *1 Enoch 91–108*, 615–16n1038.

Date: The codex seems to have been assembled by multiple hands in Brittany in the beginning of the ninth century. On the construction of the codex, see Shannon O. Ambrose, "The Codicology and Palaeography of London, BL, Royal 5 E. XIII and Its Abridgement of the Collectio Canonum Hibernensis," *Codices Manuscripti & Impressi*, no. 54 (2006): 1–6.

Contents: The codex includes a variety of works of general religious interest, like Pseudo-Jerome, and an incomplete Gospel of Nicodemus. The Enochic excerpt is immediately preceded by a piece of the Council of Compiegne on marriage within degrees of consanguinity. Immediately after the Enochic excerpt, there is a short composition found in no other manuscript known as the "De Vindictis Magnis Magnorum Peccatorum." The De Vindictis condemns the sinful pride of Satan, Adam, Cain, Lamech and David, and culminates with material suggesting the Jews' rejection of Christ led to Titus and Vespasian's destruction of Jerusalem in 70 CE. It might be possible to connect the Enochic text with its neighbors in a tenuous fashion – the focus on the parentage of Noah in the Enochic excerpt might recall the discussion of marital propriety, and the retelling of the fall of the angels and subsequent flood

There are some individual documents which attest two subsidiary works. 4Q212 contains the so-called "Narrative Bridge," and the Apocalypse of Weeks; the Chester Beatty/Michigan Papyrus codex contains the Body of the Epistle, and the Book of Noah.[16] However, no single document definitely attests more than two subsidiary works, and three of the five attest only one subsidiary work. I should also clarify that the overwhelming majority of text, though this textual bulk is here compressed into one column (Body of the Epistle, 1 En 94–105) for the sake of identifying a singular work, is apparently not attested at Qumran.[17] It is possible to argue that selective attestation is nothing more than an inevitable accident, given that none of the discussed documents are "complete." All of the five have been the object of some sort of disintegration or decay.

and destruction could echo the historical condemnations offered in the De Vindictis. On the contents of the codex, and the De Vindictis in particular, see most recently Pierre Petitmengin, "La Compilation 'De Uindictis Magnis Magnorum Peccatorum' Exemples d'anthropophagie Tirés Des Sièges de Jérusalem et de Samarie," in *Philologia Sacra. Biblische Und Patristische Studien Für Hermann J. Frede Und Walter Thiele Zu Ihrem Siebzigsten Geburtstag. Band II: Apokryphen, Kirchenväter, Verschiedenes*, ed. Roger Gryson, Hermann Josef Frede, and Walter Thiele (Freiburg, 1993), 622–38; Shannon O. Ambrose, "The De Vindictis Magnis Magnorum Peccatorum: A New Hiberno-Latin Witness to the Book of Kings," *Eolas: The Journal of the American Society of Irish Medieval Studies* 5 (2011): 44–60.

[16] One might object that, in the interest of methodological consistency with my intra-archival restoration of subsidiary works from the Book of the Watchers from one Qumran manuscript to another, I might wish to restore the Book of Noah to 4Q212 or restore the Apocalypse of Weeks to 4Q204. I would reply that my restoration with reference to the Book of the Watchers above is justified by the example of 4Q204 in which all the subsidiary works are present, as well as the Codex Panopolitanus which speaks to the later circulation of just such a work. But there is no comparable Qumran Epistle manuscript by which to establish a comparable literary whole, nor do the witness of later manuscripts establish co-circulation.

[17] This observation is contingent upon rejecting the possible identification of the Body of the Epistle in as many as seven Greek fragments from Cave 7 – maximally, the proposed fragments are 7Q4, 7Q5, 7Q8, and 7Q11–14. These identifications were proposed, and subsequently supported, by G. Wilhelm Nebe, Ernest A. Muro Jr., and Émile Puech. But the 7Q fragments are sufficiently fragmentary that a wide variety of identifications might plausibly be made, with the aid of a little imagination and reconstruction. 7Q5, for instance, was infamously identified by Jóse O'Callaghan as Mark 6.52–3, but also identified by Maria Victoria Spottorno (in an exploration of other possibilities) with 1 En 15.9–10 (the Book of the Watchers), in addition to a variety of other identifications proposed with works ranging from Exodus, to the synoptic gospels, to Homer. In light of these ambiguities in interpretation, as well as the extraordinarily fragmentary nature of the material in question, scholars of 1 Enoch like Nickelsburg, Stuckenbruck, Knibb, and Drawnel have proven unconvinced by the Body of the Epistle identifications of Puech et al. If, over the objections of Nickelsburg et al, the identification were accepted, these fragments would nevertheless attest only one subsidiary work – the Body of the Epistle.

See G. Wilhelm Nebe, "'7Q4' – Möglichkeit und Grenze einer Identifikation," *Revue de Qumrân* 13, no. 1/4 (1988): 629–33; Ernest A. Muro, "The Greek Fragments of Enoch From Qumran Cave 7 ('7Q4, 7Q8, & 7Q12=7QEn Gr= Enoch' 103.3–4, 7–8)," *Revue de Qumrân* 18, no. 2 (1997): 307–12; Émile Puech, "Sept fragments grecs de la 'Lettre D'Hénoch'

Even though we are bound to enact some sort of restoration, the question is: how much? The pattern of attestation demonstrated by these five manuscripts of the Epistle suggests that restoring subsidiary works to documents in which they are not immediately manifest might be a bridge too far. There is no basis to imagine that 4Q212 contained the Book of Noah or that the Chester Beatty codex contained the Apocalypse of Weeks. It would, therefore, be a misnomer to label these as manuscripts of the Epistle, as such a classification would lead us to expect far more and varied text than is actually present in any given document. So, the lesson learned from the evidence of the "Epistle" manuscripts is different from that learned from the Book of the Watchers manuscripts: we learn from this collection to be more reserved in our practices of restoration.

This leads us to our final example: the Book of Dreams. Text belonging to the Book of Dreams is attested in four Aramaic manuscripts assembled from fragments found at Qumran: 4Q204, 4Q205, 4Q206, and 4Q207. In Greek, there are some quite deteriorated fourth-century fragments found in the Oxyrhynchus trash heap, collected into one manuscript – P. Oxy 2069 – of which two fragments seem to attest text corresponding to the Book of Dreams.[18] Finally, an extract from the Book of Dreams can be found in the

---

('1 Hén' 100, 103 et 105) dans la Grotte 7 de Qumrân (= '7QHéngr')," *Revue de Qumrân* 18, no. 2 (1997): 313–23; José O'Callaghan, "¿Papiros neotestamentarios en la Cueva 7 de Qumrān?," *Biblica* 53, no. 1 (1972): 91–100; Maria Victoria Spottorno, "Can Methodological Limits Be Set in the Debate on the Identification of 7Q5?," *Dead Sea Discoveries* 6, no. 1 (1999): 66–77; T. J. Kraus, "7Q5 – Status Quaestionis And Fundamental Remarks To Qualify The Discussion Of The Papyrus Fragment," in *Ad Fontes: Original Manuscripts and Their Significance for Studying Early Christianity* (Leiden: Brill, 2007), 231–59; George W. E. Nickelsburg, "The Greek Fragments of '1 Enoch' From Qumran Cave 7: An Unproven Identification," *Revue de Qumrân* 21, no. 4 (2004): 631–4; Stuckenbruck, *1 Enoch 91–108*, 7n21, 529n900; Knibb, "Christian Adoption," 401; Drawnel, *Qumran Cave 4*, 19–20.

[18] **P. Oxy 2069 (TM 59975/LDAB 1087):** *Provenance:* The Oxyrhynchus papyri have a reasonably sound provenance, as they were unearthed in excavations led by Bernard P. Grenfell and Arthur S. Hunt, who published P. Oxy 2069 themselves.

Text: The text is initially published in Arthur S. Hunt and Bernard Pyne Grenfell, *The Oxyrhynchus Papyri. Part XVII* (London: Egypt Exploration Fund, 1927), 6–8. Revisited in József T. Milik, "Fragments Grecs Du Livre d'Hénoch (P. Oxy. XVII 2069)," *Chronique d'Egypte* 46, no. 92 (1971): 321–43; Randall D. Chesnutt, "Oxyrhynchus Papyrus 2069 and the Compositional History of 1 Enoch," *Journal of Biblical Literature* 129, no. 3 (2010): 485–505.

Date: All of the above agree on a fourth-century date (although Hunt alleges a late fourth-century date, where Chesnutt suggests an early fourth-century date better suits the "severe style" of script).

Contents: Fragments 1 and 2 contain material corresponding to the Book of Dreams. Milik proposed that Fragment 3 contains material corresponding to the Astronomical book, though this proposal was critiqued by Larson, "The Translation of Enoch: From Aramaic into Greek" (PhD diss., New York University, 1995), 186–7; Chesnutt, "Oxyrhynchus Papyrus 2069," 496–8. A balanced appraisal rehabilitating Milik's suggestion somewhat can be found in VanderKam, *1 Enoch 2*, 345–8.

margins of a tenth century Italian Byzantine codex, Codex Vaticanus Graecus 1809, written in brachygraphic script.[19] A closer look at the attestation pattern of the Book of Dreams demonstrates with great clarity the perils of asking for Enochic books instead of subsidiary works:

Table 1.6 Subsidiary Works of the Book of Dreams in Ancient Documents

	The Book of Dreams	
	Enoch's First Dream Vision: The Flood (1 En 83–4)	The Animal Apocalypse (1 En 85–90)
4Q204		X
4Q205		X
4Q206		X
4Q207		X
P. Oxy 2069		X
Vat. Gr. 1809		X

[19] **Codex Vaticanus Graecus 1809 (Pinakes 68438):** *Provenance:* Concerning the history of ownership of the manuscript, an inserted paper page before the first folium indicates that the manuscript comes from the monastery of Grottaferrata, in the region of Lazio, Italy – additional notations on fol. 1r and 3r confirm this link. The manuscript became part of the Vatican's manuscript collection on December 12, 1615. Concerning the production of the manuscript itself, Lilla has suggested the hand of fol. 213r–7r (though this does not include the marginal insertion of the Enoch fragment) looks to be connected to Paul I., abbot of Grottaferrata, and a pupil of St. Nilus from Rossano, who established a school in southern Calabria in the last decades of the tenth century. According to Lilla's hypothesis, the manuscript landed in the library of the monastery of Grottaferrata when it was founded in 1004. See Salvatore Lilla, *Il Testo tachigrafico del "De Divinis nominibus", Vat. gr. 1809.* (Vatican City: Biblioteca apostolica vaticana, 1970), 11–13; Drawnel, *Qumran Cave 4*, 41–2.

Text: Originally spotted by the chief keeper of the Vatican Library, Cardinal Angelo Mai, deciphered and published by J. Gildemeister, the Enochic text was re-edited by M. Gitlbauer, and was collated by Black in his edition of Enoch in Greek. See J. Gildemeister, "Ein Fragment des griechischen Henoch," *Zeitschrift der Deutschen Morgenländischen Gesellschaft* 9, no. 2 (1855): 621–4; Michael Gitlbauer, *Die Ueberreste griechischer Tachygraphie im Codex Vaticanus Graecus 1809* (Wien, 1878), 55; Black, *Apocalypsis Henochi Graece*, 36–7. Note the corrective of Drawnel – the text was previously identified as tachygraphic ('speedy writing,') which substitites syllables of transcribed words with certain symbols, but is better named "brachygraphic," in which "the syllabic part of the transcribed word is substituted with a particular symbol that, differently from tachygraphy, is written separately from the following one." In Drawnel, *Qumran Cave 4*, 40–1.

Date: Tenth century, see the comments on provenance above.

Contents: The majority of the manuscript is made up of excerpts from Maximus the Confessor and Pseudo-Dionysius the Areopagite. The Enochic fragment appears in the margins of fol. 216v, amidst a five-page section which provides a collection of excerpts from Maximus' letters in brachygraphic writing. Also excerpted in the margins of fol. 216v is an excerpt from the *Dialogos* on the Life of John Chrysostomus by Palladios. Milik noted a connection

Every one of our non-Ethiopic documents contains text corresponding to the work known in scholarship as the Animal Apocalypse. None contains text corresponding to Enoch's vision of the Flood. The same caveats apply as stated above: all of these manuscripts are subject to some degree of deterioration, and the eleventh-century codex is not a standalone manuscript but rather text found in a marginal note, so we are not working from "complete" manuscripts. It is also important to note that the Animal Apocalypse is much longer than the Flood Vision – it represents five chapters rather than two, and two of those chapters (89 and 90) are among the longest in all of 1 Enoch. Its greater length might have shortened the odds of preservation among fragments for the Animal Apocalypse, and lengthened the odds for the shorter Flood Vision. But the chart above directly poses the question of *how* to complete the incomplete. With no attestations anywhere outside of medieval Ethiopia, should we really be restoring the text of "The Flood" to any one of these documents? Perhaps not.

It is generally agreed that scholars should not restore text in keeping with an understanding of a "1 Enoch" whole. So, one should not imagine the Book of Parables was once manifest in 4Q201 just because our extant fragments witness the Book of the Watchers. This section has underlined that we should not restore text on the level of a subsidiary work in keeping with an understanding of an "Enochic book" whole. I have noted scholarly suspicions that three subsidiary works not attested at Qumran were, in actuality, *absent* from Qumran. Additionally, I have provided a documentary survey that extends this conclusion to a broader rule covering the entirety of our non-Ethiopic evidence for the Book of Dreams and the Epistle of Enoch.

Part of the reason that the character of this attestation of Enochic works has not been fully recognized until now is that our expectations of Qumran and our other documents have been shaped by the impression of a work gleaned from Ethiopic tradition. Acts of restoration are especially telling examples in which "text" and "document" are subordinated to imaginations of a "work." How we fill in the blanks says as much about us as the blanks. And a library as fragmentary and as full of "blanks" as Qumran provides an unusually rich stage on which to watch these assumptions being performed.

Matthew Monger has pursued an analogous project to the revisionist documentary survey just enacted, but with respect to Jubilees, another work extant in its "fullest" form in Ethiopia, but with some fragmentary Hebrew evidence

---

between the excerpt of the Animal Apocalypse and a clause in the Palladios excerpts comparing a liar to certain animals. Drawnel suggests a better comparison is between the epic conflict narrated by the Animal Apocalypse, and the "conflict between truth and falsehood that constitutes the main topic of Palladios' extract." See Milik, *Books of Enoch*, 75; Henryk Drawnel, *The Aramaic Astronomical Book (4Q208–4Q211) from Qumran: Text, Translation, and Commentary* (Oxford: Oxford University Press, 2011), 41.

to be found at Qumran.²⁰ In a series of articles and a dissertation, Monger re-evaluates the Qumran fragments of Jubilees, especially 4Q216, and concludes:

> Jubilees may have its fullest expression in the Ethiopic tradition, but the Qumran material should neither be overlooked or relativized based on the Ethiopic text of Jubilees, but should be studied as legitimate expressions of Jubilees in the context of late Second Temple Judaism. Jubilees is perhaps better described as a constellation of writings all relating to each other, but with distinctive expressions and histories of transmission.²¹

In particular conversation with my conclusions here, Monger is sharply critical of the assumption that any or all of our Qumran manuscripts are to be correlated with the "fullest expression" of Jubilees as found in Gəʿəz. In his work, he suggests that the Qumran fragments witness an ongoing compositional and redactional process (on which, see my conclusions in Chapter 2). Jubilees admittedly represents a different case than Enoch, with a much more streamlined literary framework that retells the histories found in the Torah with an eye to jubilees and heavenly revelation. The identification of "sources" or "works" within Jubilees has never reached the consensus awarded to, for instance, the five books of Enoch.²² But Monger's work with Jubilees, like my own, guards against the imposition of a work-concept gleaned from a later Gəʿəz manuscript tradition. Monger's thesis is in line with a growing body of work in the study of the Scrolls proper that decenters a singular work-concept in favor of allowing pluriformity and textual difference in the documentary tradition to speak.²³ I would join my work to ongoing projects which are thoughtful about the

---

[20] Matthew P. Monger, "4Q216 and the State of Jubilees at Qumran," *Revue de Qumran*, no. 4 (2014): 595–612; Matthew P. Monger, "The Development of Jubilees 1 in the Late Second Temple Period," *Journal for the Study of the Pseudepigrapha* 27, no. 2 (2017): 83–112; Matthew P. Monger, "The Many Forms of Jubilees: A Reassessment of the Manuscript Evidence from Qumran and the Lines of Transmission of the Parts and Whole of Jubilees," *Revue de Qumran* 30, no. 2 (2018): 191–211; Matthew P. Monger, "4Q216: A New Material Analysis," *Semitica* 60 (2018): 309–33; Monger, "4Q216: Rethinking Jubilees."

[21] See Monger, "4Q216: Rethinking Jubilees," 230. See also Eibert Tigchelaar, "The Qumran 'Jubilees' Manuscripts as Evidence for the Literary Growth of the Book," *Revue de Qumran* 26, no. 4 (2014): 579–94.

[22] Monger and Tigchelaar's above-cited work on Jubilees appears in a special issue of *Revue de Qumran* 26, no. 4 in 2014 that also features articles by James VanderKam pursuing a single-author model, Michael Segal exploring the use of sources such as that represented by so-called Pseudo-Jubilees, and James Kugel exploring the work of a possible interpolater. As Najman and Tigchelaar conclude in their introductory remarks: "there are severe disagreements around how to conceive of Jubilees as a work or as a unified text," in Najman and Tigchelaar, "Unity after Fragmentation," 495.

[23] One particularly rich network of scholarship exploring this avenue of inquiry is that undertaken in conversation with the many and heterogeneous manuscripts studied under the

pitfalls of practices of restoration at Qumran, and the ways that the potential for even greater pluriformity among our documents might be muffled by quick-triggered restoration.[24]

In keeping with the methodological priority granted to our documents established by New Philology and these recent directions in the study of the Scrolls, I propose that when it comes to subsidiary works, absence of evidence from our documents can be best interpreted as evidence of absence. If certain subsidiary works are absent from libraries such as the Dead Sea Scrolls, we can proceed as if that absence is potentially meaningful. On that note, one last factor can now be adduced to advance these potential conclusions to probable conclusions – the problem of Jewish texts in Christian transmission, and the inextricability of our missing subsidiary works from their Christian manuscripts.

The missing subsidiary works between Judaism and Christianity

Although it may not seem like it at first, a precise and detailed labeling of our material evidence opens an exciting set of new possibilities for rewriting the compositional history of 1 Enoch. Works absent from Qumran are no longer bound by a previously accepted *terminus ante quem* marking likely eras

---

heading of the Community Rule, or *serekh ha-yahad*. See especially Jutta Jokiranta, "What Is 'Serekh Ha-Yahad (S)'? Thinking about Ancient Manuscripts as Information Processing," in *Sibyls, Scriptures, and Scrolls: John Collins at Seventy*, ed. Joel Baden, Hindy Najman, and Eibert Tigchelaar (Leiden: Brill, 2017), 611–35; Sarianna Metso and James M.Tucker, "The Changing Landscape of Editing Ancient Jewish Texts," in *Reading the Bible in Ancient Traditions and Modern Editions: Studies in Textual and Reception History in Memory of Peter W. Flint*, ed. Andrew B. Perrin, Kyung S. Baek, and Daniel K. Falk (Atlanta: SBL Press), 2017, 269–88; James Nati, "The Rolling Corpus: Materiality and Pluriformity at Qumran, with Special Consideration of the Serekh Ha-Yaḥad," *Dead Sea Discoveries* 27, no. 2 (2020): 161–201; James Nati, *Textual Criticism and the Ontology of Literature in Early Judaism: An Analysis of the Serekh Ha-Yaḥad*, Supplements to the Journal for the Study of Judaism 198 (Leiden: Brill, 2021).

[24] See, e.g., Eibert Tigchelaar, "Constructing, Deconstructing and Reconstructing Fragmentary Manuscripts: Illustrated by a Study of 4Q184 (4QWiles of the Wicked Woman)," in *Rediscovering the Dead Sea Scrolls: An Assessment of Old and New Approaches and Methods*, ed. Maxine Grossman (Grand Rapids, MI: Eerdmans, 2010), 26–47; Eibert Tigchelaar, "Working with Few Data: The Relation between 4Q285 and 11Q14," *Dead Sea Discoveries* 7, no. 1 (2000): 49–56; Kipp Davis, "The Social Milieu of 4QJera (4Q70) in a Second Temple Jewish Manuscript Culture: Fragments, Manuscripts, Variance, and Meaning," in *The Dead Sea Scrolls and the Study of the Humanities*, ed. Pieter Hartog, Alison Schofield, and Samuel I.Thomas, Studies on the Texts of the Desert of Judah 125 (Leiden: Brill, 2018), 53–76; Kipp Davis, "'There and Back Again': Reconstruction and Reconciliation of the War Text 4QMilḥamaa (4Q491a–c)," in *The War Scroll, Violence, War and Peace in the Dead Sea Scrolls and Related Literature: Essays in Honour of Martin G. Abegg on the Occasion of His 65th Birthday*, ed. Kipp Davis et al., Studies on the Texts of the Desert of Judah 115 (Leiden: Brill, 2016), 125–46.

of composition, which they had formerly gained largely by analogy with actually present subsidiary works. We are asked to re-open the search.

For many scholars, this re-evaluation does not represent an especially exciting or groundbreaking endeavor, as likely provenances for these works have often been sought in the immediate environs of Qumran – in the world of Second Temple Judaea, even if they are not imagined to belong to the library of the Dead Sea Scrolls. The point of departure for the evaluation of an Enochic subsidiary work is, effectively, the *other* subsidiary works. Perhaps the works are assumed to be Second Temple Jewish, on analogy with those extant at Qumran, unless proven otherwise.

At this point, we should acknowledge a very uncomfortable truth – every substantial witness to the text of the pieces of 1 Enoch not found at Qumran was produced by Christians.[25] This is because, excepting the Scrolls, every manuscript of 1 Enoch is a Christian production. The Ethiopian Orthodox Tawahedo Church manuscript tradition is a Christian manuscript tradition. The two substantial late antique manuscripts which transmit pieces of 1 Enoch in Greek are clearly Christian – in one, the Book of the Watchers is bound alongside two Petrine apocrypha, in a codex decorated with a cross; in the other, the Body of the Epistle is bound alongside Melito's supersessionist homily on Passover and the crucifixion of Christ. When subsidiary works are attested at Qumran, it means there is evidence for a Jewish version. But there is no such thing as a non-Christian version of the Body of the Epistle, or Enoch's Version of the Flood, or the Eschatological Exhortation. It simply doesn't exist – at least, not in our material record.

These Enochic works are not the only purportedly Second Temple works for which this is the case. In fact, outside of the discoveries at Qumran, most Second Temple works exist only in Christian transmission. Such an

---

[25] P. Oxy 2069 (published by Milik, and revisited by Chestnutt), and P. Gen. Inv. 187, a Greek fragment held by the Bibliotheque de Geneve, contain quotations from 1 Enoch, but are so fragmentary that we cannot make definite conclusions about the communities which produced them. They offer such miniscule amounts of text that the rule still stands that we have 1 Enoch as transmitted by Christians, insofar as that is how we have all our long-form witnesses.

For P. Oxy 2069 (TM 59975/LDAB 1087), the text is initially published in Hunt and Grenfell, *Oxyrhynchus Papyri*, 6–8. Revisited in Milik, "Fragments Grecs Du Livre"; Chesnutt, "Oxyrhynchus Papyrus 2069."

For P. Gen. Inv. 187, see Marie Bagnoud, "P. Gen. Inv. 187: Un Texte Apocalyptique Apocryphe Inedit," *Museum Helveticum* 73, no. 2 (2016): 129–53; Marie Bagnoud and Kelley Coblentz Bautch, "5.7.5: Enoch: The Book of the Watchers: An Otherworldly Journey of an Unknown Figure (P.Gen. Inv. 187)," in *Textual History of the Bible*, vol. 2, ed. Armin Lange (Brill, 2020), https://doi.org/10.1163/2452-4107_thb_COM_0205070500; David Hamidovič, "1 Enoch 17 in the Papyrus Geneva 187," in *Apocryphal and Esoteric Sources in the Development of Christianity and Judaism. The Eastern Mediterranean, the Near East, and Beyond.*, ed. Igor Dorfmann-Lazarev, Texts and Studies in Eastern Christianity 21 (Leiden: Brill, 2021), 437–49.

observation is associated with the work of Robert Kraft, as well as Michael Stone and Marinus de Jonge, who explored over decades the provocative thesis that purportedly Jewish works found only in Christian transmission are more likely to tell us about the Christian transmitters who produced the manuscript, than any such hypothetical Jewish author imagined somewhere at the origins of the text.[26] This methodological challenge grew out of and alongside a scholarship growing increasingly suspicious of the privileging of origins over transmission and reception in our accountings of ancient literature, and critical of the extent to which these research priorities have led us to charge past the limits imposed by the diversity and situatedness of our documents.[27] In Kraft's phrasing, the burden of proof is on those who hold that Christians did *not* develop or compose these works, and hold to the possibility of reclaiming a Jewish originary moment or composition.[28]

Even more concerning is the reality that two of these works, the Body of the Epistle and Eschatological Exhortation, can be situated quite closely alongside various works belonging to the New Testament, and studied under the heading of early Christianity. The Body of the Epistle, for instance, has been studied alongside the Gospel of Luke.[29] Nickelsburg, at least, noted the

---

[26] Many of Kraft's classic contributions can be found in Robert A. Kraft, *Exploring the Scripturesque: Jewish Texts and Their Christian Contexts* (Leiden; Boston: Brill, 2009). Michael Stone's contributions are often associated with his work on Jewish texts in Armenian transmission, many of which are collected in Michael E. Stone, *Apocrypha, Pseudepigrapha and Armenian Studies: Collected Papers*, 2 vols., Orientalia Lovaniensia Analecta 144–5 (Dudley, MA: Peeters, 2006). Marinus de Jonge is best known for his work on the Testaments of the Twelve Patriarchs, on which see Marinus de Jonge, *Pseudepigrapha of the Old Testament as Part of Christian Literature: The Case of the Testaments of the Twelve Patriarchs and the Greek Life of Adam and Eve* (Leiden: Brill, 2003). Recent summaries of the state of the question can be found in Alexander Kulik et al., eds., *A Guide to Early Jewish Texts and Traditions in Christian Transmission*, A Guide to Early Jewish Texts and Traditions in Christian Transmission (Oxford: Oxford University Press, 2019); Liv Ingeborg Lied and Loren T. Stuckenbruck, "Pseudepigrapha and Their Manuscripts," in *The Old Testament Pseudepigrapha*, ed. Liv Ingeborg Lied and Matthias Henze, Early Judaism and Its Literature (Atlanta: SBL Press, 2019), 203–30.

[27] Some representative examples from different fields are Breed, *Nomadic Text*; David C. Parker, *The Living Text of the Gospels* (Cambridge: Cambridge University Press, 1997); Peter Schäfer, "Research into Rabbinic Literature: An Attempt to Define the Status Quaestionis," *Journal of Jewish Studies* 37, no. 2 (1986): 139–52; Ra'anan S. Boustan, "The Study of Heikhalot Literature: Between Mystical Experience and Textual Artifact," *Currents in Biblical Research* 6, no. 1 (2007): 130–60.

[28] Especially in Robert A. Kraft, "The Pseudepigrapha and Christianity, Revisited: Setting the Stage and Framing Some Central Questions," in *Exploring the Scripturesque: Jewish Texts and Their Christian Contexts* (Leiden; Boston: Brill, 2009), 35–61.

[29] See, for instance, Sverre Aalen, "St Luke's Gospel and the Last Chapters of I Enoch," *New Testament Studies* 13, no. 1 (1966): 1–13; George W. E. Nickelsburg, "Riches, the Rich, and God's Judgment in 1 Enoch 92–105 and the Gospel According to Luke," *New Testament Studies* 25, no. 3 (1979): 324–44. Note especially Aalen's closing query: "Was Luke personally acquainted with the man who translated I Enoch? Or was he perhaps himself this man?"

Eschatological Exhortation's particularly suggestive relationship to 1 Peter in twenty proposed textual parallels.[30] Finally, though it is a book, rather than a subsidiary work, the Book of Parables, which is also missing from Qumran, has recently seen a flurry of scholarship placing it in conversation with the Synoptics and "son of man" traditions of the early Jesus movement.[31]

Clearly, these unattested pieces of 1 Enoch provide ample and useful "background" for scholars working on the New Testament. But rather than assuming that this utility legitimates the restoration, we might want to reflect upon the extent to which an archive reflects the interests and needs of the scholars that use it. In this instance, we can think about the set of sources assigned to early Judaism as an archive, though admittedly the collection of sources here is largely a function of scholarly assignation rather than material attestation (with Qumran as a crucial exception). Archives are not static repositories, but constantly made and remade constructions that are embedded in the worlds of their modern users. For a particularly apt statement of this point, we can look to the work of Antoinette Burton, engaging Michel Foucault:

> For, as Foucault would have it, any given archive acts as "a reflection that shows us quite simply, and in shadow, what all those in the foreground are looking at. It restores, as if by magic, what is lacking in every gaze . . ." In the spirit of feminist historiography I would go so far as to say that if we fail to recognize this dynamic we neglect an obligation to investigate our sense of identification with the archive itself, as well as to ask questions about its capability (and ours) fully to know the subjects it claims to represent.[32]

Pointed directly at the field that this book engages, the simple point is that our ancient Jewish literary "archive" – the nature and limits of the sources granted titles, or numbers at Qumran, and enshrined in translations and printed on syllabi, and even the fact that we are convinced these entities can be effectively delineated at all – says just as much about modern scholarly imaginations as it does about the ancient world. The pursuit of background reveals the interests of the foreground. Even the seemingly binary phenomena of presence and absence are complicated by restoration, which can be a function of our

---

[30] In Nickelsburg, *1 Enoch 1*, 560.
[31] See the many contributions collected in Gabriele Boccaccini, ed., *Enoch and the Messiah Son of Man: Revisiting the Book of Parables* (Grand Rapids, MI: Eerdmans, 2007); James H. Charlesworth and Darrell L. Bock, eds., *Parables of Enoch: A Paradigm Shift* (London: Bloomsbury, 2012).
[32] See Michel Foucault, *The Order of Things: An Archaeology of the Human Sciences* (New York: Pantheon Books, 1971), 15; Antoinette Burton, "Thinking beyond the Boundaries: Empire, Feminism and the Domains of History," *Social History* 26, no. 1 (January 1, 2001): 66–7.

identification of what we most want to find in an archive.³³ For this reason, we should be cautious when we notice restored material lifting heavy weight in neighboring fields.

In the case of these unattested subsidiary works of 1 Enoch – the Flood Vision, the "Body" of the Epistle, and the Eschatological Exhortation – which can prove unusually helpful to scholars of the New Testament/early Christianity in providing parallels to ideas found in the literature they study, we meet the concern about Second Temple works in Christian transmission in a particularly sharp form. We can phrase it like this: we have no non-Christian evidence for these subsidiary works. They are demonstrably relevant to the concerns of New Testament exegetes and students of early Christianity, and often possess what appear to be textual and verbal parallels. The most plausible way to account for both of these factors is to hypothesize that these documents were written by Christians, or at the very least, that a Christian phase of transmission was so formative as to obliterate the possibility of reclaiming a "Jewish layer."³⁴ Why, then, is the "default" that they belong to the Second Temple period?

After all, none of the three missing subsidiary works offers especially specific guidance on sites of composition. I have noted above that perceived intertextual allusions with works belonging to the New Testament are more problematic than helpful. We are generally faced with the task of pursuing a date on largely internal grounds, hoping that something about the text will mention a certain event, or ring of a certain period, and thus extend tendrils connecting it with a particular historical context. But none of the three missing subsidiary works contain such clear historical references, and to a

---

³³ The New Philological insistence upon beginning a philological practice with manuscripts could be interpreted as an attempt at correction in light of this critique, to decenter the intellectual priority granted to "works" and the philologists who control their boundaries, in favor of a materially grounded analysis. But it would be a mistake to grant this proposed blueprint for future work for a new objectivity – there is no way to remove scholars from scholarship. Moreover, New Philology has its limits in the study of ancient Judaism, as many of the works assigned to this period are *only* extant in manuscripts from distant regions and eras. New Philology can provide a starting point and a strong caution to the scholar using later manuscripts, but scholars of ancient Judaism have no choice but to engage in some practices of restoration of text.

³⁴ Even among scholars well aware of this hypothesis, Enoch is treated as an exceptional case in the world of Second Temple works in Christian transmission. In Marinus de Jonge's call for a new approach privileging Christian attestation over hypothetical Jewish origins: "many pseudepigrapha were transmitted over a considerable period of time without noticeable adaptations, e.g. Ethiopic Enoch." In de Jonge, *Pseudepigrapha of the Old Testament*, 34. Enoch (sans the Parables) is similarly given carte blanche membership in the club of "Jewish" literature in another otherwise skeptical treatment: See James R. Davila, *The Provenance of the Pseudepigrapha: Jewish, Christian, or Other?* (Leiden: Brill, 2005), 13–15.

certain extent, each pursues relatively timeless reflections. So, the Body of the Epistle is a deliberation on community justice, economic ethics, and the eschaton.[35] The Flood is Enoch's pseudepigraphal "prophecy" of the great Flood of Genesis 6 that could have been prepared by virtually any reader of Genesis.[36] And the Eschatological Exhortation is an apocalyptically oriented reminder that the just will be rewarded and the wicked punished.[37] These works could have been composed at many historical junctures, as long as there were rich and poor, readers of Genesis, and communities anticipating the end of time. The assumed cultural, literary, and social conditions needed to trigger the composition of these works would have been present in Hellenistic Judaea, but also Roman Judaea, Byzantine Constantinople, and Aksumite Axum, and so on. In the case of the Body of the Epistle, thanks to a citation in Tertullian (*De Idololatria* 4.3, cf. 1 En 99.6–7) and material attestation in the Chester Beatty/Michigan codex, some of these later sites can be comfortably eliminated. But in the case of the Flood and the Eschatological Exhortation, witnessed for the first time in medieval Ethiopia, they remain theoretically possible. All of which is to say, internal considerations do not narrow down possible sites of composition for any of the missing works.

It is not clear to me that sufficient evidence exists to shift the burden of proof away from a documented history which speaks only to Christian text, towards a hypothetical originary Jewish phase. A lack of "obvious" Christian interpolations does not a Jewish text make.[38] This judgment is, of course, a subjective call

---

[35] Note Stuckenbruck's critique that, despite the attempts of previous scholarship to correlate the righteous in the Epistle with the Pharisees, "the language of the Epistle in general is too imprecise to pin down on this particular group." See Stuckenbruck, *1 Enoch 91–108*, 211–15.

[36] Or, perhaps, the Animal Apocalypse – note Nickelsburg's suggestion that 1 En 83–4 was created as a "companion piece" to 1 En 85–90. Note also that his discussion of date proceeds exclusively with reference to this work's relationship to other Enochic works, and no historical factors are mentioned. In Nickelsburg, *1 Enoch 1*, 346–7.

[37] As Stuckenbruck puts it, "The determination of a time of composition for the Eschatological Admonition is complicated by several factors: the absence in it of any historical allusion; its earliest (and only) attestation in the Ethiopic manuscript tradition; and its combination of motifs that can be compared with both Second Temple Jewish and early Christian writings" (Stuckenbruck, *1 Enoch 91–108*, 693).

[38] The explicit Jesus-references in the Testaments of the Twelve Patriarchs have, perhaps unfairly, set the reflexes by which we conceptualize phases of Christian transmission. So, in Michael Knibb's discussion of the transmission of Enoch by Christians, in which he is more open than most to substantial Christian intervention, he says with reference to the Parables that "it is very hard to explain the absence of any explicit Christological references in the Parables if they really are Christian, and here the contrast with the Christian Testaments of the Twelve Patriarchs is very instructive." See Knibb, "Christian Adoption," 71.

on the part of the individual scholar. But Józef T. Milik himself sought sites of composition for the Eschatological Exhortation, and (perhaps most notoriously) the Book of Parables among early Christian communities.[39] To this estimation, I would suggest that the scholarship placing the Body of the Epistle and the Gospel of Luke in conversation similarly encourages us to reckon with the possibility that Christian communities might have provided a primary site of textual development for this work as well.

The material phenomenon of absence from Qumran forces scholars to resort to, and reflect upon, their default model of the composition of the works belonging to 1 Enoch. I have suggested that one model responds to the cumulative weight of documents attested at Qumran and gives the Second Temple period conceptual priority in our compositional models. If many Enochic works were written by Jews by the time of the assembly of the Scrolls, perhaps *most* of our Enochic works were written around that time, even if they are not directly attested in documents from Qumran. But a material philological approach, in tandem with a "Christian-until-proven-Jewish" problematic, necessarily shifts the probabilities. Enochic works absent from Qumran, and therefore extant only in Christian transmission, cannot be so easily imagined in or retrojected to hypothetical Jewish environs.

To summarize, by describing the contents of our non-Ethiopic manuscripts according to the subsidiary works they attest, or do not attest, we best represent text that is present, and even more crucially for this project, clarify the extent of the text that is absent. As such, I have argued that absence of evidence for subsidiary works at Qumran most probably represents evidence of absence. Moreover, I have suggested that subsidiary works which are absent from Qumran effectively lose a *terminus ante quem* – a point at which we imagine a version of the work to have come into existence – that they had previously gained largely by analogy. When this *terminus ante quem* is removed, new and wider vistas of composition and development open up potentially stretching far beyond BCE Judaea.

Indeed, these horizons might stretch beyond the boundaries of Judaism, as defined by some, into the worlds studied under the heading of early Christianity. It becomes the job of scholars, if they are so inclined, to craft positive arguments by which to defend removing the text from its documentary contexts and projecting it into other sites of composition and development. We cannot take for granted the extraction of Jewish works from Christian documents, nor the extraction of "earlier" (e.g. Second Temple) text from late antique or medieval documents. Both must be argued.

---

[39] See Milik, *Books of Enoch*, 90–1 (Parables), 106–7 (Eschatological Exhortation).

(Not) Knowing what we're missing: on to the Animal Apocalypse

I have stated a concern that the three missing subsidiary works would be generally difficult to date on internal, or purely textual, grounds. There is, however, a perfect candidate for a re-dating on internal grounds hidden and undiscovered inside the Animal Apocalypse. The Animal Apocalypse (1 En 85–90) is the most "datable" section of the entire 108-chaptered progression, because it is a historical allegory that narrates event after event in animalistic garb. Early scholarship on 1 Enoch, which treated the entire 108 chapters as if they were written all at once, honed in on this section as the key to dating the work as they understood it. Though these scholars were incorrect in their assessment of the compositional history of the work, their instinct that this section is uniquely amenable to dating on internal grounds is demonstrably correct.

One might object that this is a moot point, as there is no missing subsidiary work: the Animal Apocalypse is understood to represent a single work, and it is attested at Qumran in no fewer than four manuscripts, as mentioned in the charts above. It is certainly the most datable section, and has been thus dated to the satisfaction of a majority of scholars, who place it in Hellenistic Judaea. In the next part of the book, I intend to demonstrate that the Animal Apocalypse breaks into two subsidiary works, only *one* of which is attested at Qumran. In keeping with the methodological conclusions of the present chapter, it then becomes my task to shift the burden of proof and argue for a new *Sitz im Leben* for the missing subsidiary work. Essentially, the rest of this project both capitalizes upon and serves as a test-case for a hypothesis proposed in this chapter. My forthcoming argument for a re-dating of part of the Animal Apocalypse in the first century CE demonstrates that we were right to suspect its absence from our second century BCE manuscripts.

The Animal Apocalypse represents a lucky break: we happen to have fragments from Qumran, and the work happens to pursue an *ex post facto* prophecy that makes a re-dating possible. But our luck does not imply that my conclusions represent a fluke or limit their applicability. Instead, I intend to demonstrate that it is practically possible to speak in a more detailed and documented manner about the compositional history of the Animal Apocalypse. My methodology in this project might not be practicable with reference to other works, such as Enoch's Vision of the Flood. But my conclusions bear important implications for the way we gauge our expectations of these other works, even if we cannot yet (or ever, barring the future discovery of new documents) substantiate these hypotheses.

In sum, in this chapter, I hope to have convinced the reader that, on principle, subsidiary works missing from Qumran *may* belong to contexts at some distance from BCE Judaea. In the next stage of my argument, I will strengthen this abstract claim with positive evidence, demonstrating that one subsidiary work – the Animal Apocalypse of Enoch – is a clear product of a later period than scholars have imagined.

CHAPTER 2

The Nature of the Beast: Literary Evidence for Animal Apocalypse(s) of Enoch

The Animal Apocalypse is an allegorical history in which various species of animals stand in for humans and groups of humans of both good and ill repute – something like Animal Farm for the ancient world. At this point, here in my opening paragraph, I would normally provide a summary of the dating, provenance, contents, and literary and theological themes of the Animal Apocalypse. It is the purpose of this chapter, however, to radically re-evaluate all of these descriptors. We should begin, then, with this: what is the Animal Apocalypse?

The Book of Dreams (1 En 83–90) contains two dreams, which seem to represent two subsidiary works, meaning (as we have previously established the function of the term "work") that they represent two separate hypothesized sites of composition. The first, corresponding to Gəʿəz Enoch chapters 83–4, is sometimes called the Flood Vision. The second, corresponding to Gəʿəz Enoch chapters 85–90, is called the Animal Apocalypse and is the independent subject of a great many articles and monographs. It is the Animal Apocalypse that will be the subject of this chapter.

Here is the crux of the issue with the Animal Apocalypse: Our documents of the work attest similar but different texts, especially when it comes to length. The documentary sets we will discuss here are fragments from Qumran sorted into three Aramaic manuscripts, as well as Ethiopic codices dating from the fifteenth century onwards.[1] There are also two Greek witnesses that contain

---

[1] The Ethiopic text of the Animal Apocalypse can be accessed in a variety of editions, with a manuscript base steadily growing as more manuscripts became available to Western scholars, through theft, purchase, or (more recently) photographs. Seventeen were available to Charles in 1893, forty-nine were used by Nickelsburg in 2002, and Loren T. Stuckenbruck and Ted Erho have, in recent years, collected photographs of at least one hundred more for a future edition of Ethiopic Enoch. Looking specifically to recent presentations of the Animal Apocalypse in Ethiopic, a critical text was prepared in transliteration by Patrick

about five verses apiece that will be addressed along the way, though their fragmentary nature limits their impact on our conclusions.[2]

Our earliest documents from Qumran contain the least amount of text. Our latest documents, the Ethiopic codices, contain the most. Scholars have granted the later Ethiopic tradition conceptual priority in determining what comprises the "work" of the Animal Apocalypse: the Animal Apocalypse *is* 1 En 85–90. This means that the Animal Apocalypse, the work, is understood to be the series of words-in-order – the text – that we find in the Ethiopic manuscript tradition. The work becomes equivalent to one text or set of words-in-order. This is a conceptual collapse between two philological levels, but imagining the full "work" by way of text that emerges from the best preserved documentary set is an understandable attraction. Our Qumran documents are, quite literally, fragments, and it is hard to know what was there before bats and humidity and amateur (and professional!) archaeologists took their toll. If there are any words-in-order matching between the Aramaic and Ethiopic documents, the match in text has been understood to justify a corresponding understanding of a match in work to which the text attests. Thus, the Animal Apocalypse, the work equivalent to the Ethiopic 1 En 85–90, is read by scholars such as József T. Milik, the first to publish an edition of the Qumran fragments, as the work lying behind our Aramaic fragments, and is thus used to restore words on lines as well as entire purportedly missing columns.

However, I will contribute the hypothesis that the purported work, the Animal Apocalypse, can be broken into two, and only one of these sections is attested at Qumran.

The first half of the Animal Apocalypse is an allegory of the history of Israel, from primeval time to the destruction of the First Temple. It corresponds to 1 En 85.1–89.58. I call this section the Vision of the Beasts.

The second half of the Animal Apocalypse is an allegory that begins with the destruction of the First Temple and seems to go until the eschaton (1 En 89.59–90.42). It contains an internal structuring device that does not appear in the first section, a chronology of seventy shepherds marking the onward march of time towards time's final end. I will call this unit the Apocalypse of

---

Tiller, and that text was provided in the Gəʿəz abugida with collations from other editions by Daniel Assefa. See R. H. Charles, *The Book of Enoch Translated from Professor Dillmann's Ethiopic Text* (Oxford: Clarendon Press, 1893); Nickelsburg, *1 Enoch 1*; Erho and Stuckenbruck, "A Manuscript History"; Patrick A. Tiller, *A Commentary on the Animal Apocalypse of I Enoch* (Atlanta: Scholars Press, 1993); Daniel Assefa, *L'apocalypse des animaux (1 Hen 85–90): une propagande militaire? : approches narrative, historico-critique, perspectives théologiques* (Leiden: Brill, 2007).

[2] These are fragments 1 and 2 of P. Oxy 2069, corresponding to 1 En 85.10–86.2 and 87.1–3, and the marginalia from Codex Vaticanus Graecus 1809, corresponding to 1 En 89.42–9.

the Birds.³ The Apocalypse of the Birds, unlike the Vision of the Beasts, is not attested at Qumran, as we will see.

In this chapter, I will suggest that the Apocalypse of the Birds can and should be separated from the Vision of the Beasts. Initial grounds for this split can be found in the double narration of the Destruction of Jerusalem at the close of the Vision of the Beasts and the start of the Apocalypse of the Birds, a duplication that has been previously noted by scholars. Additional evidence might be sought in terminological differences between the two works, alongside the long-noted literary differences between the two textual sections. This literary analysis opens up the possibility that there might be separable works, and a textual site at which they might be split from one another. But I wish to be clear that this does not represent independently conclusive evidence speaking in favor of their separation. Source-critical analyses proceeding on literary grounds are not always convincing with reference to apocalypses, given this genre's proclivity towards repetition. And source criticism of pseudepigrapha, like Enoch, can be frustrated by the reality that many of these works are only extant in much later manuscripts, with text likely impacted by centuries of transmission.

I will therefore use the material evidence to reinforce the suspicion on literary grounds that the Animal Apocalypse contains two separable works. In Chapter 1, I demonstrated that subsidiary works are the level of literary organization to which our documents, including those found at Qumran, best attest, and we should not restore missing subsidiary works to our late ancient documents. In light of the literary analysis of the Animal Apocalypse, the absence of a subsidiary work of 1 Enoch from Qumran becomes especially suggestive of actual (rather than accidental) absence. I take our evidence to indicate that the Vision of the Beasts once circulated without the Apocalypse of the Birds attached, affirming that an initial hypothesis of multiple stages of composition is on the right track. A further implication is that the Apocalypse of the Birds should not automatically be given the second century BCE *terminus ante quem* that the Qumran fragments provide for the Vision of the Beasts. This observation will pave the way for subsequent chapters seeking a new provenance for the

---

³ It is not recognized as a separate work, but this section is given its own name in German scholarship: the "Seventy Shepherd Vision" or "Siebzig-Hirten-Vision." Klaus Beyer, one of the most recent scholars to use the moniker, is notably unimpressed by the artistry underpinning this schema, calling it an "unimaginative (phantasielose) allegory." It is worth noting that "Siebzig-Hirten-Vision" is the title of a work which is sometimes understood to cover 1 En 85–90 (as in Koch), whereas I use it selectively to refer to the work beginning only at 89.59. It is also used in Uhlig's edition of the Ethiopic Enoch as a descriptive heading, similar to Nickelsburg's edition. In Uhlig it is styled as, "Die Siebzig Hirten – erste Periode," and so on. See Klaus Beyer, *Die aramäischen Texte vom Toten Meer* (Gottingen: Vandenhoeck & Ruprecht, 1984), 243n1; Klaus Koch, *Vor der Wende der Zeiten: Beiträge zur apokalyptischen Literatur* (Neukirchen-Vluyn, Germany: Neukirchener, 1996), 122; Siegbert Uhlig, *Das äthiopische Henochbuch* (Gütersloh: Gütersloher Verlagshaus, 1984), 695.

Apocalypse of the Birds. Note also that the case in future chapters for a compositional home for the Apocalypse of the Birds that postdates the assembly of the Qumran library strengthens the hypothesis that the Apocalypse of the Birds was absent from Qumran. I will propose a dating for the Apocalypse of the Birds in first-century CE Roman Palestine, and in so doing, substantiate my proposal that it should be deemed absent from the Hellenistic Qumran manuscripts.

In sum, this chapter will put forward a provisional hypothesis of multiple works – the Vision of the Beasts and the Apocalypse of the Birds – on literary grounds. The next will seek confirmation of this initial hypothesis' plausibility in the material record. I will conclude that the Vision of the Beasts is present at Qumran, but the Apocalypse of the Birds is absent. And Chapter 4 will complement this hypothesis by analyzing the flaws in arguments that assume that the Apocalypse of the Birds belongs in the Hellenistic era.

What is the Animal Apocalypse?: a current (rough) consensus

First, we should establish the current consensus on the work known as the Animal Apocalypse and provide a brief introduction to the animals roaming its chapters. The key arc of the work, as currently constituted and delineated in Ethiopic, is the decline and restoration of the people of Israel. The lineage of the Israelites is symbolized by bulls and sheep, depending on the era in question. Adam, Noah, and Seth are, perhaps, not obvious Israelites in their antediluvian settings. They are, however, the forefathers of the Israelite line which becomes the fixation of the work, so they are included in the narrative arc. In the days of Adam and Seth, this line is symbolized by white bulls (1 En 85.3–89.12). The era of white bulls sees a familiar litany of primordial events: the fall of the Watchers (here, symbolized by falling stars, in 1 En 86.1–6), the judgment of these stars and their monstrous children (1 En 87.1–88.3), and the Flood and its aftermath (1 En 89.1–10). By the time of Jacob/Israel, this line is transformed and is now symbolized by sheep, who are protected and sometimes avenged by the Lord of the Sheep – God (1 En 89.11–16). So, Abraham, a white bull (89.11), begets Isaac (white bull, 89.11) and Ishmael (wild donkey, 89.11). Isaac, the white bull, begets Esau (wild boar, 89.12) and Jacob, a sheep (89.12). Jacob then begets twelve sheep (89.12), and the descent of our protagonistal line through sheep continues from there. The sheep occasionally make their own problems,[4] but more often are set upon by a menagerie of wild animals, representing various "nations" or ethnic groups. (Wild animals are always represented as bad or, at

---

[4] This is usually narrated through the sheep being blinded, see James C. VanderKam, "Open and Closed Eyes in the Animal Apocalypse (1 Enoch 85–90)," in *The Idea of Biblical Interpretation: Essays in Honor of James L. Kugel*, ed. Hindy Najman and Judith Newman (Leiden: Brill, 2004), 279–92.

least, foreign in the Animal Apocalypse.) These episodes in the history of the sheep usually find biblical parallels, and we can spot a one-to-one animal symbolism throughout the first part of narrative. The wolves haranguing the sheep under the leadership of Moses, for instance, clearly represent the Egyptians. (Other symbols are more opaque; see the chart below for more.) These beastly antagonists are all quadrupeds up until the start of the third period (i.e. up until 1 En 90.1), then all birds for a time (1 En 90.1–17). Air and land join forces (a bit comically) just in time to be swallowed up by the earth (1 En 90.18). It is sheep versus beasts for most of the Animal Apocalypse.

Sometime around the fall of the Israelite kingdom(s), the Animal Apocalypse introduces a schema of seventy shepherds (at 1 En 89.59), who will mete out the punishment the sheep deserve, and an unfortunate little extra besides. Although the shepherds have a chronological function, they are characters in their own right. Scholars generally understand the shepherds to represent angels.[5] These shepherd-angels will shepherd Israel into the eschaton.

The shepherd schema has been a crucial factor in arguments for the dating and provenance of the Animal Apocalypse. The idea that there might be seventy *somethings* structuring a particularly dark period of Israel's existence is variously attested in Second Temple literature.[6] The most famous instance is

---

[5] It is assumed in contemporary scholarship that the shepherds represent angels, each sequentially charged with overseeing discrete periods of Israel's history. Early scholarship was convinced that these represented seventy different rulers that would be given hegemony over Israel (see, for instance, the initial translation and analysis of the "seventy princes" in Richard Laurence, *The Book of Enoch, the Prophet* (Oxford: JH Parker, 1838), xxii–xxvii.

By the time of the influential work of Schürer (though he credits von Hoffmann with the original insight), who would be followed by Charles, the consensus would shift to angelic guardians (or antagonists, as the case might be). See Emil Schürer, "Das Buch Henoch," in *Lehrbuch Der Neutestamentlichen Zeitgeschichte* (Leipzig: J.C. Hinrichs, 1874), 531–2; Johann Christian Konrad von Hofmann, *Der Schriftbeweis: Ein theologischer Versuch*, vol. 1 (Nördlingen: Beck'schen Buchhandlung, 1857), 422; Charles, *Enoch or, 1 Enoch*, 200.

This conclusion has been further buttressed with reference to parallel material we now possess from Qumran (4Q390 is considered to be especially close). On this connection, see Milik, "Fragments Grecs Du Livre," 254–5; Tiller, *Commentary*, 52–4; Devorah Dimant, "New Light from Qumran on the Jewish Pseudepigrapha – 4Q390," in *The Madrid Qumran Congress: Proceedings of the International Congress on the Dead Sea Scrolls, Madrid 18–21 March, 1991*, ed. Julio Trebolle Barrera and Luis Vegas Montaner (Leiden: Brill, 1992), 442.

I find the clinching consideration to be the constant equation of human ethnic and political groups with animal species, whereas every "human" character represents a heavenly or transfigured (i.e. Noah, Moses, Elijah) figure. Presumably "human" shepherds must, to be consistent, represent heavenly figures.

[6] See, for instance, Devorah Dimant, "The Seventy Weeks Chronology (Dan 9, 24–27) in the Light of New Qumranic Texts," in *The Book of Daniel in the Light of New Findings*, Bibliotheca Ephemeridum Theologicarum Lovaniensium (Leuven: Peeters, 1993), 187–210; Cana Werman, "Epochs and End-Time: The 490-Year Scheme in Second Temple Literature," *Dead Sea Discoveries* 13, no. 2 (2006): 229–55.

Daniel 9.25–7's interpretation of Jeremiah's prophecy of seventy years of exile to represent the seventy "weeks" up until the menace and transgression of Antiochus Epiphanes in the second century BCE. On analogy with this, and assisted by a perceived equation between Judas Maccabeus and the Ram of the fourth period,[7] it is usually assumed that the seventy-shepherd schema was meant to end at some point in the second century BCE, thus ending time as we know it and ushering in the eschaton, providing a *terminus ante quem*.

Under the dubious supervision of the shepherds, we are told the story of post-exilic Israel. In the first period (1 En 89.65–72a), the First Temple is destroyed. In the second, the Second Temple is rebuilt, and is explicitly defiled from the start (1 En 89.72b–90.1). In the third, a great flock of birds devours and decimates the sheep (1 En 90.2–5). By the fourth period (1 En 90.6), lambs are born to the sheep. The lambs seem to have new ideas about how to go about things, though the sheep largely fail to listen. Some sort of leader (symbolized by a ram, like David and Solomon, so likely a political leader) rises up and organizes the sheep.[8]

---

[7] The scholar credited by his contemporaries with establishing this equation is Friedrich Lücke, in 1852. Other nineteenth-century and early twentieth-century scholars remained convinced that the ram was meant to represent John Hyrcanus, such as, most notably, Emil Schürer and August Dillmann (in fact, Lücke would eventually switch to this position). But the tide shifted with the work of R. H. Charles, who found it unbelievable that the text would ignore Judas, "the greatest of all the Maccabees." In recent scholarship, the Judas Maccabeus equation is accepted by most of the major commentators, including József T. Milik, Matthew Black, Patrick Tiller, Daniel Olson, James VanderKam, George W. E. Nickelsburg, Devorah Dimant, and Loren T. Stuckenbruck. Notable dissenters are Menahem Kister and Eyal Regev, who feel a non-Maccabean religious reformer is in view (this will be discussed at length below).

In order of their mention here, see Friedrich Lücke, *Versuch einer vollständigen Einleitung in die Offenbarung des Johannes: oder allgemeine Untersuchungen über die apokalyptische Litteratur überhaupt und die Apokalypse des Johannes insbesondere* (Bonn: Weber., 1852), 131–3; August Dillmann, *Das Buch Henoch* (Fr. Chr. Wilh. Vogel, 1853), xliii–xlv; Schürer, "Das Buch Henoch"; Charles, *Enoch or, 1 Enoch*, 208; Milik, *Books of Enoch*, 43–4; Black, *Book of Enoch*, 276; Tiller, *Commentary*, 62–3; Daniel C. Olson, *A New Reading of the Animal Apocalypse of 1 Enoch "All Nations Shall Be Blessed,"* Studia in Veteris Testamenti Pseudepigrapha 24 (Danvers, MA: Brill, 2013), 85–6; James C. VanderKam, *Enoch and the Growth of an Apocalyptic Tradition*, Catholic Biblical Quaterly Monograph Series (Washington, DC: Catholic Biblical Association of America, 1984), 161–3; Nickelsburg, *1 Enoch 1*, 396–401; Devorah Dimant, "Ideology and History in the Animal Apocalypse (1 Enoch 85–90)," in *From Enoch to Tobit: Collected Studies in Ancient Jewish Literature* (Tübingen: Mohr Siebeck, 2017), 92; Loren T. Stuckenbruck, "'Reading the Present' in the Animal Apocalypse (1 Enoch 85–90)," in *Reading the Present in the Qumran LIbrary: The Perception of the Contemporary by Means of Scriptural Interpretations*, ed. Kristen De Troyer and Armin Lange (Atlanta: SBL Press, 2005), 95–6; Menahem Kister, "Concerning the History of the Essenes / לתולדות כת האיסיים," *Tarbiz* 56, no. 1 (1986), 1–18; Eyal Regev, "The Ram and Qumran: The Eschatological Character of the Ram in the Animal Apocalypse (1 En. 90: 10–13)," in *Apocalyptic Thinking in Early Judaism: Engaging with John Collins' The Apocalyptic Imagination*, ed. Sidnie White Crawford and Cecilia Wassen, Supplements to the Journal for the Study of Judaism 182 (Leiden: Brill, 2018), 181; Assefa, *L'apocalypse des animaux*, 220–32.

[8] It is not clear if the ram is part of the conquering army, or if it is killed before the great victory. See 1 En 90.9–17.

With divine assistance, the sheep prevail over the birds as well as the beasts (who, though ignored for most of the third and fourth periods, are now spontaneously present again).

At this point, the Lord of the Sheep sets up a throne on earth, and justice is served. The shepherds, beasts, and blinded sheep get their just desserts in the fiery pit, and something like a new Temple or new Jerusalem is brought to replace the "old house." The vindicated sheep are worshipped by all the remaining birds and beasts, very like the vision recounted in Isaiah.[9]

But at 90.31, the Animal Apocalypse outpaces Isaiah. The white sheep, whose wool is thick and pure,[10] are collectively reunited after their previous dispersion. They are gathered in the new house of the Lord of Sheep along with the beasts and birds, a curious happenstance that nevertheless makes the Lord of the Sheep rejoice. The eyes of all of them (including the beasts, perhaps) are opened, and the house is overflowing with creatures. In 1 En 90.37, a white bull is born, which terrifies the beasts and birds to no end. But in 1 En 90.38, "all their species were transformed, and they all became white bulls." At this point, the syntax is a bit ambiguous, but it seems that sheep, beasts, and birds alike are transformed into white bulls.[11] The species of the antediluvian patriarchs is restored, and ethnic divisions are apparently erased. This is a startling account of eschatological universalism, especially given the deeply particularist nature of the preceding allegory and narrative.[12] But we are given no further clarification, as the final lines are simply Enoch remarking on how strange his vision was. (On this, modern scholars tend to agree with Enoch.)

---

[9] See the expansive formulation of Daniel Olson: "The account of the New Jerusalem exhibits no distinctly Enochic themes, but it manages to fulfill a staggering array of Biblical prophecies." He provides a litany of about 25 Hebrew Bible references, 11 of which are from Isaiah. In Olson, *A New Reading*, 223. For another recent treatment, see Stefan Green, "'The Temple of God and Crises in Isaiah 65–66 and 1 Enoch,'" in *Studies in Isaiah: History, Theology and Reception*, ed. Tommy Wasserman, Greger Andersson, and David Willgren, Library of Hebrew Bible/Old Testament Studies 654 (London: Bloomsbury T&T Clark, 2017), 47–66.

[10] We were perhaps supposed to assume white sheep before, but it is uniquely emphasized here. See Rivka Nir, "'And Behold, Lambs Were Born of Those White Sheep' (1 Enoch 90:6) The Color White and Eschatological Expectation in the Animal Apocalypse," *Henoch* 35 (2013): 50–69.

[11] This understanding is defended in the recent commentaries of Tiller, Nickelsburg, and Olson. See Tiller, *Commentary*, 385; Nickelsburg, *1 Enoch 1*, 403; Olson, *A New Reading*.

[12] The strangeness of these final two verses, 37 and 38, has led some German scholarship to postulate that these verses, and these alone, are later interpolations – though by "later," they mean "later Second Temple." See Günter Reese, *Die Geschichte Israels in der Auffassung des frühen Judentums: Eine Untersuchung der Tiervision und der Zehnwochenapokalypse des äthiopischen Henochbuches, der Geschichtsdarstellung der Assumptio Mosis und der des 4Esrabuches*, SBAB (Berlin: Philo, 1999), 54–5; Karlheinz Müller, *Studien zur frühjüdischen Apokalyptik* (Stuttgart: Verlag Katholisches Bibelwerk, 1991), 164–6; Andreas Bedenbender, *Der Gott der Welt tritt auf den Sinai: Entstehung, Entwicklung und Funktionsweise der frühjüdischen Apokalyptik* (Berlin: Institut Kirche und Judentum, 2000), 208–11.

There are some inevitable pockets of disagreement, some of which I have attempted to signal in the footnotes, but this plot summary represents the basic status of scholarship on the Animal Apocalypse. It is understood as a second century BCE Hellenistic Jewish composition, likely composed in Palestine, with a unique way of presenting a symbolic total history of Israel, culminating in an unusually universalist portrait of the eschaton.

Table 2.1 Summary, Protagonists and Antagonists of the Animal Apocalypse

1 Enoch (Mashafa Henok)	Summary of Contents	Key Protagonist	Key Antagonist
85.1–9	Adam, Eve, and Progeny	White Bulls, Cattle[a]	Black Bull (Cain)
86.1–6	Fallen Watchers, and Violent Giants	White Bulls	Stars→Black Bulls, Elephants, Camels, Donkeys[b]
87.1–88.3	Judgment of Watchers and Giants	White Bulls	Elephants, Camels, Donkeys
89.1–8	Noah and the Flood	White Bulls	Black Bulls, Elephants, Camels, Donkeys
89.9–27	Flood to Exodus from Egypt	White Bulls→Sheep (Israelites)	Wild Donkeys (Ishmaelites), Wild Boars (Edomites), Wolves (Egyptians)
89.28–38	Exodus to Moses' Death	Sheep (Israelites)	Wolves (Egyptians)
89.39–50	Entrance into Land, Building of First Temple	Sheep (Israelites), Rams (Saul, David, Solomon)	Dogs (Philistines), Foxes (Ammonites), Wild Boars (Edomites)
89.51–8	Apostasy of the Two Kingdoms	Sheep, Rams	Lions (Babylonians?),[c] Tigers[d]
89.59–64	Commissioning of Seventy Shepherds	Sheep	Shepherds[e] (Angels)
89.65–72a	First Period: Twelve Shepherds	Sheep	Shepherds, Lions (Babylonians?), Tigers
89.72b–90.1	Second period: Twenty-Three Shepherds	Sheep	Shepherds, Wild Boars (Edomites)
90.2–5	Third Period: Twenty-Three Shepherds	Sheep	Shepherds, Eagles, Vultures, Kites, Ravens (Variously identified)[f]
90.6–19	Fourth Period: Twelve Shepherds Until the End Time	Sheep, Ram (Judas Maccabeus?)[g]	Shepherds, Ravens, Eagles, Vultures, Kites, Wild Sheep
90.20–7	The Judgment of Shepherds and Sheep	Sheep	Shepherds, Blinded Sheep

1 Enoch (Mashafa Henok)	Summary of Contents	Key Protagonist	Key Antagonist
90.28–37	A New Beginning: New Home for the Sheep, Transformation of All Species	White Sheep→Bulls Wild Animals→Bulls Birds→Bulls	
90.39–42	The Conclusion to the Vision	N/A	

[a] The color of bulls and cattle is narratively important. Eve and Adam, a white heifer and bull respectively, bear three progeny: Cain is a black bull-calf, Abel is red, Seth is white.
[b] Elephants, camels, and donkeys are generally understood to represent the illicit offspring of the Watchers—in other Enochic literature, or an "Enochic" reading of Genesis, the Giants. It is worth noting that these all represent animals which are neither domestic (as the sheep used to represent the Israelites), nor wild (as the animals used to represent the other nations), but instead a kind of in-between sort of animal, domesticated by some, but also known in the wild. That these would be symbolic of the Giants, the product of miscegenation between Israelites and an angelic other, is particularly artful.
[c] 89.55 states that the lions are accompanied by tigers, wolves, hyenas, and foxes. 89.56 places the lions at the head of the destructive horde, and 89.57 reminds the reader that all the wild animals are working in concert.
[d] The exact identity of the tigers (አናምርት, *anamərt*) is not so certain as the rest, and very much depends on how scholars read the progression of the rest of the account.
[e] It is not quite fair to label the shepherds as antagonists in the same way as are the Babylonian lions that devour the Israelite sheep, but it is presaged in this section that the shepherds destroy far more sheep than they were assigned to do.
[f] I will provide a new hypothesis concerning the identity of all these birds in chapter 6. There is little consensus in the secondary literature, other than the general impression that they must somehow represent the Hellenistic regimes (Macedonians, Seleucids, Ptolemies, etc.).
[g] Variously identified. I will discuss the translation of "ram" at length in chapter 6.

Textual fluidity and apocalyptic stability: a note on the text

In order to proceed, we need to think carefully about how, and whether, we might establish a pre-Ethiopic text for the Animal Apocalypse. Parallel text, or correspondence of words-in-order, is demonstrable between chapters 85–90 of Ethiopic Enoch, extremely poorly preserved Aramaic fragments from Qumran, Greek fragments from Oxyrhynchus, and the tenth-century Codex Vaticanus Graecus 1809. In the previous chapter, I suggested that the soundest practices of restoration would proceed along the lines of subsidiary works, therefore justifying the restoration of the text of a subsidiary work to contexts in which we find *parts* of that subsidiary work. Though we have affirmed our practices of restoration on the abstract level of *work*, we still need to concretely affirm them on the level of *text*. In order to talk about the Animal Apocalypse in an earlier period – Hellenistic, Roman, Byzantine, or otherwise – I need to capitalize on textual parallelism to import, on a larger-scale, text derived from the Ethiopic tradition into the possible historical archive of earlier contexts. Since I will now spend the rest of the book utilizing a text of the Animal Apocalypse primarily derived from Ethiopic tradition, this fact deserves sustained consideration.

The primary feature that would discourage the restoration of text from medieval Ethiopia to other times or places is demonstrable textual fluidity. Moments of variance between the Ethiopic and pre-Ethiopic textual traditions might suggest we simply do not know what we do not know about the text during late antiquity. But, on the other side of things, the genre of historical apocalyptic can often be shown to be uniquely connectable to earlier compositional settings, which suggests that the restoration of text might be well justified. I suggest that reflecting on both considerations leads us to a cautious optimism concerning the feasibility of using a text found in medieval Ethiopian manuscripts to discuss early Mediterranean Judaism and Christianity. Demonstrable textual fluidity reminds us not to uncritically assume the Ethiopic provides us with the text of a singular and unchanged composition dating to Maccabean times. But, at the same time, some degree of textual stability, though not total, is safeguarded by the genre of historical apocalyptic.

Most scholars working on Ethiopic Henok remain convinced that the period of Ethiopic transmission was a relatively quiet one for the text of this work. Current scholarship indicates that 1 Enoch has been the beneficiary of a relatively conservative Ethiopic scribal tradition. Once anchored in the prejudiced Orientalist evaluation of Ethiopians (and their scribes) as backwards and effectively incapable of creativity,[13] this position now has the weight of extended study of native Ethiopic scribal practices and manuscripts of Enoch.[14] After all, scribal conservativism is not a universal default for the human transmission of texts, but an active and practiced choice requiring substantial intellectual work over centuries. A conservative transmission of scriptural texts would be one of the many sophisticated reading and writing practices documented in the rich literary history of Ethiopia. However, we should not therefore assume Ethiopic documents preserve for us a Second Temple-era text. What our knowledge of Ethiopic scribal practices indicates is that the Ethiopic scribal tradition likely conservatively transmitted whatever it received at the hypothesized date of translation, usually estimated around the fourth to sixth century CE. As noted above, this likelihood does not do away with the problem of transmission, but simply shifts our focus to the earlier phases of transmission in Greek and perhaps Aramaic, as possible (and, as seen above, demonstrable) sites of textual fluidity, transformation, and dynamism.

We arrive at the question of the character of the Animal Apocalypse's transmission. Inspection of the different versions of the text evidenced in

---

[13] On which, please see my forthcoming article, "When Enoch Left Ethiopia: On Race and Philological (Im)possibilities in the 19th century."

[14] So, Erho and Stuckenbruck conclude "the scribal tradition was extremely conservative, to the point where we should probably imagine such individuals largely attempting to be human Xerox machines." See Erho and Stuckenbruck, "Gəʿəz Manuscript Tradition," 6.

Aramaic, Greek, and Ethiopic indicates that the textual tradition was relatively (though not completely) stable. Directed studies comparing the various texts of the Animal Apocalypse have been done very well elsewhere, most notably by Patrick Tiller, recently revisited and updated by Daniel Assefa and Henryk Drawnel.[15] There is no way to summarize the differences between our versions in a way that would apply to every instance. The Aramaic is shorter than the Ethiopic sometimes,[16] but occasionally longer.[17] Similarly, the Greek is shorter than the Ethiopic sometimes,[18] but occasionally longer.[19] In most cases, the kind and character of textual difference is minor, typically amounting to differences of few words in vocabulary, phrasing, or syntax.[20] There is one site where the Aramaic fragments overlap and witness text that differ by about a dozen characters at two different locations: textual uniformity cannot even be found when we restrict ourselves to a single archive![21]

Still, I do not see in our data evidence indicating ongoing textual upheaval. That the text can be profitably presented and compared in parallel columns

---

[15] Tiller, *Commentary*, 127–38; Henryk Drawnel, "5.5.2: Enoch: The Book of Dreams: Aramaic," in *Textual History of the Bible*, ed. Armin Lange (Brill, 2020), https://doi.org/10.1163/2452-4107_thb_COM_0205050200; Daniel Assefa, "5.5.1: Enoch: The Book of Dreams: Greek," in *Textual History of the Bible*, vol. 2, ed. Armin Lange (Brill, 2020), https://doi.org/10.1163/2452-4107_thb_COM_0205050200

[16] See, most notably, the substantially longer Ethiopic version of the Flood narrated at 1 En 89.1–9 compared with 4Q206 8 i. The Ethiopic contains throughout reference to an enclosure covered with a high roof, absent from the Aramaic. It is at this site that a few scholars (Olson, Tiller, Drawnel, Black) have introduced the idea of multiple recensions. I think we lack sufficient evidence to confirm the idea of Aramaic (or Greek) recensions among our very fragmentary early evidence – it seems beyond our material remains to situate them within the kind of stemmatic tree needed to substantiate the hypothesis of a recension. But I take these scholars' comments to indicate that this site presents the most substantial variance to our text-critics. See Tiller, *Commentary*, 258; Drawnel, "5.5.2: Enoch"; Black, *Book of Enoch*, 262; Olson, *A New Reading*, 160–1.

[17] A longer Aramaic text can be found at 4Q204 15 ll. 9–10, compared with 1 En 89.35, including in the Aramaic some sort of oath sworn by the Israelites that is mentioned in no other textual version.

[18] 1 En 89.43 is longer by about 10 words in Codex Vaticanus Gr. 1809 than in the Ethiopic text. See the discussion in Assefa, "5.5.1: Enoch."

[19] 1 En 89.49 is shorter by about 30 words in Codex Vaticanus Gr. 1809 than in Ethiopic.

[20] For a representative example showing quite minimal variation (until the last line), compare 4Q204 15 to the Ethiopic, as discussed in Tiller, *Commentary*, 288–97. On this fragment, Drawnel concludes, "In most cases, the Aramaic text is faithfully reflected in the Ethiopic versions." In Drawnel, "5.5.2: Enoch."

[21] This is not demonstrated with reference to overlapping text, of which there is not sufficient to pass judgement. Rather one fragment, 4Q205 6 (cf. 1 En 89.10–15), as it has been reconstructed, has enough room to fit a certain amount of textual material restored from the Ethiopic. But another fragment, 4Q206 8 ii (cf. 1 En 89.12–15) is short by 16 letters at the section paralleling 1 En 89.11 and 14 letters at the section paralleling 1 En. 89.13, according to Tiller, *Commentary*, 270.

indicates that some sort of relationship exists.²² We are looking at different versions, and the existence of different versions does not, on its own, necessarily imply an "unstable" textual tradition. After all, there is no ancient textual tradition untouched by some degree of change. Given this relatively restrained degree of textual fluidity on a verse-by-verse basis, I understand that a link, though cautious, can be fruitfully made between later-attested text and some earlier contexts.

Finally, we can appeal to the genre of the Animal Apocalypse, as a historical apocalypse particularly indebted to the literary device of *vaticinium ex eventu*, to justify the use of the younger Ethiopic text to discuss far older and distant cultural contexts. The work presents an eschatological narrative in a specific and protracted chronological progression, and there are limits to how much history fits into this progression.²³ For instance, the introduction of four species of evil birds at 1 En 90.1 begs its readers to supply real-world referents, with particularly allegorized actions providing clues as to their identification. Similarly, 1 En 90.6–19 narrates an overwhelming Jewish military victory, an event for which there are relatively few candidates in late antiquity. Though the data within the text must be contingently interpreted, there are clearly articulated historical markers in the Animal Apocalypse.

I have gathered scholarship on Ethiopic scribal habits, pointed to the limited textual fluidity demonstrable between our versions, and referenced the dating of historical apocalyptic works to suggest that we are justified in using a text of an Ethiopic version of the Animal Apocalypse to illuminate earlier periods. A tentative hypothesis of textual stability justifying our use of a later version to speak to an earlier period does *not* imply a never-changing text or work. Indeed, I have indicated evidence for change throughout, and will argue for quite substantial textual development below. But all of the factors discussed above strongly suggest that the Ethiopic text could very well provide a version of a work that circulated within early Judaism, at least in part. We can imagine, among other possibilities, a relatively stable transmission of text belonging to 1 En 85–90, albeit one in which we must always be ready to detect a bit of chaos.²⁴ I will therefore use an Ethiopic text with caution, from this point on.

---

²² As is presented in full in Tiller, *Commentary*, 147–223.

²³ For two sharp reflections on the potential and pitfalls of dating apocalyptic texts based on historical correspondences, see Paul J. Alexander, "Medieval Apocalypses as Historical Sources," *The American Historical Review* 73, no. 4 (1968): 997–1018; Ted M. Erho, "Internal Dating Methodologies and the Problem Posed by the Similitudes of Enoch," *Journal for the Study of the Pseudepigrapha* 20, no. 2 (2010): 83–103.

²⁴ I borrow the language of "chaos" from Liv Lied's categories of "chaotic variance" and "little variance" into which we might sort the textual histories of pseudepigrapha, in Liv Ingeborg Lied, "Media Culture, New Philology, and the Pseudepigrapha: A Note on Method," (paper, SBL Annual Meeting, Chicago, 2012).

My tentative suggestion that the later text *might* be used in historical work on early periods is not a demonstration that it necessarily *should*. The merits of this hypothesis will be known not by its roots (the theoretical discussion here), but by its fruits, or by the extent to which I can make a persuasive historical case for the situation of the text in a particular context. I hope to find what Ted Erho calls "a period in which the totality of the ideas examined are simultaneously functional,"[25] and in so doing, feel confident that the words-in-order preserved in Gəʿəz once functioned in contexts far distant in time and space from those from which we receive our material evidence.

The case for two Animal Apocalypses: the promise and pitfalls of literary evidence

In this section, I will propose a literary seam at which the Animal Apocalypse can be split into two separate works. I will provide a new account of this allegorical tale, and argue that the text extant in Gəʿəz might stem from two discrete compositional stages. I want to be quite clear, however, that the upcoming identification of a double narrative and terminological differences between two hypothesized works will not, on its own, enable us to conclude the existence of two separable literary works. This is merely a starting point for further inquiry, on which I will offer further comments below.

Much simplified from the previous chart, the chart below lists the narrative progression and major episodes included in the Animal Apocalypse, with descriptive headings adopted from Nickelsburg and VanderKam's translation and edition.[26] I have provided these headings to illustrate a standard description of the Animal Apocalypse's contents from the most popular modern translation of the work. That is, they are not selected to suit my own argument (and, indeed, it will become clear that I disagree with one particular section heading).

Below, we will explore the text in more detail. But even at this level of abstraction, it should be clear that something shifts just about halfway through, when the device of the shepherds is introduced at 1 En 89.59. Up until 1 En 89.58, the text is an opinionated but roughly one-to-one allegory of Biblical events, peopled (or rather, creatured) by animals symbolizing different characters and character groups. At 1 En 89.59, a new top-level narrative device takes over, and the remainder of the story is nestled in a schema of seventy shepherds

---

[25] In Erho, "Internal Dating Methodologies," 104.
[26] I am using Nickelsburg and VanderKam's section headings here both because of the popularity of this translation, and because they were slightly fewer in number than other editions (e.g. Tiller's monograph devoted to AA contains quite a bit more). See Nickelsburg and VanderKam, *1 Enoch*.

52   THE APOCALYPSE OF THE BIRDS

Table 2.2 Summary of Contents of Animal Apocalypse

1 Enoch (Henok)	Summary of Contents
85.1–9	Adam, Eve, and Progeny
86.1–6	Fallen Watchers, and Violent Giants
87.1–88.3	Judgment of Watchers and Giants
89.1–8	Noah and the Flood
89.9–27	Flood to Exodus from Egypt
89.28–38	Exodus to Moses' Death
89.39–50	Entrance into Land, Building of First Temple
89.51–8	Apostasy of Two Kingdoms
89.59–64	Commissioning of Seventy Shepherds
89.65–72a	First Period: Twelve Shepherds
89.72b–90.1	Second period: Twenty-Three Shepherds
90.2–5	Third Period: Twenty-Three Shepherds
90.6–19	Fourth Period: Twelve Shepherds Until the End Time
90.20–7	The Judgment of Shepherds and Sheep
90.28–38	A New Beginning: New Home for the Sheep, Transformation of All Species
90.39–42	The Conclusion to the Vision

leading (and misleading) Israel, the end of whose reign marks the onset of the eschaton. This literary shift is widely noted, and at least two commentators (Olson and Nickelsburg) use it to subdivide their editions of the text.[27]

Nickelsburg's commentary splits the text as follows: Part One is "History from Adam to the Fall of Jerusalem (85.1–89.58),'" Part Two is "History from the Destruction of Jerusalem to the End Time (89.59–90.19)." At 89.59, according to Nickelsburg, "the author changes dramatically the manner in which Israel's history is depicted."[28] Olson's commentary splits things at the same place. Olson treats 85.1–89.58 in one chapter, and 89.59–90.19 in the next, and remarks that at 89.59 "the allegory abruptly changes its focus."[29]

We might find it helpful to split the material as follows. (I have marked in grey the section we will focus on next).

---

[27] Tiller notably does not, as he is convinced the text abides by a tripartite literary structure, each division of which is led by a different white-bull-styled patriarch. So, Adam leads the "First Division: The Primordial Age" (85.1–89.9), Noah leads the "Second Division: The Present Age" (89.10–90.36), and the ambiguous white bull of 90.37 leads the "Third Division: The Future Age" (90.37–42). This leads to a very uneven division of text (the final age only contains 5 verses). See his discussion in Tiller, *Commentary*, 15–20.

[28] Nickelsburg, *1 Enoch 1*, 389.

[29] Olson, *A New Reading*, 190.

LITERARY EVIDENCE 53

Table 2.3 Two Allegories within the Animal Apocalypse

1 Enoch (Henok)	Vision of the Beasts	Allegory inside the Apocalypse of the Birds
85.1–9	Adam, Eve, and Progeny	
86.1–6	Fallen Watchers, and Violent Giants	
87.1–88.3	Judgment of Watchers and Giants	
89.1–8	Noah and the Flood	
89.9–27	Flood to Exodus from Egypt	
89.28–38	Exodus to Moses' Death	
89.39–50	Entrance into Land, Building of First Temple	
89.51–8	Apostasy of Two Kingdoms	
89.59–64		Commissioning of Seventy Shepherds
89.65–72a		First Period: Twelve Shepherds
89.72b–90.1		Second period: Twenty-Three Shepherds
90.2–5		Third Period: Twenty-Three Shepherds
90.6–19		Fourth Period: Twelve Shepherds Until the End Time
90.20–7		The Judgment of Shepherds and Sheep
90.28–37		A New Beginning: New Home for the Sheep, Transformation of All Species
90.39–42		The Conclusion to the Vision

If we check the text at the proposed site of transition, we will find further evidence that suggests different compositional contexts. Here is the text of 1 En 89.54–72. The first paragraph represents the last material from the allegory written in a simpler style. The second and third paragraphs represent the first material from the seventy-shepherd narrative.[30]

(54) And after this I saw how when they left the house of the Lord of the Sheep and his tower, they went astray in everything, and their eyes

---

[30] All the translations of the Gəʻəz text of 1 En 89–90 are courtesy of Michael Knibb, unless specific annotations indicate I have made changes. I chose Knibb's translation because his English and Gəʻəz text is drawn from one manuscript, Rylands MS 23. Even though he collates copious variants in an apparatus to the Gəʻəz, Knibb's translation is ultimately an attempt to translate one document, and thus engages in very little speculative reconstruction, which suits my document-driven approach. See Michael A. Knibb, *The Ethiopic Book of Enoch: A New Edition in the Light of the Aramaic Dead Sea Fragments*, vol. 2, Introduction, Translation and Commentary (Oxford: Clarendon Press, 1978).

were blinded; and I saw how the Lord of the Sheep wrought much slaughter among them in their pastures until those sheep invited that slaughter and betrayed his place. (55) And he gave them into the hands of the lions and the tigers and the wolves and the hyenas, and into the hands of the foxes, and to all the animals; and those wild animals began to tear those sheep in pieces. (56) And I saw how he left that house of theirs and their tower and gave them all into the hands of the lions, that they might tear them in pieces and devour them, into the hands of all the animals. (57) And I began to cry out with all my power, and to call the Lord of the Sheep, and to represent to him with regard to the sheep that they were being devoured by all the wild animals. (58) But he remained still, although he saw it, and rejoiced that they were devoured and swallowed up and carried off, and he gave them into the hands of all the animals for food.

[End of Vision of the Beasts, Beginning of the Apocalypse of the Birds]

(59) And he called seventy shepherds and cast off those sheep that they might pasture them; and he said to the shepherds and to their companions: "Each one of you from now on is to pasture the sheep, and do whatever I command you. (60) And I will hand them over to you duly numbered and will tell you which of them are to be destroyed, and destroy them. And he handed those sheep over to them. (61) And he called another and said to him, "Observe and see everything that the shepherds do against these sheep, for they will destroy from among them more than I have commanded them. (62) And write down all the excess and destruction which is wrought by the shepherds, how many they destroy at my command, and how many they destroy of their own volition; write down against each shepherd individually all that he destroys. (63) And read out before me exactly how many they destroy of their own volition, and how many are handed over to them for destruction, that this may be a testimony for me against them, that I may know all the deeds of the shepherds in order to hand them over, and may see what they do, whether they abide by my command which I have commanded them, or not. (64) But they must not know (this), and you must not show (this) to them, nor reprove them, but (only) write down against each individual in his time all that the shepherds destroy and bring it all up to me.

(65) And I looked until those shepherds pastured at their time, and they began to kill and to destroy more than they were commanded, and they gave those sheep into the hands of the lions. (66) And the lions and the tigers devoured and swallowed up the majority of those sheep, and the

wild-boars devoured with them; and they burnt down that tower and demolished that house. (67) And I was extremely sad about the tower, because that house of the sheep had been demolished; and later that I was unable to see whether those sheep went into that house. (68) And the shepherds and their companions handed those sheep over to all the animals that they might devour them; each one of them at this time received an exact number, and of one of them after the other there was written in a book how many of them he destroyed.

The first and third paragraphs are uncomfortably similar to one another. I say uncomfortably not because repetition is an unsettling fact in and of itself, but rather because it forces great contortions in scholarship looking for a unified, onward-marching chronology of the history of Israel. The final paragraph above, with the reference to the burning of the tower (likely a symbol for the Temple) and demolition of the house (likely Jerusalem), seems to be an obvious reference to the destruction of Jerusalem at the hands of Nebuchadnezzar and the Babylonians. Scholarship begins with that near-certain reference, and works backwards – the lions of 1 En 89.65 and 89.66 (the first two lines of the final paragraph) must be the Babylonians.[31] But, if this is the case, what are the lions/Babylonians doing at the helm of the destruction narrated in the first paragraph?

There have been two key solutions to this interpretative crux. The first posits an inconsistent use of symbolism to stand for historical groups; perhaps the lions are Assyria at first, and Babylon later.[32] The immediate problem with this argument is that this would be a lapse in the key literary device of the Animal Apocalypse, which very clearly seems to imagine certain species having a one-to-one relationship with certain ethnic or national groups. The second solution grants that the lions stand for Babylon, and goes hunting through biblical literature for a precedent to establish the referent behind 1 En 89.54–8 (our first paragraph above). Tiller and Nickelsburg read the lion as a symbol for Babylon throughout, and reinterpret 89.54–8 (our first paragraph above) as chronologically proximate events leading up to, but *not including* the destruction of Jerusalem.[33] An updated version of this position can be found in

---

[31] The wild boars are established elsewhere as the Edomites, who seem to rejoice over the destruction of the Temple in Psalm 137.7, Lamentations 4.21–2, Obadiah 12–13, and Ezekiel 25.12–14. They seem to be responsible for the burning of the Temple, as here, in Esdras 4.45. The tigers have yet to be satisfactorily solved by any modern interpreter.

[32] To be more specific, one stream of largely earlier scholarship suggested that the lions were the Assyrians throughout, with the incidentally mentioned tigers being the Babylonians, taking over in verse 66. And R. H. Charles, in an influential variation on this position, suggested the symbolism was loose and inexact, with lions and tigers together referring to Assyria and Babylonia.

[33] Tiller, *Commentary*, 34–6; 318–21; Nickelsburg, *1 Enoch 1*, 384–6.

the work of Daniel Olson, where he argues that the three times where lions pursue the sheep (89.55; 89.56; 89.65) refer to three separate Babylonian campaigns by Nebuchadnezzar against Judah.[34]

This solution from Olson contains a key observation: the Animal Apocalypse seems to narrate something very similar multiple times, namely, the sheep being delivered into the hands of the lions, who hungrily devour them. This repetition has not occasioned much concern in the secondary literature,[35] perhaps understandably, given the way the Animal Apocalypse is understood to function. Each allegorical episode has a unique referent, progressing chronologically alongside the history of Israel. Repetition in the text must indicate history repeating itself, and it is the task of the scholar to find the matching events.

Carol Newsom, in an unpublished seminar paper, makes the following observation: "A literary seam appears in the repetition of the destruction of Jerusalem (En 89.55–8, 65–7)."[36] She does not provide any further support for this suggestion, and does not address it any further in the remainder of the paper, but it strikes me as completely correct. We can now substantiate her instinct, and demonstrate that our first and third paragraphs represent a double narration of the same event – the fall of Jerusalem at the hands of the Babylonians – albeit with very different literary functions.[37]

---

[34] Olson, *A New Reading*, 130–5.

[35] Matthew Black obliquely suggests that verses 89.55 and 89.65 might represent a double narration, but his treatment of this section is quite agnostic on exactly what historical referents are behind the narrative. So, his comment on verse 65: "the lions appear here to be the Assyrians and the reference to their conquest of the Northern Kingdom, unless this has been described at 89.55–6, in which case some later events are made." See Black, *Book of Enoch*, 272. The only other observation of this repetition of which I am aware comes from Carol Newsom and will be addressed below.

[36] Carol A. Newsom, "Enoch 83–90: The Historical Resume as Biblical Exegesis," (unpublished paper, Harvard University seminar, Harvard, 1975), 23. This unpublished paper, which I received in a private email communication from Newsom, has nevertheless had quite the impact on scholarship on the Animal Apocalypse. It is cited in Tiller, *Commentary*, 25–7; Olson, *A New Reading*, 3n5; Anathea Portier-Young, *Apocalypse Against Empire*, 347n1.

[37] The terminology attached to purported double narratives, as has been developed with reference to source criticism of the Hebrew Bible, is something less than precise. As Aulikki Nahkola points out, "'Double narrative,' though readily recognized by anyone acquainted with Old Testament scholarship, is not a well-established technical term that would ensure that it is only used and understood in one way. Nor is there agreement whether double narrative means the same as 'doublet,' 'variant' or 'duplicate stories,' or how these relate to 'type-scenes,' 'conflation' or 'embellishment' or, simply 'repetitions,' all terms used by scholars to denote similarity and/or suggest interdependence in two or more narratives." In Aulikki Nahkola, *Double narratives in the Old Testament: the foundations of method in biblical criticism*, Beihefte zur Zeitschrift für die alttestamentliche Wissenschaft 273. (New York: Walter de Gruyter, 2001), 162.

Table 2.4 Destruction of Jerusalem in Vision of the Beasts and Apocalypse of the Birds

Motif	Vision of the Beasts (89.54–8)	Apocalypse of the Birds (89.65–8)
1. Reason for Destruction	54: And after this I saw how when they left the house of the Lord of the sheep and his tower, they went astray in everything, and their eyes were blinded; and I saw how the Lord of the sheep wrought much slaughter among them in their pastures until those sheep invited that slaughter and betrayed his place.	65a: And I looked until those shepherds pastured at their time, and they began to kill and to destroy more than they were commanded.
2. Initial handing over to the Lions	55: And he gave them into the hands of the lions (wäḥädägomu wəstä 'ədä 'änabəst) and the tigers and the wolves and the hyenas, and into the hands of the foxes, and to all the animals. And those wild animals began to tear those sheep in pieces.	65b: and they gave those sheep into the hands of the lions (wäḥädägu 'əläktä 'äbagə' wəstä 'ədä 'änabəst).
3. Devouring of Sheep; Fate of House and Tower	56: And I saw how he left that house of theirs and their tower and gave them all into the hands of the lions, that they might tear them in pieces and devour them, into the hands of all the animals.	66: And the lions and the tigers devoured and swallowed up the majority of those sheep, and the wild-boars devoured with them; and they burnt down that tower and demolished that house
4. Enoch Protests	57: And I began to cry out with all my power, and to call the Lord of the sheep, and to represent to him with regard to the sheep that they were being devoured by all the wild animals	67: And I was extremely sad about the tower, because that house of the sheep had been demolished; and later that I was unable to see whether those sheep went into that house.
5. Handing Over Sheep to All the Animals	58: But he remained still, although he saw it, and rejoiced that they were devoured and swallowed up and carried off, and he gave them into the hands of all the animals for food (wäḥädägomu wəstä 'ədä k"əllomu 'ärawit lämäble')	68: And the shepherds and their companions handed those sheep over to all the animals that they might devour them (mäṭäwəwwomu lä'ələku 'äbagə' läk"elu 'ärawit kämä yəblə'əwwomu).

Motifs 2–5 contain a striking amount of overlap (we will return to the question of tradition 1, the "why," below). Motif 2 narrates the handing over of the sheep into the hands of the lions.[38] Motif 3 tells us that the sheep were devoured by the lions,[39] and that both the house (Jerusalem) and tower (Temple) are forfeit.

This is a crucial parallel to establish, as this is not normally how scholars have understood the Vision of the Beasts's reference to the house and tower (89.56). It is near universally held that this verse reflects God abandoning the Temple, leaving it ripe and ready for destruction in punishment for Israel's transgressions, but *not yet destroyed*. It is just as syntactically possible, however, that this verse narrates the handing over of Jerusalem and Temple to the lions, or the Babylonians. Here is 89:56:

ወርኢኩ ፡ ከመ ፡ ኃደገ ፡ ለዝኩ ፡ ቤተ ፡ ዚአሆሙ ፡ ወማኅፈዶሙ ፡ ወወደዮሙ ፡ ለኵሎሙ ፡ ውስተ ፡ እደ ፡ አናብስት ፡ ከመ ፡ ይምሥጥዎሙ ፡ ወከመ ፡ ይብልዕዎሙ ፡ ውስተ ፡ እደዊሆሙ ፡ ለኵሎሙ ፡ አራዊት ፡፡

wärə'iku kämä ḫädägo läzəku betä ziʾahomu wämaḫafädomu wäwädäyomu läkʷəllomu wəstä ʾədä ʾanabəst kämä yəmśäṭəwwomu wäkämä yəblə'əwwomu wəstä ʾədäwihomu läkʷəllomu ʾärawit

And I saw how he left that house of theirs and their tower and gave them all into the hands of the lions, that they might tear them in pieces and devour them, into the hands of all the animals.

It is usually understood that God left the house and tower, and then (separately) gave all the sheep into the hands of the lions. The house and tower are not yet obliterated, unlike the lives of the unlucky sheep. This makes some sense, as the text will then clarify that the lions will tear and eat whatever has been handed over and sheep are edible; houses and towers, generally not so. However, the word that seems to make a dependent clause out of this subsequent devouring is *kämä* (ከመ), which is a very common conjunction, and can flex to create different understandings here. This verse is normally read as if the syntactic unit terminates with "their tower (maḫəfädomu)." Something like, "He left that house of theirs and their tower. And gave them all into the hands of the lions." The implication here is that the house is vacant, but not yet fallen. The sheep are forfeit, but the house is still standing.

---

[38] The Vision of the Beasts mentions other animals (tigers, wolves, hyenas, foxes) here, in verse 55. The Apocalypse of the Birds mentions companion animals (tigers, wild boars) in verse 65. In both accounts, it is clear that the lions are the key actors (so, they are the sole animals mentioned in 89.56, and 89.65).

[39] And tigers, in the Apocalypse of the Birds. See footnote above.

This is in keeping with scholarship that interprets this passage as narrating events prior to 586.

But it would be equally possible to read with the following sense: "And I saw: a) how he left that house of theirs and their tower and gave them all [i.e. the house and tower, and sheep besides] into the hands of the lions; b) how they might tear them in pieces and devour them, in the hands of all the animals." Thus it is possible that this verse communicates the fall of both city and Temple, as well as the terrible fate of the sheep.[40]

The reference to the burning of the Temple makes 89.66 an unusually clear reference to the events of 586 BCE, and this has seemed to preclude 89.56 for consideration under this same rubric. But the basic tradition, narrated in both accounts, is the giving over of the city and Temple to the Babylonians. There might not be fire in 89.56, but there is smoke. The syntactical ambiguity here means that any discernment of the referent of the passage will need to be arrived at contextually.

To return to the parallels, Motif 4 contains the protestation of Enoch, colored slightly differently in each account. In the Vision of the Beasts, Enoch is upset with God because of the devouring of the sheep. In the Apocalypse of the Birds, Enoch is "extremely sad" because of the destruction of the city and Temple. In each account, Enoch protests what has just happened at the end of the previous verse. So, in the Vision of the Beasts, the city and Temple are handed over, and then the sheep are devoured. Enoch cries out against the devouring. In the Apocalypse of the Birds, the sheep are devoured, and then the city and Temple are demolished. Enoch is sad about the demolition.

Finally, Motif 5 narrates the handing over of the sheep to all the animals (ለኩሉ ፡ አራዊት, läkʷəllu 'ärawit, in both 89.58 and 89.68). In this verse especially, the vocabulary and sequential parallels between the two accounts are substantial.

The largest difference between the two accounts has to do with the prime movers behind the destruction of Jerusalem. In the Vision of the Beasts, it is entirely God's doing, in punishment for Israel's apostasy (symbolized by their blindness). It is the Lord of the Sheep who wreaks slaughter among them (89.54, Motif 1), who gives them to the lions (89.55, Motif 2), who leaves city and Temple (89.56, Motif 3). It is to the Lord of the Sheep that Enoch makes fruitless petition (89.57, Motif 4), and the Lord of the Sheep who gleefully watches their demise (89.58, Motif 5). God is entirely in control of the situation, and everything that happens to Israel happens with his direct approval.

In the Apocalypse of the Birds, the tragedy is the shepherds' fault. Although these shepherds are ultimately appointed by God, their appointment results in a quite different narration than in the Vision of the Beasts. The forfeiture of

---

[40] I am grateful to James Nati for his help with the Gəʽəz on this point.

Judah to Babylon was orchestrated by the shepherds (89.65a, Motif 1); it was *they* who handed over the sheep to the lions[41] (89.65b, Motif 2), and ultimately hand over the sheep to the collection of beasts (89.68, Motif 5). We can also note that God is removed from Motifs 3 and 4; this is especially notable in 89.67, where Enoch does not make a petition to the Lord of the Sheep (as in the parallel at 89.57), but is simply sad.

It is possible to be nonplussed by the repetition here and nestle the Apocalypse of the Birds's account within the theological framework of the Vision of the Beasts. Israel strayed from the path; therefore, God vacated the Temple and threw Israel to the lions, and (perhaps in a fed-up sort of way) appointed mediators to take over the thankless task of punishing Israel's mishaps. Or perhaps incompetence or malice is the leadership God thinks the sheep deserve. The two accounts must refer to two different historical events, even if the actual events are a bit obscure. This is how the work has generally been read until now.

Another option is that the Animal Apocalypse includes a repetition of the same event for as-of-yet unexplained literary reasons. That this option has not been much pursued in the secondary literature reflects the scholarly assessment of the nature of the Animal Apocalypse generally. The repetition of a single historical event would represent a breach of the one-to-one allegorical device structuring the remainder of the work. In this instance, a literary hypothesis about the feasibility of repetition in one location would clash with a strong consensus about the narrative style of the work, a consensus with which I generally agree. In the case of this particular apocalypse, at this juncture in the story, repetition would be surprising enough that it has been largely left aside by previous scholarship as a means of explanation.

Instead, I think there is a strong possibility that the double narration points to different moments of composition, since both of these passages are most sensibly read as referring to the fall of Jerusalem at the hands of the Babylonians, as well as because of the marked linguistic and narrative similarities between the two accounts. This likelihood has great implications for the compositional history of the Animal Apocalypse. If this repetition is, as Carol Newsom named it, a literary seam, we are alerted to the possibility of multiple fabrics. Or, using the terms I introduced at the start, we might be looking for multiple works.

As already noted, the first work that emerges once we pull at the seam, I have called the "Vision of the Beasts." It is an allegory of the history of Israel that goes from Adam and Eve until the destruction of the First Temple. The second work that emerges I have called the "Apocalypse of the Birds." It

---

[41] I have noted this difference in the table in transliteration. In the Vision of the Beasts, a singular actor (God) gave them (*wāḥādāgomu*) into the hands of the lions (89.55). In the Apocalypse of the Birds, plural actors (shepherds) give them (*wāḥādāgu*) into the hands of the lions. (89.65)

begins at 89.59, with the destruction of the First Temple, and tracks the history of Israel under the dominion of seventy shepherds, culminating in the arrival of the eschaton.

At one time, the Vision of the Beasts likely narrated past the Destruction, and perhaps even overlapped with some of the contents of the Apocalypse of the Birds.[42] For all we know, a once-extant version of the Vision of the Beasts contained a narration of the return from exile, and the rebuilding of the Second Temple, and other events besides, including its own vision of the eschaton. There may be some small traces of the repurposing of earlier Vision of the Beasts material in the first (89.65–9) and second (89.72–7) periods of the Apocalypse of the Birds. These two textual sections feature quadrupeds. But, at 90.1, things shift more completely to the unique menagerie of the Apocalypse of the Birds, with birds primarily antagonizing the Israelites, and I will suggest below that something about bird symbolism may have been one of the animating impulses fueling the composition of the Apocalypse of the Birds.[43] I would therefore estimate based on the preserved quadrupeds that the Vision of the Beasts, at one time, covered events stretching into the Persian period, and that some of that textual material might have been reused and transformed to create what are now the Apocalypse of the Birds's first and second periods. The hypothesis that the Vision of the Beasts might have once included material extending into the Persian period works in concert with my comments offered about the dating of the Vision of the Beasts offered in the next chapter, which explores the Persian and early Hellenistic periods as especially likely sites of composition for this Aramaic work. However, we no longer have the text (words-in-order) corresponding to this (hypothetical) part of the Vision of the Beasts. What we have of the Vision of the Beasts closes at 89.58.

A traditional source-critical analysis would next go hunting for further evidence of literary and terminological discontinuity. On that note, I can briefly survey some terminological differences between the two works. We are a

---

[42] One of the quirks of the Animal Apocalypse is that 1 En 89 is the longest chapter (by far) belonging to 1 Enoch. I will suggest the possibility that 90.1 might represent a switch from one style of source-use to another, perhaps transitioning from reused material in parts of chapter 89 into an entirely new composition at 90.1, but this is speculation. It is curious to think about the possibility that internal chapter organizations might correlate with hypotheses of textual development, but it is unclear to experts when the chapter divisions took over, and why they are placed where they are. However, Loren T. Stuckenbruck suggested in a private communication on September 14, 2018 that these stem from the Ethiopic tradition as they are not attested anywhere else. I will go on to suggest that the composition of the Apocalypse of the Birds necessarily predates the translation into Ethiopic. I would hazard a guess that the chapter divisions in this instance might reflect an ancient reader's grasp of literary transitions, rather than being a reflector of anything having to do with the composition of the Apocalypse of the Birds.

[43] See Chapter 6.

bit constrained here by the nature of the evidence. We have the Apocalypse of the Birds in Gəʻəz only, which is either a secondary (assuming a Greek language original) or tertiary (if hypothesizing an Aramaic original) translation. We have the Vision of the Beasts in some Aramaic fragments, and one Greek extract, but also most of its text must be retrieved from a tertiary Gəʻəz translation. I think it is likely that some of the literary differences I note might authentically be preserved in translation, but it is also possible that they were introduced at a later stage.

First, on species: Quadruped animals are the only symbolic antagonists in the Vision of the Beasts (i.e. lions, wolves, camels, etc.), and they generally seem to work independently. Conversely, the Apocalypse of the Birds shifts the focus to a network of birds, who work in concert with one another to take on the sheep.

Second, on terminology: the Gəʻəz might preserve different vocabulary preferences for similar entities.[44] So, in the Vision of the Beasts, the children of the sheep are called "their little ones" (*däqiqomu*, 3X at 89.15), or "little sheep" (*nəʼusan* at 89.37; *bägəʻ nəʼus* at 89.48). These words never appear in the Apocalypse of the Birds, where the children of the sheep are called lambs (*mähasəʻat* 90.6, and *mähäsəʻ* 3X at 8, 9).[45] In the Vision of the Beasts, the term for horned sheep, presumably rams, is *härge* (12X at 89.42–9).[46] This word similarly never appears in the Apocalypse of the Birds, as the term for horned sheep is *dabela*

---

[44] One complicating factor is that the exact identity or species of the animals is not entirely clear, as Aramaic, Greek, and Ethiopic all have multiple lexemes by which similar flock animals (and male flock animals in particular) might be represented, and there is no reason to expect a particularly stringent or internally consistent zoemic schema, unlike, for instance, the zoemics of the priestly writings explored in Naphtali S. Meshel, *The "Grammar" of Sacrifice: A Generativist Study of the Israelite Sacrificial System in the Priestly Writings with the Grammar of [Sigma]* (Oxford: Oxford University Press, 2014), 29–61. This is compounded by the problem of connecting the multiple translations noted above, so that Tiller suggests, "the Greek text is not necessarily a reliable indicator of the specific term used in Aramaic, and the Ethiopic is certainly not a reliable indicator of the Greek term used," in Tiller, *Commentary*, 310. For that reason, I have only treated what I take to be the most extreme examples: animals with multiple attestations in one possible source, and none in the other.

[45] There is no Aramaic evidence for any of these citations. In the Codex Vaticanus Graecus 1809, text corresponding to verse 89.45 narrates a "lamb (ἄρνα)," symbolizing King David, who is appointed as a "ram (κριόν)." The Ethiopic tradition has here a "sheep (*bägəʻ*)" who is appointed as a "ram (*härge*)." It is possible that the Gəʻəz represents an earlier version without a species distinction made between sheep and lambs. The tenth-century Codex Vaticanus 1809 could then represent a later version of a Greek text of the Vision of the Beasts that has been transformed through its transmission alongside the Apocalypse of the Birds, a work whose text obviously contains a species distinction between sheep and lambs, and which we might posit may have contributed this to the ongoing tradition.

[46] We have some Aramaic and Greek evidence here. In 4Q205 8, the Aramaic term is דכר. In the Codex Vaticanus Graecus 1809, the Greek term is κριός.

(6X at 90.9–14, 31).[47] I think it probable that there were further terminological differences that were smoothed away over centuries of transmission.[48]

Third, there are some rhetorical preferences distinctive to each work. A good example is the first-person formulae by which Enoch's vision and his role as visionary are continually reintroduced. Both the Vision of the Beasts and the Apocalypse of the Birds include first-person asides every few verses or so, but the frequency of their chosen phrases differ. The Vision of the Beasts, for instance, eight times uses the transitional phrase "Again, I saw . . . (wäka ʿəbä rə'iku)."[49] There is no use of this phrase in the text of the Apocalypse of the Birds. The Apocalypse of the Birds, for its part, relies much more heavily on the transitional phrase, "I saw until (wärə'iku ʾəskä)," which is used occasionally in the Vision of the Beasts, but not with the same frequency as the Apocalypse of the Birds. It is used eight times in the Vision of the Beasts,[50] and 15 times in the Apocalypse of the Birds.[51] This pattern is deepened by recognizing that the Vision of the Beasts is about 1.5 times as long as the Apocalypse of the Birds, and that the latter has therefore used less text to reach a greater number of references. It becomes especially notable in chapter 90, in which 14 of the 22 transitional phrases used by the Apocalypse of the Birds are "I saw until" or a slight variation thereon. For comparison, this phrase only appears at 85.7 in all of chapters 85–8 (the first four chapters of the Vision of the Beasts). There is, then, some evidence on the level of text that seems to respect the split I proposed between the two works. Or, to return to the phrasing used at the outset of this discussion, there is enough literary and terminological discontinuity that we might want to explore the possibility of multiple sites of composition.

---

[47] Olson notes the differing terminology (härge/dabela), but suggests this is a semantic distinction between the rams of the former and present day. In Olson, *A New Reading*, 209–10.

[48] Tiller's chart tracking "Translation Equivalences for Sheep in the Animal Apocalypse" demonstrates the use of "*bägəʿ/ʾäbagəʿ*" at sites where the preserved Aramaic demonstrates multiple lexemes (דכר די ען/אמר/ען). At 89.45, similarly, *bägəʿ* is used where the Greek Codex Vaticanus has ἀρήν (lamb?). Though this is limited evidence, it does suggest that the Gəʿəz reflects a process of streamlining, so that *bägəʿ/ʾäbagəʿ* came to stand in for variety of terms all generally meaning sheep. This points to the limits of our knowledge in light of an extended and often undocumented transmissional history, but also the likelihood that there was once greater terminological variance which is no longer extant to us. See Tiller, Commentary, 275.

[49] Exactly as cited, this is at 86.1, 86.3, 87.1, 89.3, 89.7, and 89.51. In this count, I have also included: 87.2, "And I raised my eyes again to heaven and saw (*wäʾänsaʾku ʾäʿyəntəyä kaʿəbä wəstä sämay wärə'iku*)," and 89.2, "And again, I raised my eyes toward heaven, and I saw (*wäʿalä ʿaləku kaʿəbä ʾäʿyəntəyä mängälä sämay wärə'iku*)."

[50] At 85.7, 89.21, 89.36, 89.37, 89.37 (again), 89.39, 89.40, 89.47.

[51] At 89.65, 90.1, 90.4, 90.5, 90.9, 90.9 (again), 90.13, 90.14, 90.15, 90.18, 90.19, 90.20, 90.29, 90.34, 90.38. It is important to note the terminological overlaps between 89.65–90.19, and 90.20–42, as this indicates the extent to which these sections share a common context of textual development.

I have proposed above that the Animal Apocalypse might be split into two works, or sources. In so doing, I made use of many of the classic tools and methods of argumentation associated with source criticism. I identified a literary shift at a certain point in a narrative, spotted a duplicate narration at the moment of literary transition, and subsequently collected terminological inconsistencies between two possible "sources" making up the Animal Apocalypse.[52] At some junctures in the history of scholarship on biblical and classical texts, source-critical analyses proceeding on purely literary grounds such as these might have been generally deemed persuasive. But recent scholarship has highlighted the flaws of a solipsistic source criticism for ancient Jewish and Christian works.[53]

Literary arguments, critics note, are inherently slippery. What looks to be "coherent" and suggest a literary unity to one might appear "incoherent" and suggest a composite work to another.[54] Repetition can similarly be interpreted as a redactional accident or a literary choice depending who you ask.[55] This problem is all the more concerning in conversation with apocalyptic works in which repetition is quite common. Take, for instance, a classic example from Revelation 19.9 & 22.8–9:

19.9: καὶ ἔπεσα ἔμπροσθεν τῶν ποδῶν αὐτοῦ προσκυνῆσαι αὐτῷ. καὶ λέγει μοι· ὅρα μή· σύνδουλός σού εἰμι καὶ τῶν ἀδελφῶν σου τῶν ἐχόντων τὴν μαρτυρίαν Ἰησοῦ· τῷ θεῷ προσκύνησον. ἡ γὰρ μαρτυρία Ἰησοῦ ἐστιν τὸ πνεῦμα τῆς προφητείας.

Then I fell down at his feet to worship him, but he said to me, "You must not do that! I am a fellow servant with you and your comrades who hold the testimony of Jesus. Worship God! For the testimony of Jesus is the spirit of prophecy."

---

[52] For a recent summation of a source-critical methodology that sees features such as these as problems to be solved, see the treatment (and grouping of phenomena into "contradictions," "doublets," and "discontinuities") in Joel S. Baden, *The Composition of the Pentateuch: Renewing the Documentary Hypothesis* (New Haven: Yale University Press, 2012), 16–20.

[53] This methodological discussion has progressed in earnest with reference to Pentateuchal studies, on which see, most humorously, the satirical piece by David J. A. Clines, "New Directions in Pooh Studies: Überlieferungs-Und Religionsgeschichtliche Studien zum Pu-Buch," in *On the Way to the Postmodern. Old Testament Essays, 1967–1998. Vol. II*, Journal for the Study of the Old Testament Supplement 293 (Sheffield: Sheffield Academic, 1998), 830–9.

[54] An in-depth recent reflection on this problem can be found in Teeter and Tooman, "Standards."

[55] See the classic summary of scholarship on Revelation, charting out the "two fundamental options" for explaining repetition in Revelation, source criticism or "recapitulation theory," in Adela Yarbro Collins, *The Combat Myth in the Book of Revelation* (Missoula, MT: Scholars Press for Harvard Theological Review, 1976), 8–13.

22.8–9
καὶ ὅτε ἤκουσα καὶ ἔβλεψα, ἔπεσα προσκυνῆσαι ἔμπροσθεν τῶν ποδῶν τοῦ ἀγγέλου τοῦ δεικνύοντός μοι ταῦτα. καὶ λέγει μοι· ὅρα μή· σύνδουλός σού εἰμι καὶ τῶν ἀδελφῶν σου τῶν προφητῶν καὶ τῶν τηρούντων τοὺς λόγους τοῦ βιβλίου τούτου· τῷ θεῷ προσκύνησον.

And when I heard and saw them, I fell down to worship at the feet of the angel who showed them to me; but he said to me, "You must not do that! I am a fellow servant with you and your comrades the prophets, and with those who keep the words of this book. Worship God!"

In the work of R. H. Charles and David Aune, this passage is a "doublet," and the sign of a later textual gloss or interpolation.[56] The thinking goes that two passages as near-identical as these would represent a breach of coherence and thereby require multiple authors or moments of composition in which to vest multiple and divergent coherences. But for Craig Koester, the repetition serves to remind the audience to be teachable: "since he [the speaker] accepts repeated correction, the implication is that readers should do the same."[57] And Bruce Longenecker maintains the repetition is an aesthetic choice constructed by the same author to highlight the relatedness of the two incidents.[58] The problem here is that nobody can quite agree on the standard or character of literary coherence scholars expect of Revelation, nor of apocalyptic literature more generally. When writers are exploring events that bend space and time, such as creation or cosmic war or the eschaton, perhaps our standards of coherence ought to stretch to include a little more narrative strangeness. John J. Collins states:

> The problem with the source-critical method is obviously one of degree. No one will deny that it is sometimes possible and necessary to distinguish sources and identify interpolations. We have learned that the apocalyptic writings are far more tolerant of inconsistency and repetition than [previous scholars] realized. The burden of proof falls on the scholar who would split the text into multiple sources.[59]

---

[56] R. H. Charles, *A Critical and Exegetical Commentary on the Revelation of St. John*, vol. 2 (Edinburgh: T&T Clark, 1920), 128–9; David E. Aune, *Revelation 17–22* (Grand Rapids, MI: Zondervan, 2017).

[57] Craig R. Koester, *Revelation: A New Translation with Introduction and Commentary*, Anchor Yale Bible 38A (New Haven: Yale University Press, 2014), 840.

[58] Bruce W. Longenecker, "Revelation 19,10: One Verse in Search of an Author," *Zeitschrift für die Neutestamentliche Wissenschaft und die Kunde der Älteren Kirche; Berlin* 91, no. 3 (January 1, 2000): 230–7.

[59] In John J. Collins, *The Apocalyptic Imagination: An Introduction to Jewish Apocalyptic Literature*, 3rd ed. (Grand Rapids, MI: Eerdmans, 2016), 23.

At the same time, what we know about the composition and transmission of ancient literature encourages us to think about multiple voices drawing out and developing text and work over time. As Collins recognizes, the identification of sources is sometimes "possible and necessary." With factors pointing in both directions, repetition in apocalyptic literature, in and of itself, neither necessitates nor precludes a hypothesis of multiple sources. This is not an insuperable problem, but our ability to use repetition to talk about the textual history of an apocalypse depends on the ascertainment and consideration of other factors.

As an additional concern, we have no way of knowing what happened during the undocumented phases of transmission of the text on which source criticism is practiced. John Bryant summarizes the situation this way: "each document is like a whale breaching from time to time at the surface of a dark sea that at all other times conceals the twists and turns of its submarine navigations."[60] "Coherence" and "incoherence" can be augmented or lessened in the process of transmission, a process that is largely invisible to us.[61] For some works – and at least part of the Animal Apocalypse obviously counts among this group – there are hundreds or thousands of years of undocumented transmission. How, then, could we be confident that the sources that might be excavated on literary grounds from the received text have any kind of historical utility?

I take these questions to be generative, not rhetorical. These are important and trenchant critiques, but I do not understand them to vacate source-critical tools, such as the identification of double narratives or terminological differences, of their utility. Instead, I understand these voices to raise the bar for the level, quality, and diversity of evidence that the field needs to be persuaded that a work should be broken into two (or more). Literary observations can be incorporated into multiple compositional models. Spotting a double narrative or a terminological inconsistency is not enough to shift the burden of proof away from the reasonable skepticism outlined above. In many cases, it is impossible to gather the kind of corroborating evidence needed to break a careful scholar's threshold, because of our minimal documentation – notice, for instance, the dismal outlook on source criticism in the study of the Hebrew Bible espoused in a few recent treatments.[62] But, in the case of the Animal Apocalypse, there is suggestive material evidence supporting the hypothesis of separable works. And, as will become clear in future chapters, the text

---

[60] Bryant, *The Fluid Text*, 34.
[61] "Transmission historians must reckon with the probability or elimination of transmission-historical markers in the manuscripts before us." In David McLain Carr, *The Formation of the Hebrew Bible: A New Reconstruction* (New York: Oxford University Press, 2011), 147.
[62] E.g. R. F. Person and R. C. Rezetko, "Introduction: The Importance of Empirical Models to Assess the Efficacy of Source and Redaction Criticism," in *Empirical Models Challenging Biblical Criticism*, ed. R. F. Person and R. C. Rezetko (Atlanta: SBL Press, 2016), 35.

addresses itself so directly to historical affairs that it enables a kind of provenancing that is impossible for other literary works.

With all this in mind, my work in this section establishes a starting point for the line of inquiry which the remainder of my book will pursue. I propose that there might be two Animal Apocalypses, guided in no small part by literary considerations to a site at which the text might be split. But the plausibility of the division of the text cannot and will not be tested solely on literary grounds, but will be queried in this and future chapters by attending to material evidence, the witness of early readers and the text's interaction with contemporary historical events.

CHAPTER 3

Material Evidence for Animal Apocalypse(s) of Enoch

Fragments sorted into four manuscripts at Qumran seem to attest the Animal Apocalypse. Said with my particular terminology: these documents contain text which aligns closely enough with the text of the Gəʿəz Animal Apocalypse, to which we accord "work" status, that we feel comfortable saying these documents attest the work, the Animal Apocalypse. But what changes in the interpretation of these documents if we hold open the door for the possibility of multiple works?

As it turns out, quite a bit changes. As I will demonstrate in this chapter, every fragment found at Qumran attests text corresponding to the Vision of the Beasts. Not one attests to text corresponding to the Apocalypse of the Birds. In the following chart, the sections in grey are those for which we have at least one fragment at Qumran containing text which parallels the Gəʿəz text.

Table 3.1 Contents of the Animal Apocalypse Present and Absent at Qumran

1 Enoch (Mashafa Henok)	Vision of the Beasts	Apocalypse of the Birds
85.1–9	Adam, Eve, and Progeny	
86.1–6	Fallen Watchers, and Violent Giants	
87.1–88.3	Judgment of Watchers and Giants	
89.1–8	Noah and the Flood	
89.9–27	Flood to Exodus from Egypt	
89.28–38	Exodus to Moses' Death	
89.39–50	Entrance into Land, Building of First Temple	
89.51–8	Destruction of Jerusalem	
89.59–64		Commissioning of Seventy Shepherds

1 Enoch (Mashafa Henok)	Vision of the Beasts	Apocalypse of the Birds
89.65–72a		First Period: Twelve Shepherds
89.72b–90.1		Second period: Twenty-Three Shepherds
90.2–5		Third Period: Twenty-Three Shepherds
90.6–19		Fourth Period: Twelve Shepherds Until the End Time
90.20–7		The Judgment of Shepherds and Sheep
90.28–37		A New Beginning: New Home for the Sheep, Transformation of All Species
90.39–42		The Conclusion to the Vision

This visual representation quickly clarifies that we have no material evidence for the Apocalypse of the Birds at Qumran. This is not necessarily conclusive evidence of its absence, but it is a fascinating absence of evidence. It may help texture the quality of our data to look at what we do have preserved, noting that our manuscripts occasionally overlap in the sections they preserve. These four manuscripts – 4Q204, 4Q205, 4Q206, and 4Q207 – are dated on paleographic grounds from the early Hasmonean period (4Q207) to the early Herodian period (4Q204).[1]

Table 3.2 Qumran Manuscripts of the Vision of the Beasts

1 Enoch (Mashafa Henok)	Vision of the Beasts	Qumran MSS
86.1–6	Fallen Watchers, and Violent Giants	4Q207
87.1–88.3	Judgment of Watchers and Giants	4Q206[a]
89.1–8	Noah and the Flood	4Q206[b]
89.9–27	Flood to Exodus from Egypt	4Q205, 4Q206[c]
89.28–38	Exodus to Moses' Death	4Q205, 4Q206[d]
89.39–50	Entrance into Land, Building of First Temple	4Q204, 4Q205[e]

[a] To be specific, using Drawnel's new sigla: 4Q206 7 I; 4Q 206 8 i
[b] 4Q206 8 I; 4Q206 9.
[c] 4Q205 6; 4Q206 8 ii; 4Q206 10; 4Q205 11
[d] 4Q205 7; 4Q206 11; 4Q 206 12
[e] 4Q204 15; 4Q205 8

[1] As dated in the recent re-edition by Henryk Drawnel (in consultation with the paleographic eye of Emile Puech), in Drawnel, *Qumran Cave 4, 2–4*.

Three sections of the text are found in two manuscripts at Qumran apiece. It is surely going too far to say that this is evidence of "popularity" of these sections at Qumran (or in another imagined site where writing occurred), but it is multiple attestation nevertheless. Our documents may provide some, albeit limited, data on the frequency with which this work was copied and/or read.

We can also observe that we have directly overlapping text in multiple documents. The sections narrated above, after all, are a scholarly convention that I have borrowed from prominent voices in the field to make sure I can clearly communicate the macro-structure of a long literary composition. A document attesting more than one section might not indicate actual overlap all that directly. But there are three instances where we have more than one fragment attesting the same text:

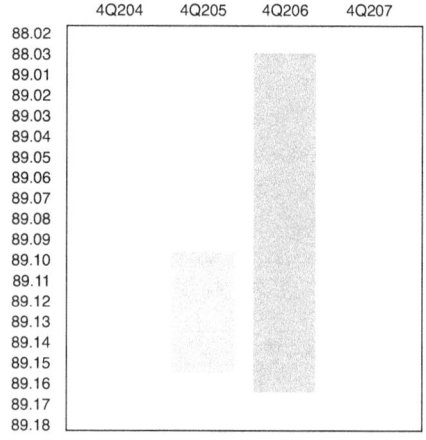

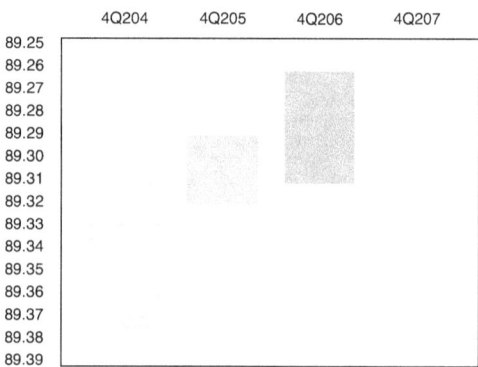

Figure 3.1 Overlaps Between Qumran MSS of Vision of the Beasts

This overlap provides a stronger foundation for the claim that these documents attest the same work.

I have demonstrated in my first chapter that the absence of a subsidiary work from Qumran need not be immediately deemed accidental. Rather, when we contextualize the attestation patterns of Enoch among our ancient evidence, such a finding can represent positive evidence for absence. I argued for a literary split creating two works within the Animal Apocalypse. I further observed that our Qumran material evidence corresponds to only one of the two works. I conclude that Qumran does not attest the Animal Apocalypse – it attests only the Vision of the Beasts. The hypothesis that the Vision of the Beasts circulated separately from the Apocalypse of the Birds finds possible confirmation in the material presence of the former, and absence of the latter, among the Dead Sea Scrolls.

The Scrolls (among a great many other functions in scholarship on ancient Judaism) can sometimes provide a material check upon literary-critical hypotheses of textual development, often pertaining to material collected in the Hebrew Bible. Perhaps the most famous example is the discovery of Hebrew manuscripts of Jeremiah corresponding to the shorter version of Jeremiah, a version previously known only from the later manuscripts of the Septuagint, thereby validating a scholarly theory about the shape of the text in the post-exilic period. A less famous but more directly analogous case for our purposes is that of Judges 6. On literary grounds (narrative discontinuity, contradiction), scholars from the nineteenth century onwards suspected that Judges 6.7–10 was a secondary addition to the text. This analysis proceeded on purely literary grounds, as Judges 6.7–10 is a part of every major witness of Judges 6. But 4Q49 presents a version of Judges that includes Judges 6.5–6, followed immediately by 6.11.[2] Judges 6.7–10, the purported secondary addition, is completely absent in this manuscript. In other words, this manuscript preserves the earlier textual version that scholars, working purely on literary grounds, guessed might have existed. Reinhard Müller, Juha Pakkala, and Bas ter Haar Romeny note with reference to Judges 6 that, "in an ideal case a theory about the literary growth of a text is corroborated by the evidence of textual witnesses in which the postulated older version is still preserved."[3] They adduce Judges 6 as a "striking" example of one of these ideal cases. I suggest that the Animal Apocalypse – the

---

[2] Published in Julio Trebolle Barrera, "4Q49: 4QJudges a," in *Discoveries in the Judaean desert. Qumran cave 4, IX: Deuteronomy, Joshua, Judges, Kings XIV*, ed. Eugene Ulrich and Frank Moore Cross (Oxford: Clarendon Press, 1995), 161–4.

[3] Juha Pakkala, Baas ter Haar Romeny, and Reinhard Müller, *Evidence of Editing: Growth and Change of Texts in the Hebrew Bible*, Resources for Biblical Study 75 (Atlanta: SBL Press, 2014), 59. See also the treatment in Eugene Ulrich, *The Dead Sea Scrolls and the Developmental Composition of the Bible*, Supplements to Vetus Testamentum 169 (Boston: Brill, 2015), 67–73.

attestation of the Vision of the Beasts but not the Apocalypse of the Birds at Qumran – represents another.

Material evidence has similarly been used to substantiate the proposed division of apocalyptic and pseudepigraphal texts into separable components, guiding the way we understand their processes of growth. Aramaic and Hebrew Dead Sea fragments with text similar to the Testaments of Naphtali and Levi from the Testaments of the Twelve Patriarchs evidence an earlier stage of textual development of material concerning the twelve patriarchs, while also indicating the separate circulation of patriarchal material before the formation of one collection in the Testaments of the Twelve Patriarchs.[4] An Oxyrhynchus fragment of 6 Ezra apparently evidences an early compositional stage for this work in which 6 Ezra circulated separately from 4 Ezra.[5] Most closely analogous to my own attention to absence here, Matthew Monger's recent work with 4Q216 at Qumran, which he concludes to be missing Jubilees 1:15b–25 and 2:25–33 (previously posited sites of "redactional seams") situates this manuscript as "historical evidence of the transmission of these chapters of Jubilees in a form that did not contain these passages, both of which should be understood as later, redactional additions to the Jubilees tradition, reflecting the literary development of Jubilees."[6] Our documents are, as Lied and Lundhaug name them, snapshots of an evolving tradition.[7] It is crucial, then, to carefully account for what is in-frame, and what is not.

The compositional history of the "Animal Apocalypse": a working hypothesis

I have presented above literary features that might be mustered to identify multiple works within the Animal Apocalypse – a literary seam at the Destruction of Jerusalem, different macro-structural devices employed by the Vision of the Beasts and Apocalypse of the Birds, and terminological differences. I have also remarked upon significant evidence for literary continuity which would need to be incorporated into any hypothesis of compositional history – the simplest

---

[4] For a general statement geared towards the collection in the Testaments of the Twelve Patriarchs, see Marinus de Jonge, "The Main Issues in the Study of the Testaments of the Twelve Patriarchs★," *New Testament Studies* 26, no. 4 (July 1980): 512–16. For studies of other trajectories for the Naphtali material, see Martha Himmelfarb, "R. Moses the Preacher and the Testaments of the Twelve Patriarchs," *AJS Review* 9, no. 1 (1984): 55–78; Michael E. Stone, "The Genealogy of Bilhah," *Dead Sea Discoveries* 3, no. 1 (January 1, 1996): 20–36.

[5] See, recently, Theodore A. Bergren, "Sixth Ezra," in *Old Testament Pseudepigrapha: More Noncanonical Scriptures*, ed. Richard Bauckham, James R. Davila, and Alexander Panayotov (Grand Rapids, MI: Eerdmans, 2013), 1:483–97.

[6] Monger, "4Q216: Rethinking Jubilees," 223.

[7] Lied and Lundhaug, *Snapshots of Evolving Traditions*.

and most conclusive shared features to which we can point are the distinctive use of animal species to represent non-Israelite people groups, and the ongoing use of sheep to represent Israelite protagonists. I have provided new precision concerning the state of our material evidence for each work in historical time. The Vision of the Beasts is attested in Aramaic by the second century BCE. The Apocalypse of the Birds is nowhere attested in Aramaic, and its earliest manuscripts are late medieval Gəʿəz. Given this precarious gap in our manuscript evidence, as we are facing a text with an undocumented transmission history of perhaps a millennium or more, it probably will not reward our attention overmuch to develop an exacting and specific compositional history. I would be wary of attempts at a granular source criticism that sought to provide isolated and separate contexts for particular words or verses. But I do think we can speak in general terms about the possible relationships between the Vision of the Beasts and Apocalypse of the Birds.

I propose the Apocalypse of the Birds represents a secondary addition to or expansion of the Vision of the Beasts. The Apocalypse of the Birds was likely composed by parties who knew the Vision of the Beasts, but were interested in developing a new account of the history and future of Israel from exile to eschaton. The second work was not written in isolation from the first work, but rather was written to augment and follow (and complete, if we consider the end of time to be a good stopping point) a previously existing account.

This compositional model makes intuitive sense (why not update a historical prophecy so that it includes more historical events?), but we are on sounder ground if we contextualize it among similar models of textual development. The general hypothesis that works grew through the addition of a conclusion, or other kinds of revision focused at the end of a work, is widely recognized for ancient Mediterranean literature. For some relevant, well-known, widely recognized examples, we might look to the "shorter" and "longer" endings of the Gospel of Mark now comprising chapter 16,[8] and the appending of Zechariah 9–14 ("Deutero-Zechariah") after 1–8.[9] There are also works in which scholars have hypothesized textual growth by updating with reference to recent history, such as Daniel, the Oracle of the Potter, and the Akkadian Dynastic Prophecy.[10]

---

[8] On which see the ongoing digital humanities project "The Mark 16 Project," accessible at https://mark16.sib.swiss/

[9] On which see, recently Hervé Gonzalez, "Zechariah 9–14 and the Continuation of Zechariah during the Ptolemaic Period," *The Journal of Hebrew Scriptures* 13 (January 1, 2013).

[10] E.g. Daniel 12.11–12 (this is a textual gloss, rather than a new work, but is an instructive example for many scholars on the logic of historical textual growth – see John J. Collins, *Daniel: A Commentary on the Book of Daniel*, ed. Frank Moore Cross (Minneapolis: Fortress Press, 1993), 400–1). On the Oracle of the Potter see L. Koenen, "A Supplementary Note on the Date of the Oracle of the Potter," *Zeitschrift für Papyrologie und Epigraphik* 54 (1984): 9–13. On the Akkadian Dynastic Prophecy see Matthew Neujahr, "When Darius Defeated Alexander: Composition and Redaction in the Dynastic Prophecy," *Journal of Near Eastern Studies* 64, no. 2 (2005): 101–7.

And most closely analogous to the emergence of the Animal Apocalypses, there are works for which we can watch this updating take place through the appending of historical narration to cover subsequent events at the end of the work. We might think of the way that Jeremiah 52, for instance, represents a later historical appendix added to a Jeremianic collection, which not only "updates" the work in light of current events, but also recasts the work so that its import is directed squarely at historical prophecy.[11]

The growth of the fourth Sibylline oracle provides a close analogue to my hypothesis concerning the compositional history of the Animal Apocalypses.[12] The fourth Sibylline contains what appears to have been a Hellenistic historical prophecy of four empires, and ten generations, that once culminated in the ascent of the Macedonians.[13] But, as David Flusser puts it, "this scheme was unacceptable" to a Jew living in Roman times, who appended a continuation of the oracle stretching into Roman times, and incorporated the events of their own day (the destruction of the Temple, the eruption of Vesuvius, etc.).[14] As the text is currently extant, we would phrase things to say that the

---

[11] On which see Alexander Rofé, "Not Exile but Annihilation for Zedekiah's People: The Purport of Jeremiah 52 in the Septuagint," in *VIII Congress of the International Organization for Septuagint and Cognate Studies, Paris 1992*, ed. Leonard Greenspoon and O. Munnich (Atlanta: Scholars Press, 1995), 165–70. I am additionally grateful to Nathan Mastnjak for sharing work on Jeremiah 52 that will be published in Nathan Mastnjak, *Before the Scrolls: A Material Approach to Israel's Prophetic Library* (Oxford: Oxford University Press, forthcoming).

[12] For a recent treatment of the "forward moving transformation" of the Fourth Sibylline, particularly with reference to its use of the four kingdoms motif, see Olivia Stewart Lester, "The Four Kingdoms Motif and Sibylline Temporality in Sibylline Oracles 4," in *Four Kingdom Motifs before and beyond the Book of Daniel*, ed. Andrew B. Perrin and Loren T. Stuckenbruck, Themes in Biblical Narrative 28 (Brill, 2020), 121–41.

[13] For a text and translation see John J. Collins, "Sibylline Oracles," in Charlesworth, *The Old Testament Pseudepigrapha*, 1:381–9.

[14] It is often assumed that the Fourth Sibyl came together in 80 CE shortly after the eruption of Vesuvius – Collins avers that "all scholars agree" on this matter, and the precise date of 80 CE is supported by Nikiprowetsky, Neujahr, and Stewart Lester. But I am quite interested in Sheila Redmond's suggestion that the *terminus ante quem* is later than generally supposed, especially given my methodological remarks below on the difficulty of setting *terminus ante quem* for historical apocalyptic works. See Valentin Nikiprowetsky, "Reflexions sur quelques problemes du quatrième et du cinquième livre des Oracles Sibyllins," *Hebrew Union College Annual* 43 (1972): 30; Matthew Neujahr, *Predicting the Past in the Ancient Near East: Mantic Historiography in Ancient Mesopotamia, Judah, and the Mediterranean World*, Brown Judaic Studies 354 (Providence, RI: Brown Judaic Studies, 2012), 235; Olivia Stewart Lester, *Prophetic Rivalry, Gender, and Economics: A Study in Revelation and Sibylline Oracles 4–5*, Wissenschaftliche Untersuchungen zum Neuen Testament 2nd ser., vol. 466 (Tübingen: Mohr Siebeck, 2018), 144; Sheila A. Redmond, "The Date of the Fourth Sibylline Oracle," *Second Century: A Journal of Early Christian Studies* 7, no. 3 (Fall 1989–1990): 129–50. Redmond's arguments are made more fully in Sheila A. Redmond, "The Date and Provenance of the Fourth Sibylline Oracle" (master's thesis, University of Ottawa, 1985).

supplementation begins at the end of the pre-Roman oracle. But it is possible that the pre-Roman oracle had an ending of its own, which was excised and replaced by the Roman-era supplementer.[15] In future chapters, I will suggest that the Apocalypse of the Birds, too, represents a Roman-era supplement to a pre-Roman historical oracle.[16] But even when we bracket out the possibility that they might have been composed around the same time, I want to suggest at this juncture that the Fourth Sibylline and the Animal Apocalypse (via the addition of the Apocalypse of the Birds) grew in the same way.

It is, of course, possible to overemphasize the universality of the extent to which ancient scribes felt the need to "update" a received work to include later historical events. After all, if this were such a universal scribal instinct, certain texts (such as the Animal Apocalypse) would simply never stop developing.[17] But we nevertheless have ample evidence for the growth of texts through the addition of historically updated concluding material to provide a strong precedent for my model here.

The postulate that the Apocalypse of the Birds was a secondary, and later, addendum is most fully demonstrated with reference to our material evidence. I have noticed its absence from Qumran, but this is just the beginning of this line of argumentation – which will be developed in its fullest form in future chapters but can be foreshadowed here. I will establish a *terminus post quem* for the Apocalypse of the Birds on internal grounds in the first century CE. This compositional window postdates the second century BCE *terminus ante quem* granted to the Vision of the Beasts by the Qumran fragments, and confirms that we were right to suspect its absence from the Scrolls. Our Qumran manuscripts, in such a light, would represent material evidence for the separate and earlier circulation of the Vision of the Beasts, and the secondary nature of the Apocalypse of the Birds.[18]

---

[15] Collins suspects the concluding material beginning at verse 173 is "inherited material," and is actually the original conclusion. In John J. Collins, "The Place of the Fourth Sibyl in the Development of the Jewish Sibyllina," *Journal of Jewish Studies* 25 (1974): 365–80. In his OTP translation, he notes that this proposal, "of course, cannot be conclusively demonstrated." See Collins, "Sibylline Oracles," 381.

[16] I will argue below that the Apocalypse of the Birds similarly mentions events datable to the mid-late first century CE, which would strengthen the similarities between these works.

[17] This is an area in which scholars working on dynamic models of textual development might reflect more. Why *do* works stop developing, even those which (according to the way we conceptualize other instances of textual development) apparently clamor for updating? Why wasn't the Animal Apocalypse, for instance, updated when the Roman Empire converted to Christianity?

[18] This precludes the possibility that, for instance, the Vision of the Beasts was composed as an introduction to the already circulating Apocalypse of the Birds, in keeping with Sara Milstein's work on revision through introduction in ancient near eastern and biblical literatures. See Sara J. Milstein, *Tracking the Master Scribe: Revision through Introduction in Biblical and Mesopotamian Literature* (New York: Oxford University Press, 2016).

The preserved double narration of the Destruction of Jerusalem can be adequately explained within this two-stage framework, without an answer deemed to be fully satisfying in every respect. I acknowledge that in some kinds of source-critical argumentation, the preserved double narration might demand the postulate of a third party, a later conflating redactor with a maximal approach to source preservation, and who left the text of their sources untouched in this instance (helpfully enabling the work of the modern source critic). To that end, some evidence can be mustered for a post-Qumran ancient reader knitting the two works closer together. So, at 89.10 in the Gəʿəz Animal Apocalypse (corresponding to the work I have called the Vision of the Beasts), all the quadrupeds and birds found in the work are introduced. We actually have Qumran fragments for text around this purported verse, but this list of animals is absent.[19] Previous commentators have noted the inconsistencies of 89.10 in the Gəʿəz, as there are species included here and then never mentioned again (swine, hyraxes), or species not included that are mentioned later (wild asses, vultures). Patrick Tiller notes that "copyists are often prone to add to lists such as this."[20] I would modify this observation to say that copyists are often prone to *add* lists such as this. But this evidence, showing that some redaction took place, tells us little about when or where that might have been. One could imagine a Greek (or Gəʿəz) scribe working contemporaneous with or after the larger-compositional work of the Apocalypse of the Birds had been completed, adding just such a list to harmonize a felt disparity.

Another route of explanation that integrates more readily into a two-stage model is that repetition of the sort we find here might be, as Adela Yarbro Collins puts it, "a common redactional device for returning to the major source after making an insertion."[21] In support of this postulate, the text of the double narrative that is found at 89.54–8 and 89.65–8 is split up by 89.58–65:

---

[19] It is important at this juncture to critique the reconstruction by Drawnel at 4Q206:

"[and vultur]es, [and] rave[ns and black eagles and hawks]"   [ונשר]יה[ו]ער[בי]א ועוזיא ונציא]

This restoration is speculation enabled by parallelism with the Ethiopic tradition (albeit in acknowledgement of difference from the Ethiopic version, as he notes "the order of the birds of prey in the Aramaic list was different from the one attested in E"). But as the typography indicates, only four letters are possibly legible. Note that Milik does not restore this verse in his edition, and Tiller also treats it as lacking. (I have been unable to access Drawnel's plates to check the readings for myself.) I find Drawnel's reconstruction to be already quite speculative, and the remainder of this study tracing the introduction of the birds to the Animal Apocalypse to the first-century composition of the Apocalypse of the Birds will militate against accepting this reconstruction. See Drawnel, *Qumran Cave 4*, 328–31; Milik, *Books of Enoch*, 222; Tiller, *Commentary*, 166, 269.

[20] See the discussion in Tiller, *Commentary*, 30–2.

[21] Collins, *Combat Myth*, 102.

the introduction of the device of the seventy shepherds. As has been noted, the first period (Babylonian, as discussed in this chapter) and second period (Persian-and-later, as discussed in a later chapter), as extant in the Apocalypse of the Birds feature quadruped animals. I have above suggested this might be a sign that these verses once belonged to an earlier version of the Vision of the Beasts before they were transposed to and transformed in their current context. In this framework, I suggest that the scribes of the Apocalypse of the Birds themselves acted as redactors, intervening at the end of the Vision of the Beasts, and renarrating the Destruction so as to restart the story within their chosen macrostructural device. In this case, the preserved double narration would not be an accidental clue left by a maximalist redactor, but a signal of a secondary textual redirection. It would not be unreasonable to suggest that minor redactions to the Vision of the Beasts, such as 89.10 discussed above, belonged to this stage of composition, as the Vision of the Beasts came into conversation with its new literary context.

If we hypothesize the Apocalypse of the Birds was written with knowledge of the Vision of the Beasts, we will need to account for discontinuity, especially the terminological and rhetorical differences presented above. One way would be to propose a translational gap. While the Apocalypse of the Birds is extant only in Gəʿəz, it is extremely likely that it circulated in Greek as well.[22] However, we have evidence at Qumran for an Aramaic version of the Vision of the Beasts, and some vestiges from the Codex Vaticanus 1809 of a Greek translation. It is possible that the Apocalypse of the Birds was composed in Greek by a) direct readers of an Aramaic Vision of the Beasts, or b) recipients of a different Greek translation of the Vision of the Beasts than that which provides the Vorlage for our extant Gəʿəz version. Either one of these hypothetical scenarios could explain why the Apocalypse of the Birds inherits the symbolism but does not inherit the Vision of the Beasts's terminology for lambs or horned sheep. So, for example, let us return to the example of the different works' different ways of naming rams. The Vision of the Beasts's term for horned sheep is *ḫärge*. We actually have Aramaic and Greek versions of relevant verses of the Vision of the Beasts, in this case, corresponding to 89.45. In 4Q205 8, the Aramaic term is דכר. In the Codex Vaticanus 1809, the Greek term is κριός. The Apocalypse of the Birds's term for horned sheep is *dabela*. Obviously, we lack textual versions of the Apocalypse of the Birds from outside of Ethiopia, but Dillman nevertheless suggests the Greek behind *dabela* might be τράγος, itself a functional translation of דכר.[23] Thus,

---

[22] For further evidence on the circulation of the Apocalypse of the Birds in Greek, see the discussion of early readers in Greek in Chapter 5.

[23] See August Dillmann, *Lexicon linguae aethiopicae cum indice latino* (Leipzig: Weigel, 1865), 1101. I have been unable to uncover any documented instances in which τράγος translates Aramaic דכר, but the semantic field in which these terms operate is sufficiently flexible to imagine the pair being made.

perhaps we should imagine the writers of the Apocalypse of the Birds reading a different translation of the Vision of the Beasts in which King David is appointed a τράγος (later translated *dabela*), not a κριός (later *härge*), and developing their own story accordingly. The attendant problem with this solution is that it does not explain how we have come to possess the textual version we have in Gəʿəz, with a version of the Vision of the Beasts tending towards one terminology and the Apocalypse of the Birds tending towards another, yet combined together. We would need to postulate a later redaction together of the two versions, which is not impossible, but is certainly undocumented.

Another way to solve this problem would be to imagine the terminological differences as literary choices. Perhaps the rams (*dabela*) of the later period were simply meant to be different entities than those of the earlier period – a new generation of (masculine) leaders, quite different from those of old. Similarly, perhaps the Apocalypse of the Birds's different terminology for the lambs reflects a newly specific referent, something like the difference between conservative and Conservative.

A similar problem is confronted with reference to the thematic differences between the Vision of the Beasts and Apocalypse of the Birds. The Apocalypse of the Birds inherits the unique animal symbolism of the first work, but uses it for purposes that are not exactly inherent or necessitated by their original function in the Vision of the Beasts. In the Apocalypse of the Birds, the Vision of the Beasts's tradition of the antediluvian patriarchs as white bulls is resurrected and reappropriated to describe the restored fate of righteous humans at the eschaton. Most surprisingly, given the expectations created by the Vision of the Beasts, the Apocalypse of the Birds seems to end with the coming of a messianic figure and obliteration of the ethnic particularity of Israel at the eschaton, as gentiles and Israelites alike are all transformed into a new species of animal. They become white bulls, which is not new to the Animal Apocalypse, considering that the pre-Jacob patriarchs are all symbolized by white bulls. It is new, however, for this generation of Israelites (previously sheep) and gentiles (previously birds). That this universal transformation might be an unexpected plot twist is clear when set alongside the key feature of this work – that is, the very animal symbolism that makes this work distinctive operates on equivalences made between ethnic and/or national groups and animals. A universalist ending might be a startling conclusion for a work which draws its fundamental literary device from a very strict particularism. Such a literary difference might suggest a different compositional stage and literary interests. But it could also indicate a writer with a keen sense of a final twist.

At this point, we reach an objection that is worth addressing head-on. I have now revisited the import of the literary elements which I initially used to intuit textual incoherence and enact a possible split – such as the double narration of Jerusalem and terminological differences – as if they were the effect not of imperfect redaction or a bumpy transmissional road, but instead of literary choices. One might then ask: why postulate multiple agents making different literary choices, when such difference could simply be addressed to a single writer developing a dynamic story? The determinative factor, to my mind, is the material evidence. The literary differences that I have described are the sort that might fit into multiple different compositional models – one in which the Animal Apocalypse was written all of a piece, and one in which the Animal Apocalypse was written in stages. The second model is one that has yet to be fully imagined in the secondary literature, a gap which I have redressed in this chapter. But the articulation of another compositional schematic in which literary observations might be nestled does not tell us much about the relative probability of that model. However, the material evidence, and apparently independent attestation of the Vision of the Beasts, forces us to reckon with the possibility of a two-stage composition. Future chapters, which address the necessary setting of the Apocalypse of the Birds after the scribing of the Qumran fragments, will confirm that we were right to further develop this model.

In summary, my working hypothesis as to the compositional history of 1 En 85–90 is a broad scheme that does not seek to explain every datum or line of text, but proceeds in two general stages. The Vision of the Beasts circulated independently for a time, and the Apocalypse of the Birds was composed later by parties interested in stepping into and continuing this stream of tradition. The Vision of the Beasts was composed in Aramaic by the second century BCE. The Apocalypse of the Birds was likely composed at a later date by scribes who knew the Vision of the Beasts, but wanted to bring the Animal Apocalyptic tradition into a new historical era. I think it likely that the Apocalypse of the Birds was composed in Greek, as there is no evidence for its existence in Aramaic, and evidence will be mustered in a future chapter to demonstrate a Greek readership. I would further posit that the Vision of the Beasts had already been translated into Greek by the time of the composition of the Apocalypse of the Birds, though the process of translation and composition of the Apocalypse of the Birds might be linked. I do not think the Apocalypse of the Birds was designed to be a free standing work, but represents an addendum to the Vision of the Beasts.[24]

---

[24] I noted above Liv Ingeborg Lied's observation that scholars are prone to excerpt textual sections from the pseudepigrapha and promote them to the status of "work," even though there is no historical evidence they existed as discrete products. I have suggested here that I do not think the Apocalypse of the Birds was designed to represent a product discrete from the Vision of the Beasts. Nevertheless, I believe our material evidence suggesting that the Vision of the Beasts represents a product discrete from the Apocalypse of the Birds in its earlier standalone circulation, suffices to meet Lied's challenge and provide material grounds for source criticism of the Animal Apocalypse. I will thereby continue the pursuit of the Apocalypse of the Birds under the conceptual heading of "work." I will offer more comments on this in my final chapter.

The Apocalypse of the Birds may very well have originated or developed orally, and may have taken shape in the mouths of few or many readers of the Vision of the Beasts, so I do not want to collapse the processes of composition and writing as if they were necessarily equivalent.[25] Nevertheless, it is worth providing an educated guess as to how I imagine the early circulation and materiality of the Apocalypse of the Birds. I do not imagine a written Apocalypse of the Birds circulating separately from the Vision of the Beasts. Given the disruption evident in the Vision of the Beasts, particularly through the apparent loss of an earlier ending, it seems unlikely that supplementation of the Vision of the Beasts materially took place through, for instance, the sewing of an additional sheet to the end of a scroll.[26] Or, if this did happen, it did not produce a version that was the direct ancestor of the textual progression we now possess. Instead, I imagine the production of a new document altogether, beginning with the copying of text belonging to the Vision of the Beasts, followed by the setting down of the Apocalypse of the Birds. From this point onwards, at least one version of the Vision of the Beasts would circulate with the Apocalypse of the Birds attached, and it is something like this version that was translated into Gəʿəz by the sixth century CE.[27] And thus I hypothesize that the entity scholars have called the Animal Apocalypse as extant in Gəʿəz was created out of two Animal Apocalypses.

At the heart of this two-stage hypothesis is the implication that the Vision of the Beasts, like other ancient works, opened up literary horizons within which others moved. John Bryant describes a work not as static production, but as energy – "flowing," "coursing," and "enlivening" writers, readers, and

[25] On orality and the composition of apocalyptic literatures of the early common era, see the dissertation-in-progress of Rebekah Haigh at Princeton University.
[26] We have difficult and fragmentary evidence guiding our hypotheses on the manner in which the Vision of the Beasts circulated, and whether it might be circulated apart from other Enoch works or at the "end" of manuscripts. 4Q207 might be a standalone manuscript of the Vision of the Beasts, as there are no other fragments belonging to other works assigned to this manuscript. Meanwhile, the fragments of the Vision of the Beasts are placed in Milik and Drawnel's editions at the "end" of 4Q205 and 4Q206, and in the "middle" of 4Q204 but the extent of these fragmentary manuscripts is uncertain, and the placement of fragments belonging to the Animal Apocalypse after the Book of the Watchers is done on analogy with the order of the works in Ethiopic, rather than being grounded in any material reasons specific to the Qumran manuscripts. See the comment by Devorah Dimant: "It is not even possible to tell whether in the more complete manuscripts, i.e. 4Q204–206, the works were originally in a sequence identical to that of the Ethiopic collection, as Milik assumes as a matter of course," in Devorah Dimant, "The Biography of Enoch and the Books of Enoch," in *From Enoch to Tobit: Collected Studies in Ancient Jewish Literature* (Tübingen: Mohr Siebeck, 2017), 61.
[27] It would not be unreasonable to expect that a Vision of the Beasts without the Apocalypse of the Birds might have continued to circulate alongside a Vision of the Beasts to which the Apocalypse of the Birds had been added, though my subsequent discussion of early readers in Chapter 5 will not find positive evidence for an ongoing circulation of the Vision of the Beasts alone.

events.[28] One might almost imagine the animals of the Vision of the Beasts bounding off of the leather (perhaps) on which they were inscribed, roaming the environs of the writers of the Apocalypse of the Birds, inspiring new animalistic envisionings of an ever-changing world.

Conclusions: on the identification of the Vision of the Beasts & Apocalypse of the Birds

This chapter demonstrates that the textual entity called the Animal Apocalypse can be split into two identifiable literary works. The first is the Vision of the Beasts, which provides a history of Israel from Adam to the exile. This work is attested at Qumran, attested in Aramaic, and is thereby justly awarded a *terminus ante quem* in the second century BCE. The second is the Apocalypse of the Birds, which provides a history of Israel from the exile to the eschaton. This work is not attested at Qumran, and not attested in Aramaic. I initially enacted the split of these two works by identifying a doublet in the double narration of the Destruction of Jerusalem, as well as literary and terminological differences between the two works. I also argued that the presence of the Vision of the Beasts and absence of the Apocalypse of the Birds from Qumran represents suggestive material evidence for the independent circulation of the Vision of the Beasts.

Twenty-first-century scholars do not always share their nineteenth- and twentieth-century colleagues' zeal for source criticism of apocalyptic and pseudepigraphic works. The optimism of R. H. Charles and others that 1 Enoch could be perfectly sliced, and the subsequent layers assigned to particular historical moments, has been justifiably critiqued on multiple fronts. John J. Collins has cautioned that source criticism of apocalyptic literature often blithely ignores the extent to which repetition is a hallmark of the genre.[29] And, as noted in the first chapter, Liv Ingeborg Lied critiques the promotion of textual excerpts from pseudepigraphal works to the status of independent works because these "works" have no or insufficient material evidence speaking in favor of their autonomy from the larger works in which they are attested.[30] But I understand the combination of literary and material evidence presented in this chapter to adequately counter Collins' and Lied's forceful critiques of an abstract source criticism of apocalyptic and pseudepigraphal works such as those collected in 1 Enoch, shifting the balance of probability towards imagining multiple works.

---

[28] Bryant, *The Fluid Text*, 62.
[29] In Collins, *Apocalyptic Imagination*, 23.
[30] In Lied, "Text–Work–Manuscript."

More generally, David Carr has suggested that only a "methodologically modest" form of transmission history might be pursued.[31] I submit that the source criticism of the Animal Apocalypse, as enacted in this chapter, represents a "modest" but promising pursuit. I have been quite cautious about the extent to which literary and terminological considerations can substantiate a historical argument. I use literary analysis to tentatively begin, not authoritatively conclude, a line of inquiry. And I will direct the remainder of this study towards supplying additional evidence to bolster the probability of this case. I have also argued in this chapter that, in light of the literary evidence, the materials from Qumran document textual absence, and support a corresponding postulate of later textual growth.[32] I have also argued that the Apocalypse of the Birds developed in a relatively well-known manner for ancient works, through the addition of a new conclusion. I agree that the source criticism of apocalyptic works such as 1 Enoch, and the source criticism of ancient works more generally, faces steep methodological challenges. But specific features of the documentation and character of the Animal Apocalypse stand up well to that challenge, and enable concrete historical work.

I will now draw out the historical implications of the literary and material hypothesis proposed in this chapter. I will consider how the Animal Apocalypses of Enoch have been, and might be, set in historical time.

---

[31] Carr, *Formation of the Hebrew Bible*, 148–9.
[32] As Charlotte Hempel puts it, "the antiquity of the manuscripts allows us a close experience of the growth of these texts that biblical scholars can only dream of." In Charlotte Hempel, "Sources and Redaction in the Dead Sea Scrolls: The Growth of Ancient Texts," in *Rediscovering the Dead Sea Scrolls: An Assessment of Old and New Approaches and Methods*, ed. Maxine Grossman (Grand Rapids, MI: Eerdmans, 2010), 178.

CHAPTER 4

Dating the Animal Apocalypses

This chapter argues that the Animal Apocalypses of Enoch need to be redated. More specifically, I will demonstrate that the decoupling of the Apocalypse of the Birds from the Vision of the Beasts bears significant implications for the dating of both works.

Previously, scholars assuming a single Animal Apocalypse combined material evidence for the Vision of the Beasts with historical references within the Apocalypse of the Birds to assign the entire work a date in the second century BCE. But if the Animal Apocalypse breaks into two as argued in my previous chapter, this analysis quickly becomes untenable. I will argue that, since the Vision of the Beasts is bereft of the particular text that brought the work into the Hellenistic era, its window of composition could widen considerably to include much more of post-exilic Judaism. I will also demonstrate that the text of the Apocalypse of the Birds, now bereft of the material attestation that seemed to domesticate the work in the second century BCE, does not inevitably point towards the Maccabean Revolt or even the Hellenistic era at all. The windows of composition for both works are wider than has ever been imagined. This realization opens the way for a new envisioning of the development of the works in historical time, as will be endeavored for the Apocalypse of the Birds in upcoming chapters.

On dating the Vision of the Beasts

The Vision of the Beasts, as identified in my previous chapter, runs from 1 En 85.1–89.58. Its *terminus ante quem* is established by the four manuscripts in which its text is found at Qumran. The earliest of these manuscripts appears to date to the second century BCE.¹ *The terminus ante quem*, or latest possible date, of the Vision of the Beasts, then, is still the second century BCE.²

But the question of an earliest possible date, or *terminus post quem*, is fundamentally transformed. If we wanted to attempt a dating based on historical events mentioned, the "latest" reference in the extant text of the Vision of the Beasts is to the sixth-century BCE destruction of Jerusalem. The possibility that the Vision of the Beasts, or any Enochic work, might be dated to the sixth or fifth century BCE might seem quite shocking at first. The composition of the earliest literature that would one day be collected in 1 Enoch is generally traced to the third century BCE.³ But, if we operate purely on the basis of demonstrable historical references in the Vision of the Beasts, earlier centuries are theoretically in play.

In the previous chapter, I noted that I think it possible that the text belonging to the first (Babylonian/exilic, 1 En 89.65–9) and second (post-exilic, 1 En 89.72–7) periods of the Apocalypse of the Birds might have once belonged to an earlier version of the Vision of the Beasts, because of the text's continued reliance upon quadruped animals as the key antagonists. If true, this would extend our historical references for the Vision of the Beasts into the Persian period, and perhaps beyond.⁴ Unfortunately, the only version of the text that we now have is that belonging to the Apocalypse of the Birds, and the references that we might seek have been effectively cut off by the history of transmission. As the text is extant to us, then, the last historical reference still belongs to the sixth century BCE.

---

¹ This is 4Q207, a manuscript comprising a single fragment corresponding to 1 En 86. In the recent appraisal of Henryk Drawnel (in consultation with the paleographic eye of Emile Puech), "The script belongs to the earliest phase of the Hasmonean semiformal book hand, hence it can be dated to ca. 150–125 BC." In Drawnel, *Qumran Cave 4, 4*.

² In the context of a discussion on methods in dating, it is worth noting some critique levied against the formalism that has guided Qumran paleography since the pioneering work of Frank Moore Cross, especially criticizing an attendant confidence that certain styles correspond to certain historical windows. See Colette Sirat, "Les manuscrits en caractères hébraïques: réalités d'hier et historie d'aujourd'hui," *Scrittura e Civiltà*, no. 10 (1986): 273–5; Colette Sirat, "Les rouleaux bibliques de Qumrân au Moyen Âge: du Livre au Sefer Tora, de l'oreille à l'œil," *Comptes rendus des séances de l'Académie des Inscriptions et Belles-Lettres* 135, no. 2 (1991): 418.

³ Note, for instance, the "rare consensus" reported by James Charlesworth from the First Enoch Seminar of 2001: "we all agreed that sometime between 300 and 200 BCE ... a group of learned Jews began to compose what we know as the Astronomical Books of Enoch and the Book of the Watchers. The time for the earliest Enoch composition had been narrowed to one hundred years; it was composed sometime between 300 and 200 BCE." In James H. Charlesworth, "A Rare Consensus Among Enoch Specialists," *Henoch* 24 (2002): 234.

⁴ See my comments in Chapter 6 expanding the locus of reference for the second period from the Persian era to include Hellenistic-era events.

The next step in dating the Vision of the Beasts might be in suggesting it belongs to one or another literary movement or historical moment based on its language, themes, and theological perspective. As the dating stood in previous scholarship, it was treated as a second-century work, and scholars would therefore attend to the consonance of its text with second-century literature and culture. But, as Benjamin Sommer has noted, the dating of individual texts by matching "ideas" to a particular historical period is wholly problematic, as "it is always possible that an author at one period came up with ideas that turned out to be peculiarly relevant at another period."[5] Scholarly literature connecting the Vision of the Beasts with the second century might be capitalizing upon a second or third (or fifteenth) wave of relevance for this text. And, indeed, the supposition that the Apocalypse of the Birds seems to be a later continuation of the Vision of the Beasts demonstrates that this work did not go entirely out of vogue, but had an ongoing attraction. Were there further firm historical references, perhaps we might be hopeful of finding a more specific historical context. (Though, as I note later in this study, identifying the last historical reference does not necessarily suffice to date an apocalyptic work!) We will explore this promise with reference to the Apocalypse of the Birds shortly. But for the Vision of the Beasts, as for many of the biblical texts treated by Sommer, "general rubrics are the best we can apply with any intellectual honesty."[6] The general rubric that is operative, at this point, stretches from the sixth century (the last historical reference in the extant text) to the second century (the first extant manuscript). We can briefly explore whether it is possible to be more specific.

If we wanted to attempt a dating based on reliance upon sources, we might note that the Vision of the Beasts seems to be conversant with traditions found in another early Enoch work, the Book of the Watchers (1 En 1–36, cf. 4Q201, 4Q202, 4Q204, 4Q205, 4Q206). In particular, 1 En 86.1–88.3 tell the story of the fall of certain stars, their transformation into bulls with horse-like genitalia, their procreation of elephants, camels, and donkeys, and their ultimate punishment. This story sounds extremely similar to the fall of the Watchers, sexual transgression with human women, procreation of the giants, and punishment of the Watchers as found in 1 En 6–11, chapters belonging to the Book of the Watchers.[7] It is further suggestive that three manuscripts at

---

[5] Benjamin D. Sommer, "Dating Pentateuchal Texts and the Perils of Pseudo-Historicism," in *The Pentateuch: International Perspectives on Current Research*, ed. Thomas B. Dozeman, Konrad Schmid, and Baruch J. Schwartz, Forschungen zum Alten Testament 78 (Tübingen: Mohr Siebeck, 2011), 85.

[6] Sommer, 106.

[7] E.g. "1 Enoch 6–11 is the main source for the Animal Apocalypse apart from the Bible," in Karina Martin Hogan, "The Watchers Traditions in the Book of the Watchers and the Animal Apocalypse," in *The Watchers in Jewish and Christian Traditions*, ed. Angela Kim Harkins, Kelley Coblentz Bautch, and John C. Endres (Minneapolis: Fortress Press, 2014), 114.

Qumran – 4Q204, 4Q205, and 4Q206 – contain the Book of the Watchers and the Vision of the Beasts, as these manuscripts provide some historical evidence for reading practices in which these works were brought into conversation, perhaps suggesting a close textual history. Since the Book of the Watchers is usually dated to the third century BCE, we might thereby assign the Vision of the Beasts a third century BCE *terminus post quem*.[8] That said, we might want to be more minimalist in how we describe the scope of the textual relationship, as the closest parallels between the Book of the Watchers and the Vision of the Beasts are in the latter's use of traditions corresponding to chapters 6–11 from the Book of the Watchers (see especially the close parallels between chapters 10 and 88–9). 1 En 6–11 likely represents an originally independent subsidiary work and some of the oldest material that would eventually be redacted into the Book of the Watchers, perhaps dating as early as the fourth century.[9] Moreover, the scholarly consensus is that 1 En 6–11 represents a complex amalgam of multiple strands of traditions, making it difficult to explain whether purported

---

[8] The dating of the Book of the Watchers begins from the paleographic dating of the Qumran manuscripts, the earliest of which seems to be 4Q201 which has been paleographically dated to the early second century CE. Milik hypothesized that this manuscript "seems to have been made from a very old copy, dating from the third century at the very least," at least partially on selected orthographic grounds, in Milik, *Books of Enoch*, 140–1. Note, however, that Drawnel objects: "The semicursive form of the *pe* in the manuscript can hardly be a sufficient proof for Milik's opinion concerning the antiquity of the manuscript archetype," in Drawnel, *Qumran Cave 4*, 71.

From there, there are several pathways in scholarship by which the Book of the Watchers has been fruitfully located in the literature and social-history between the fourth and second centuries CE, with particular interest in the third century. A few notable approaches: Suter and Himmelfarb have explored the possibility that the Book of the Watchers encodes a critique of improper priestly marriages, not unlike that found in Aramaic Levi, 4QMMT, and the Damascus Document. Nickelsburg and Portier-Young explored the possibility that the Book of the Watchers encodes (and critiques) references to contemporary Hellenistic leaders such as the Diadochoi or Seleucids. Broader treatments in a third-century context can be found in the earlier work of Michael Stone, as well as recent work by Annette Yoshiko Reed pursuing a contextualization of the Book of the Watchers within the third century as, among other things, a participant in "broader intellectual trends in the early Hellenistic age, including the archival turn noted in the previous chapter but also the redeployment of Near Eastern scribal Listenwissenschaft." For the cited works, see David W. Suter, "Fallen Angel, Fallen Priest: The Problem of Family Purity in 1 Enoch 6–16," *Hebrew Union College Annual* 50 (1979): 115–35; Martha Himmelfarb, "Levi, Phineas, and the Problem of Intermarriage at the Time of the Maccabean Revolt," in *Between Temple and Torah: Essays on Priests, Scribes, and Visionaries in the Second Temple Period and Beyond* (Tübingen: Mohr Siebeck, 2013), 25–47; George W. E. Nickelsburg, "Apocalyptic and Myth in 1 Enoch 6–11," *Journal of Biblical Literature* 96, no. 3 (1977); Portier-Young, *Apocalypse Against Empire*, 15–23; Michael Stone, "The Book of Enoch and Judaism in the Third Century B.C.E.," *The Catholic Biblical Quarterly* 40, no. 4 (1978): 479–92; Annette Yoshiko Reed, *Demons, Angels, and Writing in Ancient Judaism* (Cambridge: Cambridge University Press, 2020), 189–246.

[9] As suggested in Nickelsburg, "Apocalyptic and Myth," 391.

interaction with this material (as 1 En 88–9) reflects knowledge of the work called the Book of the Watchers, or the subsidiary work 1 En 6–11, or the latter's no-longer-extant sources.[10] The Vision of the Beasts, for example, seems to reflect material concerning angelic sexual transgressions, which is linked to the angel Shemihazah in the Book of the Watchers, and often treated by scholars as one source of 1 En 6–11. But the Vision of the Beasts presents minimal engagement with material concerning the illicit teachings of the angels, which is associated with Asael in the Book of the Watchers, and often assigned by scholars to an independent source lying behind 1 En 6–11. To that end, Tiller, after a detailed discussion, concludes that the Animal Apocalypse depends on "both the Book of the Watchers and on an independent oral tradition that predates the Book of the Watchers."[11] However, if the chronological priority of the works is yet to be established, perhaps we ought to trace the entirety of the Watchers material in the Vision of the Beasts to this "independent oral tradition" or else a purported source undergirding 1 En 6–11 or something similar.[12] Ultimately, while it is clear that the Book of the Watchers shares traditional material concerning the Watchers with the Vision of the Beasts, I think it unclear exactly what is to be made of these parallels. I will offer further comments on this below.

Another avenue of dating the Vision of the Beasts derives from language. Our early manuscripts of the Vision of the Beasts are in Aramaic, suggesting we would want to look to a period when Aramaic was in wider use. I am unaware of any analyses that attempt to locate the syntax or lexemes of the Aramaic of the Animal Apocalypse within the historical development of Aramaic, which might be a promising direction of research, though I would also be cautious here because of the later manuscript attestation, and the controversial status of linguistic dating.[13] The merits of linguistic dating are controversial, but suffice

---

[10] For some attempts to parse the sources just of 6–11, see Carol A. Newsom, "The Development of 1 Enoch 6–19: Cosmology and Judgement," *The Catholic Biblical Quarterly* 42, no. 3 (1980): 310–29; Devorah Dimant, "1 Enoch 6–11: A Fragment of a Parabiblical Work," *Journal of Jewish Studies* 53, no. 2 (2002): 223–37; Siam Bhayro, *The Shemihazah and Asael narrative of 1 Enoch 6–11: Introduction, Text, Translation and Commentary with Reference to Ancient Near Eastern and Biblical Antecedents*, Alter Orient und Altes Testament 322 (Münster: Ugarit-Verlag, 2005).

[11] See the detailed treatment in Tiller, *Commentary*, 83–96. Quotation from 117n53.

[12] Note that Tiller's discussion begins with the assertion that "there can be no question that the Book of the Watchers is older than the Animal Apocalypse," at Tiller, 83n1.

[13] Linguistic dating can be problematic, as it is possible (though contested!) that scribes might transform a received text to be more in line with contemporary norms. For two opposing views of the state of the discussion with reference to dating Hebrew biblical texts, see Robert Rezetko and Ian Young, "Currents in the Historical Linguistics and Linguistic Dating of the Hebrew Bible: Report on the State of Research as Reflected in Recent Major Publications," *HIPHIL Novum* 5, no. 1 (July 2, 2019): 3–95; Na'ama Pat-El and Aren Wilson-Wright, "Features of Archaic Biblical Hebrew and the Linguistic Dating Debate," *Hebrew Studies* 54, no. 1 (2013): 387–410.

it to say it can be difficult to be definitive when sorting our extant Aramaic compositions studied under the heading of Judaism into different periods on purely linguistic grounds. Given the documented use of Aramaic in the southern Levant from the sixth century onwards,[14] it is difficult to exclude the sixth century as an impossible site of composition for an Aramaic work such as the Vision of the Beasts, though our preserved evidence in Aramaic for literary compositions comes from the fifth century and onwards.[15]

Within our extant Aramaic literature, we might note thematic connections demonstrable between the Vision of the Beasts and a network of Aramaic texts usually dated between the fourth and second centuries BCE. The Genesis Apocryphon (1Q20), the Aramaic Levi material (1Q21, 4Q213–4), and the Visions of Amram (4Q543–8) all use pseudepigraphal frames to explore new avenues on biblical history and legendary figures, as does the Vision of the Beasts. But such literary parallels do not necessitate the texts being dated together, though they might provide a hint.[16] An even closer set for comparison comes from other examples of early apocalyptic literature in Aramaic attributed to Enoch: the aforementioned Book of the Watchers and Astronomical Book (1 En 72–82, cf. 4Q208–211).[17] Like the Vision of the Beasts as we now have it, these two works are also not "particularly interested

---

[14] For a recent example, see Madadh Richey, David S. Vanderhooft, and Oded Lipschits, "Two Private Babylonian Period Stamp Impressions from Ramat Rahel," *Maarav* 23, no. 2 (2019): 289–306.

[15] I am grateful to Madadh Richey and Daniel Machiela for discussing this point with me at length. On Aramaic in the sixth century and early Persian period in particular, see Holger Gzella, *A Cultural History of Aramaic: From the Beginnings to the Advent of Islam* (Leiden; Boston: Brill, 2015), 104–53, 190–3, 205–8. If seeking an earlier Persian provenance for the Vision of the Beasts, it would likely belong among the texts Gzella treats as "national literatures in Aramaic," including Aḥiqar, and some of the older strata now belonging to Ezra and Daniel.

[16] Scholarship on the Genesis Apocryphon, Aramaic Levi materials, and Visions of Amram might provide helpful blueprints for future directions in dating the Vision of the Beasts. See the constellation of factors cited by Daniel Machiela with reference to the Genesis Apocryphon: "None of these points is very convincing on its own, but their cumulative weight is more significant." In Daniel A. Machiela, *The Dead Sea Genesis Apocryphon: A New Text and Translation with Introduction and Special Treatment of Columns 13–17* (Leiden: Brill, 2009), 142.

[17] I noted above treatments of the Book of the Watchers that pursue dates between the fourth and second centuries BCE, with a rough consensus that the third century is especially suitable. The Astronomical Book is a trickier case. The textual history of the Astronomical Book is heavily complicated by the uncertain relationship of the earliest manuscript (4Q208) with later manuscripts (4Q209–4Q211), not to mention the many differences between the Aramaic Astronomical Book and the Gəʽəz Book of the Luminaries. It is unclear what exactly what we get back when asking after the earliest Astronomical Book – can we be satisfied with a lunar calendar, devoid of an Enochic framing, as might be manifest in the earliest manuscript 4Q208?

The earliest copy of the Astronomical Book, 4Q208, is dated on paleographic grounds to the end of the third or beginning of the second century CE. It is often stated that the work fits comfortably in the third century BCE as in VanderKam, *Enoch and the Growth*, 88; Milik, *Books*

in eschatology."[18] Instead, all three Aramaic works use Enochic pseudepigraphy to communicate privileged disclosures about primordial time and the nature of the cosmos. It is important to remember that, with the removal of the text belonging to the Apocalypse of the Birds, the Vision of the Beasts no longer has an account of the eschaton. The examples of the Book of the Watchers and Astronomical Book might caution us against assuming that the (now-lost) ending of the Vision of the Beasts would have contained an account of the eschaton, as the Apocalypse of the Birds would later supply. The Book of the Watchers and Astronomical Book allow us to imagine that the Vision of the Beasts might have been an Aramaic Enoch work that probes some of the mysteries of history, but does not necessarily follow that speculation to extended reflections on the end of time. In any case, such literary consonances do not bear necessary conclusions for dating.

Furthermore, the Vision of the Beasts, now bereft of the eschatological account that made it such an obvious participant in the genre called apocalyptic, could also be profitably situated alongside streams of ancient Israelite and Judaean historiographic literature with which it has not been previously compared. The Vision of the Beasts recounts key events in the history of Israelite kings Saul, David, and Solomon, and shows no small interest in this line, uniquely marking off these three figures as rams among sheep (1 En 89.39–50). It seems likely that this narration developed with knowledge of other sources now called biblical, like Samuel and Kings. In this case, we might thereby think of the Vision of the Beasts as a kind of rewriting, and new attempt at historiography for this royal line. Perhaps, then, we ought to read the Vision of the Beasts more closely alongside works such as Chronicles, which rewrite Samuel and Kings (though in a far more prolix manner) with a keen eye to Davidic kingship.[19] Moreover, the span of history taken on by Chronicles – from Adam until the fall of Jerusalem and return under Cyrus – roughly matches

---

of Enoch, 7; Drawnel, *The Aramaic Astronomical Book*, 51; Reed, *Demons, Angels, and Writing*, 136. The problem is that the astronomical model of the Astronomical Book is archaic – perhaps intentionally so – complicating the idea of dating in accordance with astronomical trends. For one estimation, see Eshbal Ratzon: "The terminus post quem relies on derivations of Mesopotamian astronomical terms, developed only during the fifth century BCE." In Eshbal Ratzon, "The First Jewish Astronomers: Lunar Theory and Reconstruction of a Dead Sea Scroll," *Science in Context* 30 (June 1, 2017): 114n2. And so, while the Astronomical Book is often treated as a third-century composition, I think it important to hold open the door to earlier centuries.

[18] Martha Himmelfarb, *The Apocalypse: A Brief History*, Blackwell Brief Histories of Religion. (Malden, MA: Wiley-Blackwell, 2010), 3.

[19] On practices of rewriting in Chronicles read alongside other works not belonging to the Hebrew Biblical canon, see recently Molly M. Zahn, *Genres of Rewriting in Second Temple Judaism: Scribal Composition and Transmission* (Cambridge: Cambridge University Press, 2020), 74–97.

the narrative extent of the Vision of the Beasts.[20] It is interesting that the Vision of the Beasts and Chronicles both represent kinds of total histories from Eden to Exile. Chronicles is mired in its own controversies when it comes to dating, and the window in which dates for the work(s) are generally pursued is as expansive as our window for the Apocalypse of the Birds, ranging from the sixth to the second century BCE.[21] Again, these literary parallels are not invoked as a guide to dating. Rather, with the extent of the Vision of the Beasts's text newly delineated, we notice the prominence of certain textual sections (such as the recounting of the line of Israelite kings), and need to weight these more heavily in our accounting of literary parallels. The Vision of the Beasts should not be conceptually situated alongside the exact same texts as have been invoked in the scholarly study of the Animal Apocalypse, and new comparisons are possible. Identifying new literary similarities might not enable necessary and firm conclusions concerning the dating of the Vision of the Beasts, nor do they suffice to establish a network of dependency. Still, they allow us to contextualize some of the literary choices, extant and hypothesized, made by the Vision of the Beasts.

Ultimately, the Vision of the Beasts is to be dated somewhere between the sixth and second centuries BCE. This cautious but expansive dating could look to be a step backwards, from a narrow consensus provenance to a wider and more uncertain window. But I think my conclusions here, though brief, represent an important methodological advance. There are works which can be precisely dated, or invite reasonable conjecture by supplying scholars with the documentation or internal clues needed – and there are also those that cannot. The Vision of the Beasts is an example of the latter: a work that is, as it turns out, very difficult to date.

The Apocalypse of the Birds, however, is more amenable to precision in dating, but as I will demonstrate, not necessarily the way the field has pursued things thus far.

On dating the Apocalypse of the Birds

Without Qumran fragments, the case for dating the Apocalypse of the Birds to the second century BCE rests on the historical account found at 90.6–19. I have noted the modern consensus that this passage refers to Judas Maccabeus.

---

[20] See my comments above on the possibility that the Vision of the Beasts included Persian-era material. As it currently stands, the last event narrated is the fall of Jerusalem to the Babylonians.

[21] See Kai Peltonen, "A Jigsaw without a Model? The Date of Chronicles," in *Did Moses Speak Attic?: Jewish Historiography and Scripture in the Hellenistic Period*, ed. Lester L. Grabbe (London: Bloomsbury Publishing, 2001), 225–72. Note the conclusion of Ralph Klein that "perhaps a majority of scholars, including myself, argue for a fourth century date." In Ralph Klein, *1 Chronicles: A Commentary*, ed. Thomas Krüger, Hermeneia – A Critical and Historical Commentary on the Bible (Minneapolis: Fortress Press, 2007), 14.

Part of the reason that Maccabean referents were so passionately pursued in late twentieth- and early twenty-first-century scholarship is that our earliest fragment corresponding to the Animal Apocalypse (in my description, the Vision of the Beasts) is 4Q207, dated paleographically to the early Hasmonean period.[22] The work, the thinking goes, must be completed by the time of this first fragment. Therefore, all its historical referents must predate approximately 150 BCE. However, as I have noted, this *terminus ante quem* applies to the Vision of the Beasts (though "completion" hardly means that textual development has ended); it does not necessarily apply to the Apocalypse of the Birds, which is not found at Qumran. Therefore, we need not limit our sphere of inquiry for the provenance of this latter work to second century BCE Judea.

To open new historical horizons, I will demonstrate that scholars do not always agree on the provenance and dating of text corresponding to the Apocalypse of the Birds. I will highlight scholarship that is critical of a Maccabean dating and purported allusions to the Maccabean Revolt. I will also bring to bear a lineage of scholarship that is unbothered by any purported Qumran *terminus ante quem* – namely, scholars working in an era before the discovery and publication of the Scrolls, who often dated the Animal Apocalypse to the Roman period, and/or the earliest centuries CE. Finally, I will argue that the diverse and conflicting "solutions" to the apparent chronography of the Apocalypse of the Birds indicate an opaque internal chronology that cannot provide us with guidance on dating. In essence, there is no theoretical reason that the Apocalypse of the Birds belongs in the second century, or even in Hellenistic Judea.

Playing Judas: identifying the ram of 1 Enoch 90.9

We begin with the passage in question. At this point in the story, the sheep have fallen prey to the arrival of flocks of aggressive birds – eagles, vultures, kites, and ravens. The birds, with eagles at the forefront, decimate the population of the sheep (1 En 90.2–4). We enter a new chronological period (1 En 90.5), after which the text reads:

> (90.6) And small lambs were born from those white sheep, and they began to open their eyes, and to see, and to cry to the sheep. (7) But the sheep did not cry to them and did not listen to what they said to them, but were extremely deaf, and their eyes were extremely and excessively blinded. (8) And I saw in the vision how the ravens flew upon those lambs, and took one of those lambs, and dashed the sheep in pieces and devoured them. (9) And I looked until horns came up on those lambs,

---

[22] As in Milik, *Books of Enoch*, 244; Drawnel, *Qumran Cave 4*, 4.

but the ravens cast their horns down; and I looked until a big horn grew on one of those sheep, and their eyes were opened. (10) And it looked at them, and their eyes were opened, and it cried to the sheep, and the rams saw it, and they all ran to it.

(11) And besides all this those eagles and vultures and ravens and kites were still continually tearing the sheep in pieces and flying upon them and devouring them; and the sheep were silent, but the rams lamented and cried out. (12) And those ravens battled and fought with it, and wished to make away with its horn, but they did not prevail against it. (13) And I looked at them until the shepherds and the eagles and those vultures and kites came and cried to the ravens that they should smash the horn of that ram in pieces; and they fought and battled with it, and it fought with them and cried out that its help might come to it. (14) And I looked until that man who wrote down the names of the shepherds and brought up before the Lord of the sheep came, and he helped that ram and showed it everything, its help was coming down. (15) And I looked until that Lord of the sheep came to them in anger, and all those who saw him fled, and they all fell into the shadow before him.

(16) All the eagles and vultures and ravens and cranes gathered together and brought with them all the wild sheep, and they all came together and helped one another in order to dash that horn of the ram in pieces. (17) And I looked at that man who wrote the book at the command of the Lord until he opened that book of the destruction which those twelve last shepherds had wrought, and he showed before the Lord of the sheep that they had destroyed even more than (those) before them. (18) And I looked until the Lord of the sheep came to them and took in his hand the staff of his anger and struck the earth; and the earth was split, and all the animals and the birds of heaven fell from those sheep and sank in the earth, and it closed over them. (19) And I looked until a big sword was given to the sheep, and the sheep went out against all the wild animals to kill them, and all the animals and the birds of heaven fled before them.

In the Maccabean reading, the lambs of 90.6 represent the Hasidim, the ravens of 90.8 ff represent the Seleucids, Onias III is the lamb taken away by the ravens in 90.8, and Judas Maccabeus is the ram who arises in 90.9, calling all the sheep and rams to fight against the birds with him.[23] There is then some conflict in

---

[23] For a particularly Maccabean reading, see Jonathan Goldstein, *I Maccabees*, Anchor Yale Bible Commentaries 41 (Garden City, NY: Doubleday, 1976), 40–2.

the literature on which specific battles, if any, are referred to in verses 13–15 (and the similar, and perhaps duplicated, 17–19).[24] So, Charles, Milik, Tiller, and Nickelsburg (the last two more cautiously) have all seen in verses 13–15 a reference to the Battle of Beth-zur, especially the tradition found in 2 Maccabees 11.8–9 that the Maccabean forces are led by an angelic horseman and go on to decimate Lysias' forces.[25] In the Apocalypse of the Birds, there is some help from an angel, but it seems to be in the form of a personal consultation between leader and angel (1 En 90.14). Excitement at the Maccabean equation may outpace what the Enochic text can reasonably support.

We are also missing some of the phenomena that our (limited) accounts of the Maccabean Revolt have trained us to expect: where, for instance, are the Hellenizers?[26] And there are deeply discordant clashes between this work and other accepted Maccabean literature: The Apocalypse of the Birds uses ram symbolism, as does Daniel 8, but in Daniel, the ram refers to the enemy kings of Media and Persia. If the ram is Judas Maccabeus, here, such usage would represent a very different use of symbolism for literature purportedly produced in the same decade.

A set of Israeli scholars – first Menahem Kister, but also, more recently, Eyal Regev, Cana Werman, and Rivka Nir – see here a reference not to the Maccabean Revolt, but rather to a second century BCE religious reform movement.[27] They argue that Judas Maccabeus was not viewed as a religious leader. So, although this passage is usually identified as a narration of the Maccabean Revolt, these scholars note just how *strange* a narration it would represent. After all, the ram in 90.9–16 reverses the great blindness experienced by the

---

[24] The possible duplication of 13–15 and 17–19 is a thorny and much-debated issue. See the summary of scholarship and extensive treatment in Tiller, *Commentary*, 63–78.

[25] Charles, *Enoch or, 1 Enoch*, 211; Milik, *Books of Enoch*, 44; Tiller, *Commentary*, 360; Nickelsburg, *1 Enoch 1*, 400.

[26] Kister and Regev, who mirror many of these concerns in their analyses, also suggest that the text shows no evidence of an internal schism (So, Regev: "There is no hint of an internal clash within Israel," Regev, "The Ram and Qumran", 186.) This is not exactly the case, as there seems to be a split between the lambs and the sheep who refuse to listen (90.7). There is also a reference to wild sheep who fight alongside the birds at 90.16, which seems to suggest Jews collaborating with a foreign power. This last is an uncertain textual detail – Tiller and Nickelsburg emend "wild sheep" (*'ābagəʿ gädam*) to "wild beasts" (*'ärawitä gädam*), though this is a conjectural emendation, based on Tiller's observation that the wild sheep have never been mentioned before. Some later MSS read donkeys (*'ä'dugä*) or wild donkeys (*'ä'dugä gädam*), which were used in the Vision of the Beasts previously to represent the Watchers and Ishmaelites respectively, and neither of which makes particular sense here.

[27] Kister, "History of the Essenes"; Regev, "The Ram and Qumran"; Werman, "Epochs and End-Time"; Nir, "And Behold." In their "religious" reading of 90.9, they are anticipated by Pedersen, who suggested the great horn of 90.9 was a reference to Elijah, functioning as a Messianic forerunner. See Johannes Pedersen, "Zur erklärung der eschatologischen Visionen Henochs," *Islamica* 2 (1926): 416–29.

sheep throughout the history of Israel and is heralded as the companion of the angels in 90.31. Rather, for Kister, this seems to be another account of the foundation of a sectarian community not unlike (if not exactly equivalent to) that responsible for the Scrolls. For Regev, most recently, it is an account of an eschatological leader, anticipated, but not yet arrived. Both argue that ascribing religious leadership and receipt of individual revelation to Judas Maccabeus is, at best, awkward.[28] This critique may be slightly overstated, as it is not unthinkable that supporters of the Maccabean movement might have accorded religious and political significance to their celebrated leaders, even if this is not immediately reflected in 1 and 2 Maccabees.[29] That said, the criticism does demonstrate a certain inherent weakness in the equating of the ram with Judas Maccabeus.[30]

As it is, the account is not actually so specific as to cement an equation with one, and only one, set of historical circumstances. There is a youthful reform movement of sorts (the lambs), the coming of a leader with credentials both political (the horns are previously only given to kings: Saul, David, and Solomon) and religious (opening the eyes of the sheep), and some sort of conflict between earthly nations (birds) and the sheep under the leadership of the ram. Previous scholarship has placed artificial limitations on the amount of "history" we think the Apocalypse of the Birds can narrate. So, Kister and Regev (and all scholars working after the publication of the Dead Sea Scrolls) are obliged to place their revisionist accounts in the second century BCE, no longer out of deference to a Maccabean timeline, but instead because of the perceived *terminus ante quem* for the Animal Apocalypse at Qumran. But if this is a false *terminus ante quem* for the Apocalypse of the Birds, as I have argued, the resistance narrative which emerges from 90.6–19 could find several homes in Jewish history. This passage may describe the Maccabean Revolt, albeit with significant challenges, but it could also describe the so-called Jewish Revolt of the 60s, and the Bar Kokhba revolt of the early second century CE. The historical parallels required by the allegory are relatively open-ended: an internal schism between lambs and the sheep, a Jewish leader to be the great-horned ram, followers to fill out the flock of rams, and an antagonistic fleet of enemies to be the birds. With this general narrative in mind, the Apocalypse

---

[28] A median solution is defended by Daniel Assefa, who sees the ram of 90.9–12 as a reference to a religious leader of the community producing the work, and the ram of 90.12–16 to be a pro-Maccabean interpolation telling the lore of Judas Maccabeus. See Assefa, *L'apocalypse des animaux*, 220–32.

[29] I am grateful to Martha Himmelfarb for this suggestion.

[30] Note that the apolitical readings put forward by Kister and Regev require the political conflict narrated in 90.13–19 to be placed in the eschatological future, whereas I agree with the wider consensus that some of these verses (esp. 13–15) bear historical information. See my forthcoming article, "When Does History End?"

of the Birds might have a far more flexible sphere of historical application than has been previously acknowledged.

Possible timelines, old and new: a review of prominent and forgotten scholarship

I am not the first to note these other possibilities. At least one stream of traditional Ethiopian interpretation, an Amharic commentary tradition known as the *Andəmta*, would read the end of the Animal Apocalypse as a prophecy of Roman-era events, specifically referring to the life and career of Jesus Christ.[31] The *Andəmta* in its current form has been traced by Roger Cowley to Gondar in the sixteenth–eighteenth centuries, though it seems to contain much older material.[32] According to the *Andəmta*, the Romans are introduced at 90.1, and the subsequent persecution of the lambs by the ravens refers to the persecution of Christians by the Romans.[33] Christological readings are quite common in the *Andəmta*. As Daniel Assefa puts it, "when there is no clear correlation with biblical history, the commentaries tend to make a Christological or Christian reading."[34] The prevalence of this Christological interpretative move, not just in Ethiopia or the *Andəmta* commentary tradition but as a broadly demonstrated Christian tendency in the interpretation of Jewish texts (especially Jewish texts taken to be chronologically pre-Christian by the tradition), mean that we need not take the *Andəmta* as a control on how modern scholars read the text. But it is nevertheless worth emphasizing that at least some members of the tradition

---

[31] For a brief introduction to the *Andəmta*, see the recent treatment in Kirsten Stoffregen-Pedersen and Tedros Abraha, "Andəmta," in *Encyclopaedia Aethiopica*, ed. Siegbert Uhlig and Alessandro Baussi vol. 1 (Wiesbaden: Harrassowitz Verlag, 2003), 258–9. A more extensive treatment can be found in Roger W. Cowley, *The Traditional Interpretation of the Apocalypse of St. John in the Ethiopian Orthodox Church*, University of Cambridge Oriental Publications 33 (New York: Cambridge University Press, 1983), 1–60. The *Andəmta* to 1 Enoch has been minimally translated. Note, however, the translation of its introduction from an Amharic text "dictated to me from memory by Māggabé mesṭir Géra wārq Tebābu, a teacher at the Menelik II Memorial Schoo, Addis Ababa," in Roger W. Cowley, "Old Testament Introduction in the Andəmta Commentary Tradition," *Journal of Ethiopian Studies* 12, no. 1 (1974): 159–60. Ralph Lee has provided a partial translation of the *Andəmta* on 1 En 6–9, in Ralph Lee, "The Ethiopic 'Andəmta' Commentary on Ethiopic Enoch 2 (1 Enoch 6–9)," *Journal for the Study of the Pseudepigrapha* 23, no. 3 (March 2014): 179–200. Daniel Assefa has brought the *Andəmta* commentary tradition to bear upon the study of 1 Enoch in many articles cited throughout.

[32] Cowley, *Traditional Interpretation*, 23–34.

[33] I am grateful to Daniel Assefa for sharing and discussing with me his unpublished translation of this material. Assefa and Ralph Lee are currently working on a full translation of the *Andəmta* commentary on 1 Enoch.

[34] Private communication of May 17, 2019.

that transmitted the Animal Apocalypse for over a thousand years found no insuperable textual problem preventing its chronology from stretching beyond the Maccabean Revolt.

Similarly, modern scholars working before the discovery of the Scrolls proposed sites of composition for the Animal Apocalypse in both the Hasmonean period and the Roman period.[35] Reviews of this often-overlooked era of Western scholarship can be found in a few places, but a brief summary is in order.[36] Dillmann and Schürer held to a Hasmonean hypothesis, not entirely incompatible with the Maccabean interpretation, suggesting the activities of Judas Maccabeus are narrated in a cursory fashion (90.8) before the narrative proceeds into the Hasmonean period.[37] The great ram of 90.9–14 would be John Hyrcanus, though interpreters differ on whether the historical progression is arrested there, or whether it continues into the reign of his son Alexander Jannaeus. There was a final round of defense for the Hyrcanus hypothesis in the 1950s, but Daniel Olson observes: "Reicke's [1960] identification of the 'horned ram' of *1 En* 90:9 as the Hasmonean ruler John Hyrcanus may be the last serious attempt to defend this interpretation, which

---

[35] Nineteenth- and early twentieth-century scholarship can be problematic as it was working with understandings of Judaism and Christianity that are no longer tenable, especially concerning why we might prefer denizens from one camp or another to compose certain pieces of 1 Enoch. For one representative example, the initial publication of Richard Laurence is notably excited that the Book of Parables provides proof that "Jews before the birth of Christ" held to the doctrine of the Trinity. Laurence, *Book of Enoch*, 1838, lii–liv. Or, we might note Emil Schürer's accusation that his colleagues Hoffmann and Philippi only want a Christian date for the Book of Enoch so as to skirt around the uncomfortable fact that the New Testament's Epistle of Jude seems to cite a non-canonical work such as this. See Emil Schürer, "The Book of Enoch," in *A History of the Jewish People in the Time of Jesus Christ*, trans. Peter Christie vol. 3.2 (New York: Charles Scribner's Sons, 1891), 59. Relatedly, Volkmar's contention that the Book of Enoch is a second century composition has much to do with his dogmatic commitment to a late dating for all the Catholic Epistles, Jude included. See Gustav Volkmar, "Über die katholischen Briefe und Henoch," *Zeitschrift für wissenschaftliche Theologie* 4 (1861): 422–36.

[36] A short overview is provided by Tiller. Moshe Gil, in an idiosyncratic article, gives a substantial audience and recitation to this generation of scholarship, not least because he is convinced of a Christian-era gnostic-styled Enoch written by a single author, and finds support for this simple compositional model and extensive timeline in this early school. Going back a century (and a half), George Schodde provides, in English summary, a balanced appraisal of his contemporaries, in a continuation of the German language review provided by Emil Schürer. Tiller, *Commentary*, 4–13; Moshe Gil, "The Ethiopic Book of Enoch Reconsidered," in *Related Worlds: Studies in Jewish and Arab Ancient and Early Medieval History* (Aldershot, Hampshire; Burlington, VT: Ashgate, 2004), 43–50; George Henry Schodde, *The Book of Enoch: Translated from the Ethiopic, with Introduction and Notes, by ... G.H. Schodde, Etc* (Andover, MA: W. F. Draper), 20–30; Schürer, "Das Buch Henoch."

[37] For influential early expositions, see Dillmann, *Das Buch Henoch*, 1853, xliv; Schürer, "Book of Enoch," 66.

has been abandoned since the publication of the Qumran fragments of the Animal Apocalypse."[38] (And note Olson's formulation aptly shows the extent to which the publication of the Qumran fragments served to cut off the pursuit of the Animal Apocalypse past the Maccabean Revolt.)

Roman-era hypotheses never took on quite the popularity of their Hasmonean counterparts. They came in a few varieties of which I can provide a representative sampling. At the very beginnings of Western scholarship on Enoch, Richard Laurence thought the Animal Apocalypse culminated in the reign of Herod the Great.[39] Ferdinand Philippi dates the entirety of 1 Enoch, including the Book of Parables, to a Christian author working in the second century CE.[40] And Gustav Volkmar, idiosyncratically, understands the Animal Apocalypse to culminate in the messianic revolt of Bar Kokhba, and to be written by a member of Rabbi Akiva's school.[41]

That said, in dating the Apocalypse of the Birds, nineteenth-century scholars were often trying to account for the composition of much larger swathes of material. Pre-twentieth-century scholars lacked the modern conviction that (at least) the five books comprising 1 Enoch represent five autonomous works, and were often trying to find a context which would produce particular slices of 1 Enoch that scholars do not now group together. So, Philippi's proposal that the Apocalypse of the Birds represents a Christian composition capitalizes on his belief that the Animal Apocalypse and Book of Parables (with its speculation about an exalted messiah) are to be necessarily traced to a single location.[42] At the time, even if the Book of Parables was recognized as an independent composition, the Animal Apocalypse was often traced to the same community as (and thus dated in lockstep with) the Book of the Watchers, and/or the Epistle of Enoch.[43] Contemporary scholarship now understands all

---

[38] See Bo Reicke, "Official and Pietistic Elements of Jewish Apocalypticism," *Journal of Biblical Literature* 79, no. 2 (1960): 137–50; Menahem Stern, "The Relations between Judea and Rome during the Rule of John Hyrcanus / הורקנוס יוחנן בימי ורומא יהודה בין היחסים על," *Zion* 26, no. 1 (1961): 1–22; Charles C. Torrey, "Alexander Jannaeus and the Archangel Michael," *Vetus Testamentum* 4, no. 2 (1954): 208–11; Olson, *A New Reading*, 6n7.

[39] Richard Laurence, *Book of Enoch*, 1838, xxxv–xxxvi.

[40] Ferdinand Philippi, *Das Buch Henoch: sein Zeitalter und sein Verhältniss zum Judasbriefe: ein Beitrag zur neutestamentlichen Isagogik: nebst einem Anhange über Judä V. 9 und dis Mosesprophetie* (Stuttgart: S.G. Liesching, 1868).

[41] Gustav Volkmar, "Beiträge zur Erklärung des Buches Henoch: nach dem Äthiopischen Text," *Zeitschrift der Deutschen Morgenländischen Gesellschaft* 14, no. 1/2 (1860): 87–296.

[42] Philippi, *Das Buch Henoch*. This is the chosen solution revived by Gil, "Ethiopic Book," esp. 49–50.

[43] For a contemporary's summary of this era of scholarship, specifically remarking on this stratification of compositional layers, see Schürer, "Book of Enoch," 60–70; Schodde, *Book of Enoch*, 20–30; Charles, *Enoch or, 1 Enoch*, xxx–xliv. For a modern retrospective, see the reviews of literature found in Tiller, *Commentary*, 1–11; Olson, *A New Reading*, 1–13.

of these to represent independent works. We also have proof at Qumran that some of the more outlandish proposals for late dating of large swathes of 1 Enoch (e.g. Philippi's suggestion that the entirety of 1 Enoch was a Christian composition) cannot be true.[44] That said, some of the observations of these pre-Qumran scholars are suggestive, when read with specific and limited reference to the Apocalypse of the Birds.

Importantly, early generations of scholarship demonstrate that the chronological schema of the Apocalypse of the Birds can accommodate more than one historical interpretation. The text narrates a progression of seventy shepherds, the end of whose reign ushers in the eschaton. Below is a summary with excerpts of the relevant portions of the text giving "chronological" information:

Table 4.1 Chronological Information in Apocalypse of the Birds

89.65–72	Destruction of the Temple
89.72a: "And after this, I saw how the shepherds pastured for twelve hours."	
89.72b–7	Rebuilding of Second Temple, Scattering and Mixing of Sheep with Beasts
90.1: "And I looked until the time that thirty-seven shepherds had pastured in the same way, and each individually, they all completed their time like the first ones; and others received them into their hands to pasture them at their time, each shepherd at his own time."	
90.2–4	Coming of the Birds, Devouring of Sheep
90.5: "And I looked until the time that twenty-three shepherds had pastured; and they completed, each in his time, fifty-eight times."	
90.16–19	Final Battle of Sheep and Birds
90.17: And I looked at that man who wrote the book at the command of the Lord until he opened that book of the destruction which those twelve last shepherds had wrought, and he showed before the Lord of the sheep that they had destroyed even more than (those) before them.	

Although much ink has been spilled over the historiography and chronography of the Animal Apocalypse, this table makes clear just how little text is dedicated to providing any sort of chronological schema – four verses only.

Even with such limited material, there are already syntactic ambiguities. So, in 89.72a, one wonders if we are meant to understand the Destruction of the Temple as marking the beginning of a period of twelve hours, or if this period has yet to begin. In 90.1, we might interpret references to the rebuilding of the temple and the decline of Israel by way of "mixing" as comprising the reign of

[44] The curious recent defense by Gil of Philippi's all-at-once, Christian-era compositional account of 1 Enoch is readily explained once the reader realizes that Gil understands the Qumran fragments to be non-Second Temple documents, scribed in the common era by "Jewish Manichaeans." See Gil, "Ethiopic Book," 55–6.

thirty-seven shepherds all on its own.⁴⁵ But we might equally consider this to be a cumulative tally of the first twelve shepherds' reign, with the addition of a new set of twenty-three. This latter suggestion seems to fit the logic of 90.5, which notes that twenty-three additional shepherds have had their time to reign, and fifty-eight periods have been concluded. Since the total of fifty-eight periods is the sum of 12+23+23, perhaps there has been a cumulative logic all along! But the text itself could also be read to suggest that twenty-three shepherds completed fifty-eight "times." In this case, the shepherds are not mere stand-ins for intervals of time. Finally, the last twelve periods needed to jump from fifty-eight to seventy are mentioned obliquely at 90.17, though it is not clear when exactly they drew to a close. Clearly, certain threads of logic are woven through the passage, but the text provides little help in untangling some of the knottier issues.

Contemporary scholarship tends to agree that the Apocalypse of the Birds presents four historical periods, narrated cumulatively, such that the ascending numbers in the text indicate the rising tally of shepherds whose reigns have come and gone. The quadripartite divisions run as follows: twelve shepherds ruling over the first period, twenty-three over the second, twenty-three over the third, and twelve over the fourth.⁴⁶ This arrangement effectively does away with two of the four ambiguities noted above: 90.1 and 90.5 are easily understood as marking the number of shepherds that have served altogether. However, it leaves little guidance on the remaining two issues having to do with the purported start and end points of the schema. At this point, consensus breaks down.

Due to the ambiguities at 89.72a, some interpretations of the schema begin in the Assyrian period,⁴⁷ others begin with the exile,⁴⁸ and still others with the return from exile.⁴⁹ And as a result of the scarcely mentioned fourth and

---

⁴⁵ Note that even though every single one of our Ethiopic manuscripts reads thirty-seven, this is always emended to read thirty-five, so as to arrive at a total count of seventy.

⁴⁶ There are dissenters at this point, though their solutions have not found broader support. See the 23+12+23+12 schema in Martin Hengel, *Judaism and Hellenism: Studies in Their Encounter in Palestine during the Early Hellenistic Period* (London: SCM Press, 1974), 187–8; see also Frölich's suggestion that there are four periods lasting for seventy weeks, with the fourth comprising 23 shepherds tending the flocks for 58 periods, in Ida Frölich, "The Symbolical Language of the Animal Apocalypse ('1 Enoch' 85–90)," *Revue de Qumrân* 14, no. 4 (1990): 629–36.

⁴⁷ Nickelsburg, for a representative example, starts the clock with the reign of Manasseh. See Nickelsburg, *1 Enoch 1*, 391–3.

⁴⁸ E.g. Tiller, *Commentary*, 55–60.

⁴⁹ So, "the first part of 12 periods covers the Return and attempts at reform under Ezra and Nehemiah," in Black, *Book of Enoch*, 274. A few pages earlier, however, Black seems to suggest that the Apocalypse of the Birds is "here extending from the Assyrian invasion and the fall of Samaria (721 B.C.) to the writer's own time, the 'eschatological' era (c. 200 B.C.)." This suggests that he sees two operative schema – seventy periods, stretching from the Assyrian to Maccabean periods, and seventy shepherds, stretching from the post-exilic to Maccabean periods. Elsewhere, the majority of scholars are convinced that the periodization is accomplished through the device of the shepherds, and there is no need to postulate dual schemas.

final period, some interpreters understand the final era of twelve shepherds to be mostly or completely elapsed at the time of writing,[50] while others see the final era as largely yet to come,[51] and a further few see it as a red herring, not meant to represent twelve time-intervals in the style of the previous periods at all![52] The situation of the schema in historical time is very much up for debate.

Also confusing is the number of years implied in the Apocalypse of the Birds. Is it seventy intervals of seven, as in Daniel 9.24, and thus 490 years?[53] If so, this can bring us to an awkward calculation of turning points, at least if we are relying upon modern chronologies.[54] Starting with the Babylonian exile of 586, some scholars have wondered whether it really makes sense to think of a new period being initiated in 502. Does this mean the end of time was predicted to be the relatively inconspicuous 96 BCE (being 586 minus 490 years)? This, then, leads some to suggest that the most important aspect of the periods is actually what takes place in the middle, rather than at the boundary lines, though this results in an undermining of the idea of periodization altogether.[55] Finally, it is difficult to correlate these periods with modern chronologies of the period. The Babylonian or exilic period, as calculated by modern historians, might stretch from 586–39 BCE (47 years), or perhaps until 519 or 516 (67–70 years) if tied more directly to the completion of the Second Temple. The Persian period might stretch from 539–332 (207 years), or begin later if one wishes to make the start-date the completion of the Second Temple. There is no easy way to make any of these ratios work, with twelve groupings of years equaling the Babylonian period, and twenty-three proportional groupings of years equaling the Persian period. This is an incongruity that has led to confusion in the secondary literature.[56] While it is loosely true that the

---

[50] Nickelsburg, *1 Enoch 1*, 392; Fröhlich, "Symbolical Language," 631–2. Though, here, note that Nickelsburg is sympathetic to the suggestion that a slightly earlier Vision (written around the turn of the second century BCE, with an imagined end-time date of 181 or 171 BCE) was updated by someone with knowledge of the Maccabean Revolt (now past the imagined end-time date of the original chronologist).

[51] See, for example, Antti Laato, "The Chronology in the Animal Apocalypse of 1 Enoch 85–90," *Journal for the Study of the Pseudepigrapha* 26, no. 1 (2016): 3–19; Charles, *Enoch or, 1 Enoch*, 201.

[52] Olson suggests that the final twelve periods are actually *shorter* on earth than they are in heaven, and actually last only three and a half earth years apiece, as opposed to the earlier periods which last the normal seven. See Olson, *A New Reading,*" 107.

[53] Gustav Volkmar, for one, felt that there was no reason to ally the chronology to Daniel too closely, and assigned each shepherd ten years, rather than seven. This led him to a date around the Bar Kokhba revolt. See Volkmar, "Beiträge zur Erklärung," 100.

[54] There is good evidence indicating that ancient Jews' chronological reckonings of the post-exilic period diverged from our current chronologies of the period, discussed at length in Chapter 6.

[55] This is the chosen solution of Nickelsburg, *1 Enoch 1*, 392.

[56] As Charles observed long ago, "No system ... which attributes a like number of years to each shepherd can arrive at any but a forced explanation of these numbers." In Charles, *Book of Enoch Translated*, 244.

Persian period was about twice as long as the Babylonian period, this reckoning is based on our own modern historical calculations, which might not be easily transferred to ancient readers.

The Apocalypse of the Birds also does not present a consistent narrative style, if we are looking for something akin to a total history, even a total history of a limited period. It seems reasonably clear what the first and second periods are chronicling (the first, at 89.65–71, the Babylonian exile; the second, at 89.72–7, return and rebuilding of the Second Temple). But the third period is far shorter (3 verses, compared to 7 and 6 verses for the first and second periods respectively) and quite cryptic. And after 90.5, the close of the third period, the narrative provides little further comment on the progression of the chronology. Given the total quantity of seventy shepherds, and the passing of the tenure of fifty-eight shepherds by the end of the third period (we are reminded of the latter fact explicitly at 90.5), we assume that twelve shepherds will reign over the fourth and final period (a conclusion elliptically confirmed at 90.17). However, this does not mean that we must imagine a certain duration of years elapsing before the "end" of the schema.[57] Exactly how long it will take for the fourth, and final, period to elapse cannot be extrapolated based on "given" ratios of shepherds to years, for no such ratios have been firmly established. The general point here is that the chronology or duration of the periods cannot be predicted (or reverse-engineered) based on a consistent internal numerical scheme.

Additionally, the fourth period could be the era of the Seleucid empire, on analogy with Daniel's fourth kingdom. Such a view is near-universally accepted by modern commentators. But we might note that by the Roman period, Daniel's fourth kingdom was quickly re-read as a reference to Rome.[58] It is certainly not the case that a fourth epoch styled after Daniel must reflect the original or earliest referent retrievable for Daniel's fourth kingdom, especially since the commonly understood referent changed so drastically within a few centuries of composition.

The schema, as many have concluded, might be something less than interested in, or less than capable of providing, historical accuracy. As Paul Kosmin memorably puts it: "[it] is in no sense chronologically accurate; the Apocalypse of Animals, importantly, does not count years."[59] This inherent limitation of

---

[57] A very similar schema is found in 4 Ezra 11–12, where the fourth kingdom of Daniel is identified as Rome, and the tenures of twelve leaders are enumerated as the final antagonists before the onset of the eschaton. This will be explored at length below.

[58] See especially William Adler, "The Apocalyptic Survey of History Adapted by Christians: Daniel's Prophecy of 70 Weeks," in *The Jewish Apocalyptic Heritage in Early Christianity*, ed. James C. VanderKam and William Adler (Leiden: Brill, 1996), 201–38.

[59] Paul J. Kosmin, *Time and Its Adversaries in the Seleucid Empire* (Cambridge: Harvard University Press), 169.

the text, when met with the everlasting optimism of historically minded scholars, has inevitably produced a sea of literature promising to solve the problem, though no particular solution has met with the approval of many.

I will not provide one here. Indeed, the Apocalypse of the Birds seems to defy any exact match with historical time. I wish mostly to note that the chronology does not inevitably lead us to a particular historical period in and of itself – it can, however, be worked to be in consonance with just about any landing point we might choose, from the career of Judas Maccabeus to Herod to Bar Kokhba.

Therefore, our horizons for the possible provenance of the Apocalypse of the Birds are not necessarily limited by material attestation at Qumran, internal chronology, or even a particularly strong scholarly consensus on a Maccabean date.

Conclusions: redating the Animal Apocalypse(s) of Enoch

In the last two chapters, I have explored where, how, and why we establish the work known as the Animal Apocalypse. I enacted a split of the "work" of the Animal Apocalypse into two works, in response to both literary cues within the text, and their different documentary records. The first work, the Vision of the Beasts, corresponding to 1 En 85.1–89.58, is multiply attested at Qumran. The second work, the Apocalypse of the Birds, corresponding to 1 En 89.59–90.42, is nowhere attested among the Dead Sea Scrolls.

In addition to this documentary evidence, considerations on the level of text further bolster the case for such a division: I highlighted the double narration of the destruction of Jerusalem by the Babylonians, and literary and terminological differences between the Vision of the Beasts and Apocalypse of the Birds. Additionally, I have demonstrated the weakness of the commonly accepted hypothesis of a Maccabean provenance, and the flexibility of the never-quite-solved heptadic chronology of the Apocalypse of the Birds, in an attempt to show that the Apocalypse of the Birds cannot be comfortably dated on internal grounds to the Maccabean period.

Having summarized the case made in these chapters, I want to carefully situate the nature of my intervention in the secondary literature. As my engagement with previous scholarship above indicates, I have benefited greatly from centuries of work on the Animal Apocalypse in particular, and on 1 Enoch more generally. The reader will have noted that I owe particular debts at significant junctures in my analysis:

First, a lineage of scholarship exploring the possibility of multiple works within the Book of Dreams, culminating in the work of Anathea Portier-Young and Philip L. Tite in some ways inspires my search for multiple works within a member of the Book of Dreams, the Animal Apocalypse.[60] Second, Carol Newsom identified a literary seam with the double narration of the Destruction of Jerusalem at 1 En 89.55–8, 65–7.[61] Third, George W. E. Nickelsburg and Daniel Olson, among others, subdivide their text into two parts in keeping with the literary shift at 89.59.[62] Fourth, Menahem Kister and Eyal Regev have provided a significant recent challenge to the Maccabean hypothesis, as grounded out of the historical narrative at 1 En 90.9–19.[63] Fifth, nearly all previous scholarship has expressed frustration at chronological imprecision and inconsistency in the general "periodization" of the Apocalypse of the Birds. Sixth, and finally, scholars working before the discovery of the Scrolls, such as Gustav Volkmar and Friedrich Philippi, provide conceptual blueprints for reconstructions of the Apocalypse of the Birds that stretch past the second century BCE into the common era.[64]

At the same time, the case presented in these chapters departs significantly from previous scholarship. Previous scholarship has explored the possibility that 1 En 83–4 and 1 En 85–90 should be considered separate works. None, to my knowledge, has explored the possibility that the Animal Apocalypse (1 En 85–90) breaks into multiple works. It is also the innovation of this chapter to build upon the literary cues flagged by Newsom, Nickelsburg, Olson (et al.) and hypothesize the existence of two works. In light of this hypothesis, I contribute a re-evaluation of the works attested by our Qumran fragments and conclude that the Apocalypse of the Birds is nowhere attested at Qumran. I combine Kister and Regev's critiques of the Maccabean hypothesis with general scholarly frustration concerning the imprecise periodization of the Animal Apocalypse to suggest that not only does the text not lead us to the Maccabean Revolt, but (against Kister and Regev) it does not even necessarily lead us to the second or first century BCE. I find precedent for this extended chronological timeline in pre-Scrolls scholarship, though am not persuaded by any particular provenance proposed by pre-Qumran-discovery scholars.

I present this summary because I am aware that the conclusion reached in these chapters – that the Apocalypse of the Birds a) is a separable work within the Animal Apocalypse, and b) does not have a second century BCE

---

[60] See Portier-Young, *Apocalypse Against Empire*, 347–8; Philip L. Tite, "Textual and Redactional Aspects," 106–20.
[61] In Newsom, "Enoch 83–90."
[62] In Nickelsburg, *1 Enoch 1*, 389; Olson, *A New Reading*, 190.
[63] In Kister, "History of the Essenes"; Regev, "The Ram and Qumran."
[64] In Volkmar, "Beiträge zur Erklärung"; Gustav Volkmar, *Eine Neu-Testamentliche Entdeckung und deren Bestreitung: oder, die Geschichts-Vision des Buches Henoch im Zusammenhang* (Kiesling, 1862); Philippi, *Das Buch Henoch*.

terminus ante quem – represents a significant departure from previous scholarship and would serve to redirect a scholarly consensus. Nevertheless, I understand many elements of my case to be inspired by and affirmed in the history of scholarship on the Animal Apocalypse, even though the conclusions that emerge from their amalgamation lead us towards an entirely new direction of study.

CHAPTER 5

The Early Christian Readers of the Apocalypse of the Birds

So far, I have established that the text of the work I have called the Apocalypse of the Birds appears for the first time in our material record in fourteenth-century Ethiopia. From there, we can imagine ourselves walking along a timeline backwards, looking for hints that a version of the work has come into existence. The material shape of the work we are looking for is something like the Animal Apocalypse we have attested in Gəʿəz; I have suggested above that the Apocalypse of the Birds most likely functioned as an addendum to the Vision of the Beasts, and did not circulate as a freestanding work. But we are looking in particular for references to the distinctive content and traditions of the Apocalypse of the Birds, since it is also possible to imagine the circulation of a version limited to the Vision of the Beasts, akin to what our Qumran manuscripts might have represented. This chapter will collate evidence from early readers of the Apocalypse of the Birds – Barnabas and the Testaments of the Twelve Patriarchs – to establish a *terminus ante quem* in the second century CE.

Moving backward from the fourteenth-century, we can begin with our next available evidence: a tenth-century Byzantine codex featuring not only an extract from the Vision of the Beasts, but also a summary of the work from which the extract was drawn that seems to include the Apocalypse of the Birds. This document, the Codex Vaticanus Graecus 1809, features an extract from 1 En 89.42–9 in the margins of excerpts from the letters of Maximus the Confessor.[1] The quoted section of the Vision of the Beasts tells the tale of David's conflict with the Ammonites, Amalekites, and Philistines. But after the quotation, an explanation is provided, identifying the animals (the foxes are Ammonites, and so on), and stating: "In this vision things are recorded in this manner from Adam until the consummation (Ἐν ταύτῃ τῇ ὁράσει ἀναγέγραπται τοιούτῳ τρόπῳ ἀπὸ τοῦ Ἀδὰμ μέχρι τῆς συντελείας)." The Vision of the Beasts, as it

---

[1] The most recent treatment of the text can be found in Drawnel, *Qumran Cave 4*, 40–1; Assefa, "5.5.1: Enoch."

has come down to us, does not include any reference to the eschaton, nor do we have strong reason to restore one in our imagination of its now-lost ending. The Apocalypse of the Birds does, on the other hand, include an eschatological account. It is possible that this explanatory gloss thereby demonstrates knowledge of a text in which the Vision of the Beasts and Apocalypse of the Birds have been redacted together, stretching from Adam (as is uniquely covered by the Vision of the Beasts) to the eschaton (as is uniquely covered by the Apocalypse of the Birds). It is a suggestive reference, though ultimately too tiny to burden with responsibility for establishing the shape of the Animal Apocalypse.

Moving backwards in time still, scholars of Ethiopic literature generally hold that the Gəʿəz text of *Henok* can be traced to a translation made from Greek to Gəʿəz between the fourth and sixth centuries CE, a judgment made on analogy with the translation of other Ethiopic biblical materials.[2] If this is the case, this window – fourth to sixth century CE – would represent a rough *terminus ante quem* for not only the emergence of the Apocalypse of the Birds, but also its circulation together with the Vision of the Beasts, as a textual entity comprising 1 En 85–90 (the Animal Apocalypse, as named by modern scholars). I find this commonly accepted proposition to be reasonable, on the basis of arguments from analogy with other Ethiopic biblical works to Enoch.

This chapter will provide sounder ground on which to establish an even earlier *terminus ante quem*, or latest possible date at which we imagine the Apocalypse of the Birds to have taken shape, in the second century CE. I will present quotations or allusions indicating that a version of the Apocalypse of the Birds left an impression on several second-century readers: the Epistle of Barnabas and the Testaments of the Twelve Patriarchs. The Epistle of Barnabas has been identified as a possible reader of the Animal Apocalypse before, but I propose to sharpen this hypothesis and show that it seems to know material specific to the Apocalypse of the Birds. The Testaments of the Twelve Patriarchs has received some minimal attention for its possible knowledge of the Animal Apocalypse, but I will provide a more robust portrait of this work's use of the Apocalypse of the Birds. Given that there is no documentary evidence for the Apocalypse of the Birds outside of medieval Ethiopia, these indications of an early readership are, in fact, our earliest evidence of the existence of the work at all.[3] I conclude

---

[2] See Chapter 1 for references.

[3] For quotations in medieval Ethiopic literature, see the discussions in Knibb of *Mashafa Milad* and the *Acts of Ezra* from Gunda Gunde. In Michael A. Knibb, "The Text-Critical Value of the Quotations from 1 Enoch in Ethiopic Writings," in *Interpreting Translation: Studies on the LXX and Ezechiel in Honour of Johan Lust, Louvain*, ed. Florentino García Martínez and M. Vervenne, BETL 192 (Leuven: Leuven University Press; Peeters, 2005), 225–35. On quotations from the Book of the Mysteries of Heaven and Earth, see Loren T. Stuckenbruck, "The Book of Enoch: Its Reception in Second Temple Jewish and in Christian Tradition," *Early Christianity* 4 (2013): 7–40, esp. 34n121–2.

that the evidence of Barnabas and the Testaments of the Twelve Patriarchs establishes a second century *terminus ante quem* for the Apocalypse of the Birds. I will also demonstrate that readers from the earliest contexts of reception and interpretation extant to us read the Apocalypse of the Birds as a narration of the events of the first century CE, including the birth and life of Jesus, the Jewish Revolt, and the fall of Jerusalem.

Barnabas, Enoch and the destruction of the Second Temple

We begin with the Epistle of Barnabas. Barnabas first appears in our documentary record in the fourth-century Codex Sinaiticus. It may have been written in Alexandria – at least, the work received a favorable reception in Alexandria – though suggested provenances have ranged across the ancient Mediterranean.[4] A second-century citation by Clement of Alexandria provides an external *terminus ante quem* for the work. Scholars have pursued a more specific dating on internal grounds, with a particular consensus that the work post-dates 70 CE since it refers to the destruction of the Second Temple.[5] It is

---

[4] See the summary of scholarship in James Carleton Paget, *The Epistle of Barnabas: Outlook and Background* (Tübingen: Mohr-Siebeck, 1994), 30–42. Clare K. Rothschild, currently preparing the Hermeneia commentary on Barnabas, takes the theory of Alexandrian provenance to be "current consensus," in Clare K. Rothschild, "Ethiopianising the Devil: Ὁ Μέλας in Barnabas 4," *New Testament Studies* 65, no. 2 (April 2019): 225n10.

[5] Barnabas reflects upon the meaning of the destruction of the Second Temple (at 16.3–4, as will be discussed below), meaning it post-dates 70 CE. It might also be possible to establish an internal *terminus ante quem* of 132 CE, if one is convinced that the work demonstrates a lack of knowledge of the events of the Bar Kokhba Revolt (as in Leslie W. Barnard, "The 'Epistle of Barnabas' and Its Contemporary Setting," *ANRW* II.27.1 (1993): 159–207; Paget, *Epistle of Barnabas*), though other scholars are convinced the work instead demonstrates knowledge of the building of Hadrian's temple to Jupiter atop the Temple Mount (as in Reidar Hvalvik, "The Struggle for Scripture and Covenant: The Purpose of the Epistle of Barnabas and Jewish-Christian Competition in the Second Century" (PhD diss., Det teologiske menighetsfakultet, 1994), 26–7). I find attempts to establish a dating limit with reference to the Bar Kokhba Revolt to engage in undue speculation on how Barnabas ought to have felt about Judaism and the events of the revolt, and to be generally unpersuasive.

There have also been many attempts to precisely exegete key verses in Barnabas (16.3–4, and 4.3–6, as will be discussed below) to establish a date in particular windows – the reigns of Vespasian, Nerva, and Hadrian, are popular suggestions. But I agree with skeptical appraisals, as found in Prigent and Kraft, which note that Barnabas' obvious reliance upon sources (Danielic and Enochic) in these passages makes it very difficult to suggest that these passages directly reflect what has and has not happened in recent history, outside of the destruction of the Temple. See Pierre Prigent, "Introduction," in *Épître de Barnabé* (Paris: Éditions du Cerf, 1971), 26–7; Robert A. Kraft, *Barnabas and the Didache*. Vol 3 of *The Apostolic Fathers: A New Translation and Commentary* (New York: Nelson, 1965), 42–4.

infamous for its abrasive and detailed critique of Judaism.⁶ With this rhetorical fury in mind, it is curious that Barnabas seems to provide us with one of the only previously noted references to the Animal Apocalypse in antiquity.

Barnabas is easily situated as a reader of a work attributed to Enoch, as it introduces a prophecy "about which it has been written, just as Enoch says," in Barn 4.3. The prophecy in question in Barn 4 does not appear to reflect any of our extant texts.⁷ More germane to our current inquiry, Barn 16.5 has been long-recognized as a reference to some part of the work known as the Animal Apocalypse:

---

⁶ "The anti-Judaic content of Barnabas is not its most disturbing feature ... what disturbs the reader most is the virulence with which these themes are presented." In Martin B. Shukster and Peter Richardson, "Temple and Bet Ha-Midrash in the Epistle of Barnabas," in *Anti-Judaism in Early Christianity. Volume 2. Separation and Polemic*, ed. Stephen G. Wilson, Peter Richardson, and David M. Granskou (Waterloo: Wilfred Laurier University Press, 1986), 17.

⁷ The Enochic reference at Barn 4:3 is: "The final stumbling block is at hand, about which it has been written, just as Enoch says. For this reason the Master shortened the seasons and the days, that his beloved may hurry and arrive at his inheritance."

There is some question as to whether the intended Enochic citation is 4.3a ("the final stumbling block") or 4.3b ("the Master shortened the seasons and the days"). Pierre Prigent & Robert Kraft opt for the former, where John C. Reeves opts for the latter. Ultimately, neither hypothetical intended citation looks like any extant Enochic text we now possess, which has led to creative solutions such as assuming 4.3a+b represent a brief citation with loose commentary (Priget & Kraft), or that 4.3b is a citation of a text extant to us without explicit Enochic ascription (see Reeves proposing the Oracles of Hystaspes, while assuming that the source-text extends to Barn 4.4; or Menahem Kister proposing 4Q Ps–Ezek(?), 4Q385).

Interestingly, Kirsopp Lake's edition of Barnabas understands 4.3 to be a reference to "1 Enoch 89.61–4; 90.17," which are the passages introducing the seventy shepherds and commanding that their future misdeeds be committed to writing (89.61–4), as well as the verse in which a written record of their now-completed misdeeds is shown to the Lord of the Sheep (90.17). Although Lake makes no further comment, his assumption seems to be that the intended citation is not just "the final stumbling block is at hand," but "the final stumbling block is at hand about which it has been written," and the Enochic citation is assumed to have something to do with a written record concerning the eschaton. The problem is that the cited Enochic verses are not really about written records outlining a "final stumbling block," but rather written records concerning the previous excesses of the seventy shepherds, which apparently need to be consulted by the Lord of the Sheep in order to close out this era of historical time.

So, it does not seem to me tenable to suggest that 4.3a is a reference to a particular verse within the Apocalypse of the Birds. As things currently stand, a convincing textual match between 4.3 and an extant Enochic text does not exist.

See Kirsopp Lake, *The Apostolic Fathers*, vol. 2 (London: Heinemann, 1912); Prigent, "Introduction"; Menahem Kister, "Barnabas 12:1; 4:3 AND 4Q Second Ezekiel," *Revue Biblique* 97, no. 1 (1990): 63–7; John C. Reeves, "An Enochic Citation in Barnabas 4:3 and the Oracles of Hystaspes," *Pursuing the Text: Studies in Honor of Ben Zion Wacholder on the Occasion of His Seventieth Birthday* (Sheffield: Sheffield Academic Press, 1992), 260–77.

Table 5.1 1 Enoch 89 and Barnabas 16

1 Enoch 89.56		Barnabas 16.5[a]	
		Again it was revealed how the city, the Temple, and the people of Israel were about to be handed over.	πάλιν ὡς ἔμελλεν ἡ πόλις καὶ ὁ ναὸς καὶ ὁ λαὸς 'Ισραὴλ παραδίδοσθαι, ἐφανερώθη.
wärä 'iku kämä ḫädägo läzəku betä zi 'ähomu wämaḫfädomu wäwädäyomu läk^wəlomu wəstä 'ədä 'änabəst kämä yəmśəṭəwomu wäkämä yəblə 'əwomu wəstä 'ədäwihomu läk^wəlomu 'ärawit[b]	And I saw how he left that house of theirs and their tower and gave them all into the hands of the lions, that they might tear them in pieces and devour them, into the hands of all the animals.	λέγει γὰρ ἡ γραφή καὶ ἔσται ἐπ' ἐσχάτων τῶν ἡμερῶν, καὶ παραδώσει κύριος τὰ πρόβατα τῆς νομῆς καὶ τὴν μάνδραν καὶ τὸν πύργον αὐτῶν εἰς καταφθοράν. καὶ ἐγένετο καθ' ἃ ἐλάλησεν κύριος.	For the Scripture says, "It will be in the last days that the Lord will hand over to destruction the sheep of the pasture along with their enclosure and tower." And it has happened just as the Lord said.

[a] The text and translation of Barnabas come from Bart D. Ehrman, *The Apostolic Fathers, Volume II: Epistle of Barnabas. Papias and Quadratus. Epistle to Diognetus. The Shepherd of Hermas*, Loeb Classical Library 25 (Cambridge, MA: Harvard University Press, 2003).
[b] In the Gə'əz abugida: ወርኢኩ ፡ ከመ ፡ ኃደገ ፡ ላዝኩ ፡ ቤተ ፡ ዚአሆሙ ፡ ወማኅፈደሙ ፡ ወወደዮሙ ፡ ለኩሎሙ ፡ ውስተ ፡ እደ ፡ አናብስት ፡ ከመ ፡ ይምሥጥዎሙ ፡ ወከመ ፡ ይብልዕዎሙ ፡ ውስተ ፡ አደዊሆሙ ፡ ለኩሎሙ ፡ አራዊት ።

There is clearly some relationship between Barnabas and a text he calls Scripture (ἡ γραφή), which we now call Enoch. Although there is no particular line that it matches perfectly, 1 En 89.56 is the verse generally supplied as the closest fit. The strange trio of the sheep, the enclosure, and the tower are unique to the Animal Apocalypse.

But the quotation from Barnabas also includes the peculiar coda that its prophecies take place "in the last days." Such a pronouncement is certainly inapplicable to the historical destruction of the First Temple for a writer of Barnabas' own day. Scholars have suggested that the citation is simply inexact,[8] or a pastiche of Septuagintal prophetic material.[9] Granting that the citation is periphrastic, Milik goes on to suggest that the quotation was actually meant to be of 1 En 90.26–8, which seems to narrate the purging

---

[8] Tiller, *Commentary*, 321–2. On Barnabas' own idiosyncratic quotational style, see first, Robert A. Kraft, "The Epistle of Barnabas: Its Quotations and Their Sources: A Thesis" (PhD diss., Harvard University, 1961).
[9] Olson, *A New Reading*, 246–9.

of the wicked sheep and removal of the earthly Temple in an eschatological scenario.[10]

(26) And I saw at that time how a similar abyss was opened in the middle of the earth, full of fire, and those blinded sheep were brought, and they were all judged and found guilty, and cast into the fiery abyss, and they burned: this abyss was to the right of that house. (27) And I saw those sheep burning and their bones burning. (28) And I stood up to look until he rolled up that old house,[11] and they removed all the pillars, and all the beams and ornaments of that house were rolled up with it; and they removed it and put it in a place in the south of the land.

---

[10] Milik, *Books of Enoch*, 47–8.

[11] The reading of Rylands MSS 23: ጠወሞ, or *ṭawämo*, is translated by Knibb as "he folded up," and this is the reading followed by Olson. The reading of the majority of manuscripts is ጠምዖ (*ṭam'o*), meaning "he immersed" or "submerged," though this is rarely the choice of translators (it is written in the margins of Knibb's Ryland MSS). Uhlig notes that his colleague Bairu Tafla suggests it might also mean "he caused it to disappear," though he offers no further comment on or support of this fascinating possibility. Charles' 1906 edition, followed by Tiller, Nickelsburg, and Assefa, conjectures that ጠምዖ (*ṭomawo*), either: "it was folded up" or "they folded up") was the original reading, corrupted over time. Although conjectural emendation is not an immediately attractive way to approach the text, the benefit here is that it provides a streamlined account of plural actors. These actors, continuing on from the previous section, are the archangels doing the Lord of the Sheep's bidding (cf. 90.24 "they threw them into an abyss"; 90.26 "they brought those blinded sheep.") The Lord of the Sheep will be introduced by name twice in the next verse – 90.29 – and it is perhaps not obvious that we should imagine an unnamed God at the helm of the removal of Jerusalem, instead of continuing the previous pattern of angels doing God's bidding. For these opinions, see Michael A. Knibb, *Enoch: A New Edition*, 2:215; Olson, *A New Reading*, 225; Uhlig, *Das äthiopische Henochbuch*, 702; R. H. Charles, *The Ethiopic Version of the Book of Enoch* (Oxford: Clarendon Press, 1906), 187; Tiller, *Commentary*, 374–5; Nickelsburg, *1 Enoch 1*, 403; Assefa, *L'apocalypse des animaux*, 40.

I find a more promising translation here to be "he rolled up" (or "it was rolled up," or "they rolled up" – there are other text-critics of the Gəʿəz better qualified to discern the "earliest" textual form, if indeed this is even possible to decide). The immediately helpful benefit of this translation is that it enables a connection with the famous passage in Revelation 6:14 in which "the sky was rolled up like a scroll (Gəʿəz ወሰማይኒ ተጠዉመት ከመ ከርታስ, *wäsämayəni täṭäwmät kämä kərətas*)." Dillmann's lexicon connects Revelation 6.14 and 1 En 90.28 in their use of this term, in Dillmann, *Lexicon linguae aethiopicae cum indice latino*, 1865, 1238.

At 90.29, the term ተጠብለለት (*täṭäblälät*) is rendered "[which] had been rolled up," by Tiller, *Commentary*, 373; Olson, *A New Reading*, 225; Nickelsburg, *1 Enoch 1*, 402. Knibb and Charles translate "[which] had been folded up," to preserve the parallelism with 90.28, even though the term at 90.29 is different, in Knibb, *Enoch: A New Edition*, vol. 1, Text and Apparatus, 215; Charles, *Enoch or, 1 Enoch*, 214. I agree with Knibb and Charles' streamlining approach, but think that both should be translated as a rolling up, rather than a folding up, as will be adopted here.

According to Milik, Barnabas is a reader of what I have called the Apocalypse of the Birds, sees prophecies satisfied in the failed Jewish Revolt, and destruction of Jerusalem in the first century CE. This suggestion can be substantiated, but only if we sew the excised citation back into its place within Barn 16 proper. I have bolded the purported quotation for ease in reference, and supplied the verses before and after.

> (4) Moreover he says again, "See, those who have destroyed this temple will themselves build it." This is happening. For because of their war, it was destroyed by their enemies. And now the servants of the enemies will themselves rebuild it. (5) Again it was revealed how the city, the Temple, and the people of Israel were about to be handed over. **For the Scripture says, "It will be in the last days that the Lord will hand over to destruction the sheep of the pasture along with their enclosure and tower."** And it has happened just as the Lord said.

The context of the quotation is the aftermath of the Jewish Revolt ("because of their war"), and the destruction of the Temple by the Romans in 70 CE. If we follow Milik's suggestion that this is a reference to the end-time scenario imagined by the Apocalypse of the Birds, it is interesting to note that, for Barnabas, pieces of this scenario have already been fulfilled by history: the removal of the Temple in 1 En 90.28 is interpreted as a reference to its destruction.

We might find continuing engagement with the Enochic account as Barnabas remarks upon the arrival of what Barnabas calls the "spiritual temple" (πνευματικός ναός, Barn 16.10), "gloriously built" (Barn 16.8), and "imperishable" (Barn 16.9). This "temple of God" (ναὸς θεοῦ) exists, as he (presumably God) is "making and completing it (Barn 16.6)." In the Enochic framework just presented, Milik suggests that this could easily be a reference to the very next Enochic verse, 1 En 90.29:[12]

> And I looked until the Lord of the sheep brought a new house, larger and higher than that first one, and he set it up on the site of the first one which had been rolled up; and all its pillars (were) new, and its ornaments (were) new and larger than (those of) the first one, the old one which he had removed. And the Lord of the sheep (was) in the middle of it.

Although the Enochic account speaks directly of a material temple (with pillars, ornaments, greater dimensions, etc.), it would not be difficult for an interpreter such as Barnabas to spiritualize this entity, especially in a chapter of history where most of the once-material temple had been razed to the ground.

---

[12] Milik, *Books of Enoch*, 47.

If we borrow Barnabas' interpretive lenses and think more holistically, we might place other Enochic details in historical time. Perhaps, as Milik suggested, the blinded sheep cast into the fiery pit of 90.26–7 are the many Jews killed in the Revolt (punished for their folly in investing so much in an earthly Temple, in Barnabas' unflinching portrayal). And perhaps Jesus himself is to be found somewhere in the historical progression, such as the white bull at 90.37.

Accordingly, I understand this direct reference to shift the probabilities by which we interpret the unknown citation of Enoch in Barn 4. I noted above that there is no exact textual match to be made between Barnabas' explicit citation of Enoch at Barn 4.3, and any extant Enochic text, including the Apocalypse of the Birds. To that end, the two Enoch references within Barnabas would be unrelated and disconnected from one another: one from a known source, but one from an unknown source. But these passages are connected in some way. In fact, virtually all discussions concerning the date of Barnabas reckon with precisely these two passages – Barn 4.3–6 and Barn 16.1–4 – suggesting we should not sever the connection between the two just yet, and should attend to the possibility that Barn 4 reflects the same Enochic historical source as was demonstrable behind Barn 16: the Apocalypse of the Birds.

Barn 4.3–6 focuses on the wicked leaders of the time, and the subsequent hope that "the Master's beloved" might arrive to reverse the world's fortunes. Barn 4.3 contains a reference to an Enochic prophecy unknown to modern scholars. This text is followed by apparent references to Daniel 7.24 ("ten kingdoms") and 7.8 ("I saw the fourth beast.") Most scholars agree that the Danielic references provide a schematic portrayal of recent Roman imperial history, though scholars disagree on the emperors and historical progression in question. For our purposes, we can note the Enochic framing is adduced by Barnabas to support this historical review – as if Enoch, too, spoke of the end of a sequential legacy of overseers – of ten kingdoms, or of four beasts. Among the extant Enochic corpus, the Apocalypse of the Birds provides the strongest fit for this schematic eschatological presentation. Indeed, it is directly cited by Barnabas later. So, perhaps Barnabas is loosely alluding to the Apocalypse of the Birds here, as a prophecy witnessing to the rapid, if bumpy, onset of the final days.

Attempts at greater specificity are possible, but inevitably are problematized by their speculative nature. So, it is interesting that the honorific for God in Barn 4.3 – a citation from the Enochic source – is Master (ὁ δεσπότης), which could represent a Greek version of the Animal Apocalypse's own preferred title for God: እግዚአ አባግዕ, ʾəgziʾä ʾäbagəʿ meaning Lord, or Master, of the Sheep. Or we might think of the inheritance of the beloved as a possible reference to the figure of 1 En 90.37–8 whose transformation into the white bull indicates his inheritance of the line of Jacob.

Unfortunately, Barnabas is not explicit on any of these allusions. However, the way that Barnabas interprets verses often assumed to be eschatological (1 En 90.26–9) as narrations of historical events creates the conditions for the possibility of a new way of understanding the Apocalypse of the Birds. The witness of Barnabas suggests that 90.28 could be read as a reference to the events of 70 CE, an interpretative move we will see again in the Testaments of the Twelve Patriarchs.[13]

Testaments of the Twelve Patriarchs: Greek readers of the Apocalypse of the Birds?

The Testaments of the Twelve Patriarchs represents a curious waypoint in Enochic reception history. This work repeatedly references insights derived from scriptures or books of Enoch, yet those references rarely match the text of the work we now call 1 Enoch. This mismatch can be quickly demonstrated: a recent survey of the history of scholarship by John C. Reeves and Annette Yoshiko Reed reviews ten references to Enoch or Enochic texts in the Testaments of the Twelve Patriarchs.[14] They find that none has earned a scholarly consensus with respect to the purported verse or verses in Enoch to which any of the ten allude. In fact, the Testaments of the Twelve Patriarchs are occasionally used as evidence for the existence of non-extant Enochic texts.[15]

---

[13] It is possible that the establishment of the Apocalypse of the Birds as the "source" for Barn 16 might complicate the use of this chapter as a reference and reaction to contemporary historical events – if it could glean the reference to the Destruction of the Temple from a literary source, then firsthand historical knowledge is not a necessary postulate. For my part, I find the reference to be a sufficiently accurate recitation of 70 CE to indicate it was written later, but recognize it is a matter of interpretation.

[14] These are, in alphabetical order: T. Benj 9.1, T. Dan 5.6, T. Jud 18.1, T. Levi 10.2–4, T. Levi 10.5, T. Levi 14.1, T. Levi 16.1, T. Naph 4.1, T. Sim 5.4, and T. Zeb 3.4. See the updated identifications and summaries of the literature in the footnotes to these references in John Reeves and Annette Yoshiko Reed, *Enoch from Antiquity to the Middle Ages. Vol. 1. Sources from Judaism, Christianity, and Islam.* (Kettering: Oxford University Press, 2017), 32–4; 142; 306–7. But the consensus has not advanced much past the opinion of Lawlor in 1897 that "the citations therefore must be very free, or rather very much garbled – so much so as perhaps in some cases to be unrecognizable." In Hugh J. Lawlor, "Early Citations from the Book of Enoch," *The Journal of Philology* 25, no. 50 (1897): 169.

[15] So, in the words of Michael Stone and Jonas Greenfield: "Citations from writings or books of Enoch in the Twelve Patriarchs which do not occur in extant Enochic works also attest to [a larger body of Enochic literature, not preserved at Qumran]." In Jonas C. Greenfield and Michael E. Stone, "Enochic Pentateuch and the Date of the Similitudes," *Harvard Theological Review* 70, no. 1–2 (1977): 56.

Here I explore the hypothesis that the Testaments of the Twelve Patriarchs indicate knowledge of the Apocalypse of the Birds. By restoring greater literary context around a few of the granular "references" to Enoch in the Testaments previously studied, I hope to illustrate ways that some of the quotations of Enoch in the Testaments, placed back in their respective contexts, narrate an eschatological scenario that looks very like that found in 1 En 90. These re-readings parallel my proposal for Barnabas' reading of the Apocalypse of the Birds: as a prophecy come to fulfillment in the events of the first century CE. I will explore the possibility that the Testaments might provide supporting evidence for the same *terminus ante quem* established already by our discussion of Barnabas.

This argument relies upon, and potentially reinforces, the position that the Testaments of the Twelve Patriarchs is best understood as a work that reached something like the form we now have in a tenth-century-and-onwards manuscript tradition, by about the second century CE.[16] It may have been written in

---

[16] A famous impasse in scholarship on the Testaments of the Twelve Patriarchs has to do with whether to consider it a Jewish or Christian work. The Jewish hypothesis generally correlates with a second-century BCE dating, a la R. H. Charles, and a Christian reading is generally tied to a second-century CE dating, a la Marinus de Jonge. A "Jewish" version of the Testaments of the Twelve Patriarchs, however, needs to be created by the scholar, by means of the removal of various Christian glosses and interpolations. However, every document by which we glean the text of the work we now call the Testaments of the Twelve Patriarchs contains these Christian interpolations – materially, there is no such thing as a non-Christian Testaments of the Twelve Patriarchs. The burden of proof, to use Bob Kraft's language once again, is very much on scholars arguing for a Jewish provenance for what is a manifestly Christian work. I will assume this context going forward, and submit that my own analysis of ways that it might use the books or writings of Enoch to narrate the events of the first century CE further strengthen this proposed provenance.

For Charles' influential take on the purported Jewish origins and composition of the text, see R. H. Charles, *The Testaments of the Twelve Patriarchs* (London: Adam and Charles Black, 1908), xxxviii–lxiv. For the most recent defense of the purported Jewish origins of the work specifically directed against the critiques raised by Kraft and de Jonge, see David A. DeSilva, "The Testaments of the Twelve Patriarchs as Witnesses to Pre-Christian Judaism: A Re-Assessment," *Journal for the Study of the Pseudepigrapha* 23, no. 1 (September 1, 2013): 21–68.

The work of Marinus de Jonge on the Testaments is too extensive to list here, but a recent monograph treatment is de Jonge, *Pseudepigrapha of the Old Testament*, esp. 71–181. See also the history of research culminating in a strong case for Christian provenance in Robert Kugler, *Testaments of the Twelve Patriarchs* (Sheffield: Bloomsbury Publishing, 2001), 11–39. Largely following de Jonge, but with special interests in settings sometimes called Jewish-Christian, see Joel Marcus, "The Testaments of the Twelve Patriarchs and the Didascalia Apostolorum: A Common Jewish Christian Milieu?" *The Journal of Theological Studies* 61, no. 2 (October 2010): 596–626; David Frankfurter, "Beyond 'Jewish-Christianity': Continuing Religious Sub-Cultures of the Second and Third Centuries and Their Documents," in *The Ways That Never Parted: Jews and Christians in Late Antiquity and the Early Middle Ages*, ed. Adam H. Becker and Annette Yoshiko Reed (Minneapolis: Fortress Press, 2007), 131–43; Annette Yoshiko Reed, *Jewish-Christianity and the history of Judaism: collected essays*, Texte und Studien zum antiken Judentum 171 (Tübingen: Mohr Siebeck, 2018), 92–103.

Syria, if certain parallels between the Testaments and late antique Syrian baptismal rituals indicate a geographic provenance.[17] Indeed, I take it as confirmation of my view, which situates these passages in an early Christian historical milieu, that elements of every single passage from the Testaments discussed in this section have been flagged as evidence of so-called Christian interpolation by scholars committed to a Jewish Testaments of the Twelve Patriarchs, as I will note in the footnotes throughout.[18] I suggest these passages are, in the only form which we now have them, self-evidently common-era Christian compositions, as are the Testaments of the Twelve Patriarchs generally. And if my hypotheses in this section are accepted, alongside my treatment of Barnabas, it becomes difficult to escape the determination that the Apocalypse of the Birds was a potent and lively springboard for interpretation by Christians of the events after the turn of the millennium.

Here is a summary of the ways all the selections from the Testaments[19] seem to understand their Enochic source, with the help of this brief chart:

Table 5.2 Common Elements in Passages Attributed to Enoch in the Testaments of the Twelve Patriarchs

	T. Benj 9.1–4	T. Dan 5.4–13	T. Jud 18.1–24.1	T. Levi 10; 14; 16	T. Naph 4	T. Sim 5.4–6.7
Direct Reference to Enoch	X (9.1)	X (5.6)	X (18.1)	X (10.5, 14.1, 16.1)	X (4.1)	X (5.4)
"In the last days" or similar		X (5.4)	X (18.1)	X (10.2, 14.1)	*X (8.1)*	
Population Collapse	X (9.1)		X (21.7–8)		X (4.3)	X (5.6)

---

[17] I find Joel Marcus' appeal to parallels between T. Levi 8.4–5 and a distinctively Syrian baptismal order to be compelling evidence in this regard, in Marcus, "Testaments," 597–8. But as with Barnabas, above, there is precious little firm ground on which to balance discussions of geographic provenance. Note, for instance, the Syrian conclusion of Kee, reached because "the knowledge of Palestinian place-names but the lack of accuracy as to their location may point to a neighboring land such as Syria, while almost certainly ruling out Palestine proper," in Howard Clark Kee, "Testaments of the Twelve Patriarchs," in Charlesworth, *The Old Testament Pseudepigrapha*, 1:778. It is not clear to me what level of geographic knowledge we should or should not be ascribing to any given scribe in Palestine, or elsewhere.

[18] This is most readily demonstrated with reference to the full translations and commentaries by R. H. Charles and Howard Clark Kee. See Charles, *Testaments*; Kee, "Testaments," 1:775–828.

[19] The one Testamentary account attributed to Enoch not discussed here is T. Zeb 3.4: "It is on account of this that it is inscribed in a writing of a law of Enoch that one who does not wish to raise up seed for his brother will have his sandal taken off and his face spat upon." This is profoundly dissimilar to every other Enochic reference in the Testaments of the Twelve Patriarchs (Reeves and Reed cautiously suggest it might be "a periphrastic form of LXX Deut 25.9"), and therefore does not belong in the same group as all the rest collated and summarized in the table below. See Reeves and Reed, *Enoch from Antiquity*, 142.

	T. Benj 9.1–4	T. Dan 5.4–13	T. Jud 18.1–24.1	T. Levi 10; 14; 16	T. Naph 4	T. Sim 5.4–6.7
Warfare		X (5.4)	X (22.1)			X (5.5)
Sodomy, Sexual Transgression	X (9.1)	X (5.5)		X (10.2, 14.5–6)	X (4.1)	
Opposition to Gentile "race" or "seed"			X (21.6–8)			X (6.3–4)
Destruction of Jerusalem (70 CE)	X (9.4)		X (23.3)	X (10.3, 15.1, 16.4)		
Coming of New Jerusalem	X (9.2)	X (5.12)		X (10.5)		
Inheritance of Gentiles	X (9.2)		X (22.2)		X (8.3)	X (7.2)
Coming of Jesus	X (9.2)	X (5.13)	X (24.10	X (10.2, 14.2, 16.3)	X (4.5)	X (6.5; 6.7)

In every case, Enoch is cited as the direct source for an account of the decline of Israel, reversed by the coming of Jesus Christ.[20] It is crucial to establish the character of such attributions to determine that we are not pursuing parallelism needlessly. In every Testamentary account surveyed, a writing or book of Enoch is cited as the source for the subsequent (or, in a few cases, antecedent) eschatological narrative.[21] As such, we are more justified in hoping to find a written account as a source.

No two accounts are exactly the same, but there are common components to multiple renditions.[22] So, four out of six testaments clarify that the

---

[20] For a treatment of each one of these references to writings of Enoch, see Robert A Kraft, "Enoch and Written Authorities in Testaments of the Twelve Patriarchs," in *Exploring the Scripturesque: Jewish Texts and Their Christian Contexts*, JSJSup 137 (Leiden: Brill, 2009), 165–9. Note here also Kraft's assessment of the "battle in the background of the preserved texts of the Testaments over the presence or absence of explicit references to Enoch," with the most "anti-Enoch" manuscript family being c (and its "allies," h i j). Kraft suggests it is more likely that Enochic references were removed from an earlier text, either because they failed to find parallels in extant Enoch literature or because of growing discomfort with the implied high status of Enochic writings. I agree, and therefore have presented the textual versions including, rather than those omitting, the Enochic ascription.

[21] The key words: "a book of Enoch the righteous (βίβλος Ἐνὼχ τοῦ δικαίου)" in T. Levi 10.5; "from a scripture of Enoch (ἀπὸ λόγων γραφῆς Ἐνώχ)" in T. Levi 14.1; "in a book of Enoch (ἐν βιβλίῳ Ἐνώχ)" in T. Levi 16.1; "according to the words of Enoch the righteous (ἀπὸ λόγων Ἐνὼχ τοῦ δικαίου)" in T. Benj 9.1; "in books of Enoch the righteous (βίβλοις Ἐνὼχ τοῦ δικαίου)" in T. Jud 18.1; "in a book of Enoch the righteous (βίβλῳ Ἐνὼχ τοῦ δικαίου)" in T. Dan 5.6; "in the writing of the scripture of Enoch (ἐν χαρακτῆρι γραφῆς Ἐνώχ)" in T. Sim 5.4; "in a holy scripture of Enoch (ἐν γραφῇ ἁγίᾳ Ἐνώχ)" in T. Naph 4.1.

[22] Many of these passages have already been grouped with one another in previous form-critical scholarship. T. Benj 9.1–4, T. Jud 18.1, T. Levi 10.2–5, T. Levi 14, T. Levi 16, and T. Naph 4.1 are

narrated events will happen at the end of time. For example, T. Levi 14.1: "I have learnt from the writing of Enoch that at the end (ἐπὶ τέλει) you will act impiously."[23] Four testaments predict a substantial population collapse, including the Testament of Judah, which uses animalistic language similar to that of the Animal Apocalypse to prophesy: "those who reign as kings will be like sea monsters, swallowing men like fishes . . . they will wrongfully feed ravens and cranes with the flesh of many" (T. Jud 21.7–8).[24] A different set of four out of six suggest that sodomy and other sexual transgressions will be rife in this evil time, which I will correlate to the repeated chastising of "blindness" in the Apocalypse of the Birds.[25] Three of the six account for the coming of a New Jerusalem, perhaps including a new Temple: so, in T. Levi 10.4, we read: "For the house which the Lord will choose will be called Jerusalem, as the book of Enoch the righteous contains."[26] A different set of four of the six seems to be deeply interested in the coming inclusion of and even preference for Gentiles.[27] Three imagine some sort of warfare,

all grouped by de Jonge under the heading of "S E R Passages," following a "sin, exile, return," pattern. T. Sim 5.4–6.7, T. Jud 21.1–6 and T. Dan 5.6 are grouped under L. J., or "Levi-Judah" passages. For our purposes, the distinction is not so important, as we are seeking to understand each individual passage as a potential interpretation of the stated Enochic source. Even if there is a common eschatology underlying each set of passages, this does not distance us from the necessity of accounting for why and how it is each time attributed to an Enochic work. For more, see the treatment and review of scholarship in Marinus de Jonge and H. W. Hollander, *The Testaments of the Twelve Patriarchs: A Commentary* (Leiden: Brill, 1985), 39–41, 53–61.

[23] See also T. Dan 5.6: "For I know that in the last days (ἐν ἐσχάταις ἡμέραις) you will depart from the Lord"; T. Jud 18.1: "All the evil things you will do in the last days (ἐν ἐσχάταις ἡμέραις)"; T. Levi 10.3: "All your ungodliness and transgression which you will commit at the consummation of the ages (ἐπὶ συντελείᾳ τῶν αἰώνων)"; T. Naph 8.1: "Behold, my children, I have shown to you the last times (καιροὺς ἐσχάτους), all these things will come to pass in Israel."

[24] See also T. Benj 9.1: "And you will perish, all save a few"; T. Naph 4.3: "After you have been diminished and made few, you will repent"; T. Sim 5.5: "They will be few in number, divided among Levi and Judah."

[25] See also T. Benj 9.1: "You will act impurely with impurity of Sodom"; T. Levi 14.8: "Your union will be like Sodom and Gomorrah in ungodliness"; T. Naph 4.1: "You will perform every lawless deed of those who inhabited Sodom"; T. Dan 5.7: "Acting impurely with women of the lawless ones, and in all wickedness."

[26] See also T. Benj 9.2: "The temple of God will be in your portion, and the last will be more glorious than the first"; T. Dan 5.12: "And the saints will rest in Eden and the righteous will rejoice in the new Jerusalem which will be to the glory of God forever."

[27] T. Benj 9.4: "And the veil of the temple will be rent, and the spirit of God will pass on to the Gentiles, as a fire that is poured out, and he will rise from Hades and ascend from earth unto heaven"; T. Jud 22.2: "My kingship will be brought to an end, until the salvation of Israel comes, until the appearing of the God of righteousness to give Jacob rest in peace, and all the Gentiles"; T. Naph 8.3: "For through his tribe God will appear dwelling among men on earth to save the race of Israel, and he will gather together the righteous from among the Gentiles"; T. Sim 7.2: "For the Lord will raise up from Levi someone as a high priest and from Judah someone as a king, God and man. This one will save all the Gentiles and the race of Israel."

or battle of the sword.²⁸ Two of the accounts characterize non-Jews as a race or seed, similar to the Apocalypse of the Birds's use of differentiated species as a literary device.²⁹

Finally, and most specifically, four accounts seem to read the 70 CE destruction of Jerusalem as part of Enoch's prophecy, in a manner similar to that proposed for Barnabas above.³⁰ If we wish to read all the Testaments together, we might say something like this: Enoch is explicitly cited by multiple Testaments as the source for a historical prophecy that marches through to the eschaton, tracing a disastrous decline in the actions and fortunes for the children of Israel, the fall of Jerusalem, and the subsequent coming of a messianic figure identified in the Testaments as Jesus Christ.

The examples cited above have been selected because they share certain points of agreement, but they represent a rich and heterogeneous set of eschatological accounts that would reward further individual study. That said, although the traditions summarized above are all attributed to an Enochic source, it would be pushing the bounds of probability to suggest that they all attest a singular underlying account that can be traced to another extant work, Enochic or otherwise. And so, rather than pursuing a case in the aggregate, or with reference to an essentialized version of the common elements, I will

---

[28] T. Dan 5.4: "For I know that in the last days you will depart from the Lord and be wroth with Levi and fight against Judah, but you will not prevail against them for an angel of the Lord guides them both, because Israel will stand by them"; T. Jud 22.1: "But the Lord will bring upon them divisions one against the other, and there will be continuous wars in Israel, and among men of other nations, my kingship will be brought to an end, until the salvation of Israel comes"; T. Sim 5.5: "But they will not prevail against Levi, because he will wage the war of the Lord and will conquer all your hosts."

[29] T. Jud 21.6: "Every race (γένος) of men (will be tossed) on you" (note also T. Naph 8.4–6: "If you work that which is good, my children ... the wild beasts will fear you ... But him who does not do what is good ... every wild beast will master him."); T. Sim 6.3: "Then the seed (σπέρμα) of Canaan will perish, and there will not be a remnant to Amalek, and all the Cappadocians will perish, and all the Hittites will be utterly destroyed."

[30] The most explicit is T. Jud 22.3: "For which things' sake the Lord will bring upon you famine and pestilence, death and an avenging sword, siege and dogs of enemies for tearing to pieces and revilings of friends, destruction and blighting of the eyes, slaughter of children and carrying off of wives, plundering of possessions, burning of the temple of God, laying waste of the land, enslavement of yourselves among the Gentiles, and they will castrate some of you to be eunuchs for their wives." See also T. Levi 10.3–4: "He will not bear Jerusalem because of your wickedness, but will rend the covering of the temple so as not to cover your shame. And you will be scattered as captives among the Gentiles. And you will be for a reproach and a curse and for trampling under foot." Slightly more elliptical phrasings, though clarified as references to the events of 70 CE greatly in context; T. Benj 9.4: "And the veil of the temple will be rent, and the spirit of God will pass on to the Gentiles"; T. Levi 16.4: "Because of him your holy place will be desolate, polluted to the ground, and your place will not be clean."

focus on three excerpts to demonstrate ways that some of these texts (T. Benj 9.1–5, T. Levi 10.1–5, and T. Levi 16.1–5) indicate remarkable parallels to the Apocalypse of the Birds.

Narrative parallels in the Testament of Benjamin

Of all the Testaments cited, the account in the Testament of Benjamin most closely follows the same narrative progression as is found in the Apocalypse of the Birds.[31] First, a look at the account in context:

> (9.1) But I surmise that there will be also evil-doings among you, from the words of Enoch the righteous, for you will act impurely with impurity of Sodom, and you will perish, all save a few, and you will renew wanton deeds with women, and the kingdom of the Lord will not be among you, because straightaway he will take away. (2) But the temple of God will be in your portion, and the last will be more glorious than the first; and there the twelve tribes and all the Gentiles will be gathered together, until the Most High will send forth his salvation in the visitation of an only-begotten prophet. (3) And he will enter into the first temple, and there the Lord will be outraged and set at nought and lifted upon a tree. (4) And the veil of the temple will be rent, and the spirit of God will pass on to the Gentiles, as a fire that is poured out, and he will rise from Hades and ascend from earth unto heaven. And I knew how humble he will be on earth and how glorious in heaven.[32]

In the Benjaminite telling, the words of Enoch the righteous inform us that there will be a precipitous increase in sexual transgression, with the "impurity of Sodom" as the key misstep. There will be a population collapse ("you will perish, all save a few,") and there is an elliptical reference to the kingdom of the Lord being taken away as a kind of punishment. The historical progression seems to jump around a bit – in verse 2 we learn that the last temple will exceed the first, and be the site of a future gathering of Jews and Gentiles alike. In verse 3, we skip back to the time of the "first" temple (certainly what modern scholars call the Second Temple), and we are told of Jesus' crucifixion,

---

[31] All translations of the Testaments of the Twelve Patriarchs are from de Jonge and Hollander, *Testaments* (1985). Greek text is from Marinus de Jonge and H.W. Hollander, *The Testaments of the Twelve Patriarchs: A Critical Edition of the Greek Text* (Leiden: Brill, 1978).

[32] Note that Kee calls verses 3–4 "the most explicit of all the Christian interpolations." Charles calls (at least 9.3–5) "obviously Christian." See Kee, "Testaments," 1:827; Charles, *Testaments*, lxiv.

accompanied by the ripping of the temple veil.³³ With this cataclysmic rupture, the "spirit of God will pass on to the Gentiles," and Jesus will ascend into heaven.³⁴ Verse 2 is revealed to take place after verse 3, clarifying that both the tribes and the Gentiles will await in the last temple the arrival (or return) of the "only-begotten" prophet.

This account is similar to the eschatological account given in the Apocalypse of the Birds, in both content and narrative progression. In T. Benj 9, we find a precipitous moral decline (à la 1 En 90.6–7). In T. Benj, and many of the other Testaments cited in our opening table, if this tradition is being cited, it is specifically understood as sexual sin. There is, however, no explicit mention of sexual transgression in the Apocalypse of the Birds (except for, perhaps, the reference to some kind of "mixing" at 1 En 89.75). But the Apocalypse of the Birds contains the often-invoked device of blindness, which frequently symbolizes apostasy of some sort. At 1 En 90.6–7, this blindness reaches new and "exceeding" levels, right at the start of the final historical and eschatological battles which will culminate in the arrival of the day of judgment. In the Testaments of the Twelve Patriarchs, blindness and blinding are often-invoked devices used to describe ways in which human emotions such as jealousy, lust, and anger mislead the patriarchs who experience them.³⁵ Especially relevant are Judah's complaints that wine and lust "blinded my heart" at T. Jud 11.1–3 (cf. T. Jud 13.6), or his admonition to "Beware, therefore, my children, of impurity and love of money . . . because these things draw you away from the law of God and blind the disposition of the soul." Here, blindness is an apt descriptor of the state in which sexual sinners, such as the now-repentant Judah, find themselves trapped. Given this established function of blindness within the language of the Testaments, it seems far more possible that a source which chastises the people of Israel for their perpetual blindness would be read as providing a specific condemnation of sexual sin. So, while sexual transgression is certainly not the only option for how to understand blindness available to readers of the Apocalypse of the Birds, nor is it even one that naturally emerges from the Enochic text read on its own, it is nevertheless a plausible interpretative option for communities fixated on the urgency and relevance of that particular subset of sin, such as, for instance, the community which produced the Testaments.

---

³³ In the similar account in T. Levi, this is not linked quite so explicitly to the figure of Jesus. Here in T. Benj, the reference to the ripping of the temple veil more explicitly links in with Christian traditions such as are found in the Synoptics (Mark 15.37; Matt 27.51; Luke 23.45) about the tearing of the veil at the moment of Jesus' death. On the intersection of this and the Marcan account, see Joel Marcus, *Mark 8–16: A New Translation with Introduction and Commentary* (New Haven: Yale University Press, 2009), 1067; Marcus, "Testaments," 612–13.

³⁴ See the manifold references spotted to early Christian literature in these verses recounted in de Jonge and Hollander, *Testaments* (1985), 436–7.

³⁵ For a selection of passages, see the cross-references in de Jonge and Hollander, 113.

T. Benj 9 continues by narrating the replacement of the old temple with a glorious new model (as in 1 En 90.28–9), the coming of a messianic figure (as in 1 En 90.37–8), and the subsequent inclusion of the Gentiles within the framework of eschatological salvation (as in 1 En 90.38). It is also notable that both the Testament of Benjamin and the Apocalypse of the Birds execute a temporal flashback at the same juncture, just after the removal of the Old House (Enoch) or destruction of the Temple (Benjamin), to a previous pre-Judgment time marking the advent of the Messiah.

Identifying an Enochic source might explain why the chronology in T. Benj 9 is so confusingly expressed. Just above, I noted that verse 2 seems to narrate events happening after the destruction of the Temple – at a time when the eschatological Temple holds the gathered-in-anticipation Jews and Gentiles, and the first is no more. Immediately following this, verse 3 cycles back however many years to the birth of Jesus that seems to begin this scenario, and verse 4 creates the conditions for the possibility the Gentiles to be positively involved in this eschatological arrangement. This counterintuitive arrangement could be easily explained by Benjamin's interaction with the Apocalypse of the Birds.

Indeed, Benjamin's reading lens might even help us explain a particularly peculiar part of the text preserved in Ethiopic. At 1 En 90.31 – after the removal of the old house, and replacement with the new – we are told that Enoch is taken by three angels and the *dabela* (ram) and set down among the sheep "before the judgment took place" (እንበለ ፡ ትኩን ፡ ኩነኔ, *'ənbälä təkun kwənnäne*).

This clause is met with confusion throughout the secondary literature. Some, such as Knibb, Charles, and Tiller, find it entirely insoluble.[36] Uhlig and Black consider it corrupt.[37] Olson translates so as to preclude any apparent flashback.[38] Nickelsburg, Schodde, and Assefa consider this clause to be somehow ill-at-ease in its current location, whether because it was mislocated from a more sensible place, or is the product of a later gloss.[39] It is not, however,

---

[36] So, Knibb notes "these words are confusing and appear to be out of place;" Charles calls them "most confusing;" Tiller concludes "the text is unclear and probably completely corrupt." See Knibb, *Enoch: A New Edition*, 2:215–16; Charles, *Book of Enoch Translated*, 257; Tiller, *Commentary*, 379.

[37] Uhlig hypothesizes an Aramaic original of קדם דין which would idiomatically mean "before the [throne of] judgment," that accidentally lost its idiomatic meaning in translation. Black calls it a "difficult clause" of suspicious authenticity and postulates the very different Aramaic original די בלא דינא. See Uhlig, *Das äthiopische Henochbuch*, 703; Black, *Book of Enoch*, 279.

[38] Olson uses a variant translation of *'ənbälä* to arrive at the translation "unrelated to the judgment that took place," suggesting "a flashback at this point is awkward." See Olson, *A New Reading*, 226.

[39] Nickelsburg suggests it has been transposed from its "chronologically correct location between vv 19–20" (though also notes it could be a scribal gloss having to do with Enoch and Elijah). Schodde suggests the phrase is there to belatedly explain how Enoch was able to behold the judgment at all from verse 16 onwards. Assefa offers two suggestions: first, that the verse has been mistakenly transposed, or second, that it was a later gloss added by a reader disappointed by the fact that the end of time had not yet arrived. See Nickelsburg, *1 Enoch 1*, 405; Schodde, *Book of Enoch*, 241; Assefa, *L'apocalypse des animaux*, 133–5.

unprecedented to accept the phrase as written! Dillmann makes just such a suggestion, asserting that this verse is there to clarify that the judgment (20–7) will come after verses 28–31.[40] I have not, however, found any scholarship defending the plainest reading of the text: that what *follows* (31–8) comes before the judgment scene just narrated (20–31). It requires Enoch's vision to time-travel backwards a bit, but this hardly seems impossible. It is this final reading that I have adopted.

With Benjamin's account in mind, this reading makes sense. Such a transitional phrase jumps the reader back in time to events taking place before the day of judgment. Everything from 90.30–8 chronologically takes place *before* the final judgment of 90.20–9. Positing a chronological jump at this narrative juncture not only enables the interpretation found in T. Benj 9, but, since Jesus has to have lived before the final judgment day, all the other Christological readings of the texts to which I will point throughout my analysis of the Testaments.

The parallels between T. Benj 9 and the Apocalypse of the Birds are summarized below:

Table 5.3 Testament of Benjamin 9 and the Apocalypse of the Birds

Apocalypse of the Birds	Testament of Benjamin 9
Exceeding blindness and deafness (90.6–7); Final Judgment (90.20–6)[a]	Moral Decline and Judgment (9.1)
Removal of Old House, Replacement with New (90.28–9)	Last Temple greater than the first (9.2a)
Gathering of sheep, birds, and beasts therein (90.30–6)	Gathering of Jews and Gentiles therein (9.2b)
Birth of White Bull (90.37–8)	Life and Death of Jesus (9.3)
Transformation of birds and beasts into white bulls (90.38)	Pouring out of "spirit of God" onto Gentiles (9.4)

[a] Note that the warfare in 90.9–19 is apparently absent from the Benjamin account.

With the help of Barnabas, we have established precedent for some of the apparent leaps from the Enochic text to early Christian interpretations summarized in the table above. So, we already surmised from Barnabas' account that some early Christians read 1 En 90.28 as a prophecy of the destruction of the Temple. But Benjamin's account, insofar as we judge it an interpretation of the Apocalypse of the Birds, seems to suggest (not surprisingly) that some early Christians read 1 En 90.37–8 as a prophecy of the advent and messiahship of Jesus. The precedent of T. Benj 9 will be crucial in linking this and all

[40] Dillmann *Das Buch Henoch*, 286.

EARLY CHRISTIAN READERS 123

the other Testamentary accounts attributed to Enoch with the Apocalypse of the Birds. Accordingly, I will demonstrate ways in which early messianic and Christological readings of 1 En 90.37–8 might have been executed.

(Christian?) messiahs at 1 Enoch 90.37–8

At the very end of the Apocalypse of the Birds, there is an ambiguous reference to the arrival of a controversial figure. At this point in the account, the ram has already defeated the birds (90.6–19); the fallen stars and blinded sheep have been judged and thrown into the fire (90.20–7); and the old Jerusalem has been replaced by the new (90.28–9). Sheep, birds, and beasts alike are all gathered in the New Jerusalem, worshipping the Lord of the Sheep (90.30–6). Next comes the birth of a white bull, and a subsequent transformation of all species into white bulls.

(37) ወርኢኩ ፡ ከመ ፡ ተወልደ ፡ ፩ ላህም ፡ ፀዓዳ ፡ ወአቅርንቲሁ ፡ ዓቢይት ፡ ወኩሉ ፡ ዓራዊት ፡ ገዳም ፡ ወኩሉ ፡ አዕዋፈ ፡ ሰማይ ፡ ይፈርሀዎ ፡ ወያስተበኍዕዎ ፡ በኩሉ ፡ ጊዜ ፡
(38) ወርኢኩ ፡ እስከ ፡ ተወለጠ ፡ ኩሉ ፡ አዝማዲሆሙ ፡ ወኮኑ ፡ ኩሎሙ ፡ አልህምተ ፡ ፀዓድወ ፡ ወቀዳማዊ ፡ ኮነ ፡ በማእከሎሙ ፡ ነገረ ፡ ወውእቱ ፡ ነገር ፡ ኮነ ፡ አርዌ ፡ ዓቢየ ፡ ወቦ ፡ ውስተ ፡ ርእሱ ፡ አቅርንት ፡ ዓቢያት ፡ ወጸሊማት ፡ ወእግዚአ ፡ አባግዕ ፡ ተፈሥሐ ፡ ዲቤሆሙ ፡ ወዲበ ፡ ኩሎሙ ፡ አልህምት ።

(37) *wärəʾiku kämä täwäldä 1 lahm ṣäʿada wäʾäqrəntihu ʿabäyt wäk^wəllu ʾärawitä gädam wäk^wəllu ʾäʿwafä sämay yəfärəhəwo wäyastäbäq^wəʾəwo bäk^wəllu gize (38) wärəʾiku ʾəskä täwälläṭä k^wəllu ʾäzmadihomu wäkonu k^wəllomu ʾälhəmätä ṣäʿadəwä wäqädamawi konä bämäʾkälomu nägärä wäwəʾətu nägär konä ʾärwe ʿäbiyä wäbo wəstä räʾəsu ʾäqrənt ʾäbiyat wäṣälimat wäʾəgziʾä ʾäbagəʿ täfäśśəhä dibehomu wädibä k^wəllomu ʾälhəmt.*

(37) And I saw that one white bull was born, and his horns were large, and all the beasts of the wild and all the birds of the heavens feared him, and made petition to him constantly. (38) And I saw until all their kinds changed, and they all became white bulls: and the first among them was the "nägär" (lit: thing, word), and that "nägär" became a great animal, and had great black horns on its head, and the Lord of the Sheep rejoiced over them and over all the bulls.

This is a tricky passage. Sheep are the protagonists throughout most of the Animal Apocalypse, from Jacob onwards. But before Jacob (the last of the bulls, who became the first of the sheep), humans were symbolized by white bulls. The return of the white bull thereby represents the return of a species that has not roamed the earth since the day of the patriarchs. Its appearance triggers the transformation of either a) all the birds and beasts mentioned explicitly in 90.37, or b) all the birds and beasts, as well as the sheep mentioned in 90.33–4 and thus implicitly involved.[41] Ultimately, "all their kinds" (*kʷəllu 'äzmadihomu*) are transformed, and the distinctions of species of birds, beasts, (and perhaps sheep) disappear, as all become white bulls. The first among this revived patriarchal race is the *nägär*, a term I've left untranslated for now, who becomes a great-horned animal, and causes the Lord of the Sheep to rejoice.

For some scholars, such as August Dillmann and R. H. Charles, this is an obvious messianic passage.[42] For others, such as John J. Collins and Matthew Novenson, it hardly qualifies.[43] After all, it never uses the term Messiah, or any other particularly salvific terminology.[44] All we know is that this creature represents a return to the patriarchal generations of old, he is horned like some Davidic kings in the Animal Apocalypse, and he is feared by the birds and beasts alike. The dis-synchronicities between this portrait of an eschatological figure and what scholars generally assume about early Jewish messianism has led at least a few scholars to postulate that these verses must be a later gloss.[45]

---

[41] This latter understanding is defended in the recent commentaries of Tiller, Nickelsburg, and Olson. See Tiller, *Commentary*, 385; Nickelsburg, *1 Enoch 1*, 403; Olson, *A New Reading*, 19–21. The former is adopted in Terence L. Donaldson, *Judaism and the Gentiles: Jewish Patterns of Universalism (to 135 CE)* (Waco, TX: Baylor University Press, 2007), 111–17; Matthew Thiessen, "Paul, the Animal Apocalypse, and Abraham's Gentile Seed," in *The Ways That Often Parted: Essays in Honor of Joel Marcus*, ed. Lori Baron, Jill Hicks-Keeton, and Matthew Thiessen (Atlanta: SBL Press, 2018), 70–1.

[42] So, see Dillmann, *Das Buch Henoch*, 286; Charles, *Enoch or, 1 Enoch*, 215–16; Jonathan Goldstein, "How the Authors of 1 and 2 Maccabees Treated the 'Messianic' Promises," *Judaisms and Their Messiahs at the Turn of the Christian Era*, 1987, 72; E. Isaac, "1 Enoch," 1:6.

[43] Note the critical treatment in two large-scale studies of Jewish messianism: John J. Collins, *The Scepter and the Star: Messianism in Light of the Dead Sea Scrolls*, 2nd ed. (Grand Rapids, MI: Eerdmans, 2010), 41; Matthew V. Novenson, *The Grammar of Messianism: An Ancient Jewish Political Idiom and Its Users* (New York: Oxford University Press, 2019), 28–9.

[44] Part of the problem is that scholars have different understandings of what threshold would need to be crossed in order for the text to be classified as "messianic." There are ample studies concerning the nature of the white bull within the secondary literature which show some functional or practical similarities to the role and status of a messianic figure, but which are nevertheless reticent to use the word messianic or title Messiah. So, we might look to the classification of the white bull as an eschatological second-Adam or new Adam, proposed by Pedersen, and echoed in Milik, Tiller, and Nickelsburg. Or we could look to Olson's characterization of the white bull as an "exalted, idealized, true-Jacob." See Johannes Pedersen, "Zur erklärung," 216; Milik, *Books of Enoch*, 45; Tiller, *Commentary*, 384–5; Nickelsburg, *1 Enoch 1*, 406–7; Olson, *A New Reading*, 26–31.

[45] The strangeness of these final two verses, 37 and 38, has led some German scholarship to postulate that these verses, and these alone, are later interpolations – though by "later," they mean "later Second Temple." See Reese, *Die Geschichte Israels*, 54–5; Müller, *Studien*, 164–6; Bedenbender, *Der Gott*, 208–11.

Most interpretations of this passage, however, have been hamstrung by the lexeme attached to one of these creatures: "*nägär,*" literally meaning "word" or "thing."[46] For scholars committed to a second century BCE provenance for the Apocalypse of the Birds, or even just expecting an animal here in the so-named Animal Apocalypse, this term needs to be explained away, and there

---

[46] Assefa, and Knibb to a certain extent (Knibb opines in a brief footnote "it is not clear" whether these two creatures are to be identified), object that *nägär* is not to be attached to the white bull of verse 37, and that there are two creatures in view here. Assefa's suggestion is born out of the *Andəmta* commentary tradition of Ethiopia, which may seem to grant the reading a strong priority from a material philological perspective, as this tradition grew up alongside the manuscripts and text of the Animal Apocalypse and is a direct response to the Gəʽəz text in question. I do not accept this reading and explain why below.

Assefa is interested in the possibility that the white bull of 37, and *nägär* of 38, are different creatures. In particular, he proposes that the *nägär* of 38 might be the Antichrist, as is the interpretation in the *Andəmta* tradition. He notes what I discuss below, that *nägär* is little-used in Gəʽəz to refer to Christ. Other objections he raises are that the term *ʼärwe* is negatively used in the Animal Apocalypse to refer to wild beasts, and that the beast's black horns represent a similarly negative character trait, which would be different to reconcile with the positive white bull of 37.

There are a few problems here. First, I do not think that black horns are necessarily a signal of a negative entity all on their own (Dillmann, for instance, suggests these are simply the natural color of the imagined animal's horns). Second, although I recognize that *ʼärwe* is often used on its own to refer to non-Israelite antagonists throughout the Apocalypse of the Birds (89.58, 90.18, 90.19b), it is just as often accompanied by the qualifier "wild" (e.g. *ʼärawitä gädam* at 89.57, 90.19a, 90.33). Indeed, at 90.37, the white bull is feared by the "beasts of the wild," or "*ʼärawitä gädam.*" In the verse in question, 90.38, we have *ʼärwe* without *gädam*. This leaves space for the possibility that *ʼärwe* might mean, as it does elsewhere in Gəʽəz translations of scriptures, something more generally like "animal" rather than exclusively referring to evil creatures or predators (e.g. Dillmann's lexicon lists Dan 5.21, Job 37.7, Sir 17.4). Third, and finally, *nägär* may not be a Christological term in Gəʽəz, but if it represents a translation of *logos*, as Assefa suggests, we need to think about a Christological possibility at some point in the textual history of the Apocalypse of the Birds. And so, although Assefa brilliantly accounts for tension with a Christological interpretation made by specific lexical choices evidenced in the Gəʽəz, it is possible that this tension might not have been reflected in a Greek version from which it was translated. But the biggest problem with the two-creature hypothesis is 90.38c: "And the lord of the sheep rejoiced over them and over all the bulls." This qualifier implies that whatever was just described is a good thing. Assefa suggests, in line with the *Andəmta*, that this divine rejoicing over an evil creature is actually a rejoicing over this creature's destruction, but this suggestion relies on assuming an implied connection with a different set of events and ultimately goes very far beyond the text narrated here.

Assefa's work is critically important because it demonstrates one local and historical direction in which the Gəʽəz 90.37–8 might have been pulled, and the commitments of some of the scribes through whom the text was transmitted. I would hazard to guess that at least some of the many difficult readings that puzzle scholars in these verses have to do with the text's historical entanglement with changing and diverse envisionments of great figures present at the eschaton.

For the works cited, see Daniel Assefa, "The Enigmatic End of the Animal Apocalypse in Light of Traditional Ethiopian Commentary," in *Proceedings of the XVth International Conference of Ethiopian Studies Hamburg 2003*, ed. Siegbert Uhlig, vol. 1 (Wiesbaden: Harrassowitz Verlag, 2012), 552–60; Knibb, *Enoch: A New Edition*, 2:216; Dillmann, *Das Buch Henoch*, 288.

are multiple competing explanations as to how a more "normal" term like "lamb" or "ram" was corrupted to the reading we universally possess today.⁴⁷

Daniel Olson's recent commentary provides an excellent summary of interpretations, organized below:

Table 5.4 "Corruptions" of 1 Enoch 90.37–8

Aramaic	Error	Scholars
ראמא ("wild ox")	ρημα (transliteration)	Dillmann, Charles (1893), Milik, Knibb, Uhlig, Black …
טלא ("lamb")	Misread as מלה ("word")	Goldschmidt, Charles (1912)
אִמַּר ("lamb")	Misread as אֲמַר ("word")	Charles, Lindars, Olson
ראימא ("wild ox")	Misread as מאמרא ("word")	Torrey
דבר ("leader")	Read as if it were Hebrew דבר ("word")	Nickelsburg, Tiller
מלה ("word")	No corruption—*nāgār* of 38 different from bull of 37	Assefa

All of these solutions rely upon a hypothetical Aramaic phase of transmission for these verses, for which I have noted we have no material evidence. It is possible that these verses represent a later development. Indeed, it is worth considering that this passage found only in Christian transmission appears quite consonant with language and theologies developing in Jesus-following contexts. So, for instance, one early scholar, Ferdinand Philippi, who was committed to a Christian provenance for the Animal Apocalypse, and 1 Enoch more generally, found these two verses to represent such an obvious referent to the advent of Christ as Johannine-styled "Word" that it cemented his suspicions of the Christian authorship of the whole book.⁴⁸ We may come to suspect that there is a very heavy burden of proof on those who might postulate retrieving a "Jewish" version from beneath it.⁴⁹

---

⁴⁷ So, Nickelsburg's characterization that "it is universally agreed that 'word' reflects a textual corruption," in Nickelsburg, *1 Enoch 1*, 403. On the many solutions as to how this textual corruption came about, see the recent summary in Olson, *A New Reading*, 22–5.
⁴⁸ This is not to say that a Christianizing opinion should be adopted without reflection. So, Ferdinand Philippi observes that the Messiah is called the "word," but then goes on to suggest that this metaphysical designation of the Messiah would be anathema to Judaism, and is therefore proof of Christian authorship. In the century and a half since this work was composed, scholarship on logos theologies in Philo and the Judaism of the New Testament, just to name two, has made this an untenable assumption. That said, it is still a valuable piece of information to realize just how easily and without friction these verses could be incorporated into a Christian reading. See Ferdinand Philippi, *Das Buch Henoch*, 69.
⁴⁹ I am borrowing the language of burden of proof from the work of Robert Kraft, especially in his discussion in Kraft, "Pseudepigrapha and Christianity."

Here is the passage, with *nägär* simply translated as "word:"

> And I saw that a white bull was born, and his horns were large, and all the beasts of the wild and all the birds of the heavens feared him, and made petition to him constantly. And I saw until all their kinds changed, and they all became white bulls. And the first among them was the word, and the word became a great animal, and had great black horns on its head, and the Lord of the Sheep rejoiced over them and over all the bulls.

The word was the first of the white bulls, he who was born with large horns. Horns throughout the Vision of the Beasts and Apocalypse of the Birds seem to indicate some sort of kingship or right to rule. They are given only to Saul, David, Solomon, and the lamb/ram protagonists of 90.9–19.[50] He is worshiped and feared by all the foreign nations (birds and beasts, non-Israelites), who then transform to become like him. The clarification that the Word "became a great animal (*konä 'ärwe 'äbiyä*)" is a simple but crucial rhetorical move within the progression of the Apocalypse of the Birds.[51] The Word is therefore not an angel or a heavenly being (always signified by men in the Enochic work), but instead became a human, which in the symbolic logic of the text means it became an *animal*.[52] In the Gospel of John, the Word became Flesh (cf. Gəʿəz John 1.14: ወውእቱ ቃል ሥጋ ኮነ, *wäwə'ətu qal śəga konä*)[53]; in the Apocalypse of the Birds, the Word became Animal (ወውእቱ ነገር ኮነ አርዌ *wäwə'ətu nägär konä 'ärwe*).[54]

The resonances with Christian accounts of Jesus are clear. Notably, this equation seems to be resisted within Ethiopic reading contexts. So, the lexeme used to refer to Jesus as the "Word" is usually *qal*, not *nägär* (see, for instance, the many uses of the former in the Gəʿəz Gospel of John). Additionally, the *Andəmta* commentary tradition seems to understand not Jesus, but another creature to be present in 90.38: Jesus is the white bull of 90.37, where the *nägär* of 90.38 represents the anti-Christ.[55] It is possible that these two incongruities

---

[50] E.g. 90.9: "And I looked until horns came up on those lambs, but the ravens cast their horns down; and I looked until a big horn grew on one of those sheep, and their eyes were opened."

[51] Note that Gəʿəz does not have a definite article, so an implied difference between word and Word (if there is such a difference operative in this passage) must be supplied from context.

[52] What the *nägär* was before it became an animal is unclear. If this is, in fact, a Christological reference, I take comfort in my confusion in the fact that the nature of Jesus' preexistence has been debated for much of Christian history.

[53] I take the Ethiopic text of John from Michael G. Wechsler, ed., *Evangelium Iohannis Aethiopicum*, Corpus scriptorum Christianorum Orientalium 617 (Leuven: Peeters, 2005).

[54] I am anticipated in the recognition of Johannine language here in a brief note on this verse by André Caquot, "1 Hénoch," in *La Bible. Écrits Intertestamentaires.*, ed. André Dupont-Sommer and Marc Philonenko (Paris, 1987), 464–525.

[55] See Assefa, "Enigmatic End."

might help to explain one another. So, an Ethiopic interpretative commitment to the idea that Christ was not to be found in 90.38 may have influenced the use of a non-Christologically loaded synonym (*nägär*, rather than *qal*), or vice versa. In light of this history of translation, Ethiopian translators of Enoch such as Ephraim Isaac and Daniel Assefa have opted to translate *nägär* more abstractly, as "something."[56] And, as Daniel Assefa puts it, "If it were an intentional Christian interpolation the author would have undoubtedly used the term *qal*."[57] Assefa is entirely correct, but we should nuance his claim – *qal* would be used if it were an intentional Christian interpolation *in Gəʿəz*. I think the powerful Christian consonance of *nägär* as "word" signals the need to look more closely, not only at the Gəʿəz, but the Greek from whence it likely came.

Let us consider whether a Greek stage of composition and/or transmission might illuminate some of our problems here. I find a Greek stage of transmission likely, and perhaps even proven, by the substantial knowledge that the Greek Barnabas and the Greek Testaments of the Twelve Patriarchs have of the work. It has been suggested by Barnabas Lindars that the Gəʿəz *nägär* is a mistranslation of the Greek *logos*, which itself is a Christologically fueled translation of the Aramaic term for lamb אמר.[58] As noted above, I find recourse to Aramaic to be speculative, given that we have no positive evidence for the circulation of this section of the Animal Apocalypse in Aramaic. Without this part of the chain, we are brought to the conclusion that *nägär* translates *logos*.

Once we imagine *logos* in the text of 1 En 90.38 being read by the minds behind the Testaments of the Twelve Patriarchs, all of a sudden, the conviction of second-century readers that the book of Enoch provides a prophecy of the advent of Jesus Christ becomes intelligible. Such readings, when arriving at the end of a work that they already understood to narrate the moral decline of the children of Israel, and destruction of Jerusalem, would find a closing prophecy of the advent of the Word, who would become human (or animal, in the symbolism of the Enochic text), and transform Gentiles and Jews alike into a renewed kind of humanity. The evidence of our earliest readers provides us with guidance on the kind of text they accessed, and the kind of interpretations that were possible in a stage of transmission for which we no longer have documentary evidence.

I am not arguing here that the composition of 1 En 90.37–8 is necessarily to be traced to Jesus-following contexts. I do not believe that there is enough

---

[56] In Isaac, "1 Enoch," 71; Assefa, "Enigmatic End," 560.
[57] Assefa, "," 555.
[58] See the claim of Lindars that the Ethiopic translators produced "a meaningless text prov[ing] only that they did not understand the intention of the Greek." I have thus characterized his claim as being that the Gəʿəz transmission represents mistranslation, where the more accurate assessment would be that it is simply a translation. See Barnabas Lindars, "A Bull, Lamb and a Word: I Enoch XC. 38," *New Testament Studies* 22, no. 04 (1976): 486.

evidence in these brief snippets to indicate one way or the other. I *am* arguing, however, that the instinct to emend them so that they are less consonant with a demonstrable Christian usage is fundamentally flawed. 1 En 90.37–8 culminated in an account of the arrival of a man who was likely called *logos* in Greek. Jesus followers, such as the writers of the Testaments of the Twelve Patriarchs, might easily have seen Jesus in these verses. I do not find consonance with Christian ideas to be a problem that justifies conjectural emendation of the sort as has been typically pursued (especially with reference to a hypothetical Aramaic version, of which I am generally suspicious). But, in this instance, I also do not find consonance with Christian ideas to necessitate talking about "Christian composition" so long as we are looking to the first and second centuries CE, when the boundary between Jew and Jesus follower was porous and uncertain. And Jesus followers were certainly not the only people in antiquity interested in the role and function of an entity named in Greek *logos* – one might look to Philo of Alexandria, or Plotinus.

Our work with this ambiguous figure brings out some of the nuances of Kraft's Christian-until-proven-Jewish heuristic for the reading of the pseudepigrapha.[59] Works, such as this one, which appear to belong to centuries in which Jew and Christian were not so readily differentiable or identifiable cannot be Christian-until-proven-Jewish, for the framing imposes a false and anachronistic binary. Our primary challenge is to account for the text as is, without effacing or emending details that seem, at first, to defy our categories – such as a celebration of a logos-turned-man (1 En 90.37–8) in a work that has been treated as Jewish.

Regardless of the origins of the text (which I think might be beyond our ken), we can readily conclude that 1 En 90.37–8 could be easily read as a prophecy of the advent of the Messiah and applied to the life and career of Jesus. With the messianic, and even Christian messianic, interpretative possibilities of 1 En 90.37–8 established, we can return to the Testamentary accounts which capitalize upon them.

Prophecies of Jerusalem, and a heptadic schema: references in the Testament of Levi

The Testament of Levi comes closest to direct references to the Apocalypse of the Birds (T. Levi 10.5 and 16.1) as exist in the Testaments. Indeed, the first of the texts discussed below has been flagged by previous scholarship as a likely reference to the Animal Apocalypse.[60] What looked like abstract narrative parallelism in the Testament of Benjamin, might be promoted to a more concrete

---

[59] See especially his discussion in Kraft, "Pseudepigrapha and Christianity."
[60] From the very earliest scholarship, Dillmann connected 1 En 89.50 to T Levi 10.5, in Dillmann, *Das Buch Henoch*, 263.

reference when we incorporate the evidence of these two parallel attestations of an attributedly Enochic eschatological account in the Testament of Levi.

We can begin with the first reference, at T. Levi 10:[61]

> (10.1) Now, therefore, observe the commands which I give to you children because whatever things I have heard from my fathers I have declared to you. (2) I am clear from all your ungodliness and transgression which you will commit at the consummation of the ages (ἐπὶ συντελείᾳ τῶν αἰώνων) against the Saviour of the world,[62] acting impiously, leading Israel astray, and stirring against it great evils from the Lord, (3) and you will act lawlessly together with Israel, so that he will not bear Jerusalem because of your wickedness, but will rend the covering of the temple so as not to cover your shame. (4) And you will be scattered as captives among the Gentiles. And you will be for a reproach and a curse and for a trampling under foot. (5) For the house which the Lord will choose will be called Jerusalem, as the book of Enoch the righteous contains.

This passage prophesies that Israel's transgressions will prompt the Lord's abandonment of Jerusalem, and the rending of the temple veil. The same progression (transgression, anger of the Lord, culminating in the rending of the temple veil) is provided by T. Benj 9.1. There, the entire section is introduced under the auspices of the words of Enoch the righteous (λόγων Ἐνὼχ τοῦ δικαίου), and it is clear from Benjamin's many references to the life and death of Jesus that it narrates the events of the first century CE. So, concerning T. Levi, the qualifier "at the consummation of the ages," and juxtaposition alongside sins committed against the "Saviour of the world," on analogy with the similar account in T. Benj 9.1, clarifies that the passage in T. Levi refers to the events around the destruction of Jerusalem in 70 CE.

Finally, we notice that unlike the Testament of Benjamin, the account in T. Levi 10 ends with what looks like a direct reference to an extant Enochic text. In previous scholarship, the final verse (T. Levi 10.5: "for the house which the Lord will choose will be called Jerusalem, as the book of Enoch the righteous contains") has been understood as a reference to 1 En 89.50.[63] Alongside

---

[61] The book of Enoch the righteous (βίβλος Ἐνὼχ τοῦ δικαίου) is cited at the end of this passage, but on analogy with other citations of Enoch within the Testaments as the source of information on the events of the eschaton (see the chart above), it seems reasonable to include the entire passage selected above within the framework of prophecies derived from a conversation with Enoch.

[62] Here, Kee muses that "much of this chapter appears to have been modified by a Christian hand." See Kee, "Testaments," 792n10a. Charles, in a more limited manner, suggests that verse 2 is the primary site of interpolation, in Charles, *Testaments*, lxii; 48–9.

[63] As in Dillmann, *Das Buch Henoch*, 263; Lawlor, "Early Citations," 170; Charles, *Enoch or, 1 Enoch*, lxxvi; Black, *Book of Enoch*, 269; Reeves and Reed, *Enoch from Antiquity*, 32. See also the discussion in de Jonge and Hollander, *Testaments* (1985), 160–1.

an explicit sourcing to Enoch, this parallel is quite strong, especially given the Animal Apocalypse's use of "house" to symbolize Jerusalem, 1 En 89.50 is a verse introducing the Second Temple from the text comprising the work we called the Vision of the Beasts.[64] Just as with our reading of Barnabas, however, context dictates that we should switch the proposed Animal Apocalypse reference from the Vision of the Beasts to the Apocalypse of the Birds. Set alongside the parallel accounts in other testaments, T. Levi 10 cannot be referring to the building of the Second Temple, since it has no place in a narrative on the "consummation of the ages." Rather, it must refer to the new "house," or New Jerusalem, of 1 En 90.29. This Jerusalem presumably has yet to appear, but the text understands Enoch to mean that it will do so one day. The best extant match for the content of this "book of Enoch the righteous" that provides such a tradition about the future house of Jerusalem seems to be the Apocalypse of the Birds.

There is another place in T. Levi where we might spot a reference to the Apocalypse of the Birds:

(16.1) And now I have learnt in the book of Enoch that for seventy weeks you will go astray and profane the priesthood and pollute the sacrifices, (2) and you will make void the law and set at naught the words of the prophets, in perverseness persecute righteous men and hate godly men, loathe the words of faithful men, (3) and a man who renews the law in the power of the Most High you will call a deceiver, and, at last, you will kill him, as you suppose, not knowing that he would be raised up, taking innocent blood, in wickedness, on your heads. (4) Because of him your holy place will be desolate, polluted to the ground, (5) and your place will not be clean, but among the Gentiles you will be for a curse and for dispersion, until he will again visit and in pity receive you through faith and water.

T. Levi 16.1 tells the reader that the Book of Enoch prophesies the decline of either the priesthood, or Israel more generally, over a period of seventy weeks.[65] Although a heptadic schema is not unique to Enoch, the only place to our knowledge that such a reckoning is pursued within extant Enochic literature is the Apocalypse of the Birds.

[64] Note that in nineteenth- and early twentieth-century scholarship, a parallel to the description of the house-as-Second Temple was especially necessitated by understanding both the Testaments of the Twelve Patriarchs and the Animal Apocalypse as pre-Christian works.

[65] Speaking in favor of the former is the specific charge that the narrative audience, imagined to be the children of Levi, will commit the priestly infractions of profaning their office, and polluting the sacrifice. Speaking in favor of the latter is the prophecy of a decline of fortunes among the Gentiles, which would be shared by all Jews in the aftermath of the events of the first century CE. It is also likely that we need not choose just one option. The addressees imagined within the Testaments are certainly the children of their patriarchal lines, but the prophecies of their fortunes are often of more general application.

Verses 2–5 of Levi's rendition of Enoch's prophecy are not addressed in the secondary literature as part of this quotation, but are in fact crucial additional evidence. Without taking into account the subsequent eschatological prophecy, the Enochic reference in T. Levi 16.1 amounts to a) a heptadic schema, and b) a condemnation of the priesthood. The latter is not a hallmark of the Apocalypse of the Birds, though it is the basis of one reading of the Aramaic Book of the Watchers as an anti-priestly discourse, leading Lawlor to propose that this verse is an elliptical reference to the Book of the Watchers.[66] Nevertheless, the initial application of a heptadic schema to a priestly field of concern should not preclude attention to the remainder of the passage. I understand the subsequent eschatological narrative to present strong parallels to the Apocalypse of the Birds. So, in T. Levi 16.2–5, after a period of transgression, the children of Levi will reject Jesus, a sin for which they will be punished by the destruction of their (already defiled) holy place and subsequent subjugation to the Gentiles.[67] We have demonstrated above ways in which these events – an era of transgression, the fall of the Temple, the coming of Jesus – might be reasonably understood as interpretative possibilities spotted by early Christians reading the Apocalypse of the Birds, from Barnabas to the writers behind the Testament of Benjamin. If we hypothesize that the entirety of the narrative arc at T. Levi 16.1 is to be attributed to the book of Enoch cited at 16.1, then we have a heptadic schema interwoven with a historically minded march to the eschaton. The strongest match among our extant Enoch literature would be the Apocalypse of the Birds.

The Testaments as readers of Enoch

This brief exploration concerning the Testaments' relationship to Enochic texts and traditions suggests that, rather than representing piecemeal preservations of now-lost exemplars, at least some of the Enochic passages in the Testaments may indicate engagement with the work I have called Apocalypse of the Birds.

If the case for the reliance of the Testaments upon the Apocalypse of the Birds is granted, a few larger conclusions emerge. First, unlike Barnabas, the Testaments all seem to "translate" the allegory out of its animalistic garb into a more straightforward presentation of its assumed referents – there are almost

---

[66] See Lawlor, "Early Citations," 170. Cited by Reeves and Reed, *Enoch from Antiquity*, 307.

[67] We can again note here the conviction of Kee that "chapter 16 gives evidence, not of interpolation, but of reworking by a Christian editor in light of the gospel tradition about the complicity of Jewish priests in the death of Jesus," as further confirmation that this passage seems to operate in light of the events of the first century CE. Charles' typically granular suggestion is that verse 3 alone should be bracketed as a Christian interpolation. See Kee, "Testaments," 794n16a; Charles, *Testaments*, 59–60.

no sheep, lambs, houses, or towers remaining. This confirms what we had already surmised from the tenth-century Greek brachygraphic excerpt of the Vision of the Beasts: the allegorical conceit of the work known as the Animal Apocalypse was quite transparent, and easily understood by ancient readers. On the one hand, this highlights the individuality of the vision of the Vision of the Beasts and Apocalypse of the Birds's vision – not everyone thinks in images, as did our animalistically inclined Enoch writers.[68] On the other hand, it also reminds us that citations of and allusions to the Animal Apocalypse need not be animalistic, and this may open up new avenues for understanding and theorizing its reception history.

Second, the possible interest of the Testaments in the Apocalypse of the Birds has to do with its portrait of the eschaton, not with the allegorical history of Israel that precedes it. For this reason, I think it is inconclusive as to whether the Testaments know a form of Enoch in which the Vision of the Beasts and Apocalypse of the Birds have already been redacted together. The Vision of the Beasts does not serve the rhetorical interest of the Testaments, and the absence of citations and references in the Testaments of the Twelve Patriarchs could have as much to do with a lack of interest as a lack of knowledge on the part of the composers and transmitters of the Testaments. Third, the mere suspicion that the Testaments relied so heavily on this Enochic work is notable in and of itself. It would provide evidence alongside Barnabas for the status of Enochic texts in early Christianity, and a Christian community for whom Enoch was an authoritative predictor of the eschaton. Fourth, the example of the Testaments impacts how we imagine the circulation of Enochic texts, as here we seem to find, yet again, evidence of engagement with a limited selection of text belonging to 1 Enoch, rather than the super-entity we call 1 Enoch.

Finally, the Testaments demonstrate knowledge of far more material from the Apocalypse of the Birds than Barnabas, enabling us to have greater confidence in the restoration of text from medieval manuscripts to earlier contexts. I have made the case above that Barnabas either cites or directly capitalizes upon two (or potentially more) verses in the Apocalypse of the Birds (1 En 90.28–9). But finding a reader of two verses might not suffice to establish the entire textual progression existed by the second century. Here, I am not exploring a historical claim about the Apocalypse of the Birds, as I am not implying that any evidence suggests the Apocalypse of the Birds circulated in a piecemeal form (though that is a theoretical possibility). Instead, the concern is that the text might have changed drastically in transmission without us knowing or realizing and make the practice of textual restoration from medieval manuscripts to earlier historical contexts quite problematic.

---

[68] I am grateful to Elaine Pagels for this suggestion.

The holistic pattern engagement of the Apocalypse of the Birds by the Testaments of the Twelve Patriarchs that I have proposed would greatly expand the amount of Enochic text for which we can demonstrate an early Christian readership, and thereby restore with greater confidence to an early period. I have suggested that pieces of the Testaments of the Twelve Patriarchs demonstrate knowledge of the following elements within the Apocalypse of the Birds: the heptadic schema (1 En 89.59–64), a precipitous moral decline (1 En 90.6–7), the final Judgment (1 En 90.20–6), the fate of the Temple (1 En 90.28–9), the reunion of Israel and other nations/species (1 En 90.30–6), the coming of a Messiah (1 En 90.37), and the subsequent transformation of Gentiles into a revitalized people group (1 En 90.38). It is my view that these broadly distributed parallels allow us to upgrade the hypothesis gleaned from Barnabas (that textual pieces of the Apocalypse of the Birds were known by the second century CE), to this larger conclusion: the Apocalypse of the Birds was a work known in broad strokes to Christian readers by the second century CE.

Therefore, the function of my analysis of the Testaments of the Twelve Patriarchs is not only to reinforce the conclusion of a second-century *terminus ante quem* for the Apocalypse of the Birds, already reached in the discussion of Barnabas, but also to move from work to text, and legitimate the application of this *terminus ante quem* to a good amount of the text of the Apocalypse of the Birds.

Conclusions: second-century readers of the Apocalypse of the Birds

In this section, I sought to discover the earliest readers of the work known as the Animal Apocalypse, and thereby sharpen our understanding of their reading. I have matched the Apocalypse of the Birds to sources which narrate a similar schema, including vocabulary and narrative parallels, *and* attribute it to an Enochic source. I suggested that Barnabas and the Testaments of the Twelve Patriarchs represent readers and interpreters of the work I have called the Apocalypse of the Birds. I thereby established a *terminus ante quem* for the Apocalypse of the Birds in a form close to that in which we now have it in the second century CE and provided substantial evidence for its transmission and circulation in Greek.

It is interesting that these early readers of the Apocalypse of the Birds do not show definite knowledge of material exclusive to the Vision of the Beasts. An absence of engagement with the Vision of the Beasts might simply be a feature of our readers' lack of interest in earlier Israelite history. I therefore find nothing to contest my previous hypothesis that the Apocalypse of the Birds materially circulated as an addendum to the Vision of the Beasts. Intriguingly, we have almost no evidence (perhaps the tenth-century codex featuring a marginal excerpt) for an ongoing circulation of the Vision of the Beasts without the Apocalypse of the Birds. The evidence of our early readers might provide provisional confirmation that a Vision of the Beasts plus Apocalypse of the Birds textual progression outpaced a Vision of the Beasts-only version in popularity.

I also demonstrated that both Barnabas and the Testaments of the Twelve Patriarchs read and use the Apocalypse of the Birds as a prophecy of the tumultuous events of the first century CE, understanding Enoch to predict the decline in the political fortunes of Israel, the coming of Jesus, and the destruction of the Temple. These Christian interpretations of their Enochic source often overlap in their reading strategies. For instance, I have argued that Barnabas and the Testaments recognize 1 En 90.28 as an oblique prediction of the events of 70 CE, and the cited Testaments seem to read 1 En 90.37–8 as a Christ-prediction.

That this evaluation of an early readership has not been done before has, in my view, as much to do with the granular method in which the field has attempted to match Enochic quotations with text, as with a mistaken understanding of the Apocalypse of the Birds as a Maccabean-era work, fixated on the issues of second-century BCE Hellenistic Judea. The reading strategies utilized by Barnabas and the Testaments would be far more extreme if this is the provenance in which we imagine the work to be most properly domesticated. Any hypothesized readings which match the Apocalypse of the Birds to first-century CE referents would be classed as substantial re-readings, out of line with how scholars understand the text's original function. However, my previous chapter argued that the assumption of Maccabean-era provenance for the Apocalypse of the Birds is groundless. We need not be warned off by imagined dissonance between "original text" and our earliest readers – in fact, these earliest readers represent our earliest datable evidence for the state of the text itself! Said differently, the first datable evidence for the Apocalypse of the Birds that we possess ably reads and cites the work as an account of the events of the first century CE.

It is now time to explore the extent to which the text itself, though preserved only by medieval Ethiopian scribes, fits into the context to which its earliest readers imagined it to speak.

Appendix: non-readers of the Apocalypse of the Birds, including the Book of Jubilees

Here I introduce the sources that I have excluded from this discussion of the reception of the Apocalypse of the Birds and defend the rationale for their exclusion.

First, there are papyrus fragments from Oxyrhynchus – P Oxy 2069 fragments 1 and 2 (TM 59975/LDAB 1087) – with text corresponding to the Vision of the Beasts (cf. 1 En 85.10–86.2, 87.1–3). Because these do not tell us about Apocalypse of the Birds, I do not address them in the body of the chapter. Even so I have, below, updated the table from Chapter 1 in light of my new compositional hypothesis, so as to clarify that all of our non-Ethiopic manuscripts attest text belonging to the Vision of the Beasts, and none attest text belonging to the Apocalypse of the Birds.

Table 5.5 Updated: Subsidiary Works of the Book of Dreams in Ancient Documents

	The Book of Dreams		
	Enoch's First Dream Vision: The Flood (1 En 83–4)	The Vision of the Beasts (85.1–89.59)	The Apocalypse of the Birds (89.60–90.42)
4Q204		X	
4Q205		X	
4Q206		X	
4Q207		X	
P. Oxy 2069		X	
Vat. Gr. 1809		X	?

Previously, I found this frequency of attestation to amount to a remarkable pattern in the case of the Qumran manuscripts. However, I feel less confident in the interpretation of the likely extent of our later manuscripts (P. Oxy 2069 and Vat. Gr. 1809). It is interesting to think about the possibility that the Oxyrhynchus fragments might witness the ongoing circulation of the Vision of the Beasts, without the addendum of the Apocalypse of the Birds, though the fragments (like those found at Qumran) are too poorly preserved to encourage total confidence in this judgment. Again, some knowledge of the Apocalypse of the Birds might be implied in an interpretative note in Vat. Gr. 1809 that provides a brief summary of the work from which its excerpt was drawn, even if none of its text is included in the excerpt itself.

Second, I do not use the "Enochic biography" in Jubilees 4 as a *terminus ante quem* for the Apocalypse of the Birds. Jubilees is usually dated to the second century BCE. If its reliance upon the Apocalypse of the Birds was accepted, this would accordingly establish a *terminus ante quem* for the work in the second century BCE. As I argue elsewhere, I feel the evidence for dependency is too weak to sustain such a conclusion.[69] My comments in the next chapter, arguing for a

---

[69] On which, see my forthcoming article, "On Late Ancient Readers of 1 Enoch: Suspected, Suspicious, and Supposed."

first-century provenance for the Apocalypse of the Birds, will further confirm the suspicion that Jubilees did not and could not know the work in question.

Third, and finally, Jean Marc Rosenstiehl, Matthew Black, József T. Milik, and Daniel Olson (the latter most extensively), have suggested that there is a reference to 1 En 90.22–7 in the third/fourth century CE Coptic Apocalypse of Elijah.[70] The correspondence between this text and the Apocalypse of the Birds is loose at best.

Briefly stated, the verse which seems to recommend itself most strongly as evidence is Coptic Apocalypse of Elijah 5.31: "He will judge the shepherds of the people. He will ask about the flock of sheep, and they will be given to him, without any deadly guile existing in them." Sheep and shepherds are all over the Hebrew Bible, even in discourses of judgment, and their invocation need not refer us immediately to the Apocalypse of the Birds. As even Olson notes, "the language is no closer to 1 En 90.22–5 than it is to Ezekiel 34.1–10 and Jeremiah 23.1–2."[71]

The next verse in the Coptic Apocalypse of Elijah (5.32) narrates the return of Enoch and Elijah, their transfiguration, and the pursuit and killing of the Son of Lawlessness. Olson and Black allege that these events find parallel in 1 En 90.31, in which Enoch is taken up by angelic figures and a ram. Olson translates *dabela* as "male sheep" and suggests it is Elijah, previously mentioned (in the Vision of the Beasts) at 1 En 89.52. But the term *dabela* is specific to the Apocalypse of the Birds and is only used to refer to the generation that rises up against the birds from 1 En 90.9–19. It is not obvious to me that Elijah is in view here. Moreover, the text of the Apocalypse of the Birds at 90.31, and surrounding, does not suggest in any way that Enoch and/or Elijah play an active role in judgment. Rather, it is the Lord of the Sheep and his angels who are the prime actors.

Olson bases his argument for an Enoch/Elijah reading of the Apocalypse of the Birds on the Ethiopic *Andəmta* commentary upon 1 En 90.37–8. He notes that, in the Ethiopic commentary tradition (*Andəmta*) to 1 En 90.37–8, presented at length by Daniel Assefa, it is assumed that Enoch and Elijah have played a crucial role in ushering in the final battle with the Antichrist.[72] The influence of the Enoch/Elijah pairing evident in the Ethiopic tradition suggest to Olson a Christian exegesis of the book shared by the Coptic Apocalypse and the Ethiopic *Andəmta*. But whereas the *Andəmta* is a commentary dedicated to

---

[70] See Jean Marc Rosenstiehl, *L'Apocalypse d'Élie: Introduction, Traduction et Notes* (Paris: Paul Geuthner, 1972), 55; Milik, *Books of Enoch*, 47; Matthew Black, "The 'Two Witnesses' of Rev. 11: 3f. in Jewish and Christian Apocalyptic Tradition," *Donum Gentilicium: New Testament Studies in Honour of David Daube*, 1978, 228–9; Olson, *A New Reading*, 252–6; Assefa, "Enigmatic End," 552–60.

[71] Olson, *A New Reading*, 253.

[72] Assefa, "Enigmatic End."

1 Enoch, the Coptic Apocalypse is an unverified allusion. It would be circular to suggest that it provides evidence for a certain Christian exegesis of a portion of the Apocalypse of the Birds when we need to make recourse to the later exegesis to prove it is reading the book at all.

To summarize, I do not accept Jubilees or the Coptic Apocalypse of Elijah as probable readers of the Apocalypse of the Birds. There is no pre-Ethiopic manuscript evidence for the Apocalypse of the Birds (we have Greek fragments only for Vision of the Beasts). I have argued for Barnabas and the Testament of the Twelve Patriarchs as probable readers. To my knowledge, this is the full extent of our material and literary evidence for the Apocalypse of the Birds outside of medieval Ethiopia.

CHAPTER 6

The Apocalypse of the Birds and the First Jewish Revolt

At this point, I have established that the Apocalypse of the Birds should be separated from the Vision of the Beasts and needs a new compositional home. I have provided evidence that the earliest readers of the Apocalypse of the Birds understood it to be a prophecy of the events of the first century CE and were reading it by the early second century CE. I will now endeavor to bring these two lines of inquiry together and read the Apocalypse of the Birds as a narrative of the events of the first century CE.

Specifically, I will establish a *terminus post quem*, or earliest possible date, for the Apocalypse of the Birds in 66 CE, arguing the text encapsulates some of the significant events of the early Jewish Revolt. I will be a bit more circumspect about the placement of a *terminus ante quem*, as well as when, and whether, the compositional window for this work closed. The major contribution of this chapter is the identification and detailing of ways that the text of the Apocalypse of the Birds is entangled with the early Jewish Revolt, though I will stop short of suggesting the entire work was necessarily composed during these tumultuous years.

A note on dating historical apocalyptic, and the problem with a *terminus ante quem*

To make this argument, I will now correlate the text of the Apocalypse of the Birds with historical events. This effort is built on a key assumption: that the text can be dated by following the trail left by the *post facto* prophecy narrated in 1 En 89.59–90.19. But what appears to be a commonsense theory requires substantial explanation. In this section, I want to demonstrate why I feel quite confident about the identification of a *terminus post quem* but less confident about the identification of a *terminus ante quem* with respect to the Apocalypse of the Birds.

The Apocalypse of the Birds is a historical apocalypse particularly indebted to the literary device of prophecy after the fact, or *vaticinium ex eventu*. But, it might be objected, historical apocalypses are prone to a little updating. We have ample evidence of the proclivity of later scribes to rescue valued prophecies from irrelevance by changing the received text, in ways both major and minor.[1] In cases with constantly updated historical references, the possibility of a single compositional window slips away.[2] Even in the context of these methodological problems, I understand the progression of text handled in this chapter, 1 En 89.59 to 1 En 90.19, to be a unified composition, generally speaking.[3] This textual selection takes place within the confines of a heptadic schema, whose start and finish delineate a literary whole. Such a conclusion may also find confirmation in the special vocabulary set employed in this textual section, which I have studied in contrast to other textual units such as the Vision of the Beasts. But part of my choice is methodological – in Chapter 2, I established that I would be operating within a general framework of a two-stage model of composition, particularly because granular source-critical models reap diminishing returns as they grow in detail, especially with reference to the often repetitive and allusive textual world of apocalyptic literature. There is some tension in my thought here, as I acknowledge the historical reality of complex and protracted compositional processes, even as we recognize the limits of our modern access to these processes. I therefore employed the working assumption that, at this stage of research on the Apocalypse of the Birds, we must begin with the establishment of simpler models. Within such a model, I assume that the Apocalypse of the Birds as a whole can be awarded a *terminus post quem* in accordance with the latest-mentioned historical event. Since the last event identifiable took place in 66 CE, I am inclined to set 66 CE as the earliest date for a window of composition.

I have suggested that the Apocalypse of the Birds can be dated in accordance with the historical events it "knows." In so doing, I have invoked the

---

[1] For representative examples see Neujahr, "When Darius Defeated Alexander"; Brian Schultz, "Not Greeks but Romans: Changing Expectations for the Eschatological War in the War Texts from Qumran," in *The Jewish Revolt against Rome: Interdisciplinary Perspectives*, ed. Mladen Popović (Leiden: Brill, 2011), 107–28; Collins, "Fourth Sibyl"; Alexander, "Medieval Apocalypses."

[2] As Hillel Newman puts it, "implicit in this method is the assumption that the texts in question are unitary works, created by a single author according to a systematic plan. In practice, our texts are often composite or even anthological works, each of whose components requires separate investigation and which may or may not have undergone editorial changes." See Hillel I. Newman, "Dating Sefer Zerubavel: Dehistoricizing and Rehistoricizing a Jewish Apocalypse of Late Antiquity," *Adamantius* 19 (2013): 325.

[3] I previously noted my suspicion that text belonging to the first and second periods of the Apocalypse of the Birds may have belonged to an earlier version to the Vision of the Beasts, but, even if this were the case, I understand them to be transformed and functional in their current context.

historians' hunch that texts which participate in a literary paradigm known as *vaticinium ex eventu*, or prophecy after the fact, can be dated in accordance with the last event that they mention.[4] I find this approach to be generally appropriate in the case of the Apocalypse of the Birds, given the protracted and detailed historical progression found herein. In an otherwise critical treatment of the validity of historical-allusional dating as an absolute tool in dating ancient texts, Ted Erho isolates the Animal Apocalypse (and especially, the sections corresponding to the work I have called the Apocalypse of the Birds) as one of the few bona fide "purveyor[s] of vaticinia ex eventu."[5]

Even so, the use of this methodology is an art rather than a science. Readers of apocalyptic works are often confronted with a difficult combination of myth and history. David Frankfurter summarizes the problem well: "historical antecedents to symbols can be identified, but ... the symbols themselves are often arranged in such a manner as to reflect mythological order rather than a chronicle's endeavor toward identifiability."[6] We have already grappled with one way that mythic frameworks can obscure matters for the historian in our discussion about the inexactitude of the chronology of seventy shepherds. In a similar fashion, it can also be hard to date an apocalypse like the Apocalypse of the Birds which culminates in a triumphant military victory. This victorious reversal of fortunes could represent an allusion to historical events; it could also represent a lucky prediction later fulfilled by the events of history, or simply wishful thinking.[7] The line between history and prophecy, and between events and eschaton, is not often clear in this, or any apocalyptic, text.[8] I offer comments below on where I understand history to turn into eschatology in the Apocalypse of the

---

[4] "Eschatology is one of the rare fields in which we can hope to find traditions susceptible of hard dating on external grounds." In Michael Cook, "Eschatology and the Dating of Traditions," *Princeton Papers in Near Eastern Studies* 1 (1992): 29.

[5] In Erho, "Historical-Allusional Dating," 507.

[6] David Frankfurter, *Elijah in Upper Egypt: The Apocalypse of Elijah and Early Egyptian Christianity*, Studies in Antiquity and Christianity (Minneapolis: Fortress Press, 1993), 196.

[7] This insight with reference to military victories in apocalyptic literature can be found in Alexander, "Medieval Apocalypses," 1005. He also notes, "the historian should never lose sight of the possibility that the author may have been an intelligent observer of current affairs," in Alexander, 1000. An analogous case is pursued with reference to non-apocalyptic literature by Benjamin Sommer, writing on Pentateuchal literature, who notes that over-certitude with reference to historical events that a writer could or could not have known or written about, "ignores or belittles the individual genius or even denies that such a genius could exist." In Sommer, "Dating Pentateuchal Texts," 104.

[8] Lorenzo DiTommaso suggests that the scholar must be alert to "details such as the names of kings, the lengths of their reigns, the particulars of and participants in battles," which "smack of historical content." In Lorenzo DiTommaso, *The Book of Daniel and the Apocryphal Daniel Literature* (Leiden: Brill, 2005), 106. András Kraft calls DiTommaso's heuristic "the principle of particularity," in András Kraft, "The Last Roman Emperor 'Topos' in the Byzantine Apocalyptic Tradition," *Byzantion* 82, no. 2 (2012): 215.

Birds, but acknowledge that other interpretations are possible. It is up to the individual scholar to decide where to draw the line, a decision that inevitably and necessarily prompts speculation to some degree, and a falling back upon assumptions about the kinds of people and circumstances that produce literature more generally, and apocalyptic literature in particular.

For instance, it is sometimes taken for granted that the arrived-upon *terminus post quem* of eschatological or apocalyptic works also provides an attendant *terminus ante quem*. And Florentino García Martínez, in his discussion of how to date Enochic apocalypses, tasks scholars to look for "the determination of the moment when the description of the past is replaced by the announcement of the future, since *this transition fixes the time during which the author lived and composed his work* [emphasis mine]."[9] Part of this overlapping of *terminus post quem* and *terminus ante quem* arises from an assumption that apocalyptic literature is a response to specific moments of crisis, and that its composition is marked by a certain amount of urgency.[10] This portrait of apocalyptic composition might be a helpful heuristic but it is not a robust methodology to guide dating.[11] For this reason, I do not assume that a *terminus post quem* automatically provides a *terminus ante quem*.

Another way to pursue the dating of a historical apocalypse is to postulate that a work can be given a *terminus ante quem* by the first historical prediction that it gets wrong. As with the above, what we know about the history of transmission of apocalyptic texts urges us to be cautious in the application of this principle. Modern scholars might value inaccuracy, but ancient and medieval scribes loathed it. When studying other works that have multiple versions preserved, we can frequently spot and reverse-engineer later redactions to restore an earlier version.[12] In the case of the Apocalypse of the Birds, a millennium of transmission has gone undocumented. It is more than reasonable to posit that our extant Gəʿəz text provides us with a later, and much-cleaned-up

---

[9] García Martínez, *Qumran and Apocalyptic*, 85. See also Paul Alexander's suggestion that "Every apocalypse must have been written not long after the latest event to which it alludes," in Alexander, "Medieval Apocalypses," 999.

[10] E.g. "As a rule, apocalypses seem to be written in close proximity to their target date. They are usually the literary expression of eschatological tension and urgency." In Newman, "Dating Sefer Zerubavel," 325.

[11] Erho collects examples of cases in which scholars "try to be overly particular by this method [e.g. historical-allusional dating], even to the point of refining the dating of a document down to a single year or two without due cause, as the available evidence only supports a wider timeframe." I suggest these cases result from the cited scholars' assumptions that *terminus post quem* and *terminus ante quem* can be effectively collapsed in the case of apocalyptic compositions, for the reasons discussed above. See Erho, "Internal Dating Methodologies," 87n4.

[12] Kraft's suggestion, trained on more voluminously manuscripted Byzantine apocalyptic works, is that a complex motif is more likely to devolve into multiple fragmented traditions than otherwise. See Kraft, "Last Roman Emperor," 216.

set of predictions. Perhaps there were inaccurate predictions that were wiped away by well-meaning scribes.

Complicating the application of this principle further, the Apocalypse of the Birds has very little text that operates in the nebulous area between history and eschatology, by which we might judge the limits of the work's knowledge. We can trace historical referents until 1 En 90.16 or 90.19, at which point the text springs into explicitly otherworldly speculation, by way of narrating a final and ultimate victory against all of Israel's enemies, and subsequent arrival of the Day of Judgment. We have, therefore, little in the way of historically minded predictions that are demonstrably inaccurate, and the expected eschaton is never assigned an actual date. The idea of dating based on inaccurate predictions does not offer much guidance in our particular case, and this will not help us establish a *terminus ante quem*.

This recognition leaves us with a related, but slightly different, principle: that we can establish a *terminus ante quem* with reference to events the work does not know, but assumedly would have mentioned. This kind of negative inquiry relies on speculating what a writer would or would not disclose.[13] Even so, the strongest candidate for consideration under this heading with reference to the Apocalypse of the Birds is the destruction of the Temple in 70 CE, often used as a "watershed" moment by which to relatively date a variety of first-century works.[14] One can argue that the Apocalypse of the Birds, committed as it is to a relatively detailed narration of a historical progression, would be even more likely than other works to include this event if it had already taken place. If this work in particular lacks an explicit mention of this event, then it would seem to provide extremely strong guidance in dating, and a possible *terminus ante quem* of 70 CE.

But the extent to which 70 CE should truly be considered a watershed moment in Jewish and Christian history, so cataclysmic that it *must* be

---

[13] Although differently pointed, note the comment of Newman, "We must ... recognize the limitations of our sense of what someone would or would not 'just make up' as a reliable measure of historicity in apocalypses." In Newman, "Dating Sefer Zerubavel," 326.

[14] The perceived relevance of 70 CE to the dating of first-century works can be spotted on a work-by-work basis, with particularly direct statements on the matter to be found in studies on works such as Mark and Matthew which contain possible but contested references to the events of 70 CE. So, on Matthew, Ulrich Luz opens his section on dating with the clear statement that "the terminus post quem is the formation of the Gospel of Mark and the destruction of Jerusalem," in Ulrich Luz, *Matthew 1–7: A Commentary*, ed. James E Crouch and Helmut Koester, Hermeneia – A Critical and Historical Commentary on the Bible (Minneapolis: Fortress Press, 2007), 58. Or, in the even more ambiguous formulation of Mark, Adela Yarbro Collins situates the scholarly discussion around the controversy of "whether the Gospel was written before or after the destruction of the temple," in Adela Yarbro Collins, *Mark: A Commentary*, Hermeneia – A Critical and Historical Commentary on the Bible (Minneapolis: Fortress Press, 2007), 11.

mentioned in any post-dated text, is being re-evaluated.[15] Optimism about the Temple's fortunes, perhaps expressed by treating it as if it were still standing, did not cease in the immediate aftermath of the Temple's destruction.[16] We might imagine that it waned over time, or it became a less functional idea. It is not clear whether this process was completed by the second century CE when we have evidence for readers of the Apocalypse of the Birds. In my discussion of 1 En 90.28–9 below, I will suggest that there is no definite reference to the destruction of the Temple. But given the contested role that we imagine 70 CE played in Jewish and Christian thought, it is not clear to me whether non-reference indicates a lack of knowledge, or simply focus elsewhere. We strike out, once again, in the search for methodological grounds by which to establish an internal *terminus ante quem*.

Ultimately, I understand the Apocalypse of the Birds to be uniquely amenable, among other ancient Jewish works, to an internal dating in light of the sequential and detailed nature of its historical progression and its demonstrable correlation with externally known events. I will demonstrate the functionality of the preserved text in the late first century CE. Moreover, I will uncover historical referents by which I push its *terminus post quem* of the Apocalypse of the Birds to 66 CE. Were we pursuing the provenance of the apocalypse in a traditional manner, we might immediately hypothesize the quick development of this work in the immediate environs of 66 CE.

But, though I find it quite plausible, the early Revolt does not represent the only possible option for the generation of text. The text does not provide sufficient grounds upon which to establish a *terminus ante quem*. There might have been a gap between known or identifiable historical referents and the process of composition. Benjamin Sommer has said, with reference to the dating of Pentateuchal texts:

> Even if a text's ideas do somehow correspond to the date of its composition, there is no one way of deciding how they correspond – through a logic of presence, according to which a text's ideology reflects its

---

[15] See Daniel R. Schwartz, "Introduction: Was 70 CE a Watershed in Jewish History? Three Stages of Modern Scholarship, and a Renewed Effort," in *Was 70 CE a Watershed in Jewish History?: On Jews and Judaism Before and after the Destruction of the Second Temple*, ed. Daniel R. Schwartz and Zeev Weiss (Leiden: Brill, 2012), 1–19.

[16] One possible analogue might be found in rabbinic literature: Jacob Neusner influentially suggested the ongoing centrality of the Temple in the Mishnah was a reaction to its destruction, representing a counter-factual insistence that "nothing has changed." In Jacob Neusner, "Map without Territory: Mishnah's System of Sacrifice and Sanctuary," *History of Religions* 19, no. 2 (1979): 118, 122. Recent work has been a bit more nuanced in differentiating the Temple's demonstrable ongoing importance in rabbinic literature from a model in which rabbinic literature is somehow hiding from, or ignoring, history. See, for instance, Naftali S. Cohn, *The Memory of the Temple and the Making of the Rabbis* (Philadelphia: University of Pennsylvania Press, 2013).

setting positively, or through a logic of absence, according to which a text's author yearns for what is missing.[17]

We read historical apocalypses as if they operate absolutely according to a logic of presence, but this need not be the case. And so, although placing the composition of the Apocalypse of the Birds after 70 CE might suggest patterns of literary engagement that we might find surprising (e.g. a historical apocalypse glossing over a tumultuous historical event), this does not mean such circumstances are impossible to imagine. Just because scholars' imaginations have prioritized one model by which we understand the composition of historical apocalypses – namely, a single author writing a unified account in frenzied haste, assiduously including events up until their present day – this approach does not represent a stringent methodology of dating.

Therefore, my proposal for the latest possible date does not come from an independent evaluation of the text, but is that established in the previous chapter, by second-century readers who know of a "book" or "writing" of Enoch that matches the Apocalypse of the Birds. An important benefit of this external *terminus ante quem*, in dialogue with the literature on the methodology of dating cited here, is that it eliminates a host of possible historical sites before even approaching the internal allusions itself, and in so doing, encourages a focus on earlier sites such as the first century, and even the early Jewish Revolt. In so doing, I hope to meet Sommer's challenge that, "when scholars claim that a text is obviously appropriate for a particular moment in history, they are often correct, but they fail to acknowledge that the idea or text is equally appropriate for some other moment as well."[18] The previous chapter has narrowed the window of possible sites to exclude much of late antiquity.

In short, I think it probable the Apocalypse of the Birds developed at some point between 66 CE and the early second century CE. The arguments upon which such reasoning is based are detailed below.

A first-century CE reading of the Apocalypse of the Birds

I propose interpreting the Apocalypse of the Birds as a narrative of the events of the first centuries BCE–CE, culminating in the Jewish Revolt. To review what has already been established: in the second and third chapters, I rejected the argument that either the Qumran manuscripts or the Maccabean Revolt provide a *terminus ante quem* for the Apocalypse of the Birds. In the previous

---

[17] Sommer, "Dating Pentateuchal Texts," 101.
[18] Sommer, 94.

chapter, I argued that Barnabas, and the Testaments of the Twelve Patriarchs provide a second century CE *terminus ante quem* for the Apocalypse of the Birds.

Building on this argument, I will demonstrate that the "eagles" of 1 En 90.2–16 most probably symbolize Rome, impelling us to a site of textual development in the Roman period. Within these newly established chronological limits, the Jewish Revolt, especially in its earliest years, provides the most fertile grounds for the emergence of the kinds of conflict narrated in the bloody and militaristic historical review of 1 En 90.1–15. I will make an attempt at stricter identifications (I will present one possible reading of the Enochic allusions as cognizant of some of the events of 66 CE), though I acknowledge such a close pairing is difficult to establish with a high degree of certainty (due to the allusive nature of the Enochic text and the singularity and unreliability of our only internal literary source for the events of the Jewish Revolt, Josephus).[19] Still, more than any other proposed option, the First Jewish Revolt provides the best historical backdrop for the allegorical allusions of the Apocalypse of the Birds.

Periods 1 & 2: post-exilic, pre-Roman Judaism

The first and second periods of the four outlined by the Apocalypse of the Birds are often identified in the secondary literature as the Babylonian and Persian periods, respectively. For the Maccabean hypothesis, the second period must be

Table 6.1 The Babylonian and Persian–Hellenistic Period

Verses	Summary	My Reading
89.59–64	Commissioning of Seventy Shepherds	
89.65–72a	First Period: Twelve Shepherds	Babylonian Period
89.72b–90.1	Second period: Twenty-Three Shepherds	Persian–Hellenistic Period
90.2–5	Third Period: Twenty-Three Shepherds	
90.4	Attacks of Dogs, Eagles, Ibises	
90.6–7	Resistance of Lambs, Apathy of Sheep	
90.8–11	Attacks of Ravens, Rise of Rams and Great-Horned Sheep	
90.12–15	Intervention of Lord of the Sheep on Ram's Behalf	
90.16–19	Battle at End of Seventy Shepherds' Reign	
90.28–9	Removal of Old Jerusalem, Replacement with New Jerusalem	

---

[19] "Attempts to see historical significance in minor details represent speculation rather than legitimate historical inference. Such speculation, if properly controlled, is not out of place in a study of this type, but it should and will be explicitly labeled as such." In John A. Brinkman, *A Political History of Post-Kassite Babylonia: 1158–722 B.C.* (Rome: Pontificum Inst. Biblicum, 1968), 33. I am grateful to Ted Erho for this reference.

the Persian period, in order for the third period to represent the Hellenistic era, and for the fourth to represent the Seleucid era. But in this section, I suggest the second period expansively covers post-exilic, pre-Roman Jewish history.

We have addressed the text corresponding to the introduction of the seventy shepherds, and the first period (clearly an allegory of the Babylonian destruction of the Temple) in the previous chapter. There is little to add at this point, other than to reiterate the foundational nature of this set of initial conditions – i.e. a schema of seventy shepherds.

The second period, however, should be addressed:

(72) And after this I saw how the shepherds pastured for twelve hours, and behold, three of those sheep returned and arrived and came and began to build up all that had fallen down from that house; but the wild-boars hindered them so that they could not. (73) And they began again to build, as before, and they raised up that tower, and it was called the high tower; and they began again to place a table before the tower, but all the bread on it (was) unclean and was not pure. (74) And besides all (this) the eyes of these sheep were blinded so that they could not see, and their shepherds likewise; and they handed yet more of them over to their shepherds for destruction, and they trampled upon the sheep with their feet and devoured them. (75) But the Lord of the sheep remained still until all the sheep were scattered abroad and had mixed with them, and they did not save them from the hand of the animals. (76) And that one who wrote the book brought it up, and showed it, and read (it) out in the dwelling of the Lord of the sheep; and he entreated him on behalf of them, and petitioned him as he showed him all the deeds of their shepherds, and testified before him against all the shepherds. (77) And he took the book, and put it down by him, and went out. (90.1) And I looked until the time that thirty-seven shepherds had pastured (the sheep) in the same way, and, each individually, they all completed their time like the first ones; and others received them into their hands to pasture them at their time, each shepherd at his own time.

In most previous scholarship, this passage has been identified as an allegory for the Persian period of Jewish history.[20] But it is not as clearly centered on Persian

---

[20] As in Dillmann, *Das Buch Henoch*, 264–7; Charles, *Book of Enoch Translated*, 244; Tiller, *Commentary*, 336–8; Nickelsburg, *1 Enoch 1*, 391–3; Assefa, *L'apocalypse des animaux*, 202n45; Olson, *A New Reading*, 196–8; Laato, "Chronology," 14–15.

Note that Black and Fröhlich identify these same verses with the events from Cyrus to Alexander, even though they differ with most other scholars, both holding that the schema of seventy starts with Cyrus. The majority position, against these two scholars, is that the reigns of twelve shepherds have already elapsed by the coming of Cyrus. See Black, *Book of Enoch*, 273–4; Fröhlich, "Symbolical Language," 631.

affairs as this titling may lead us to believe. It is curious, for instance, that the Persians are nowhere allegorized in the text. The only animals actually mentioned are the wild boars, who are likely the Edomites or Samaritans, and who hinder the construction of the Second Temple.[21] There is no new species of animal marking the arrival of a new era, and there is nothing like the coming of the lions and tigers in the first period, or the arrival of the birds in the third period. The 'second period' operates under the auspices of the shepherds, not animals who might stand for the Persians, and so it is doubtful the extent to which we should think about exclusively Persian kingship overseeing or structuring this period.

To this point, I think that scholarship has overassumed the extent to which these four periods are meant to represent the four-empire schematic attested in Daniel and elsewhere in Second Temple literature.[22] The association of four periods in the Apocalypse of the Birds with four empires is a scholarly construct which adequately describes the quadripartite divisioning of the heptadic schema, but is never once mentioned in the text. The periods are also not so uniformly structured. It is only the first and third periods which introduce new earthly antagonists; the second and fourth do not. It is not obvious that we have here a succession of four discrete national hegemonies as the dominant structuring device of four discrete periods. Just as likely, we are presented with a chronological continuum sliced into sections irrespective of the changing of the imperial guard. So a hypothesis concerning the second period could stretch from 520–332 BCE, or 520–200 BCE, or 520–100 BCE, so long as we account for all its encapsulated events.

Now, to account for the events: while the second period certainly references events and grievances associated with the Persian period, many of these are the abiding concerns of the Hellenistic period as well. So, it is beyond a doubt that 1 En 89.72–3 allegorizes the rebuilding of the Second Temple, with some negative editorializing about the subsequent impurity of the offerings in said Temple. But we should look more carefully at 1 En 89.74–5:

(74) ወዲበ ፡ ኵሉ ፡ እሉ ፡ አባግዕ ፡ ጽሉላን ፡ አዕይንቲሆሙ ፡ ወኢይሬእዩ ፡ ወኖሎቶሙኒ ፡ ከማሁ ፡ ወይሜጥውዎሙ ፡ ለኖሎቶሙኂ ፡ ለሐጕል ፡ ፈድፋደ ፡ ወበእገሪሆሙ ፡ ኬድዎሙ ፡ ለአባግዕ ፡ ወበልዕዎሙ ፡፡

wädibä k^wəllu ʾəlu ʾäbagəʿ ṣəlulan ʾäʿyəntihomu wäʾiyəreʾəyu wänolotomuni kämahu wäyəmeṭəwəwwomu länolotomuhi lähäg^wəl fädfadä wäbäʾəgärihomu kedəwwomu läʾäbagəʿ wäbäləʿəwwomu

---

[21] For the Samaritans, see Charles, *Enoch or, 1 Enoch*, 203. For the Edomites, see Tiller, *Commentary*, 339–40.
[22] See the explicit comments in Nickelsburg, *1 Enoch 1*, 360; Matthias Henze, "Enoch's Dream Visions and the Visions of Daniel Reexamined," in *Enoch and Qumran Origins: New Light on a Forgotten Connection*, ed. Gabriele Boccaccini (Grand Rapids, MI: Eerdmans, 2005), 19.

And besides all (this) the eyes of the sheep were blinded so that they could not see, and their shepherds likewise; and they handed yet more of them over to [their shepherds?][23] for destruction, and they trampled upon the sheep with their feet and devoured them.

(75) ወእግዚአ : አባግዕ : አርመመ : እስከ : ተዘርዛሩ : ኩሉ : አባግዕ : ገዳመ : ወተደመሩ : ምስሌሆሙ : ወኢያድኀነዎሙ : እምእደ : አራዊት ።

wä'əgzi'ä 'äbagə' 'ärmämä 'əskänä täzärzäru kʷəllu 'äbagə' gädamä wätädämäru məsləhomu wä'iyadḫänəwwomu 'əm'ədä 'ärawit.

But the Lord of the Sheep remained still until all the sheep were scattered abroad and had mixed with them, and they did not save them from the hand of the animals.

This section of text communicates two key complaints. The first, in verse 74, is that the sheep are continuing to be punished and devoured, but also "trampled" – a phrase that occurs only here in the Apocalypse of the Birds. But the narrative here does not match closely what we know about the (relatively peaceable) Persian period. As Knibb puts it, "What was in the mind of the author when in v. 74b he refers to the destruction of large numbers of the sheep during the second, i.e. the Persian, is not entirely clear."[24] It is possible that the absence of animal representation for the Persians is indicative of a more positive attitude towards this particular empire.[25] If this is the case, we should find a non-Persian climate in which to situate the accounts of death and destruction at 1 En 89.74–5. A better way to make sense of this bloody narrative is to view it as an allusion to the imperial successions that took place in the post-exilic period, when the Persian empire gave way to Alexander the Great and the warring Hellenistic kings and kingdoms that fought for succession in his wake. Indeed, I think there is a clue that points us directly towards the Hellenistic period, in the unique detail that the sheep were not simply handed over (which happens often) and devoured (which also happens often), but that they were "trampled" (ኬድዎሙ, kedəwwomu).

---

[23] Although the syntax is unfortunately ambiguous, the shepherds do hand over the sheep to a new set of somebodies: either another set of shepherds ("their shepherds" is the confusing reading found in all manuscripts), or some kind of wild beasts (this logical suggestion is the conjectural emendation made by Nickelsburg). In Nickelsburg, *1 Enoch 1*, 389.

[24] Michael A. Knibb, "The Exile in the Literature of the Intertestamental Period," *The Heythrop Journal* 17, no. 3 (1976): 257–8. Note also Olson's somewhat forced attempts to restore Persian-era events in and around this verse in Olson, *A New Reading*, 197–8.

[25] I am grateful to Martha Himmelfarb for this suggestion.

Surprisingly, given the usual predilection towards reading Enoch and Daniel together (both are theriomorphic historical apocalypses, after all),[26] there has been no mention in previous scholarship of the curious overlap between the phrasing of 1 En 89.74, and the "trampling" and "devouring" specifically enacted by the Hellenistic kings and empires in Daniel.[27] Such a connection would not be the first time the use of "trampling" in a historical apocalyptic text has flagged Danielic intertextuality – there is precedent in scholarship which connects 4Q246, called an "Aramaic Apocalypse," with Daniel 7–8, on just these grounds.[28]

---

[26] E.g. Stephen Breck Reid, *Enoch and Daniel: A Form Critical and Sociological Study of the Historical Apocalypses*, BIBAL Monograph Series 2 (Berkeley, CA: BIBAL Press, 1989).

[27] Likely because of the majority consensus that the Hellenistic period cannot have started yet, for it is needed to fill out the references of 1 En 90. Note also that the parallel between the Gəʿəz Apocalypse of the Birds and Daniel must be made with reference to the Gəʿəz of Daniel 7 and 8. There are, of course, some methodological challenges inherent in this comparison of works in their secondary (or tertiary, in the case of Daniel) translations. Although Daniel is extant in Aramaic (Daniel 7)/Hebrew (Daniel 8) and Greek, I have provided a Gəʿəz text of Daniel below, since it allows us to spot vocabulary similarities between the Danielic account and the Enochic account, in the only version in which the latter is extant.

It is possible that parallel phrasing of the Gəʿəz Daniel and Enoch might point to similarities that existed in a Greek phase of transmission, and help us recover some of the Greek behind the Gəʿəz of the Apocalypse of the Birds. Ethiopic versions of Daniel seem to be translations of the Theodotionic version of Daniel. If we imagine the Ethiopic to be a translation of a Greek Daniel, with what we have extant demonstrating a specific relationship to a Theodotionic text, we can supply a possible Greek Vorlage behind the Gəʿəz Daniel. So, the Gəʿəz root ከደ (*kedä*, trample) always translates the Theodotion συμπατέω, where በልዐ (*bälə'ä*, devour) translates ἐσθίω and the related κατεσθίω. Thus the textual history of Daniel could provide us with an indication as to the Greek behind the Gəʿəz for these same terms in the Apocalypse of the Birds. It is also possible, however, that the Gəʿəz translation of 1 Enoch was impacted by the Gəʿəz translation of Daniel (or vice versa), and that joint or affected translation has produced our similarities in vocabulary and phrasing, thereby getting us no closer to the Greek Apocalypse of the Birds in this section, and perhaps limiting the extent to which we should imagine these textual parallels existing outside of Ethiopia.

I will present the parallels as evidence that Enoch 89.74–5 is veering especially close to Gəʿəz Daniel's account of the Hellenistic period. I am, however, ultimately uncertain concerning the extent to which we can retroject this parallelism into earlier periods.

[28] Aided especially by the shared Aramaic lexeme דוש. See Collins, *Daniel*, 77–8. At greater length, and more convinced of 4Q246's dependency upon Daniel, see Årstein Justnes, "4Q Apocryphon of Daniel AR (4Q246) and the Book of Daniel," in *The Seleucid and Hasmonean Periods and the Apocalyptic Worldview*, ed. Lester L. Grabbe, Gabriele Boccaccini, and Jason M. Zurawski (London: Bloomsbury T&T Clark, 2016), 183–93, esp. 187–8. Note also that in Joseph L. Angel's included response to Justnes, Angel highlights the use of the word דוש by both Daniel and 4Q246 as among the "most impressive" of the many parallels highlighted by Justnes.

In the Gəʿəz of Daniel 8, both the initial arrival of Alexander the Great (Daniel 8.5–8, 21),[29] and the career of his despised (by Daniel) Seleucid successor Antiochus Epiphanes (Daniel 8.9–13, 23–5) are characterized by "trampling." Alexander the Great comes to "trample" (ኬደ, *kedo*, Daniel 8.7) a ram symbolizing the vanquished kings of Persia. This is followed by a subsequent evil king who will "trample [them]" (ኬደን, *kedon*) – "them" being the heavenly bodies (Daniel 8.10) – and be responsible in Daniel 8.13 for the "trampling of the host" (ኀይል ተኬየዳ, *həyəl täkäyədä*). The evils of this and other Seleucid kings are outlined in Daniel's portrait of the fourth beast in Daniel 7, which includes not only the requisite "trampling," but another action with parallels to Enoch, "devouring." So, at Daniel 7.7, the seer glimpses a terrifying beast that "devoured" (ይበልዕ, *yəbälə'*) and "crushed and trampled underfoot (ይኬይድ በእግሩ, *yəkäyəd bäʾəgru*) what remained."[30] The exposition at Daniel 7.23 explains that this is a kingdom which will "devour (ተበልዕ, *täbälə'*) all the kingdoms of earth, and trample (ይኬይድ, *yəkäyəd*) and crush [them]."[31] In other words, in Gəʿəz (and the Theodotion Greek assumed behind it), Daniel consistently presents the marauding of the Hellenistic kings as "trampling" (from the root ኬደ, *kedä*) and "devouring" (ወበልዖሙ, *wäbälə'əwwomu*; from the root በልዐ, *bäl'ä*).

In this light, it is suggestive that the new set of antagonists introduced in 1 En 89.74 are responsible for "trampling with their feet" (ወበአገሪሆሙ ኬደዎሙ, *wäbäʾəgärihomu kedəwwomu*; using the root ኬደ, *kedä*) and "devouring" (also using the root በልዐ, *bäl'ä*) the sheep. Parallel phrasing in Daniel may allow us to hypothesize that the post-exilic antagonists in the Apocalypse of the Birds who enter the scene devouring and trampling are the Hellenistic kings.

Such a re-evaluation has implications for the next verse, 1 En 89.75, which can also be profitably identified with events of the Hellenistic age. 1 En 89.75 expresses anguish at the reality of the diaspora, and subsequent "mixing" of the sheep with third parties (contextually, the wild beasts). If the

---

[29] In this passage, a goat (*dabela*), who symbolizes the "king of Greece (cf. Daniel 8.21)," comes to obliterate and wrest power from the two-horned ram, who symbolizes the kings of Media and Persia. This rings some bells, but we must be specific and limited in our comparisions. So, here and throughout Daniel 7 and 8, the Danielic and Enochic accounts share a general literary commitment to presenting national history in the guise of theriomorphic allegories. We should not be fooled by the stylistic similarities, as there exists a kind of oppositional correlation between their casting philosophies – where a *dabela* is the hero of the Apocalypse of the Birds (1 En 90.10–19), in Daniel 8, it is the symbolic representative for the rampaging of Alexander the Great.

[30] The full account at 7.7: ይበልዕ ወየሐርጽ ወዘተርፈ ይኬይድ በእግሩ, *yəbälə' wäyäḥäräṣ wäzätärfä yəkäyəd bäʾəgru*. See also the similarly phrased account at 7.19: ወይበልዕሂ ወየሐርጽሂ ወዘተርፈ ይኬይድ በእግሩ, *wäyəbäl'əhi wäyäḥäräṣhi wäzätärfä yəkäyəd bäʾəgru*.

[31] The full account at 7:23: ወተበልዕ ኵሎ መንግሥታተ ምድር ወይኬይድ ወይመትራ, *wätäbäl' kʷəllo mängəśtätä mədr wäyəkäyəd wäyəmätra*.

possible historical arena of application is limited to the Persian period, then the verse looks like a specific reference to the kinds of conflicts over intermarriage that we imagine took place in the immediate post-exilic period and are reflected in Ezra–Nehemiah.[32] But concerns about "mixing" certainly did not end with Ezra–Nehemiah.[33] Indeed, the concern evolves to encapsulate much more than intermarriage. We need not read the Gəʽəz word "ተደማሩ, *tädämäru*" to point us directly, and without exception, to discourses concerning (and concerned by) intermarriage. Knibb employs the more flexible "mix[ing] with," which could refer to cultural or social assimilation, or exchange of any kind. With the implied transition to Hellenistic-era (and especially Seleucid-era) events in my reading of 1 En 89.74, one might read the kinds of cultural conflicts with Hellenization and assimilation that texts such as 1 and 2 Maccabees insist prompted the outbreak of the Maccabean Revolt behind 1 En 89.75[34]

One of the benefits of understanding 1 En 89.74–5 as referring to the Hellenistic era is that it preserves the veneer of "history" by which we identify the Apocalypse of the Birds as a work of historical apocalyptic. If we identified the second period as Persian history only and went on to identify the third period as Roman history (as I will do shortly), this would mean that the Hellenistic era went entirely unaccounted for. On the one hand, this omission might not be so surprising given the inconsistent and selective nature of "historiography" in the work as a whole. There are plenty of omissions that already disqualify the "Animal Apocalypse" from consideration under the heading of rigorous historiography, even in the sections where we feel

---

[32] So, as Nickelsburg puts it, "the reference at this point in the historical account may have been triggered by the Judean problem so central to the narratives in Ezra–Nehemiah," in Nickelsburg, *1 Enoch 1*, 395. Also assuming intermarriage is in view in this verse is the topical study of William R. G. Loader, *Enoch, Levi, and Jubilees on Sexuality: Attitudes towards Sexuality in the Early Enoch Literature, the Aramaic Levi Document, and the Book of Jubilees* (Grand Rapids, MI: Eerdmans, 2007), 63.

[33] Ezra–Nehemiah is a crucial post-exilic starting point, but discourses on intermarriage would evolve and take on new significances in Hellenistic-era texts. See, for instance, Armin Lange, "Your Daughters Do Not Give to Their Sons and Their Daughters Do Not Take for Your Sons (Ezra 9,12): Intermarriage in Ezra 9–10 and in the Pre-Maccabean Dead Sea Scrolls," *Biblische Notizen* 137, no. 1 (2008): 17–39; Hannah Harrington, "Intermarriage in Qumran Texts: The Legacy of Ezra–Nehemiah," in *Mixed Marriages: Intermarriage and Group Identity in the Second Temple Period*, ed. Christian Frevel (New York: T&T Clark, 2011), 251–80.

[34] Note also Himmelfarb's conclusions on the significant silence of 1 and 2 Maccabees concerning intermarriage with non-Jews, and her conclusion that "there is no reason to believe that intermarriage was a significant issue in Palestine in the period around the Maccabean revolt." See Martha Himmelfarb, "Levi, Phinehas, and the Problem of Intermarriage at the Time of the Maccabean Revolt," *Jewish Studies Quarterly* 6, no. 1 (1999): 3.

confident in its identifications.³⁵ For instance, also unmentioned are the mishaps of David and Solomon, the Assyrian conquest of the North, the reforms of Josiah, and the post-exilic reorganization under Ezra. It is also clear that by the first centuries BCE and CE, interest in the key players of the Hellenistic era had faded and morphed into fixation on their heirs: the Romans.³⁶ The Hellenistic kingdoms, for instance, get no mention in the first-century works later collected within the New Testament, and neither do the Maccabees or Hasmoneans. Indeed, we've seen evidence of the ways that speculation about Rome directly and immediately displaced similar deliberations concerning the Greeks/Seleucids in the re-readings of Daniel's fourth kingdom surveyed in Chapter 4.³⁷ Perhaps the Hellenistic kingdoms were no longer worthy of mention to most first-century CE authors. Thus we need not be surprised to see the Apocalypse of the Birds following suit. On the other hand, the Apocalypse of the Birds does account for a great many things that we might imagine fading in relevance as time marched forward, such as the Persian period. It is undoubtedly preferable to have major historical eras accounted for in a work normally classed in the genre of "historical apocalypse". If there is an opportunity to interpret verses so as to fill in the historical blanks, the established expectations of the genre encourage us to take this opportunity very seriously.

Compressing the Persian period: a tendency in ancient Jewish historiography

If my hypothesis concerning the second period is granted, we now have to account for its unusual length. A second period covering post-exilic, pre-Roman Jewish history would be around 450 years long. If the third period were to be the same length (23 shepherds again), the fourth period would not start until the third or fourth century of the common era. However, a closer look at our assumptions about chronology and periodization allow us to reimagine the implied historical progression.

---

³⁵ In his recent book, Paul Kosmin treats the Animal Apocalypse within the framework of "total history," as a "historiography of irreducible excess and affective immediacy, a dialogical history, preceding, incorporating, and surpassing the Seleucid empire and exploding its logic of time." This is a rich new way to understand the way that the work functions within and outside of historiographical conventions and discourses. That said, my arguments concerning the two works making up the so-called Animal Apocalypse, and conviction that the more-recent Apocalypse of the Birds does not stem from the Seleucid period, make it difficult to talk about an "Animal Apocalypse" as a representative of a Seleucid-era discourse of "total history." See Kosmin, *Time*, 165–9.

³⁶ See the argument for a parallel displacement of the Seleucids by the Romans in Brian Schultz' reading of the nebulous Kittim in the many manuscripts of the War Scroll, in "The Jewish Revolt against Rome."

³⁷ See also Adler, "Apocalyptic Survey."

First, there is no evidence for any assumed firm ratio of shepherds to years, as demonstrated at length in Chapter 4.

Second, a concern for an exceptionally long second period assumes that we must place the start-date for the second period at the immediate return from exile (circa 515 BCE, according to our modern reckonings), and the end-date at the Roman invasion of Judaea (circa 63 BCE). Against this, I have suggested above that there is no reason to tie the turning points of the periods to the exact dates of imperial changing of the guard, or imperial periods at all. It is possible that the third period is meant to start around what we now call 200 BCE, but that the headlining takeaway of the period was felt to have more to do with the Romans, than with the already-defunct Seleucids or Hasmoneans, and so they were given pride of placement in the narrative of the period.

Third, we need not assume that our modern chronological knowledge is the same (or close) to that possessed by the Apocalypse of the Birds. Speaking further against this are examples from late antique Jewish and Christian literature that clash with modern chronological reckonings, especially with reference to the Persian period.

Let us begin with an excerpt from Seder Olam Rabbah, paralleled in b. Avodah Zarah 9a.[38]

ר' יוסי או' מלכות פרס במני הבית שלשי(ם) וד' ;מלכות יון מאה ושמוני(ם) ;מלכות ב"ת חשמונאי
מאה ושלש ;מלכות הירודוס מאה ושלש; מיכן ואילך צא וחשוב לחרבן הבית.

> Rabbi Yose says: The kingdom of Persia – during the time of the Temple – (existed) thirty-four years; the kingdom of Greece one hundred and eighty; the kingdom of the House of the Hasmoneans one hundred and three; the kingdom of Herod one hundred and three. From here and on go and reckon according to the destruction of the Temple.[39]

The calculations attributed to R. Yose assume 490 years between the destruction of the First Temple, and the destruction of the Second, representing one *post facto* way of correlating a Danielic prophecy with historical events. It also, clearly, flies in the face of our modern chronologies of the period in question,

---

[38] Text of Avodah Zarah 9a accessed via Maagarim is drawn from the fourteenth or fifteenth century BnF MS 1337:

והתניא ר' יוסי או' מלכות פרס בפני הבית שלשים וארבע שנה. מלכות יון בפני הבית מאה ושמונים שנה.
מלכות בית חשמונאי מאה ושלש. מלכות בית הורודוס מאה ושלש מכאן. ואילך צא וחשוב אחר חרבן הבית.

[39] English translation from Chaim Milikowsky, "Seder Olam: A Rabbinic Chronography," (PhD diss., Yale University, 1981), 546–7. Text from Chaim Milikowsky, *Seder 'olam: mahadurah mada'it, perush u-mavo* (Jerusalem: Yad Yitsḥak Ben-Tsevi: Ḳeren ha-Rav Dayid Mosheh ye-'Amalyah Rozen, 2013).

which we believe spanned around 656 years. Most fascinating, for our purposes, is the way it collapses the Persian period into a mere thirty-four years, giving pride of place (or pride of time, rather) to the so-called Kingdom of Greece (clearly an amalgam of what we would now differentiate as the Alexandrian, Ptolemaic, and Seleucid periods). Seder Olam Rabbah evidences a very compressed understanding of the duration of the post-exilic period, and limited interest in the fleeting reign of Persia.

And, though we have no other ancient Jewish chronographic account as detailed as Seder Olam Rabbah, there is additional scattered evidence for ancient Jews having what Daniel Schwartz calls "vague and inaccurate notions of the chronology and length of the Persian period."[40] Daniel 11.2 mentions only four Persian kings reigning before the arrival of a mighty king (Alexander the Great) at 11.3. Though they go mostly unnamed in Daniel, we might restore the only four Persian kings named in the Bible – Cyrus, Darius, Xerxes, and Artaxerxes from Ezra 4.5–7. While these were, indeed, names of the kings that reigned over Persia, there were multiple kings claiming these names – the Achaemenid dynasty featured Darius the I, II, and II; Xerxes I and II; and Artaxerxes I, II, III, IV, and V. Daniel's compression here is noted by Jerome, who avers, "After he has specified the four kings of Persia after Cyrus, the author omits the nine others and passes right on to Alexander. For the Spirit of prophecy was not concerned about preserving historical detail but in summarizing only the most important matters."[41] Josephus, similarly, has long beguiled historians with his compressed account of the Persian period in Book 11 of his *Antiquities*, in which he (among other things) apparently confuses Artaxerxes II and III, and Darius II and III, and "reduced the Persian period by at least as much as two generations."[42]

This should assuage our discomfort with a second period that might appear to engulf far more years (in the reckoning of our modern chronology) than its apparently equivalent third period, while providing little space to the events of the Persian period. Modern chronology might not represent the most relevant

---

[40] Daniel R. Schwartz, "On Some Papyri and Josephus' Sources and Chronology for the Persian Period," *Journal for the Study of Judaism in the Persian, Hellenistic, and Roman Period* 21, no. 2 (1990): 184 n24.

[41] Gleason L. Archer, trans., *Jerome's Commentary on Daniel* (Grand Rapids, MI: Baker Book House, 1958), 119.

[42] On this error in particular, see H. G. M. Williamson, "The Historical Value of Josephus' 'Jewish Antiquities' XI.297–301," *The Journal of Theological Studies* 28, no. 1 (1977): 64. A common suggestion is that this confusion is to be attributed to a gap in Josephus' sources. E.g. Seth Schwartz makes a distinction between Josephus "correct and fairly extensive knowledge of early Persian history" and his confusion over later Persian history concerning which "Josephus has read no Greek works." In Seth Schwartz, *Josephus and Judaean Politics*, Columbia Studies in the Classical Tradition 18 (New York: Brill, 1990), 64.

source by which we can or should ascertain the "length" or function of the post-exilic period, and compressed chronologies of the Persian period can be found at various places in ancient Jewish literature.

To conclude this section, it is universally acknowledged that 1 En 89.72–3 narrates the rebuilding of the Second Temple, implying, though not narrating explicitly, the regnant Persian dominance in the region. And, although 1 En 89.74–5 *could* belong to the Persian period, I have suggested that specific textual parallels with Daniel's account of the rise and reign of the Hellenistic kings tilt the balance of probability towards imagining these verses to further represent a reference to Alexander, his successors, and the keenly felt cultural pressures of Hellenization on diaspora and non-diaspora Second Temple Judaism. This leads us to a new characterization of the second period, as a loose account of the Persian–Hellenistic period, and the struggles facing post-exilic Judaisms more broadly.

The eagles of Rome and the birds of the Apocalypse of the Birds

I understand the third period to narrate the rise of Rome, with the Romans cast as the eagles. Here is the initial passage in question:

> (90.2) And after this I saw in the vision all the birds of heaven coming: the eagles, and the vultures, and the ibises, and the ravens; but the eagles

Table 6.2 The Beginning of the Roman Period

Verses	Summary	My Reading
89.59–64	Commissioning of Seventy Shepherds	
89.65–72a	First Period: Twelve Shepherds	Babylonian Period
89.72b–90.1	Second period: Twenty-Three Shepherds	Persian–Hellenistic Period
90.2–5	Third Period: Twenty-Three Shepherds	Roman Period
90.4	Attacks of Dogs, Eagles, Ibises	
90.6–7	Resistance of Lambs, Apathy of Sheep	
90.8–11	Attacks of Ravens, Rise of Rams and Great-Horned Sheep	
90.12–15	Intervention of Lord of the Sheep on Ram's Behalf	
90.16–19	Battle at End of Seventy Shepherds' Reign	
90.28–9	Removal of Old Jerusalem, Replacement with New Jerusalem	

led all the birds; and they began to devour those sheep, and to peck out their eyes, and to devour their flesh. (3) And the sheep cried out because their flesh was devoured by the birds, and I cried out and lamented in my sleep on account of that shepherd who pastured the sheep. (4) And I looked until those sheep were devoured by the dogs and by the eagles and by the ibises, and they left on them neither flesh nor skin nor sinew until only their bones remained; and their bones fell upon the ground, and the sheep became few. (5) And I looked until the time that twenty-three shepherds had pastured (the sheep); and they completed, each in his time, fifty-eight times.

Let us begin with the identity of the birds. In previous scholarship, this passage has been generally read as an allegory of the arrival of the Hellenistic era, and associated empires. Each bird is held to represent a particular group of people.[43] The eagles are therefore Alexander the Great's Macedonians, the ibises (usually translated "kites") are the Ptolemies, and the ravens (the soon-to-be key antagonist) are the Seleucids.[44] This hypothesis immediately runs into some problems. Alexander the Great's Macedonians do indeed "lead all the birds" (ወእንስርት ይመርሕዎሙ ለኲሎሙ አዕዋፍ, *wä'änsərt yəmärəhəwwomu läkʷəllomu 'ä'waf*) in the sense of being the first empire on the scene, but the empire splintered within a few decades. The ravens and ibises, if they are the Seleucids and Ptolemies, would supplant the eagles rather than working in concert with them. Therefore, if the eagles were Alexander the Great's Macedonian expansion force, they would cease to be mentioned after their initial appearance. Instead, the eagles resurface once again at 90.11, 90.12, and 90.15, working in coalition with the other birds, and urging the ravens to action. A Maccabean-era reading therefore runs into serious issues insofar as it contradicts what we know

---

[43] Although I differ in my identifications, I assume that this fundamental symbolism – one species to one people group – is correct. There are some scholarly treatments which compromise this principle, largely in pursuit of the goal of matching the events narrated to Maccabean-era history. So, Jonathan Goldstein suggests that the birds represent differently ranked Seleucid officials, and Charles, Milik, and VanderKam postulate that the birds symbolize the Hellenistic empires writ large upon their arrival, but come to symbolize local enemies (in what Charles calls a "fresh change of symbols") by the time of the final battle. See Goldstein, *I Maccabees*, 41n12; Charles, *Book of Enoch Translated*, 253; VanderKam, *Enoch and the Growth*, 163; Milik, *Books of Enoch*, 44. Against this, I think the Apocalypse of the Birds, like the Vision of the Beasts, shows no sign of breaking a commitment to an equivalency between one species and one group, and these kinds of arguments are therefore unnecessary.

[44] For an excellent and in-depth survey of the history of scholarship on the identifications of the birds, see Olson, *A New Reading*, 136–43. On alleged Aramaic equivalents behind the Gəʽəz lexemes, see David Bryant, *Cosmos, Chaos and the Kosher Mentality* (Sheffield: Sheffield Academic Press, 1995), 123–7.

about the succession of Hellenistic empires.[45] I have argued that 1 En 89.74–5 could just as easily be interpreted as an allegory of this very same ascendancy of the Hellenistic kings, and it would be unnecessary for this to be narrated twice.

In fact, there is a much easier equation for the eagles to be made. Early scholars who proposed a Christian or common-era date for the Book of Enoch – notably, Philippi, Volkmar, and von Hoffmann – found it so self-evident that the eagles are the Romans, that none see fit to defend it at length.[46] The close association of the Roman Republic and Empire with eagles and eagle symbolism, especially with military overtones, is not only a well-known Classical trope, but is specifically referred to throughout first-century Jewish/Christian literature. This is not to say, of course, that the Romans were the first or only ancient empire to use the symbol of the mighty eagle for its iconography. We have numismatic, archaeological, and literary evidence for the occasional use of eagles in Persian, Macedonian, Seleucid, and Ptolemaic imperial contexts.[47] In the secondary literature on Enoch, the identification of Macedonians/Greeks with Eagles is generally made contextually, since the eagles come at the start of what is assumed to be the Hellenistic era.[48] Stronger evidence, with specific instantiations in both imperial iconography and

---

[45] To get around this, one solution pioneered by Dillmann and Charles, and recently adopted by Black, Uhlig, and Olson, is that the continuing existence of the purportedly Macedonian eagles, and Ptolemaic kites in the era of the Seleucid ravens, has to do with the presence of foreign mercenaries fighting under the Seleucids. I find this to be a bit of a stretch, based as it is on an unnecessary commitment to correlating the Animal Apocalypse with the events of Seleucid-era Judaea, as well as the narrow reading that the eagles "lead" all the birds to be a necessarily chronological statement. Dillmann, *Das Buch Henoch*, 279; Charles, *Book of Enoch Translated*, 252; Black, *Book of Enoch*, 276; Uhlig, *Das äthiopische Henochbuch*, 699; Olson, *A New Reading*, 141.

[46] See Volkmar, *Eine Neu-Testamentliche Entdeckung*, 15–16; Philippi, *Das Buch Henoch*, 30–1; von Hofmann, *Der Schriftbeweis*.

[47] For a dense survey of eagle iconography employed by the Persian and Hellenistic empires, see the sources collated in Benjamin James Robert Greet, "The Roman Eagle: A Symbol and Its Evolution" (PhD diss., University of Leeds, 2015), 42–3; 50–1, http://etheses.whiterose.ac.uk/12543/. Note, on the other side of things, Ya'akov Meshorer's conclusion that the eagle is "not a common motif in Jewish numismatics," in Ya'akov Meshorer, *Ancient Jewish Coinage*, vol. 2 (Dix Hills, NY: Amphora Books, 1982), 27.

[48] One of the only instances of a scholar grounding their identification of the eagles in the empire's own iconography can be found in Nickelsburg's commentary. Unlike most other scholars, however, Nickelsburg notes extensive numismatic evidence for eagles on Ptolemaic coins, and argues the eagles represent the Ptolemies, though he though he is circumspect in his certainty when guessing the identity of this or any other bird. See Nickelsburg, *1 Enoch 1*, 396. The problem is that eagles were so often used on coins by Greek and Roman imperial authorities from the sixth century BCE onwards that eagle coinage is not necessarily distinctive to a single period or region, hence my note that I reproduce Roman coins for illustrative purposes. See the coins reproduced in Greet, "The Roman Eagle," 235–76.

Figure 6.1 Eagle on Silver Tetradrachm of Galba Antioch, 68–69 CE, American Numismatic Society

Figure 6.2 Eagle on Silver Denarius of Vespasian Ephesus, 76 CE, American Numismatic Society

refractions thereof in Jewish/Christian literature, can be provided from the Roman world. I provide here and below for illustrative purposes especially well-preserved examples of contemporary coinage with eagles.[49]

Within early Jewish/Christian literature, the strongest and most immediate parallel to the particular tradition-set found in the Apocalypse of the Birds comes

---

[49] Additional examples of eagle coinage circulating at the time can be provided from mints in Palestine or caches discovered in Roman Palestine. See: the Agrippa I coins of 41–2 CE in which a king carries an eagle tipped scepter (in Meshorer, *Ancient Jewish Coinage*, 2:53); a Tyrian silver half-shekel with an eagle on the reverse that has been intentionally defaced, found at Masada (#3670 in Ya'akov Meshorer, "The Coins of Masada," in *Masada: The Yigael Yadin Excavations, 1963–1965: Final Reports* (Jerusalem: Israel Exploration Society, 1989), 122, plate 74); the eagle coin-type minted under Herod the Great of which examples are amalgamated in Donald Tzvi Ariel and Jean-Philippe Fontanille, *The Coins of Herod: A Modern Analysis and Die Classification* (Leiden: Brill, 2011), 285–90.

from 4 Ezra, roughly dated to the end of the first century CE.[50] The eagle vision of 4 Ezra 11–12 is virtually universally understood to symbolize a succession of emperors ruling the Roman Empire by way of an eagle with twelve wings, and three heads.[51] In 4 Ezra, the fall of the eagle marks the end of the final oppressor, the inbreaking of the direct intervention of God, and the beginning of the end:

> (11.44) The Most High has looked upon his times, and behold, they are ended, and his ages are completed! (45) Therefore you will surely disappear, you eagle, and your terrifying wings, and your most evil little wings, and your malicious heads, and your most evil talons, and your whole unjust body, (46) so that the whole earth, freed from your violence, may be refreshed and relieved, and may hope for the judgment and mercy of him who made it." (12.1) While the lion was saying

---

[50] 4 Ezra states that it was written 30 years after the destruction of the Temple, which would be around 100 CE, though this is an obvious patterning on Ezek 1.1. It not only reflects obvious knowledge of the destruction of the Second Temple (though transposed into a pseudepigraphal narrative of the destruction of the First), but is in many ways focused on explaining this traumatic event, so it has a definite *terminus post quem* of 70 CE. 4 Ezra is quoted in Clement of Alexandria's *Stromateis*, which could establish a *terminus ante quem* of the end of the second century CE. Within this compositional window, the Eagle Vision of 4 Ezra 11–12 can be mined for specific historical allusions, in pursuit of a more specific date. A Flavian date in the late first century (achieved by correlating the Eagle vision to Flavian-era personages and events) was regnant for much of the twentieth century, influentially backed by Michael Stone, and is now generally accepted (though see the dissent of DiTommaso discussed below). See Michael E. Stone, *Fourth Ezra: A Commentary on the Book of Fourth Ezra*, Hermeneia – A Critical and Historical Commentary on the Bible (Minneapolis: Fortress Press, 1990), 9–10; Michael E. Stone and Matthias Henze, *4 Ezra and 2 Baruch: Translations, Introductions, and Notes* (Minneapolis: Fortress, 2013), 2–3. For a recent project using a Flavian date for 4 Ezra for social-historical analysis, see G. Anthony Keddie, "Iudaea Capta vs. Mother Zion: The Flavian Discourse on Judaeans and Its Delegitimation in 4 Ezra," *Journal for the Study of Judaism* 49, no. 4–5 (November 2018): 498–550.

[51] There is, however, some disagreement on precisely which emperors are in view. For a summary of scholarship on the particular Roman emperors that 4 Ezra sets in its sights, and a revival of a Severan-era dating see Lorenzo DiTommaso, "Dating the Eagle Vision of 4 Ezra: A New Look at an Old Theory," *Journal for the Study of the Pseudepigrapha* 10, no. 20 (October 1999): 3–38.

DiTommaso's Severan dating, which pushes beyond the purported late second-century *terminus ante quem* provided by Clement, notes that Clement's citation of one passage does not amount to proof of the existence of all of the text of 4 Ezra – it is not, for instance a citation of the Eagle Vision. But Karina Martin Hogan provides a strong critique of DiTommaso's Severan dating, noting that he has no material evidence by which to separate the Eagle Vision from the rest of 4 Ezra, and his theory depends on all of our extant manuscripts deriving from this hypothetical Severan-redaction of an earlier circulating work, with none of our manuscripts representing this earlier version. In Karina Martin Hogan, *Theologies in Conflict in 4 Ezra: Wisdom, Debate, and Apocalyptic Solution* (Leiden: Brill, 2008), 184–5.

these words to the eagle, I looked, (12.2) and behold, the remaining head disappeared. And the two wings that had gone over to it arose and set themselves up to reign, and their reign was brief and full of tumult. (12.3) And I looked, and behold, they also disappeared, and the whole body of the eagle was burned, and the earth was exceedingly terrified.[52]

In the Apocalypse of the Birds, the ultimate defeat of the eagles (and subsidiary birds) marks the very same moment – the imminent arrival of the last judgment, and advent of the eschaton. Intensifying the parallel, the Apocalypse of the Birds situates its audience in the waning years of a final period of oppression of the twelve shepherds, which strongly recalls 4 Ezra's insistence that its readers are experiencing the final days of crippling rule under the eagle's twelve wings (and three heads). It is unnecessary (and unsubstantiated elsewhere in the text) to assume that 4 Ezra is reliant upon the Apocalypse of the Birds, or vice versa. Rather, we have two refractions of a very similar tradition: the belief that Jews were living at the very end of a final period which was divided into "twelve" and were subjected to the evils of the (Roman) eagles, but not for long.

These are not the only references to eagles as Romans in first-century literature. There is some Matthean scholarship that understands the gruesome Matt 24.28 ("Wherever the corpse is, there 'οἱ ἀετοί' will gather") to be a coded reference to the Romans, as eagles. One well-trodden path in scholarship interprets this verse as a reference to the Roman destruction of Jerusalem in 70 CE.[53] Pivoting away from reading this allusive verse as strict *vaticinum ex eventu*, some recent scholarship has explored the possibility that the Roman/eagle identification encodes a critique of imperial dominion, or perhaps an eschatological prediction of the empire's eventual collapse.[54] If this is the case,

---

[52] Translation from Stone and Henze, *4 Ezra and 2 Baruch*. Note that I have not included a non-English text of 4 Ezra, largely because its complicated textual history makes it difficult to privilege supplying one tradition among the Syriac, Latin, Gəʻəz, and Arabic over the other. Stone and Henze note no significant variants in this section, and I present the English translation on which they arrive as the best available approximation of a text of 4 Ezra.

[53] See the literature cited as well as a concise summary of other interpretations in Dale C. Allison and W. D. Davies, *A Critical and Exegetical Commentary on the Gospel According to Saint Matthew XIX–XXVII*, vol. 3, International Critical Commentary on the Holy Scriptures of the Old and New Testaments (Edinburgh: T&T Clark, 1988), 355–6.

[54] So, see the work of Warren Carter and Alexandria Frisch, which accept the Roman/eagle analogy for this verse, but offer new ways of understanding its application, outside of the simple Destruction of Jerusalem. In Warren Carter, "Are There Imperial Texts in the Class? Intertextual Eagles and Matthean Eschatology as 'Lights out' Time for Imperial Rome (Matthew 24:27-31)," *Journal of Biblical Literature* 122, no. 3 (2003): 467–87; Alexandria Frisch, "Matthew 24:28: 'Wherever the Body Is, There the Eagles Will Be Gathered Together' and the Death of the Roman Empire," in *The Gospels in First-Century Judaea*, ed. R. Steven Notley and Jeffrey P. García (Leiden: Brill, 2016), 58–75.

it would represent a fascinating parallel to the eschatologically focused Enochic material. Moreover, these sources would provide the only two instances in Jewish/Christian literature of the period in which Rome is not represented by a singular eagle, but by eagles plural. The emphasis, in the Matthean as well as in the Enochic material, would thus shift from simply likening the Roman Empire to an eagle, to representing the people in whom the empire is manifest as eagles themselves.[55] If we do grant a Roman/eagle identification here at Matt 24.28, we have Roman eagles gathered around a corpse, presumably to devour it as carrion.[56] The exact identity of the corpse is not entirely clear in this case – perhaps it symbolically represents Jerusalem, or more literally

---

[55] I should clarify that I do not find in this parallel any evidence for dependency or relationship between the Matthean and Enochic materials. I am largely unconvinced by previous scholarship that has explored a possible relationship between Matthew and the works belonging to 1 Enoch, especially the Book of the Watchers, and Book of Parables. The Book of the Watchers might be a more plausible "source" in the abstract, given the early attestation of a good amount of its text, and demonstrable influence on works like Jude and 2 Peter, but the specific parallels suggested are not so exact as to demand hypotheses of direct influence (see the hypothesis of Sims, and response of Verheyden). I find the Book of the Parables (arguing for the Parables' influence on Matthew see Walck and Macaskill) to be less plausible in the abstract – given the medieval Christian attestation of its text, it seems more likely that any similarities spotted between, for example, Son of Man language in Matthew and Enoch indicate that the former exerted textual influence on the latter, rather than the other way around. Therefore, I do not consider my work here to provide positive evidence to scholarship interested in demonstrating direct Enochic influence on Matthew. For the above-cited sources, see David C. Sims, "Matthew 22.13 a and 1 Enoch 10.4 a: A Case of Literary Dependence?," *Journal for the Study of the New Testament* 15, no. 47 (1992): 3–19; Joseph Verheyden, "Evidence of 1 Enoch 10:4 in Matthew 22:13?," in *Flores Florentino: Dead Sea Scrolls and Other Early Jewish Studies in Honour of Florentino García Martínez*, ed. Anthony Hilhorst, Émile Puech, and Eibert Tigchelaar (Leiden: Brill, 2007), 449–66; Leslie W. Walck, *The Son of Man in the Parables of Enoch and in Matthew*, Jewish and Christian Texts in Contexts and Related Studies 9 (London: T&T Clark, 2011); Grant Macaskill, "Matthew and the Parables of Enoch," in *Parables of Enoch: A Paradigm Shift*, ed. Darrell L. Bock and James Charlesworth (London: Bloomsbury T&T Clark, 2013), 218–30.

[56] Here, I disagree with the above-cited articles of Carter and Frisch, who both understand the eagles, in attending a corpse, to be effectively attending the funeral of their own demise, rather than gathering to eat. Against this, I think it clear that the human corpse is to be differentiated from the eagles. I also find it telling that Matt 24.28 is still embedded in the catastrophic downturn of events, preceding the triumphal return of the Son of Man at 24.29. Therefore, I find a return to the general scholarly consensus, assumed in the commentaries of Davies and Allison, and Ulrich Luz, and read the passage as, indeed, birds gathering around carrion. See Warren Carter, "Imperial Texts," 467–87; Frisch, "Matthew 24:28"; Allison and Davies, *Commentary*, 355–6; Luz, *Matthew 1–7*, 199.

As a smaller note, part of Carter's case for rejecting the consensus understanding that the eagles are eating carrion is that eagles are rarely depicted in ancient literature as eating carrion, flesh, or really eating at all. This is, however, quickly disproven by the witness of the Apocalypse of the Birds.

the corpses littered around the city in the aftermath of the Roman siege. But, either way, the tradition of Roman eagles feasting on Jewish misfortune would find an immediate echo in the Enochic tradition of eagles devouring the sheep in 1 En 90.2–4.

Two other roughly contemporary Jewish texts cast the Romans as eagles, and particularly rapacious ones at that: 1QpHab iii 6–12 and 4 Ezra 11.35. Pesher Habbakuk is a slightly ambiguous parallel, since it borrows the language of hungry eagles from its Hebrew Biblical source, but it does apply the symbol to the Kittim, generally understood in this verse to represent the Romans[57]:

וקול מנמרים סוסו וחדו מזאבי ערב פשו ופרשו פרשיו מרחוק יעופו כנשר חש לאכול כול(ו) לחמס
יבוא מגמת פניהם קדים   פ(שר)ו על הכתיאים אשר ידושו את הארץ בסוס(יהם) ובבהמתם
וממרחק יבואו מאיי הים לאכול (את) כול העמים כנשר ואין שבעה

[Hab 1.8] Their horses are swifter than panthers; they are keener than wolves at night. Their war-horses paw the ground, gallop, from afar they come flying like an eagle, hastening to eat. [Hab 1.9] All of them come to use violence; the breath of their faces is like the East wind. Its inter[pretation] concerns the Kittim, who trample the land with horse[s] and their animals and come from far off, from the islands of the sea, to devour all the nations, like an eagle, insatiable.

Even despite multiple animals from the Hebrew text of Habakkuk from which to choose, the Kittim are here specifically likened to an eagle, not just hungry, but now insatiable.[58] It is possible that this was a pointed jab at Roman dominance, newly exerted over Judaea (assuming the accepted late first-century BCE date for the scroll is correct), by way of their prized eagle symbol. At least, the incidence of the eagles was a happy coincidence of scriptural text and contemporarily relevant symbolism, and seized upon by this composition. Further examples of the same symbolism employed in roughly contemporary

---

[57] As Moshe Bernstein puts it, the Kittim "have been virtually universally identified as the Romans." In Moshe J. Bernstein, "Pesher Habakkuk," in *Encyclopedia of the Dead Sea Scrolls*, ed. Lawrence H. Schiffman and James C VanderKam, vol. 2 (New York: Oxford University Press, 2000), 649.

On the nature of the Roman identification of the Kittim, see also a more general treatment by George Brooke, as well as the suggestion by Hanan Eshel that the Kittim layer was a secondary addition to a previous Habakkuk commentary, added in light of the Roman conquest of Judaea: George J. Brooke, "The Kittim in the Qumran Pesharim," in *Images of Empire*, ed. Loveday Alexander (Sheffield: Sheffield Academic Press, 1991), 135–59; Hanan Eshel, "The Two Historical Layers of Pesher Habakkuk," in *Northern Lights on the Dead Sea Scrolls: Proceedings of the Nordic Qumran Network 2003–2006*, ed. Anders Klostergaard Petersen et al., Studies on the Texts of the Desert of Judah 80 (Leiden: Brill, 2009), 107–17.

[58] I owe this observation to Frisch, "Matthew 24:28," 66.

(though slightly later) texts should bolster our confidence in reading this passage as a directed dig at Roman rule.

For another brief but suggestive incidence of the rapacious eagle tradition, we can return to the Eagle Vision of 4 Ezra 11.29–35. This textual section is especially important because it places the devouring action of the Roman eagles as the climax of a final catastrophe, heralding the inbreaking of the eschaton, the same juncture it occupies in our Matthean and Enochic texts. In this literary context, Ezra is being shown the infamous eagle with twelve wings and three heads – the twelve wings have reigned and collapsed, but it is now time for the three heads to battle it out for dominion:

> (11.29) One of the heads that were at rest awoke; for it was greater than the other two heads. (30) And I saw how it allied the two heads with itself, (31) and the head turned with those that were with it, and it devoured the two little wings which were planning to reign. (32) Moreover, this head gained control of the whole earth, and with much oppression dominated its inhabitants; and it had greater power over the world than all the wings that had gone before. (33) And after this, I looked, and behold, the middle head also suddenly disappeared, just as the wings had done. (34) But the two heads remained, which also ruled over the earth and its inhabitants. (35) And I looked, and behold, the head on the right side devoured the one on the left.

In 4 Ezra 11.35, one of the heads of the eagle wins supremacy by devouring the other head, its only remaining competition. In the next verse, the eagle, now reduced from a twelve-winged three-headed monstrosity to a single-headed bird, is mocked by a lion speaking with the voice of the "Most High," asking if this is "what remains of the four beasts which I had made to reign in my world, so that the end of the times might come through them?" Note that in the later interpretation of this prophecy, 4 Ezra 12.27–8, glosses the devouring as "devouring of the sword." This is a helpfully explicit statement on what exactly is being allegorized in not only 4 Ezra, but likely also the images of carnivorous eagles in 1QpHab iii 6–12, Matt 24.28, and 1 En 90.2–4: Roman warfare. Ultimately, I find this quartet of references to be mutually reinforcing, and to provide substantial evidence of the commonness of a literary choice in first-century BCE–CE Jewish literature, in which eagles (and especially, eagles at the eschaton) were not only thinly veiled references to Rome, but also represent specifically loaded encapsulations of Roman aggression. It is unsurprising to see these texts appear in the very centuries during and after which imperial Roman expansion achieved conquest of Judaea.

Outside the world of eschatological literature, the Roman/eagle association was established enough to appear twice in Josephus' accounts of the first century. Both passages affirm not only the commonplace nature of a Roman/

eagle identification in the world of first-century Judaea, but speak directly to the underlying association of this symbol with Roman military aggression. In one passage, the image of an eagle provides a political flashpoint for a Josephan tale about the Jewish demolition of a golden eagle apparently placed by King Herod atop the Second Temple (Ant 17.151–63, also alluded to in JW 2.2). It is unclear whether the eagle in this episode would have been controversial insofar as it directly symbolized Roman imperial power, Herodian power, or whether its presence would simply have been an affront to prohibitions on depicting living beings.[59] I think E. Mary Smallwood is correct in suggesting the Temple eagle "had some offensive connotation – perhaps simply as the legionary emblem, the symbol of Roman might, and thus an affront to Jewish national sentiment."[60] In a second passage, Josephus explains the import of the legionary practice of carrying an *aquila*, or eagle, as a marching standard in *Jewish War*. He describes the nature of Vespasian's forces: "Next the ensigns surrounding the eagle, which in the Roman army precedes every legion, because it is the king and the bravest of all the birds: it is regarded by them as the symbol of empire (τῆς ἡγεμονίας τεκμήριον), and, whoever may be their adversaries, an omen of victory (JW 3.122)."[61] Without assuming that Josephus speaks for all first-century Jews,[62] Josephus makes explicit what has previously been implicit in our eschatological texts: that the Roman eagle was, indeed, a symbol of the Roman Empire, especially representative of its military might.[63]

---

[59] It is not surprising that Josephus' Flavian account emphasizes the latter reason, rather than dwelling on any anti-Roman implications.

[60] Or, as Steven Fine summarizes the state of affairs, "... as tensions with Rome increased, Hellenistic imagery that smacked of Roman paganism, like the eagle and the trophy, were highly suspect." See E. Mary Smallwood, *The Jews Under Roman Rule: From Pompey to Diocletian: A Study in Political Relations* (Leiden: Brill, 2001), 99; Steven Fine, *Art and Judaism in the Greco-Roman World: Toward a New Jewish Archaeology* (Cambridge: Cambridge University Press, 2005), 75. On the incident more generally, see Jan Willem Van Henten, "Ruler or God? The Demolition of Herod's Eagle," in *The New Testament and Early Christian Literature in Greco-Roman Context: Studies in Honor of David A. Aune*, ed. John Fotopolous (Leiden: Brill, 2010), 257–87.

[61] Translation from Flavius Josephus, *The Jewish War: Volume II*, trans. Henry St. John Thackeray, Loeb Classical Library 487 (Cambridge, MA: Harvard University Press, 1927).

[62] It is important to remember that Josephus, in his framing, emphasizes that he is explaining how the eagle is regarded "by them," i.e. the Romans.

[63] A final avenue of Roman/eagle identification that might prick the ears of keen readers of the New Testament has to do with the congregational leader named Aquila mentioned multiple times (Acts 18:2, 18, 26; Rom 16:3; 1 Cor 16:19; 2 Tim 4:19). If indeed this is a Greek transliteration of the Latin name Aquila (and see Jewett for a summary of the controversy here), the very fact of the appearance of such a name might be a clue as to the popularity of Roman/eagle symbolism in the first century CE, and its networking into contemporaneous Jewish and Christian literature. But it can be problematic to extrapolate cultural paradigms solely from onomastic evidence, though I find the name curious nevertheless. See Robert Jewett, *Romans: A Commentary*, ed. Eldon Jay Epp, Hermeneia – A Critical and Historical Commentary on the Bible (Minneapolis: Fortress, 2007), 956.

Figure 6.3 Aquila between Two Standards on Silver Denarius of Nero Rome, AD 67–68. American Numismatic Society

The evidence collected above, from Pesher Habakkuk, 4 Ezra, Matthew, and Josephus, indicates that the eagle was a potent symbol in the fraught Jewish–Roman politics and associated literatures of the earliest centuries CE, as is reflected in our literary sources of the time.[64] We now have significant parallels encouraging us to identify the eagles of the Apocalypse of the Birds as Rome.[65] And we have substantial evidence that this Enochic identification is not without precedent, but is one of multiple documented reactions to and refractions of Rome's triumphant eagle. So, if the eagles of Enoch are, in fact, meant to symbolize the Romans, this identification provides us with a new (temporary, as we will move it up below) *terminus post quem* for the composition of the Apocalypse of the Birds: roughly 63 BCE, or the beginning of the Roman occupation of Judaea.

[64] Eagles were not, of course, automatically a negatively coded entity within all of Jewish antiquity. They have a rich if ambiguous poetic significance in the Hebrew Bible and early Jewish art (see Hachlili and Szkołut). An eagle also appears on at least one type of Herodian-era coinage, though it is unclear exactly what is to be made of this symbolism (see Meshorer, Ariel & Fontanille). However, the examples cited in the body should suffice to demonstrate a complex of first century CE literary sources that associated the eagles with Roman imperial power. See Rachel Hachlili, *Ancient Jewish Art and Archaeology in the Land of Israel* (New York: Brill, 1988), 332–4; Paweł Szkołut, "The Eagle as a Symbol of Divine Presence and Protection in Ancient Jewish Art," *Studia Judaica (Krakow)* 5 (2002): 1–11; Meshorer, *Ancient Jewish Coinage*, 2:29–30; Ariel and Fontanille, *Coins of Herod*, 115–19.

[65] Identifying the Enochic eagles as Rome, because it would then represent such a comparatively robust and detailed account of Roman occupation in the guise of eagle symbolism, has the potential to shift the ways we interpret the texts discussed above. I noted, for instance, that much of Warren Carter's objection to reading Matt 24:28 as a reference to 70 CE has to do with his conviction that there is no precedent for carnivorous Roman eagles – but with the Apocalypse of the Birds as an intertext, perhaps the balance of probability shifts towards a 70 CE-centric reading.

Such a reading opens the way to a new understanding of the above-cited text narrating the third period. If we accept the Roman=Eagle equation, we can re-imagine what is being communicated with the qualifier of 1 En 90.3 that "the eagles led all the birds." It is not necessarily that the eagles came first chronologically, but rather that they were atop the leadership pyramid – they were, as Josephus puts it, the king of all the birds.[66] If the Romans are eagles, then the lesser birds (and, without sinking too deep into universal symbolism, it is fair to say that ravens, ibises, and vultures are subordinate to the eagle) would be either client kingdoms, legions, or provincial leaderships – distinct from, yet subject to, the eagles. This identification would certainly explain why the eagles never quite recede to the background, and also why they are not the key antagonists of the sheep at 1 En 90.6–19. Perhaps the implication is, given that Roman rule of Palestine was not always entirely direct, even if the Romans were the power behind the coalition, they were not always its most obvious and local manifestation.

As for the other birds, if we wanted to make more specific identifications, we could look to regional powers in and around Palestine. I have already suggested that the ibises are clearly meant to symbolize Egyptians.[67] Within the Roman-era imagination of the text, this likely refers less to the native peoples of Egypt, and more to the Roman forces (with military forces, such as legions, in mind especially) who ruled Egypt on Rome's behalf. I confess to being largely stumped on the identity of the vultures, who never act alone or do anything particularly of note, though I am consoled by the realization that I am in good scholarly company.[68] The ravens are always identified in modern

---

[66] Once again, I am anticipated here by the idiosyncratic but largely forgotten work of Volkmar, who understood 1 En 90.3 to function just this way, as a statement of the Roman eagles' leadership and hegemony over the other birds. However, Volkmar wanted the third period to encompass the Hellenistic and early Roman periods (with the ultimate goal of placing the climax of the Animal Apocalypse at the Bar Kokhba Revolt). Relatedly, then, he was forced to postulate a changing symbolism, by which the ravens represented the Seleucids in the third period, and then the Roman-Syrian legions in the fourth period. This helpfully possesses some geographic continuity in the identification of the ravens, but I think it leads to a very forced reading of the text of the third period, in which the ravens are barely introduced, and are not active antagonists, even as they are meant to symbolize a powerful interim empire. So, Volkmar thinks that 1 En 90.2 is a precis of the Maccabean Revolt, even though the eagles, not the ravens, are the stated antagonists. See Volkmar, *Eine Neu-Testamentliche Entdeckung*, 14–16.

[67] In my forthcoming article, "Ibises in the Animal Apocalypse," I argue for the translation of the Enochic bird known in Gəʿəz as *hobay* as "ibis" in light of an apparent parallel phrasing in the Testament of Judah.

[68] This will not be exhaustive, but for some representative examples: for Charles, the vultures and kites (*hobay* which I have translated as ibises) are both the Ptolemies. But, since this would be the only time two species are used to refer to a single population, it seems a lacking solution. Olson dubs them the Anatolians/Thracians on analogy with Daniel's four successor kingdoms, but as I have been quite critical of the assumed twinning of Daniel and Enoch's provenance, and the Maccabean hypothesis more generally, I do not find this convincing.

secondary literature with the aid of the assumed historical context as the Seleucids. The previous hypothesis that the ravens represented the Seleucids, however, has nothing to do with any sort of raven-symbolism inherent to Seleucid culture or literature, and everything to do with the role they play in the story.[69] I will attempt an identification based on their role in the story below.

In fact, I find the weakness of our independent evidence on the identity of the other birds, in both the Hellenistic period in which the text has normally been situated, and the Roman period we are exploring now, to be quite telling. We might have here a kind of downstream symbolism, where the Roman eagles set the tone for the related but lesser creatures animating this chapter of the historical allegory. So, since the Romans were symbolized by eagles, it made sense to cast their subsidiaries or functionaries as lesser birds rather than as animals.[70]

There are also ways in which Jewish literary precedent might have encouraged upgrading one bird – the Roman eagle – to a fleet of multiple species of birds. Casting a diverse array of birds would work in concert with Jewish expectations for a conflict at the waning of historical time with a diverse coalition of foreign nations (e.g. Zech 14, Ezek 38–9, 1QM i–iii), though these nations are nowhere imagined as birds outside of Enoch. There is also some

---

Other scholars stick to functional but uncertain identifications, as nebulous allies in Asia Minor (Volkmar), or simply local allies (Schodde). Similarly, but more extensively, Nickelsburg feels exact identifications for all of the birds are outside the realm of probability, understanding the schema to stand for the Hellenistic powers writ large, though I think three (eagles, ravens, and ibises) are still strong possibilities. Below I too will offer a tentative guess from context that the vultures might at one point represent the Judaean forces donated to the Roman suppression of the Revolt by Agrippa, but this is not independently convincing and relies upon the reader accepting a series of my hypotheses along the way.

Tiller makes a very strong case for the vultures as a secondary intrusion into the text, since they never act independently of the eagles, but also because of significant evidence for variation among our Gəʻəz manuscripts when they appear. At this point, this seems a strong explanation of the data. For the cited texts, see Charles, *Enoch or, 1 Enoch*, 204–5; Olson, *A New Reading*, 136–40; Volkmar, *Eine Neu-Testamentliche Entdeckung*, 15; Schodde, *Book of Enoch*, 235; Nickelsburg, *1 Enoch 1*, 396; Tiller, *Commentary*, 31–2.

[69] One of the only details upon which scholars can capitalize is the ravens' black coloring, which lines up with previous uses of "black" coloring for animals in the Vision of the Beasts as representing special wickedness. See Lydia Gore-Jones, "Animals, Humans, Angels and God: Animal Symbolism in the Historiography of the 'Animal Apocalypse' of 1 Enoch," *Journal for the Study of the Pseudepigrapha* 24, no. 4 (2015): 278–9; Bryant, *Cosmos, Chaos*, 74–9; Kosmin, *Time*, 167–8.

[70] A similar argument about how the bird symbolism is employed especially to account for the entry of the Romans can be found in Volkmar, *Eine Neu-Testamentliche Entdeckung*, 15. He also suggests that this is meant to communicate a fundamental shift in power away from the "pagan armies of Asia" to the forces from the West, although I think this assessment might tell us more about nineteenth-century scholarly views on the merits of various Mediterranean empires than it does about first-century understandings of imperial power.

consonance with traditions concerning bloodthirsty birds picking apart corpses at the cusp of the eschaton (e.g. Ezek 39.17–19; Rev 19.17–18, 21), though these birds generally feast on the fodder of the foreign nations (Gog's armies in Ezekiel, the armies of the beast in Revelation), where in Enoch they feed on Israel. It is possible that one or both of these rich tradition-sets contributed to the proliferation of bird-species from a single, potent referent (the eagles) to a multitude under their command, though the symbolism also takes on its own life in the context of the story.

Finally, it may be worth highlighting an incident that may have been the spark that lit the Revolt's fuse: an illicit avian sacrifice. According to Josephus, on a Sabbath in 66 CE:

> When the Judeans had assembled in their meeting [place], a certain Caesarean agitator turned over a belly-style [container], placed it beside their entryway, and began sacrificing birds on it. This provoked the Judeans beyond remedy, on the ground that their laws had been outraged and their site polluted. Whereas the stable and mild [element] considered it proper to retreat to the governors, the factious [element], having become inflamed by virtue of youth, were burning for a fight. (War 2.289–90)[71]

Though the rest of the war would have little to do with sacrifice, of birds or otherwise, this particular event is often given heavy weight in narrative accounts of the war. So, in the recent account of Guy Maclean Rogers: "When the unnamed Caesarean sacrificed some birds on an upturned pot next to the synagogue in Caesarea in 66 CE, he bent the arc of history for Jews."[72] Of course, avian sacrifice had its own place within Jewish practice, and it is therefore hard to see a way that the sacrifice of this bird – however offensively done – could be the sole provider of a symbolic language by which birds came to represent non-Jews. I do not see, in other words, a direct connection with the identification of the birds with various non-Jewish peoples. That said, it is curious to note a bird at the origins of the revolt.

Ultimately, in this section, I have proposed that the eagles are best understood as the Romans, establishing a new context for the Apocalypse of the Birds in the Roman period. I have also provided some initial thoughts on how the political and literary milieu of Roman Judaea might have uniquely informed a writer's choice of avian symbolism as a means of expression, a topic

---

[71] See also Steve Mason, *Flavius Josephus: Translation and Commentary. 1B: Judean War 2* (Leiden: Brill, 2008), 235n1857.

[72] Guy MacLean Rogers, *For the Freedom of Zion: The Great Revolt of Jews Against Romans 66–74 CE* (New Haven: Yale University Press, 2022), 3.

to which I will return below. The literary repercussions of this identification will be explored below, but we first need to explore the (im)possibility of establishing a *terminus ante quem*.

The fate of Jerusalem, and the difficulty of a 70 CE terminus ante quem

I noted above that an external *terminus ante quem* is provided by an early Christian readership (Barnabas, the Testaments of the Twelve Patriarchs) of the Apocalypse of the Birds, which shows that something like the work was likely in circulation by the early second century CE.

Table 6.3 A *terminus ante quem* at 70 CE?

Verses	Summary	My Reading
89.59–64	Commissioning of Seventy Shepherds	
89.65–72a	First Period: Twelve Shepherds	Babylonian Period
89.72b–90.1	Second period: Twenty-Three Shepherds	Persian–Hellenistic Period
90.2–5	Third Period: Twenty-Three Shepherds	Roman Period
90.4	Attacks of Dogs, Eagles, Ibises	
90.6–7	Resistance of Lambs, Apathy of Sheep	
90.8–11	Attacks of Ravens, Rise of Rams and Great-Horned Sheep	
90.12–15	Intervention of Lord of the Sheep on Ram's Behalf	
90.16–19	Battle at End of Seventy Shepherds' Reign	
90.28–9	Removal of Old Jerusalem, Replacement with New Jerusalem	Terminus Ante Quem 70 CE?

Internal evidence for a *terminus ante quem* might be found in two verses narrating the fate of Jerusalem, 1 En 90.28–9.[73] I will suggest in this section that the text as received in Gəʿəz, and as read alongside explicitly post-70 CE accounts such as 2 Baruch, probably indicates a lack of knowledge of the destruction of Jerusalem. But I have previously stated problems inherent in the transmission of historical apocalyptic, and noted the curious witness of both

---

[73] At this point, I break from my previous companions, those early scholars defending a common-era date for Enoch, like von Hoffmann, Volkmar, and Philippi, all of whom place the composition of the work post-70. Philippi and von Hoffmann seem to assume that the destruction of Jerusalem is narrated somewhere herein, though neither are explicit that it is in these two verses, where Volkmar seems to ignore these verses, in pursuit of a second-century date for Enoch writ large. See Philippi, *Das Buch Henoch*, 36–9; von Hofmann, *Der Schriftbeweis*, 1:91; Volkmar, "Beiträge Zur Erklärung," 124–7.

Barnabas and the Testaments of the Twelve Patriarchs, who read this very passage as a prophecy of the events of 70 CE. I therefore want to state that my own reading of the text as lacking an explicit reference to 70 CE does not establish a firm *terminus ante quem*.

Although these verses have been treated in pieces above, they deserve a full translation and engagement here.

90.28: ወቆምኩ ፡ እርአይ ፡ እስከ ፡ ጠወሞ ፡ ለዝኩ ፡ ቤት ፡ ብሉይ ፡ ወአውፅእዎሙ ፡ ለኩሎሙ ፡ ዐማድ ፡ ወኩሉ ፡ ተክለ ፡ ወስኑ ፡ ለውእቱ ፡ ቤት ፡ ተጠውሙ ፡ ምስሌሁ ፡ ወአውፅእዎ ፡ ወወደይዎ ፡ በ፩ መካን ፡ በየማነ ፡ ምድር ።

wäqomku ʾərʾäy ʾəskä ṭäwämo läzəku bet bəluy wäʾäwḍəʾəwwomu läkʷəllomu ʾäʿmad wäkʷəllu täklu wäsənu läwəʾətu bet täṭäwmä məslehu wäʾäwḍəʾəwwo wäwädäyəwwo bäʾḥädu mäkan bäyämanä mədr.

And I stood up to look until he rolled up that old house, and they removed all the pillars, and all the beams and ornaments[74] of that house were rolled up[75] with it; and they removed it and put it in one place in the south of the land.

90.29: ወርኢኩ ፡ እስከ ፡ አምጽአ ፡እግዚአ ፡ አባግዕ ፡ቤተ ፡ ሐዲስ ፡ ወዓቢየ ፡ ወልዑለ ፡ እምነ ፡ ዝኩ ፡ ቀዳማይ ፡ ወአቀሞ ፡ ውስተ ፡ መካነ ፡ ቀዳሚት ፡ እንተ ፡ ተጠብለላት ፡ ወኩሎሙ ፡ ዐማደ ፡ ዚአሃ ፡ ሐዲሳን ፡ ወስና ፡ ሐዲስ ፡ ወዓቢይ ፡ እምቀዳሚት ፡ ብሊት ፡ እንተ ፡ አውፅአ ፡ ወእግዚአ ፡ አባግዕ ፡ ማእከላ ።

wäräʾiku ʾəskä ʾämṣəʾä ʾəgziʾä ʾäbagəʿ betä ḥäddisä wäʿabiyä wäləʿula ʾəmännä zəku qädamay wäʾäqämo wəstä mäkanä qädamit ʾəntä täṭäblälät wäkʷəllomu ʾäʿmadä ziʾähä ḥäddisan wäsəna ḥäddis wäʿabiy ʾəmqädamit bəlit ʾəntä ʾäwḍəʾä wäʾəgziʾä ʾäbagəʿ maʾkälä.

And I looked until the Lord of the sheep brought a new house, larger and higher than that first one, and he set it up on the site of the first one which had been rolled up; and all its pillars (were) new,[75] and its ornaments (were) new and larger than (those of) the first one, the old one which he had removed. And the Lord of the sheep (was) in the middle of it.

---

[74] Literally, "tooth." Emended by Dillmann from ስን (*sən*, "tooth") to ሥን (*śən*, "beauty"), in Dillmann, *Das Buch Henoch*, 285. See also the use of this term in 1 En 98.2.

[75] I addressed in Chapter 2 my choice to alter Knibb's translation of "folded up" to "rolled up," to streamline verses 28 and 29, on analogy with a similar usage in Revelation 6.14.

[76] Though omitted by most manuscripts including Knibb's Rylands 23, *wätäklä ḥäddis* ("new beams") is attested in a few manuscripts including the fifteenth-century Tana 9 and EMML 2080. See Tiller, *Commentary*, 214.

First, we need to address exactly what is being removed, and what is being constructed in its place. In 1 En 90.28, an "old house (*bet bəluy*)" is taken away, and its components placed in the south of the land. Throughout the Vision of the Beasts, and earlier in the Apocalypse of the Birds, it is often the case that "house" is a symbol for Jerusalem (e.g. in the Vision of the Beasts: 89.50–6; in the Apocalypse of the Birds: 89.66–7, 89.72). "Tower (*maḥfäd*)," not mentioned in 1 En 90.28–9, is often a clearly identifiable symbol for the Temple, alongside the house (e.g. in the Vision of the Beasts: 89.50–6; in the Apocalypse of the Birds: 89.66–7, 89.73 especially). One might surmise, then, that the references to the house at 90.28–36 are references to Jerusalem and not the Temple. If this were the case, we might conclude that the Temple would play no role in the eschatology of the Apocalypse of the Birds.

1 En 90.28–9 is a controversial passage in the secondary literature. August Dillmann, Matthew Black, and David Flusser believe the Temple to be obviously present even if lacking an explicit mention.[77] Devorah Dimant and Patrick Tiller have recently defended the idea that the Temple is not present, and the passage is envisioning a wholly new and redesigned Jerusalem. This latter approach assumes that 1 En 90.28–36 might be "solved" by establishing that a consistent house symbolism operative throughout the remainder of the Animal Apocalypse excludes the Temple.[78] I find the pursuit of a consistent house symbolism to overlook inconsistencies in the text, an argument also made by the above-cited voices who assume the Temple might well be mentioned.[79] The pursuit of a consistent symbolism also is compromised by my current hypothesis on the multi-staged compositional history of the Animal

---

[77] In Dillmann, *Das Buch Henoch*, 284; Black, *Book of Enoch*, 278; David Flusser, "Jerusalem in the Second Temple Literature," in *Judaism of the Second Temple Period: The Jewish Sages and Their Literature*, trans. Azzan Yadin (Grand Rapids, MI: Eerdmans, 2009), 45.

[78] Both rely on the concept of consistency. So: "The author is consistent in using the symbol of a house to depict the city throughout the vision," in Devorah Dimant, "Jerusalem and the Temple in the Animal Apocalypse (1 Enoch 85–90) in Light of the Qumran Community Worldview," in *From Enoch to Tobit: Collected Studies in Ancient Jewish Literature* (Tübingen: Mohr Siebeck, 2017), 125. Patrick Tiller relies and builds on an earlier version of Dimant's article, but acknowledges a bit more variability in "house" symbolism. And so, rather than relying on a uniform house symbolism, he reaches the same conclusion that 90.28 does not include the Temple, though on the grounds that "pseudo-Enoch has given consistent and clear attention to the temple and it seems inconceivable that it is here merely assumed." In Tiller, *Commentary*, 46.

[79] There are two other times in which "house" does not and cannot refer to the city of Jerusalem. At 89.36 and 89.40 in the Vision of the Beasts, for instance, "house" seems to most obviously represent the tabernacle. In Tiller and Dimant, these provide an initial symbolism for a "desert camp" which shifts at 89.50 to refer more strictly to Jerusalem. And there is another passage which is not always given its due in the literature, and which I find to be essential in stretching the semantic limits of "house" to include the Temple. In the Apocalypse of the Birds, at 89.76, we read this:

"And the one who wrote the book brought it up, and showed it, and read (it) out in the *houses of the Lord of the Sheep* ['äbyatä 'əgzi'ä 'äbagə', emphasis added] and he entreated him

Apocalypses. We need not control the references in the Apocalypse of the Birds so that they match the interpretative commitments of the Vision of the Beasts. For these reasons, I do not think there is sufficient internal evidence to determine whether 90.28–36 includes the Temple or not. It is plausible given the symbolic inconsistency that the reference to the old and new house at 1 En 90.28–9 is not a strict and exclusive reference to a city without the Temple infrastructure, but rather implicitly includes the Temple. The new house is described as "higher" (ልዑል, *lə'ulä*) than the old house, an attribute previously ascribed to the tower/temple, called the "high tower" (ማኅፈደ ነዋኅ, *maḥfädä näwaḫä*) at 89.73, though height is a relatively generic identifier for impressive structures. And it might be a bit strange to think about ornaments for the city of Jerusalem, rather than the Temple,[80] though we could also think of Rev 21's ornamentation of the New Jerusalem, explicitly imagined without a temple (Rev 21.22), with precious stones (Rev 21.19).

Indeed, the city with templic features found in Rev 21 gains in relevance to our consideration of the Apocalypse of the Birds in light of our ongoing exploration of a first-century provenance for the Enochic work.[81] Its importance has been overlooked because of the disparate provenances assigned to Revelation and the Animal Apocalypse. Tiller, for instance, notes that "the closest parallel to this is Rev 21.22 . . . [but this parallel is not] contemporary with the composition of the An. Apoc., and [is] of little help in understanding the thought of the An. Apoc."[82] Dimant similarly signals that her interpretation of 1 En 90.28 as erecting a kind of "temple-city" finds parallel in Rev 21–2, but she focuses more on second and first-century materials extant at Qumran, in line with the assumed second-century provenance of the Animal

---

on behalf of them, and petitioned him as he showed him all the deeds of their shepherds, and testified before him against all the shepherds."

I have modified Knibb's translation here, as he opts to translate *'äbyatä* as "dwelling," rather than the more obvious "houses," likely in an attempt to preserve the "house" symbolism assumed throughout the text. This translation is corrected by Tiller, *Commentary*, 342; Nickelsburg, *1 Enoch 1*, 387, 389. But in this instance, "house" symbolizes neither earthly city nor Temple, but rather the structures making up what we might imagine to be the heavenly Temple. The example of 1 En 89.76 provides us with a plural rather than the singular we find in 1 En 90.28, but nevertheless, the symbolism, especially if we restrict our sphere of reference to the Apocalypse of the Birds, proves to be a bit slippery.

[80] This point is credited by Devorah Dimant to Flusser, "Jerusalem," 45n2; Hannan Birenboim, "The Halakhic Status of Jerusalem According to 4QMMT, '1 Enoch', and Tannaitic Literature (Heb.)," *Meghillot: Studies in the Dead Sea Scrolls* 7 (2009): 3–17.

[81] Note that von Hofmann, whom Tiller credits as an early voice anticipating his own view of a Temple-free city in 1 En 90.29, understood the Animal Apocalypse to be an allegory of first-century events – namely, the life and career of Jesus. Von Hofmann, *Der Schriftbeweis*, 423. Cited by Tiller, *Commentary*, 46n60, 376.

[82] Tiller, *Commentary*, 47.

Apocalypse.[83] The Apocalypse of the Birds does not precisely match Revelation's eschatology, as it does not explicitly exclude the Temple as does Revelation. But I submit that the interpolation in 1 En 90.28–9 of objects such as columns and ornaments into the description of the house might indicate some conceptual slippage between eschatological city and temple, analogous to Revelation's adornment of the new Jerusalem with decorations associated with the Temple.[84] I think any pursuit of a more concrete envisionment of the role (or non-role) of the Temple in the eschaton will be frustrated by the text.[85] What is ultimately clear is that the entirety of the house, whatever we imagine that to encompass, is taken away, and replaced with something larger and more splendid in the following verse.

We might wish to know: under what circumstances does this old house disappear? It is possible we should understand "removal" or "rolling-up" to be a euphemism for the destruction of Jerusalem and perhaps the Second Temple in 70 CE. While it is a bit counter-intuitive, as removal is not the same thing as destruction, and the Romans go curiously un-mentioned as the agents of its destruction, there are some points speaking in favor of such an understanding.

First, Barnabas, and perhaps the Testaments of the Twelve Patriarchs, read 1 En 90.28 as a prophecy of the events of 70 CE, so the reading was presumably not strange or forced to an ancient audience.

Second, a comparison with 2 Baruch is both vexing and illuminating. There are ways in which Enoch does not meet the standards of demonstration set by 2 Baruch, a decidedly post-70 CE text, and thus encourages us to set a *terminus ante quem* at 70 CE. But there are also ways in which the text participates in the same kind of rhetorical framing and traditional discourse used in 2 Baruch.

Let us begin with their similarities. The idea that angels[86] are responsible for destroying Jerusalem, found at 1 En 90.28, is a curious but not unparalleled tradition also attested in Ezek 10.1–8, and 2 Bar 7.1–8.2. In the former, angels are commissioned to set Jerusalem aflame. The latter, most relevantly for our purposes, contains particular references to the angels' interventions concerning the realia and infrastructure of the Temple:

> And after these [things], I heard that angel, who said to these angels who were holding the torches: "Now destroy and demolish its walls to the

---

[83] Dimant, "Jerusalem," 135.

[84] E.g. the transposition of twelve stones from the high priest's breastplate to be foundation stones of the city walls (Rev 21.19–21, cf. Exod 28.17–20, Ezek 28.13). See also the detailed discussion of transpositions from Ezekiel's Temple to Revelation's New Jerusalem in Dave Mathewson, *A New Heaven and a New Earth: The Meaning and Function of the Old Testament in Revelation 21.1–22.5* (London: Bloomsbury Publishing, 2003), 112–19.

[85] I am joined in the recognition that the passage might not be clear enough to make a concrete call by Loren T. Stuckenbruck, "Reading the Present," 98; Nickelsburg, *1 Enoch 1*, 405.

[86] Note the plural actors, angels in context, in view in the syntax of 1 En 90.28.

foundations, lest the enemies should boast and say: 'We, we have demolished the wall of Zion and we have burned the place of God, the Mighty One.'" And they took me back to the place where I was standing before. Then the angels did as he had commanded them. And when they had broken down the corners of the wall, a voice was heard from within the temple, after the wall had fallen, and it said: "Enter, enemies, and come, those who hate, for he who preserves the house has left [it] behind."[87]

The parallel from 2 Baruch contains more violence than our Enochic account; so, the angels destroy, demolish, and break down the walls, whereas in the Apocalypse of the Birds the components of the city are "rolled up" and "removed." But in both cases, angels seem to be responsible for the take-down of Jerusalem, most especially its architectural elements (pillars and beams in the Apocalypse of the Birds, the walls and cornerstones in 2 Baruch).

Additionally, just previous in 2 Baruch is the famous passage (paralleled in 4 Ezra 10) in which an angel buries in the earth for safekeeping "the curtain, the holy ephod, the cover, the two tablets, the holy garment of the priests, the censer, the forty-eight precious stones, those which the priest wore, and all the holy implements of the sanctuary" (2 Bar 6.7). This passage could shed light on the strange detail that the ornaments of the house are "removed" and moved elsewhere. So, the ornaments in view at 1 En 90.28 might be the valued treasures of the Temple. 2 Baruch might also help color our interpretation of the Enochic tradition regarding the deposition of the old house to a "place in the South of the land."[88] Perhaps, in the Apocalypse of the Birds, we have an optimistic reinterpretation of 70 CE, as Jerusalem and its accoutrements are not understood to be entirely destroyed, but rather, hidden for safekeeping. All that said, in 2 Bar 8.4, the narrative goes on to explain that what remained was obliterated by the Babylonians. The Apocalypse of the Birds does not. Of course, just because 2 Baruch feels the need to account for the humiliating destruction of the Temple by the Babylonians (or Romans, as are the symbolic referents behind 2 Baruch), that does not mean this is a necessary conclusion of any tradent telling the story of the fall of Jerusalem.

There is, then, some evidence for understanding 1 En 90.28 to be clarified with reference to 2 Bar 7–8, representing a reinterpretation of the destruction of Jerusalem within a framework of total divine sovereignty. Certainly the Temple was destroyed, Enoch might say, but it was part of God's plan, and God sent agents to set things in motion on God's behalf. If this were the case, it would demand that we push the *terminus post quem* from 63 BCE to 70 CE,

---

[87] Translation from Stone and Henze, *4 Ezra and 2 Baruch*, 86–7.
[88] For post-70 CE works interested in the idea that the valuable treasures of the Temple were hidden, rather than carted off by the Romans, see 4 Baruch 3.9–11; 18–19 and *Lives of the Prophets* 2.9–14. Note also the precedent for hidden Temple objects established in 2 Macc 2.1–8.

especially given the near-total lack of precedent for a prediction of the Temple's destruction in pre-70 CE literature.[89] Within Second Temple literature, there are a few texts that anticipate the coming of an eschatological temple, or ruminate on the heavenly temple (often cited are 4Q Florilegium and the Temple Scroll). But the idea that the Second Temple would be physically destroyed or removed is nowhere to be found. Lloyd Gaston, exploring possible background to the cryptic Synoptic tradition in which Jesus prophesies the fall of the Temple, states: "We find no background in Jewish apocalyptic before 70 AD for the statement, 'I will destroy this temple and in three days I will build it.'"[90] Given this lack of precedent, if we understood 1 En 90.28 as a prophecy of the destruction of Jerusalem and the Temple, it would most probably belong to a post-70 CE context.

There are, however, strong arguments against understanding 1 En 90.28 as a historical reference at all, let alone as a bona fide reference to the destruction of Jerusalem. The first has to do with weak correspondence with the events of 70 CE. As has already been mentioned, there are substantial discrepancies between a historical event in which the Romans burned the Temple to the ground and sacked Jerusalem, and a literary account in which angels remove the city's component parts, apparently unharmed, to another location.[91] Moreover, the Second Temple was not entirely destroyed. Josephus reminds his readers that the western wall and lofty towers were spared (JW 7.1), which would contrast with the Apocalypse of the Birds's portrait of total removal. The ambiguity of the verses from the Apocalypse of the Birds comes into stark relief in comparison with the "prophecy" of 2 Baruch, which more clearly aligns with the details of what took place in 70 CE, and (along with 4 Ezra) provides a clear and directed portrait of Jewish attitudes towards and in light of these tragic events. If 2 Baruch is the standard by which we gauge "knowledge" of 70 CE, 1 Enoch will come up short.

A second argument against taking the passage as *ex eventu* prophecy has to do with the presence of 1 En 90.28 after seven verses (1 En 90.20–7) which are

---

[89] With the possible exception of the early Synoptic tradition, especially as accessed by scholarship through the Gospel of Mark, though the debate on the date of this tradition should indicate just how shaky such ambiguous references to 70 CE can be in establishing provenance! For a primer on Mark's own precarious dating, see Collins, *Mark*, 11–14.

[90] Lloyd Gaston, *No Stone on Another: Studies in the Significance of the Fall of Jerusalem in the Synoptic Gospels*, Novum Testamentum, Supplements 23 (Leiden: Brill Archive, 1970), 114. Note that 1 En 90.28 gives him the most pause, as he is forced to conclude that "this is the *only* text which explicitly mentions the destruction of the second temple[italics mine]." Of course, Gaston's argument is not only a statement about precedent, but also the grounds by which many scholars date Mark itself, thereby delineating what would be chronologically "precedent" and what would not, so it becomes a bit circular. I am grateful to Mark Letteney for this observation.

[91] We should remember that the Baruch account, apparently post-70 CE, maintains the tone of a violent demolition, even if it transposes agency from the Romans to God's own angelic troops.

clearly eschatological, and as yet unfulfilled. So, 1 En 90.16–31 seems to take place in the time after the completion of the reign of the seventy shepherds, and assumedly, the end of time as it once functioned. (This will be addressed below.) Our narrative expectations for apocalyptic literature have trained us to expect narrations of history to lead into, or be followed by, predictions of the events of the eschaton, but not the other way around.[92] These expectations suggest that 1 En 90.28 belongs to an era not yet experienced by the very earliest audiences.

A third argument against understanding 1 En 90.28 as a reference to 70 CE stems from consideration of the next verse, 1 En 90.29. Even if we were willing to grant that 1 En 90.28 should be read as a pious euphemism for the events of 70 CE, albeit one that is oddly placed in an eschatological narrative, the very next verse predicts the creation of a splendid new house. This "new house" is a decidedly material entity, built with pillars and ornaments. We do not have the immaterial "spiritual" temple of Barnabas. Rather, this is a prediction very like that found in 4QFlorilegium, that there would be an eschatological structure erected in the last days, here on earth.[93]

This event, clearly, did not happen. In order to take 1 En 90.28 as a historical reference, we must assume an implied chronological gap between destruction (v. 28) and rebuilding (v.29). Optimistic observers could have hoped for something to happen in the aftermath of 70 CE, though there is no textual evidence for any kind of imagined delay in these verses. There is, of course, no hard-and-fast time limit on hope, but we might suggest that the text was written close enough to the events of 70 CE that an immediate and glorious rebuilding could still be reasonably anticipated. Whether written before or close to 70 CE, we are still bound to read 1 En 90.29 as an eschatological prediction, which means that 1 En 90.20–7 and 1 En 90.29–38 are entirely eschatological, casting 1 En 90.28 as all the more unexpected in its apparent historical knowledge, and all the more strange in its narrative context. What seems certain is that 1 En 90.29 is not a historical reference. If it is linked to 1 En 90.28, as is syntactically and narratively simplest to conclude, then the balance shifts away from understanding 90.28 historically as well.

The fate of Jerusalem and the Second Temple is not accounted for at any point in the text prior to 1 En 90.28–9. Given the apparent interest of the text in integrating its eschatological schema with historical events, an omission here would be notable. But it is not clear whether these verses demonstrate

---

[92] My thanks to John J. Collins for this suggestion.
[93] 4QFlorilegium, notably, calls this construction the "house which will {be built} for {him} in the last days (הבית אשר {יכין} ל{וא} באחרית הימים)" which suggests that house/Temple symbolism had a natural overlap in roughly contemporary Jewish compositions. Whether this is the case for the stricter symbolism of the Apocalypse of the Birds is uncertain,.

knowledge of the events of 70 CE, though the balance of evidence leans negative. 1 En 90.28–9 is not the only first-century text to be sufficiently ambiguous concerning the events of 70 CE as to give scholars reasonable grounds for reading it as both a reference and non-reference to this "watershed" moment (we might think of debates on the situation of Mark 13.1–2, or Rev 11.1–2). Given these precedents, perhaps our expectations for how clearly demonstrated the events of 70 CE must have been in first-century literature are a bit too grandiose. In any case, my opening remarks demonstrated the significant problems associated with assigning firm end-dates to historical apocalyptic works, especially those with as protracted (and unknown) a transmission history as the Apocalypse of the Birds.

My tentative conclusion is that 1 En 90.28–9 does not reflect knowledge of the events of 70 CE and so does not provide us with a new *terminus post quem*. I have also been skeptical that a non-mention of this event would suffice to assign a *terminus ante quem* to the Apocalypse of the Birds. The firmest *terminus ante quem* is still external, the early second century CE date derived from the witness of Barnabas and the Testaments of the Twelve Patriarchs. Therefore, the window of composition within which we will seek historical identifications, at this point, stretches from the beginning of the Roman occupation of Judaea in 63 BCE to the early second century CE.

Why the Jewish Revolt?

So this is our newly updated task: we are looking for a historical site for primary composition between 63 BCE and the early second century CE in which to situate 1 En 90.1–15.[94]

Among the various events occurring between 63 BCE and the second century CE, I think the early years of the Jewish Revolt present the likeliest setting.[95] The most crucial consideration is the military victory ascribed to the sheep (the people of Israel) against the invading ravens in 1 En 90.12–15. This victory comes after a particularly intense period of persecution and population

---

[94] Like many other scholars (e.g. Martin, Charles, Tiller, and Olson), I understand 1 En 90.15 to be the last "historical" verse, or the last instantiation of *ex eventu* prophecy, with not-yet-actualized events taking place from 1 En 90.16 onwards. Further on this subject, see my forthcoming article, "Where does History End?"

[95] I use the label "Jewish Revolt" to encourage continuity with previous literature on the subject. I am quite persuaded, however, by the argument of James McLaren and Martin Goodman that labeling the events of 66–70 CE a "revolt" rather than a "revolution" unintentionally replicates a pro-Roman stance, in James McLaren and Martin Goodman, "The Importance of Perspective: The Jewish–Roman Conflict of 66–70 CE as a Revolution," in *Revolt and Resistance in the Ancient Classical World and the Near East*, ed. John J. Collins and J. G. Manning (Leiden: Brill, 2016), 203–18.

collapse (1 En 90.2–4), followed by the rise of a resistance movement, and internal-to-Israel schisms over how best to respond (1 En 90.6–11). While there were other military clashes during the period in view, as well as sporadic revolts, only the First Jewish Revolt resulted in a decisive victory of the kind that is narrated by 1 En 90.12–15. Similarly, though there are a few instantiations of Jewish resistance movements in the first centuries BCE and CE, almost none of them achieved any sort of substantial military success. Conversely, a resistance movement culminating in startling military victories against non-Jewish invading forces is the hallmark of the early Jewish Revolt.

Now, it is also possible that there are other historical contexts which would do just as well for which we no longer have independent evidence. One must keep in mind the singular and selective nature of Josephus' work as a source for the events of this period.[96] That said, I have noted that the persecution, resistance, and military victory narrated by the Apocalypse of the Birds point us, in the historical limits we have articulated, to the milieu of the Jewish Revolt. It is therefore worthwhile to build more specific hypotheses on this general probability.

In the upcoming sections, I will provide a set of possible identifications of the events narrated between the Apocalypse of the Birds and what Josephus tells us about the Jewish Revolt, especially the events of 66 CE. I caution the reader again that this approach is just one hypothetical way to "solve" the Apocalypse of the Birds within the chronological limits for composition (63 BCE–second century CE) established above. If accepted, however, the window of probable composition shrinks, with a new *terminus post quem* established by the "last event mentioned" – the events of the early Jewish Revolt in 66 CE.

66 CE: when eagles (Rome), ibises (Egypt), and dogs (non-Jewish neighbors) attack

> (2) And after this I saw in the vision all the birds of heaven coming: the eagles, and the vultures, and the ibises, and the ravens; but the eagles led all the birds; and they began to devour those sheep, and to peck out their eyes, and to devour their flesh. (3) And the sheep cried out because their flesh was devoured by the birds, and I cried out and

---

[96] At this point, I am joining a line of scholarship which matches "literary references" to "history from Josephus." Given the singularity of Josephus' testimony on the Jewish Revolt, there is a certain extent to which some kind of twinning is unavoidable. However, I want to be wary of using the self-serving Flavian work of Josephus as if it states "history" as compared to this "literature." For some reflections on this topic, see Steve Mason, "What Is History? Using Josephus for the Judaean–Roman War," in *The Jewish Revolt Against Rome: Interdisciplinary Perspectives*, ed. Steve Mason and Mladen Popovic (Leiden: Brill, 2011), 155–240.

Table 6.4 The Massacres of 66 CE

Verses	Summary	My Reading
89.59–64	Commissioning of Seventy Shepherds	
89.65–72a	First Period: Twelve Shepherds	Babylonian Period
89.72b–90.1	Second period: Twenty-Three Shepherds	Persian–Hellenistic Period
90.2–5	Third Period: Twenty-Three Shepherds	Roman Period
90.4	Attacks of Dogs, Eagles, Ibises	Massacres of 66 CE?
90.6–7	Resistance of Lambs, Apathy of Sheep	
90.8–11	Attacks of Ravens, Rise of Rams and Great-Horned Sheep	
90.12–15	Intervention of Lord of the Sheep on Ram's Behalf	
90.16–19	Battle at End of Seventy Shepherds' Reign	Beginning of Eschaton
90.28–9	Removal of Old Jerusalem, Replacement with New Jerusalem	*Terminus Ante Quem* 70 CE?

lamented in my sleep on account of that shepherd who pastured the sheep. **(4) And I looked until those sheep were devoured by the dogs and by the eagles and by the ibises, and they left on them neither flesh nor skin nor sinew until only their bones remained; and their bones fell upon the ground, and the sheep became few.** (5) And I looked until the time that twenty-three shepherds had pastured (the sheep); and they completed, each in his time, fifty-eight times.

I have previously argued that the eagles clearly represent the Romans, who are ascendant during what would prove to be a particularly gruesome period of history. The ibises are Egyptian forces of some sort; since we are told that they are led by the Roman eagles, the ibises likely refer to the provincial leadership and/or military forces of Roman Egypt. Though we are told of general eye pecking and flesh-devouring by all the birds in 90.2–3, the text also introduces an early subset of antagonists at 90.4; we are told that the dogs, eagles, and ibises are annihilating the sheep and decimating their numbers. Identifying this trio might provide us with our first entry into the events of the early Revolt in 66 CE.

Dogs are a strange inclusion in the era of the birds, but also a crucial detail clarifying the events possibly in view here. If we are comfortable inheriting the symbolism of the Vision of the Beasts, dogs stand in for the

Philistines. Given the non-existence of the Philistines in post-exilic times, scholars working within the Maccabean hypothesis have stretched the term to refer to non-Jewish populations local to Judea, which is sensible in the abstract, but difficult to substantiate with reference to Ptolemiac- or Seleucid-era conflicts.[97]

We have no difficulty at all, however, supplying a referent from the Roman period. Particularly suggestive evidence comes from the biting Jesus-saying from the synoptic gospels that "even the dogs under the table eat the children's crumbs" (Mark 7.27–8, cf. Matt 15.26–7), used to refer to a woman whose ethnicity is various identified as "Canaanite" (Χαναναία, Matt 15.22), "Greek" (Ἑλληνίς, Mark 7.26), and "Syrophoenician by race" (Συροφοινίκισσα τῷ γένει, Mark 7.26).[98] It is mostly unimportant specifically what ethnicity (if any) we wish to map onto the woman in this Marcan and Matthean passage – it is enough to note that she is marked as other, and a local neighbor of the Southern Levant, against the implied Jewish ingroup.[99] With this parallel in mind,

---

[97] See, for instance, the various suggestions of Olson to the effect that "Philistine" was a) a self-conscious identity claimed by non-Jewish residents of the coastal plane, b) an ideological category of vexation (cf. Sir 50.25–6, Jub 24.28–33), or c) simply another way to say "Greek." In Olson, *A New Reading*, 204–5. But Olson then needs to supply a historical referent for this purported third-second century BCE antagonism, proposing the Tobiad romance from Josephus' *Antiquities*, which does not seem especially strong evidence for an on-the-ground conflict from three centuries prior.

[98] After a survey of biblical, Qumranic, and rabbinic invocations of "dog" symbolism, Adela Yarbro Collins concludes that Mark 7.26 suggests that, "the metaphorical use among Jews of "dogs" for Gentiles was already current in the first century CE." See Collins, *Mark*, 366–7. Implied in her phrasing is the reality that the references cited which use "dog" to denote a non-Jew are nearly all rabbinic, with the exception of this gospel reference (and perhaps, now, the Apocalypse of the Birds).

These references are revisited by Ryan Collman, who argues that the connection between a "dog" epithet and an implied slur against or reference to gentiles is insufficiently attested in the literature, in Ryan D. Collman, "Beware the Dogs! The Phallic Epithet in Phil 3.2," *New Testament Studies* 67, no. 1 (January 2021): 105–20.

Indeed "dogs" as gentiles or non-Jews is not an absolute symbolism in contemporary literature. Amy-Jill Levine notes "dogs" is used elsewhere in Matthew and other early Christian sources simply to refer to apostates more generally (e.g. Matt 15.24; 2 Pet 2.22; Phil 3.2; Rev 22.15). See Amy-Jill Levine, *The Social and Ethnic Dimensions of Matthean Social History*, Studies in the Bible and Early Christianity 14 (Lewiston, NY: Edwin Mellen Press, 1988), 149–50.

However, the Apocalypse of the Birds might actually serve to bolster the case for the metaphorical use of "dogs" for Gentiles in first-century Palestine, as the identity of the dogs in the Vision of the Beasts is certainly the Philistines, and the contextual use of "dogs" in the Apocalypse of the Birds similarly seems to point to non-Jewish neighbors.

[99] On geography, regionalism, and ethnicity in the Marcan pericope, for instance see Sharon Ringe, "A Gentile Woman's Story, Revisited," in *A Feminist Companion to Mark*, ed. Amy-Jill Levine (Sheffield: Sheffield Academic Press, 2001), 83–92.

and the previous instantiation of dogs in the Vision of the Beasts, I propose that the dogs are meant to stand in for non-Jewish neighbors, implicated in a serious standoff against the sheep. That they are not represented by birds suggests that they are qualitatively different from the other antagonists. They are a hold-over from the era of the beasts, and seemingly less powerful for their dissociation from the Roman fountainhead of power. As a reminder, their companions in their evil pastimes are the eagles (Romans) and ibises (Roman Egyptians).

This trio not only devours the sheep (an unfortunate, though common activity, already perpetrated by lions, tigers, and wild boars in the Apocalypse of the Birds), but is described with an intensifying clause: "they left on them neither flesh nor skin nor sinew until only their bones remained; and their bones fell upon the ground, and the sheep became few." This particular complaint alludes not only to oppression and persecution, but to mass killing to the point of a kind of population collapse.[100] It is especially peculiar that it is not ascribed to all the birds (as in 90.2–3), but to this particular subset – non-Jewish residents of the surrounding region, Romans, and Egyptians.

The same trio is tagged for their accumulating body counts by Josephus in his account of the skirmishes of 66 CE leading into the First Jewish Revolt. Concerning the dogs, we might look to the urban turmoil in Syria in 66 CE. We have both literary evidence that some sort of conflict between Jews and their non-Jewish neighbors had been roiling for a while (e.g. JW 2.284–93), as well as archaeological evidence which supports a growing cultural and ethnic separation.[101] In Josephus' telling, existing tensions exploded into large-scale conflict with the "butcher[ing]"[102] of 20,000 Jews in Caesarea (JW 2.457), followed by, as Uriel Rappaport memorably put it, "Jews and pagans slaughter[ing] each other wherever the two resided in close proximity."[103] With his traditional flair for the dramatic (and a clearly marked incentive to indicate causes for the revolt outside of direct Jewish–Roman antagonism given his place within Flavian Rome), Josephus goes on to tell of Jews massacred by the "Syrians" (2.461)

---

[100] Remember that population collapse was one of the key traditions mirrored and received by multiple testaments within the Testaments of the Twelve Patriarchs.

[101] See, for instance, the conclusions of the ceramics analyses in Andrea M. Berlin, "Romanization and Anti-Romanization in Pre-Revolt Galilee," in *The First Jewish Revolt: Archaeology, History and Ideology*, ed. Andrea M. Berlin and J. Andrew Overman (London: Routledge, 2003), 57–73; Andrea M. Berlin, "Identity Politics in Early Roman Galilee," in *The Jewish Revolt against Rome: Interdisciplinary Perspectives*, ed. Mladen Popović (Leiden: Brill, 2011), 69–107.

[102] All translations from book 2 of Josephus' Jewish War/Judaean War come from Mason, *Flavius Josephus*.

[103] In Uriel Rappaport, "Jewish–Pagan Relations and the Revolt against Rome in 66–70 CE," *Jerusalem Cathedra* 1 (1981): 84.

in Scythopolis (2.466–8), Ashkelon and Ptolemais (2.477), Tyre, Hippos, and Gadara (2.478).[104]

As for the eagles of the Apocalypse of the Birds, there are a good many candidates for historical episodes of Roman aggression in the run-up to the Jewish Revolt, with a notable one being in 66 CE, which Josephus takes great pains to narrate diplomatically.[105] Though placed a bit before the violent meltdowns in Syria, we might think of the reckless "savagery" (JW 2.308) enacted in Jerusalem under the auspices of Procurator Gessius Florus, who whips, tortures, and crucifies 630[106] Judaeans, even women, children, and (most shockingly to Josephus) equestrians (JW 2.293–306).

Concerning the ibises, or Egyptians, we might remember that around the same time (66 CE), Alexandrian Jews were the victims of another massacre.[107] According to Josephus, a conflict between the Alexandrians and Jews exploded when the governor, Tiberius Alexander, "let loose on" the Jews by way of two Roman legions, who set out to kill, plunder, and burn, leaving 50,000 corpses in their wake.[108] It is this conflict that, according to Josephus,

[104] Josephus, however, is at pains to demonstrate that this outburst was, at least in part, prompted and perpetuated by Judaean aggression. The opening massacre in Caesarea happens at the same day and time, "as if because of otherworldly knowledge" [on the part of the Caesareans], as the Judaean attack of the Roman garrison (2.457). Then, the attack on Caesarea occasions Judaean retaliation against their Syrian neighbors, and so the cycle of violence takes off, in Josephus' account. If the Apocalypse of the Birds is attempting to retell these same events, it is striking that, against Josephus' account, the sheep are portrayed as entirely defenseless, slaughtered apropos of nothing at all, and not fighting back in the least, at least at this point in the story.

[105] "Eagle–sheep conflicts" might be the very episodes that Josephus might have been least inclined to place in immediate proximity to the outbreak of the revolt, lest he place the responsibility strictly upon Roman shoulders. Even in the account just mentioned, Florus comes off as an unusually bad egg. Florus prompts his own conflict by taking an enormous amount of money from the Temple, counts himself deeply offended by the inevitable local outcry, assembles a kind of kangaroo court accusing his opponents of sedition, and then, despite the Judaeans' last-minute attempts at appeasement, sends his forces on a murderous spree. He is a singularly terrible procurator, suggesting that it is Florus, rather than a "Roman," who is to blame. In his assessment of the events, Josephus reflects upon "the novelty of the Roman savagery (JW 2.308)," as if it were a break from the norm. Clearly, for Josephus, there can be bad eagles, but there is nothing wrong with the species. This is not the case for the Apocalypse of the Birds, for whom the eagles are uniformly evil – at least, at this point in the narrative.

[106] Or 3,600. See the note in Mason, *Flavius Josephus*, 264n1974.

[107] Although this is a uniquely bloody event in Egyptian Jewish history, a region for which we often have a greater number of extant sources than others, Josephus is our only source for this particular incident. See the abbreviated treatments in Smallwood, *Jews Under Roman Rule*, 364–6; Joseph Modrzejewski, *The Jews of Egypt: From Rameses II to Emperor Hadrian* (Princeton: Princeton University Press, 1995), 185–90; Aryeh Kasher, *The Jews in Hellenistic and Roman Egypt: The Struggle for Equal Rights* (Tübingen: J.C.B. Mohr, 1985), 24–5.

[108] This is no doubt an inflated number. However, Mason suggests that, even if the number is not especially accurate, there was likely a horrendous massacre of some sort, "which would otherwise be subject to disproof in Josephus' Rome." See Mason, *Flavius Josephus*, 356n3050.

Figure 6.4 Ibis [left] next to Reclining "Aegyptos." Silver Denarius of Hadrian. 134–38 CE, American Numismatic Society

makes up the mind of Cestius Gallus to end the Jewish conflicts once and for all. Cestius Gallus sends the Twelfth Legion and an associated coalition into Judaea, an important event that will be treated shortly.

But, for now, Josephus' account could provide us with possible identifications for the trio of massacres narrated by the Apocalypse of the Birds at 90.4. The dogs (non-Jewish civilians), ibises (Roman Egyptian legions and auxiliaries), and eagles (Roman troops stationed in Jerusalem, under the auspices of Procurator Gessius Florus), are blamed by the Apocalypse of the Birds for the death of thousands of sheep (Jews). We should return, once more, to the clarification of the Apocalypse of the Birds that the eagles led all the other birds, though *not* the dogs (i.e. Syrian civilians), who are placed outside the avian framework. Indeed, after their initial outburst, the dogs will not be heard from again. Instead, we are firmly in the era of the birds, and it is a bloody one indeed.

This set of identifications, if correct, would also confirm something about the nature of bird symbolism in the Apocalypse of the Birds that I suggested above. Rather than representing purely ethnic or national groups, as in the Vision of the Beasts, birds stand in for regional administrations and military forces. They are categorically differentiated from dogs, who symbolize non-military local people. This approach becomes especially fitting if we imagine that all the birds have been assigned symbols in keeping with the core identification of eagles representing Roman military might. In 1 En 90.4, we are therefore given a portrait of sporadic conflicts with both regional military units and local residents alike, hastening towards resistance and escalation, for which a close match can be found in the opening acts of the Jewish Revolt.

The rise of the revolutionaries and the calamity of Cestius Gallus in 1 Enoch 90.6–16

I will now offer a thorough integration of 1 En 90.6–16 and the portrait of the early years of the Jewish Revolt extracted from Josephus' account. I will argue

Table 6.5 Resistance and the Calamity of Cestius

Verses	Summary	My Reading
89.59–64	Commissioning of Seventy Shepherds	
89.65–72a	First Period: Twelve Shepherds	Babylonian Period
89.72b–90.1	Second period: Twenty-Three Shepherds	Persian–Hellenistic Period
90.2–5	Third Period: Twenty-Three Shepherds	Roman Period
90.4	Attacks of Dogs, Eagles, Ibises	Massacres of 66 CE
90.6–7	Resistance of Lambs, Apathy of Sheep	Early Judean Resistance
90.8–11	Attacks of Ravens, Rise of Rams and Great-Horned Sheep	Cestius Gallus's Campaign
90.12–15	Intervention of Lord of the Sheep on Ram's Behalf	Rebuffed Siege of Jerusalem, Victory at Beth Horon
90.16–19	Battle at End of Seventy Shepherds' Reign	Beginning of Eschaton
90.28–9	Removal of Old Jerusalem, Replacement with New Jerusalem	*Terminus Ante Quem* 70 CE?

1 En 90.6–7 introduces the conflict between Judaean revolutionaries (lambs) and quietist, or pro-Roman Jews (sheep), escalating with the early clashes of the Revolt.[109] The ravens at 1 En 90.8–15 are the legionary forces mustered out of Syria and led by Cestius Gallus, marauding through Galilee and the Judaean countryside, and besieging Jerusalem in 66 CE. The great-horned *dabela* introduced at 1 En 90.9 is a leader of the Judaean revolutionary forces, with an exact identification probably beyond our ken given the reticence of Josephus' account at this point. The other rams (*dabelat*) rallying around him represent fellow revolutionaries. And the account at 1 En 90.12–15 of a desperate battle culminating in an unexpected Jewish victory would refer to the calamity of Cestius Gallus' of 66 CE, in which obvious Roman military advantage disintegrated into the legion's inexplicable (according to Josephus) retreat from Jerusalem, and a rout at Judaean hands at Beth Horon. These readings are made possible by the historical-interpretative framework propounded above.

(6) And small lambs were born from those white sheep, and they began to open their eyes, and to see, and to cry to the sheep. (7) But the sheep did not cry to them and did not listen to what they said to them, but were extremely deaf, and their eyes were extremely and excessively blinded. (8) And I saw in the vision how the ravens flew upon those

---

[109] Sheep will reemerge as protagonists at 90.19, in a section of text I consider to be eschatological. In these final historical events, some sheep are clearly found lacking. But it is unclear whether the entire category of sheep is compromised, or whether the focus has simply shifted elsewhere. It is syntactically ambiguous for instance, whether the sheep and the *dabelat* run to the great horn at 90.10, or if it only the *dabelat* who do so.

lambs, and took one of those lambs, and dashed the sheep in pieces and devoured them. (9) And I looked until horns came up on those lambs, but the ravens cast their horns down; and I looked until a big horn grew on one of those sheep, and their eyes were opened. (10) And it looked at them, and their eyes were opened, and it cried to the sheep, and the rams saw it, and they all ran to it. (11) And besides all this those eagles and vultures and ravens and cranes were still continually tearing the sheep in pieces and flying upon them and devouring them; and the sheep were silent, but the rams lamented and cried out.

The passage above tells of dissent within the ovine ranks, as a younger generation (if we are to take the lamb/sheep opposition reasonably literally) achieve some sort of awakening, and appeal to the older generation (90.6). The older generation stubbornly resists the lambs' rallying cry (90.7), and both groups continue to face persecution by the birds. The birds, now represented by the ravens, take (kidnap?) a lamb, and continue their onslaught of the sheep (90.6). The lambs grow horns, becoming rams, though the ravens do away with these quickly enough (90.9). When one of the sheep grows an especially big horn himself, the rams rally behind this leader (90.10). The sheep, apparently unmoved by the ongoing witness and lament of the rams and the continued violence of the birds, remain silent (90.11).

We are looking for a group of Jews who were dissatisfied with the violence of the status quo and the rise of leaders among them.[110] Separately, we must identify a group of Jews at odds with those lambs, and apparently in line with (or, at least, not in open defiance of) the excesses of their foreign overlords. More, we need to account for a new antagonist, represented by the ravens, who show up after the eagles, ibises, and dogs have exercised their aggression, and become the key enemy from this point forwards.

I will suggest that the action of the ravens in the passage points us to the potentially deadly but failed campaign of Cestius Gallus and his Syrian legion (ravens), alongside the emergence of a Judaean resistance movement in the mid-60s CE (lambs/rams), and its activities from 66 CE onwards.[111]

---

[110] In previous scholarship, this was either identified as an allegory for the development of a breakaway religious group (e.g. Regev, Kister), or the rise of the Maccabean resistance (Charles et al).

[111] For detailed military-historical studies of this campaign, see Mordechai Gichon, "Cestius Gallus's Campaign in Judaea," *Palestine Exploration Quarterly* 113, no. 1 (January 1981): 39–62; B. Bar-Kochva, "Sēron and Cestius Gallus at Beith Horon," *Palestine Exploration Quarterly* 108, no. 1 (January 1976): 13–21; Steve Mason, "Nero's War I: The Blunder of Cestius Gallus," in *A History of the Jewish War: AD 66–74* (Cambridge: Cambridge University Press, 2016), 281–334. Note however their varied estimations of Josephus' account as a "historical" source. So, Gichon opens by averring, "the narrative of the campaign of 66 CE seems to be reasonably objective and trustworthy. Meanwhile, with characteristic suspicion, Mason remarks that "Josephus' *War* is no diary or even documentary." See Gichon, "Gallus's Campaign," 39; Mason, "Nero's War I," 283.

Returning to the timeline of the Jewish Revolt, following the conflicts of 66 CE explored in conversation with 1 En 90.4 above, the next key player to enter the field (according to Josephus) is Cestius Gallus, the legate of Syria. Apparently in an attempt to quell the bloody conflicts happening in cities all over Judea and Syria, he assembled a coalition of forces from the various legions stationed in Syria, which was augmented with tribute forces sent by local kings (2.500–2).[112] Most notably and infamously participating was the entire Legio XII Fulminata.[113] Traveling south, this coalition force left great destruction in its wake. Josephus variously reports the burning of Chabulon and its countryside (JW 2.503–5), the slaughter of 8,400 in Joppa (JW 2.507–9), and the plundering and burning of Narbata (JW 2.509), before the forces run into minor trouble in Galilee (2.511).

In the context of this southward push, Josephus introduces the action of a group for whom he has no great love – the "factious and bandit-like" element of Jewish resistance that opposes the Roman troops (flying in the face of what Josephus calls "good advice" to remain calm and welcome Cestius Gallus). This group achieves a stand-off at Mt Asamon (JW 2.511–12), and initial (albeit minor) success, but the rebel force is eventually destroyed resulting in 2,000 Judeans killed (JW 2.512). Josephus' account has already provided some hint of a resistance before (apparently, the Judaeans "disposed of" 2,000 of Cestius

Figure 6.5 Bronze Coin Countermarked by XII Fulminata with Thunderbolt and Eagle. Neopolis, Samaria. Domitian, 82–83 CE. BnF 1968/227

---

[112] Mason suggests that the other forces were likely drawn from the III Gallica, VI Ferrata, and X Fretensis, whose emblems were a bull (III and VI) and boar (X). See also Guy MacLean Rogers, *For the Freedom*, 161–3.

[113] Regarding the countermarks and emblems of the XII Fulminata, usually represented by a thunderbolt, though the pan-Roman eagle appears on some countermarks as shown in Figure 6.5, see C. J. Howgego, "The XII Fulminata: Countermarks, Emblems and Movements under Trajan or Hadrian," in *Armies and Frontiers in Roman and Byzantine Anatolia*, ed. Stephen Mitchell (Oxford: B.A.R., 1983), 41–6; Gregory G. Brunk, "A Hoard from Syria Countermarked by the Roman Legions," *Museum Notes (American Numismatic Society)* 25 (1980): 63–76.

Gallus's abandoned troops at 2.506), but this conflict and subsequent clashes with the Syrian forces formally indicate the emergence of a resistance movement and Judaean military force. (Josephus does not care to enumerate its early development in detail). When Cestius Gallus's forces draw near to Jerusalem around the time of Sukkot, Judaean forces successfully rebuff them (JW 2.517–19). Particular leaders of this resistance are marked by Josephus as the most excellent fighters in the estimation of the Judaeans – Monobazus, the convert-king (cf. Ant 20.75) of Adiabene, Niger the Perean, and Silas the Babylonian. Also named, and apparently playing a pivotal role in rebuffing the Syrian forces, is Simon bar Giora (JW 2.520–1).

This kind of historical landscape provides a strong match for the scenario narrated in 1 En 90.6–16 of the Apocalypse of the Birds, especially if we grant that just previous, 90.4 narrated the violent clashes of 66 CE.

In verse 6, the birth of the lambs and the opening of their eyes fits well with the rise of the rebel movement (no doubt with roots pre-66 CE but becoming especially vocal in the early years of the Revolt). Note that the exact circumstances which allowed for the development of such a resistance group in Judaea at the time, its leaders, and the nature of the organization and ideology of its constituent forces, is a matter of much debate among scholars.[114] If the Apocalypse of the Birds does, in fact, have the resistance in mind, as the context suggests, it does not provide much independent clarification on these matters, or what exactly they "saw" on the other side of their blindness. That said, the clarification that the lambs grow horns indicates the political/militaristic ramification of their rallying cry, and a looming conflict over leadership, territory, and governance with the Roman Empire. In the Vision of the Beasts, although there are no explicit mentions of multiple horns, Saul, David, and Solomon are each depicted as a ram (härge).[115] While

---

[114] There are no shortage of attempts to explain the outbreak of the Jewish Revolt. For a few recent treatments pointing to further literature, see Martin Goodman, "Current Scholarship on the First Revolt," in *The First Jewish Revolt: Archaeology, History and Ideology*, ed. Andrea M. Berlin and J. Andrew Overman (London: Routledge, 2003), 15–24; James McLaren, "Going to War against Rome: The Motivation of the Jewish Rebels," in *The Jewish Revolt against Rome: Interdisciplinary Perspectives*, ed. Mladen Popović (Leiden: Brill, 2011), 129–54; Steve Mason, "Why Did They Do It?: Antecedents, Circumstances, and 'Causes' of the Revolt," in *A History of the Jewish War: AD 66–74* (Cambridge: Cambridge University Press, 2016), 199–280.

[115] Bryan finds five individuals represented by the ram: Jacob, Saul, David, Solomon, and Judas Maccabeus. Note that there is a philological problem with Jacob as ram. The Gəʻəz of 1 En 89.12, 14 identifies Jacob as a sheep (በግዕ, bägəʻ), and never as a ram. It is only 4Q205 6, which seems to roughly correspond to these verses, that apparently identifies Jacob as a ram (דכר). Neither the admittedly fragmentary Aramaic, nor the Gəʻəz, mentions Jacob's horns explicitly. Perhaps in this way, Jacob is separated from the other rams.

Nevertheless, with this litany framing the parameters, he concludes "the ram represents royal leadership in the Animal Apocalypse." If this were really the case, however, it is hard to imagine why there are so *many* rams in 1 En 90.9–11 – they cannot all be kings. See Bryant, *Cosmos, Chaos*, 69.

this is not the same Gəʿəz word as that used to describe the horned-lambs (in 1 En 90.6–19, the term is always *dabela*), if we assume some continuity in symbolism, then horned animals are kings, or, to be a bit more abstract, some sort of national or political leader.[116] In the Apocalypse of the Birds, the aggression of the ravens is always focused on the horns in particular, rather than the animal to whom the horns belong. This construction of conflict is not unlike that found in other invocations of horns in the Hebrew biblical literature: so, in Lam 2.3, where the Lord in vengeance destroys "every horn of Israel."[117] In 1 En 90.9, "the ravens cast their horns down." Later, in 1 En 90.12, the ravens "wished to make away with its horn," and, in 1 En 90.13, respond to the wishes of the other birds "that they might dash the horn of that ram in pieces." Similarly, in 1 En 90.16, all the birds work together to "dash that horn of the ram in pieces." It is the horn, not the animal, that causes the friction between sheep and birds. This unusual but consistent phrasing, combined with the continuity between the horned-ram Israelite kings of the Vision of the Beasts and the horned-lambs of the Apocalypse of the Birds, suggests that horns symbolize the bearer's claim to political authority, kingship, or military autonomy.

The intransigent sheep of 1 En 90.7 would then symbolize the opposition this group faced from their fellow Judaeans, some of whom were apparently more interested in cooperating with (or ignoring the excesses of) those whom the Apocalypse of the Birds depicts as avian oppressors. This particular group of people, and the perspectives they embodied, are well represented in Josephus' account of the Revolt – probably a bit too well represented, given his literary interest in demonstrating the quiescent and peaceable instincts of his Jewish countryfolk to his Flavian readers. King Agrippa's impassioned speech urging the Judaeans to reconsider their march towards war (JW 2.345–401) is a heavily worked-over Josephan compositional accomplishment, but speaks to a likely historical perspective nevertheless.[118] And accounts of pro-Roman Jews (or, at least, Jews uncomfortable with the looming rebellion) can be

---

[116] Horns have a rich symbolic life in the literature collected in the Hebrew Bible. For horns symbolizing kings or political powers, see Ps 75.10, 148.14, Zech 1.21, Ezek 29.21, Lam 2.3, 17, Jer 48.25, and, of course, Dan 8. Specifically applied to David: 1 Sam 2.10, Ps 132.17. Applied to an heir of David: Luke 1.69. There is also some precedent within Hebrew biblical literature for identifying political leaders, both Israelite and non-Israelite, as rams. See the summary in Bryant, 70–1.

[117] I am grateful to Martha Himmelfarb for this reference.

[118] Concerning Agrippa's speech, even if Josephus put words in his mouth, it is not entirely devoid of value to the historian of the early years of the Revolt. As Tessa Rajak puts it, "we are obliged to treat Agrippa's words as evoking the ambiguous stance of the native governing class, superficially pro-Roman (in varying degrees), but harbouring doubts and even deep resentments." In Tessa Rajak, "Friends, Romans, Subjects: Agrippa II's Speech in Josephus' Jewish War," in *Jewish Dialogue with Greece and Rome: Studies in Cultural and Social Interaction* (Leiden: Brill, 2000), 158.

found throughout Josephus' wider account.[119] Within Josephus' own story, we might think of the elite party in Jerusalem that feared what would happen if Jerusalem fell "outside the pact" with Rome (JW 2.414–16), the cities such as Sepphoris that Josephus congratulates for cooperating with Cestius Gallus's forces (JW 2.512), or the messengers sent by Agrippa II to try to talk down the rebels in exchange for a "trustworthy pardon from the Romans" (JW 2.523–6).[120] Related to this group, though likely excluded from this identification as their actions hardly count as "silence," would be the Herodian house who contributed forces to the Romans, and the Syrian campaign in particular.

In keeping with this evidence for a historical group inclined to cooperate with the Roman forces, or as Paul Kosmin calls them in a different context "the Jewish allies of empire,"[121] note the Apocalypse of the Birds's specific charge against the sheep, found in verse 11: all the birds are tearing the sheep to pieces, but the sheep remain silent. The sheep are charged with apathy in the face of the birds' persecution and oppression, the apparent outcome of the extreme blindness and deafness introduced in 90.7. This blindness has been forcibly visited upon them, as the birds peck out their eyes in 90.2, and they are thus robbed of their ability to see the injustices being visited upon them. The text additionally chastises the sheep with a failure to hear (which is credited to the birds' attack on their eyes), and failure to cry out (rebel) against their oppressors.

If pro-Roman Judaeans (or, simply, quietist Jews) are the sheep of this section of the Apocalypse of the Birds, and we come to understand the text to be a contemporary statement of support for the Revolt, it makes sense that these sheep are given the most damning description of any of the many generations of blinded sheep. They are not just blind, but "extremely deaf, and their eyes were extremely and excessively blinded." The heightened rhetoric at this point could suggest the felt proximity of this conflict to the Apocalypse of the Birds's own milieu. Despite all the characters being animals, it sounds quite personal.

Moreover, given what we know about how elite a phenomenon literacy and the composition of complex works would have been in Roman Judaea, it seems we are privy here to a clash amongst the region's elite. The disdainful literary voice behind the Apocalypse of the Birds chastening the blind sheep marks one elite disparaging another, and may support scholarship on the Revolt

---

[119] See the work of Julia Wilker, "Josephus, the Herodians, and the Jewish War," in *The Jewish Revolt against Rome*, ed. Mladen Popović (Leiden: Brill, 2011), 271–89; Julia Wilker, "'God Is with Italy Now:' Pro-Roman Jews and the Jewish Revolt," in *Jewish Identity and Politics between the Maccabees and Bar Kokhba*, ed. Benedikt Eckhardt (Leiden: Brill, 2012), 157–87.

[120] On numismatic, archaeological, and literary evidence for Sepphoris as an especially peace-seeking city, see Eric M. Meyers, "Sepphoris: City of Peace," in *The First Jewish Revolt: Archaeology, History and Ideology*, ed. Andrea M. Berlin and J. Andrew Overman (London: Routledge, 2003), 110–20.

[121] Kosmin, *Time*, 168.

which emphasizes conflict among the ruling class as a key factor in the outbreak of war.[122]

The ravens are introduced in detail in 1 En 90.8. They take out their aggression on lambs and sheep alike, and will be the key antagonists of 1 En 90.8–19.[123] Importantly, the key antagonists now are not the Roman eagles, nor the Roman-Egyptian ibises, nor the non-Judaean "civilian" dogs, but a new group for whom we must account. In the immediate aftermath of the events of 66 CE symbolized by 1 En 90.4, and the subsequent emergence of a resistance in 1 En 90.6–7, I have suggested that the ravens refer to the legionary forces mustered by Cestius Gallus. Further evidence in favor of this identification will be presented below, in an exploration of 1 En 90.12–15, which depicts a retreat followed by a humiliating defeat for the ravens, not unlike that experienced by the Syrian coalition.

It might strike the reader as curious that the preeminent antagonists would be ravens rather than eagles – Cestius Gallus was a Roman senator, and it would make sense to think of him as a ready candidate for eagle symbolism. The events in question, when told by Josephus, are told as if Cestius Gallus was the protagonist and decision-maker, in keeping with Josephus' own character-driven style

---

[122] E.g. Martin Goodman, *The Ruling Class of Judaea: The Origins of the Jewish Revolt against Rome A.D. 66–70* (Cambridge: Cambridge University Press, 1987).

[123] Knibb's translation of verse 8 also includes the detail that the ravens "took one of those lambs (ላ፩ እምእልኩ መሐሰ, lä 1'əm'ələku mähäsə' in Rylands 23)." In some versions of the Maccabean hypothesis, this is taken to be a reference to the murder of Onias III, though this can be a problematic identification (why is Onias a lamb, rather than a sheep?)

Volkmar (*Eine Neu-Testamentliche Entdeckung*, 18) and more recently Pierre Cardinal ("L'Apocalypse des animaux aux sources de la Grande révolte juive," (paper, Graduate Enoch Seminar, Montreal, May 20, 2014), 5), have read 90.8 as a reference to Judas the Galilean's revolt against the census imposed by Quirinus. Judas the Galilean was remembered by Acts 5.37, and Josephus (JW 2.118, Ant 18.9) as the leader of a failed revolt against the Romans. Josephus' account, in particular, is at pains to place Judas the Galilean in a direct lineage with the (soon-to-fail) revolt of 66–70, both intellectually (he names him at Ant. 18.9 as the founder of the "fourth philosophy" which he credits as the ideology fueling the later revolt against Gessius Florus and events following), and genealogically (he suggests the leader of the First Revolt, Menahem, was his son, at JW 2.433). I think Judas the Galilean is a fine identification, though can easily imagine others (Theudas, also remembered as a failed revolutionary at Acts 5.36 and Ant 20.97–8; "the Egyptian" remembered at Acts 21.38 and JW 2.261–2) fitting the bill, depending who the writers of the Apocalypse of the Birds wanted to place in their genealogy of the currently fomenting revolution.

Note, however, that Tiller observes textual variation provided by our manuscripts on this verse, and opts to translate instead "seized those lambs" (ለእልኩ መሐሰ, läzäku mähäsə', from the seventeenth–eighteenth-century mss BM 491, as "the only reading that does not pose major difficulties," in Tiller, *Commentary*, 352. I think Tiller's standards for syntactic coherence are a little too high here, as most manuscripts have some version of one lamb in view. But, nevertheless, the variation at this point does make it difficult to lean overmuch on this verse as an anchor for historical identification.

of historiography.¹²⁴ But there is no single or superlative avian antagonist in the Apocalypse of the Birds – the scene features groups of birds. There is, then, no problem with a purported failure to represent Cestius Gallus (or any particular Roman official) in appropriate eagle garb, as the Apocalypse of the Birds does not care overmuch to account for the workings of individual antagonists. We are led to the hypothesis that the ravens represent Roman legionary forces: in the specific historical context proposed here, they would symbolize the forces assembled by Cestius Gallus, including the entire Twelfth Legion.

Another factor that might strengthen this identification is the use of black feathers atop the helmets of some legionary soldiers during the late Republic and early principate. It is important to caution that we have, to the best of my knowledge, little information about the specific outfitting of the Twelfth Legion during this campaign, or the first century more generally.¹²⁵ Theories about what the Twelfth might have worn must draw conclusions based on literary and material evidence from other regions and periods.¹²⁶ Nevertheless, since other factors suggest that we might identify the ravens as first-century legionaries, it is worth summarizing the evidence for feathers, and black feathers in particular, as a feature of Roman legionary military dress, as it might have presented to first-century observers like those behind the Apocalypse of the Birds.

Figure 6.6 Legionaries with Feathered Crests, Bronze Sestertius of Gaius/Caligula Rome, 39–40 CE. American Numismatic Society

[124] On Josephus' individually focused history in its Roman historiographic context, see Christina Shuttleworth Kraus, "From Exempla to Exemplar? Writing History around the Emperor in Imperial Rome," in *Flavius Josephus and Flavian Rome*, ed. Jonathan Edmondson, Steve Mason, and James Rives (Oxford: Oxford University Press, 2005), 181–200.

[125] Josephus provides a brief description of the Roman armies (with no particular legion in view) in *War* 3.93–7. He mentions that the footmen have helmets and breastplates (οἱ πεζοὶ θώραξιν πεφραγμένοι καὶ κράνεσιν), and the cavalry do as well (κράνη δὲ καὶ θώρακες ὁμοίως τοῖς πεζοῖς ἅπασιν). The question of plumes or feathers is not addressed.

[126] For a general treatment that addresses the possibilities and limitations of our evidence for Roman armor from Augustus to Hadrian, see J. C. Coulston and M. C. Bishop, *Roman Military Equipment: From the Punic Wars to the Fall of Rome*, 2nd ed. (Oxford: Oxbow, 2006), 73–123.

Polybius, writing in the second century BCE, describes heavy infantry (*hastati*, and he implies the same is the case for *principes* and *triarii*), wearing:

> As an ornament a circle of feathers with three upright purple or black feathers about a cubit in height, the addition of which on the head surmounting their other arms is to make every man look twice his real height, and to give him a fine appearance, such as will strike terror into the enemy (*Histories*, 6.23.13).[127]

Though these heavy infantry divisions were eliminated by the Marian reforms, we have evidence stretching into the early imperial period for helmets adorned with high feathers. Soldiers outfitted with three feathers alike to Polybius' description atop their helmets can be found on some Late Republican coins (as the silver denarius above). Though the style and form of helmets changed over time and varied regionally, the decoration of legionary helmets with feathers seems to have continued into the early Imperial period.[128] To my knowledge, we do not have archaeological remains of legionary helmets in Judaea and Syria (nor would we expect feathers or crests to have survived the centuries!), but representational evidence from across the empire shows the imaging of legionary soldiers with feathered plumes, as well as horsehair crests and other height-creating helmet decorations.[129] If the kinds of black-feathered infantry plumes Polybius saw in the second century BCE were still in use, we might arrive at an even closer identification. But I think that a band of legionary soldiers bedecked with feathered helmets, or even just the popular imagination of such a force so outfitted, could provide a possible, though speculative, referent for a swarm of birds more generally. Their coloring as black ravens could owe to use of black feathers, or simply a recourse to coloring negative creatures black as happens occasionally in the Vision of the Beasts.[130]

---

[127] Translation from F. W. Walbank and Christian Habicht, eds., *Polybius: The Histories, Books 5–8*, trans. W. R. Paton, vol. 3, Loeb Classical Library 138 (Cambridge, MA: Harvard University Press, 2011).

[128] On early Imperial helmet helmets, with particular attention to crests/plumes/feathers, see H. Russell Robinson, *The Armour of Imperial Rome* (New York: Scribner, 1975), 140–3; Raffaele D'Amato and Graham Sumner, *Arms and Armour of the Imperial Roman Soldier from Marius to Commodus, 112 BC–AD 192* (London: Frontline Books, 2010), 109–20. See also the particular case study of the helmets of Legio V Alaudae in M. C. Bishop, "Legio V Alaudae and the Crested Lark," *Journal of Roman Military Equipment Studies* 1 (1990): 161–4.

[129] See especially the drawings from friezes and sculpture in Robinson, *The Armour of Imperial Rome*, 142.

[130] E.g. the line of Cain are black bulls (85.3); the three sons of Noah are colored at 89.9 as white (Shem), and black and red (Ham and Japheth, though it is unclear which is which); Esau is a black boar (89.12). But assuming the universality of white/black symbolism can be problematic, on which see Rothschild, "Ethiopianising the Devil."

Figure 6.7 Soldier with Helmet Feathers, Silver Denarius. Rome, 100 BCE. American Numismatic Society

In 1 En 90.9, we are introduced to a key figure: a great-horned sheep (interestingly, not originally a lamb!) who will be the leader of the ovine forces from this point forward – a ram (*dabela*) at the helm of a larger force of rams (*dabelat*).[131] It can be obscured, if we focus only on identifying individual rams, that this horned sheep is *not* the only leader that emerges. Rather, in the first part of the verse, we hear that multiple lambs have grown horns, but these horns were summarily cast down by the ravens. The "great horn" of 90.9, as he is often known,[132] is not the only "horn," though he is the most successful. Nor is he the last, as a group of rams (*dabelat*) rally around him in verse 10, and lament over the devouring of the sheep in verse 11. It is possible that the great-horned ram of 90.9 is imaged as a sole aspirant to a throne, if we think the horns indicate the bearer's claim to Davidic kingship.[133] This is complicated, however, by the rather variegated use of horns in Hebrew biblical works to refer to leaders and powers of all sorts (compare, for instance, the "horns of the righteous" of Ps 75.10 with the cutting off of the "horn of Moab" of Jer 48.25). The ram with the great horn appears to be a leader of a breakaway

---

[131] Remember that previous treatments of the "ram" symbolism of 1 En 90.9–19 have collapsed the "rams" of the Vision of the Beasts, always called by "*härge*," and the Apocalypse of the Birds, where they are always called "*dabela*."

[132] Although he might not have been the very first to use the title, part of the fun of the coining can be traced to R. H. Charles who matched the "great horn" with the "greatest of all the Maccabees." In Charles, *Enoch or, 1 Enoch*, 208.

[133] Outside of the Apocalypse of the Birds, a horn is connected with a Davidic king at 1 Sam 2.10, Ps 132.17, and applied to Jesus as a purported heir to David at Luke 1.69. One treatment of the great horn of 90.9 as the purported heir to Davidic kingship can be found in Regev, "The Ram and Qumran," 12–14. This is different than scholarship which seeks to place the white bull of 1 En 90.37–8 in a Davidic lineage, e.g. Young S. Chae, *Jesus as the Eschatological Davidic Shepherd: Studies in the Old Testament, Second Temple Judaism, and in the Gospel of Matthew* (Tübingen: Mohr Siebeck, 2006), 97–113.

group, joined by allies also bearing horns. The great horn is the key target in verses 12–19, but it is not necessarily the case that we have in view a singular figure; we simply have a literary account singularly focused on his actions. We are seeking a leader around whom others rallied, who was in command of those who (in the estimation of the text) did not submit to the attacks of the birds. The early years of the Revolt provide a great many possibilities. I noted above the named figures that Josephus associates with resistance to the Syrian legions' southward campaign in 66 CE: Monobazus, the convert-king (cf. Ant 20.75) of Adiabene, Niger the Perean, Silas the Babylonian, and Simon bar Giora (JW 2.520–1). Any of these, not to mention others not named by Josephus, would make fine candidates for the ram with the great horn.[134]

It might be worth highlighting one name among the resistance fighters who would ascend to the highest heights of leadership (and ignominy, in Josephus' account): Simon bar Giora.[135] Scholars have long thought he might have presented himself, or been understood by his contemporaries, as a messianic figure, not least because he apparently robed himself in purple and stood among the razed Temple when surrendering to the Romans (JW 7.29).[136] It is hard to escape from the confines of Josephus' account and anticipate how or if to correct for ways that Josephus might have handled or downplayed such messianic pretensions in the Revolt's prominent leader.[137] Independent of whether we understand the evidence to cross the threshold at which we understand Simon bar Giora to be a messianic figure, or not, his prominence in the events of 66 CE and onwards might suggest him as the great horn of 90.9. In this case, the Apocalypse of the Birds would provide evidence for contemporaries placing Simon bar Giora's career in an apocalyptic and eschatological progression, evidence scholars have long sought to uncover by reading against the grain in Josephus' apologetics.[138]

---

[134] It also might depend how flexibly the Apocalypse of the Birds understands the category of sheep. If it does not include converts, then, for instance, Monobazus would no longer be an acceptable candidate.

[135] See Otto Michel, "Studien zu Josephus: Simon Bar Giora," *New Testament Studies* 14, no. 3 (April 1968): 402–8.

[136] For a critique of this and other arguments adduced in favor of Simon bar Giora's supposed messianicity, see Gideon Fuks, "Some Remarks on Simon Bar Giora," *Scripta Classica Israelica* 8–9 (1988): 106–19.

[137] A review of scholarship on Simon bar Giora and way forward, can be found in Matthew Novenson's recent suggestion that Josephus does not attend to messianic claims as an aspect of the Revolt because his Flavian audience would have no idea what that meant: "Josephus is constrained by literary convention, by his own chosen project of cultural translation from a Jewish idiom to a Roman one." In Novenson, *The Grammar of Messianism*, 136–48.

[138] I do not understand the Apocalypse of the Birds to illuminate Simon bar Giora's self-understanding or whether he fashioned himself as a messiah – an avenue of inquiry I understand to be basically beyond our ken.

Even if a precise identification between the great horn and Simon bar Giora is not sustained — and I do not think there is enough evidence to make it confidently — the Apocalypse of the Birds nevertheless demonstrates how some observers saw the political leaders of the Revolt standing at the brink of the fast-approaching horizon of the eschaton. It is important to remember that the "historical" account of 1 En 90.6–19 will soon be supplanted by the onset of the eschaton beginning at 1 En 90.20, featuring the construction of the Throne of Judgement, and the incineration of offending stars and sheep in fiery abysses that will crack open the very center of the earth. Though it does repay our attention to seek earthly identifications for some of the people and events of the Apocalypse of the Birds, we should always keep in mind the work's imminent pivot towards the obliteration and transcendence of these historical concerns. But, for now, we can return to the historical progression.

> (12) And those ravens battled and fought with it, and wished to make away with its horn, but they did not prevail against it. (13) And I looked at them until the shepherds and the eagles and those vultures and ibises came and cried to the ravens that they should dash the horn of that ram in pieces; and they fought and battled with it, and it fought with them and cried out that its help might come to it. (14) And I looked until that man who wrote down the names of the shepherds and brought (them) up before the Lord of the sheep came, and he helped that ram and showed it everything, (namely, that) its help was coming down. (15) And I looked until that Lord of the sheep came to them in anger, and all those who saw him fled, and they all fell into the shadow before him.

In this section, the ravens are soundly defeated. The syntax is ambiguous, but it is possible to imagine the shepherds, eagles, ibises, and vultures joining in on the (soon-to-fail) assault. Speaking against the supposition of a joint assault might be the clarifier later at 1 En 90.16 that, "all the eagles and vultures and ravens and ibises gathered together and brought with them all the wild sheep, and they all came together and helped one another." There the narration takes pains to indicate a different kind of coalition than had previously existed. If we do grant a joint assault, this need not disqualify the Syrian legionaries' campaign of 66, as this was a coalition force assembled not only from the entire Twelfth Legion, but also selected troops from other legions stationed in Syria,[139] as well as troops contributed by Antiochus IV king of Commagene, Soaemus king of Emesa, and the Judaean's very own Agrippa II (*JW* 2.500–1). I have suggested the ibises symbolize Egyptian actors, and the violence imagined to be

---

[139] Mason suggests the three legions based in Syria at the time: III Gallica, VI Ferrata, and the X Fretensis, in Mason, *Flavius Josephus*, 357n3067.

happening in parallel to but far distant from the events in view.[140] This leaves the eagles (Romans more broadly understood), ravens (Syrian legionary forces), and vultures (unknown) to represent the coalition force being confronted in Palestine, which is not altogether unsatisfying. As such, we may hazard a contextual guess that the vultures, as lowest and most loathsome of the avian species, could represent (to the Apocalypse of the Birds) the traitorous forces of Agrippa: Judaeans recruited to fight their own. But, regardless of which other birds we envision to be participating in the assault, the ravens are quite doomed.

When our Enochic allegory left off in verse 11, the ongoing marauding of the ravens had been met with apathy by the sheep, and lamentations by the rams. A leader (the "great horn") had emerged and will now be the key target of the avian aggression. That said, although the text implies that the ravens are taking on a single opponent, the great-horned ram, 1 En 90.10 establishes that the rams have run to join their leader, and are presumably fighting alongside him even here.

In this first battle account, the ravens unsuccessfully attack the rams (1 En 90.12), but are urged on not only by the other birds, but also by the shepherds, to continue their assault (1 En 90.13). In the face of the aggression of the ravens, the ram appeals to God for aid, and receives a vision indicating that help is on the way (90.14). God comes, and the forces flee. The birds are not yet entirely defeated, nor are they entirely removed from the field of battle, as the avian coalition is reassembled by verse 16. The fact that they have fled is still, however, especially remarkable within the text. Over and against the similar account in verses 16–18, we might note the first encounter features the embattled plea for aid by the ram (90.13), a personal revelation to the ram (90.14), and the curious detail that the forces flee apparently only because they "saw him" (either God, or perhaps the ram). Apparently, in this first episode, dire circumstances are resolved with a surprising and divinely engineered retreat.

Within the context of the Jewish War, there is a retreat so surprising that even Josephus concludes it must have been divinely sponsored: the sudden and inexplicable raising of Cestius Gallus's siege of Jerusalem in 66 CE.[141]

---

[140] We have very little information on what happened in Alexandria or Egypt after the massacre of 66 CE, though I think a safe assumption is that relations were not positive. Additionally, I think it very difficult to assign geographic provenance to works of the period, but the focus on Palestinian events might suggest a Palestinian provenance for the Apocalypse of the Birds, and the sidelining of Egyptian events might discourage an Egyptian (Alexandrian) provenance.

[141] Here I am paraphrasing T.E.J. Wiedemann: "An attempt by Cestius Gallus, the governor of Syria, to suppress the rebellion with military might in November 66 failed (the reasons for his withdrawal were inexplicable to contemporaries as they are to us) ..." In T. E. J. Wiedemann, "Tiberius to Nero," in *The Augustan Empire, 43 BC–AD 69*, ed. Alan K. Bowman, Edward Champlin, and Andrew Lintott, The Cambridge Ancient History 10, 2nd ed. (Cambridge: Cambridge University Press, 1996), 251.

We do not have a non-Josephan account of the particulars of this military campaign, but at least some early imperial historians remembered Cestius Gallus's campaigns as unsuccessful. Tacitus recalls, "When Cestius Gallus, governor of Syria, tried to stop it [i.e. the conflict that began under Gessius Florus], he suffered varied fortunes and met defeat more often than he gained victory (*Histories* V.10)."[142] And Suetonius knows the basics of his ignominious rout (*Life of Vespasian* 4.5).

According to Josephus' account (JW 2.527–37), Cestius Gallus's forces defeated the local countryside rebels, brushed off the urban resistance forces of Jerusalem, had smashed their way to the Northern approach of the Temple, and were "preparing to burn the gate of the Temple" (JW 2.537). Much to the dismay of Josephus, who notes multiple times that the War could have been avoided if Cestius Gallus had taken Jerusalem then (as Josephus does not doubt he could have done), this is as far as the siege goes, as it is abruptly abandoned, and the forces retreat. It is worth quoting his account in full:

> (2.538): Terrible alarm seized the insurgents: already many were running away from the city in the belief that it was going to be captured presently. It happened that the populace was encouraged by this and, to the extent that the worthless [fellows] might relent, they themselves would approach the gates with the intention of opening [them] and welcoming Cestius as benefactor – (539) who, if he had persevered a short while with the siege, would indeed have quickly taken the city. But I think that because of the worthless [fellows], God, having already been turned away even from the holy places, prevented the war from reaching a conclusion on that day. (540) Cestius, at any rate, since he comprehended neither the despair of those being besieged nor the state of mind among the populace, suddenly recalled his soldiers and, having thought better of his hopes, though without a single blow, most astonishingly decamped from the city. (541) At this unexpected turnabout of his, having regained their courage the bandits ran out against those at the rear and destroyed large numbers of the cavalry and infantry.

Josephus, gauging the political, military, and emotional advantage to be firmly in Cestius Gallus's court, is clearly shocked by the retreat, which takes place "without a single blow." Even if we correct for Josephus' quite high opinion of the Roman forces, the fact that the siege had reached the Temple walls made it a very serious threat indeed, and its abrupt lifting was a reprieve so shocking as to be baffling. The exact circumstances of the siege have some

---

[142] Translation from Tacitus, *Histories: Books 4–5. Annals: Books 1–3*, trans. Clifford H. Moore and John Jackson, Loeb Classical Library 249 (Cambridge, MA: Harvard University Press, 1931).

structural parallels with the failed Assyrian siege of Jerusalem narrated in Isa 37 and 2 Kgs 19, so we might suspect Josephus of some literary patterning.[143] Nevertheless, regardless of the specifics of the siege, it is clear that Jerusalem did not fall while Cestius Gallus was campaigning in the region, which would have been a curious "miss" for the legionary forces that warranted explanation.

I suggest identifying 1 En 90.12–15 with the non-conquest of Jerusalem. The core event, non-Jewish enemies pressing a would-be successful attack and then abruptly fleeing, is draped in loose and allusive language, but nevertheless spottable. The desperate plea of the leading-ram at 1 En 90.13 implies truly dire circumstances, and the advancement of Cestius Gallus's forces to Jerusalem and (if Josephus is correct) to the very gate of the Temple would certainly qualify. The curious historical memory that Jerusalem was spared in 66 CE would be "solved" by both Josephus and the Enochic text with recourse to divine intervention (albeit with very different valuations of that intervention).[144] Finally, the location of this anecdote in Josephus' account (insofar as his account matches the historical progression) after the rise of an organized resistance matches up nicely with the narrative progression of the Apocalypse of the Birds's historical allegory.

If we grant the identification, we still face a few open questions, but these largely come down to the limitations on our general knowledge of the period. We are still no closer to learning the identity of the great-horned ram, other than confirming what we had already suspected, that he was a leader of an organized resistance. We also have no evidence of a Jewish rebel leader claiming to receive personal revelation from God at this juncture in the Revolt. These two concerns can be easily countered with further consideration of the nature of Josephus' account. So, there are a great many military maneuvers and encounters between the Syrian forces and Judaean rebels narrated by Josephus, which would have required some kind of military leadership to ever get off the ground. Josephus is, however, apparently reluctant to give names with any kind of consistency, generally content to present the rebel forces as an undifferentiated rabble. There must have been key leaders in this chapter of Judaean military history, but Josephus does not provide them.[145] Given the fact that his is our only literary account of the Jewish Revolt, their names are likely lost to us. Similarly, the unparalleled nature of the account of personal revelation to a rebel leader is unsurprising, as Josephus would certainly not give a "parallel"

---

[143] I am grateful to Martha Himmelfarb for this suggestion.

[144] Though note that Josephus offers two explanations: at 2.531, he also suggests "The camp prefect Tyrannius Priscus, along with most of the cavalry commanders, having been enticed by money from Florus, dissuaded him from the undertaking."

[145] See the comment of Shaye Cohen: "Nowhere in this long account does Josephus name the generals of the Jews." In Shaye Cohen, *Josephus in Galilee and Rome: His Vita and Development as a Historian* (Leiden: Brill, 1979), 196.

account, even if he knew it.[146] To that end, we might even understand the curious fact that Josephus ascribes the turning back of the siege to divine intervention to be a pessimistic refraction of a popular cultural memory in which God stepped in to save the Temple.

A final concern remains. If the "house" or "tower" (to use the symbolism of the Apocalypse of the Birds) was under threat, why is this not made explicit in the text? One possible response is that the Apocalypse of the Birds has intellectually divested from the Temple infrastructure. When last it was mentioned, at 1 En 89.73, the text laments that all the bread upon the table was impure. When it is next mentioned, at 1 En 90.28, it is the "old house." Another response might take note of the especially compressed nature of the historical parallels at 1 En 90.1–19 (three verses devoted to the third period, etc.), and suggest that this implies a greater level of assumed familiarity on the part of the audience. The Apocalypse of the Birds, from 1 En 90.1 and onwards, is apparently no longer working off a literary account that we know,[147] and might be narrating contemporary events. If this is the case, and we assume an implied audience capable of filling in the blanks, perhaps certain qualifiers did not need to be stated. I think some combination of the two would suffice to explain why a failed siege of the house or tower might be an event noted for its significance, but left devoid of specifics.

After the ravens flee, the narrative ends with the curious note that "they all fell into the shadow before his face"[148] (ወወድቁ ፡ ኩሎሙ ፡ ውስተ ፡ ጽላሎቱ ፡ እምቅድመ ፡ ገጹ, wäwädqu kʷəllomu wəstä ṣəlalotu ʾəmqədmä gäṣṣu). As Knibb comments, "the expression is a little obscure."[149] Some have seen it as a loose reference to a moral "falling" for the ravens, something like falling into blindness or a state of darkness.[150] It is unclear to me, however, that the ravens could ever possibly have been understood to be in a state of awakening, from which they would then have to "fall," and I find this unconvincing. Others spot more historical heft behind the verse. In one influential version of the Maccabean

---

[146] In considering what Josephus has omitted, I am thinking alongside Arnaldo Momigliano's question concerning "What Josephus did not see," and Tessa Rajak's subsequent reframing concerning "What Josephus did see, but could not write about." See Arnaldo Momigliano, "Ciò Che Flavio Giuseppe Non Vide," in *Settimo Contributo Alla Storia Degli Studi Classici e Del Mondo Antico* (Rome: Edizioni di Storia e Letteratura, 1984), 305–17; Arnaldo Momigliano, "What Josephus Did Not See," in *On Pagans, Jews, and Christians* (Middletown: Wesleyan University Press, 1987), 108–19; Tessa Rajak, "Cio Che Flavio Giuseppe Vide: Josephus and the Essenes," in *Josephus and the History of the Greco-Roman Period* (Leiden: Brill, 1994), 141–60.

[147] Always keeping in mind Molly Zahn's challenge to theoretically account for reliance upon now-lost sources, from Zahn, *Genres of Rewriting*, 186–7.

[148] This is likely the Lord of the Sheep's face, given the divine apparition just narrated, though it could also be the great-horned ram.

[149] In Knibb, *Enoch: A New Edition*, 2:213.

[150] See Johannes Paul Gotthilf Flemming, *Das Buch Henoch: äthiopischer Text* (Leipzig: J. C. Hinrichs, 1902), 119; Olson, *A New Reading*, 219.

hypothesis, 1 En 90.15 represents an allegorization of the "rout" of Lysias' first expedition, concluding with Lysias' "shameful" flight from the scene of battle.[151] As should be quite clear by now, I do not subscribe to the Maccabean hypothesis, and I additionally would note that the Lysias battle proposed as the event behind the verse is a rout followed by a retreat, where we are apparently looking for a retreat followed by a rout. That said, this kind of reading clarifies the victory encoded within the allusive phrasing of the verse. There is something more than simply fleeing being narrated, carried by the ambiguous qualifier that the ravens "fell into the shadow."

In the aftermath of Cestius Gallus's abortive siege of Jerusalem, the fortunes of his forces sharply declined. In the process of withdrawing, they apparently suffered "considerable injury," as a slow-moving super-coalition in retreat proved vulnerable to the lightweight guerilla attacks of Judaeans moving outside the city (JW 2.542–3). This difficult retreat was only a prelude to what was easily the most humiliating defeat visited upon the Romans by Jews of this period, or, as Jodi Magness puts it, "one of the most humiliating defeats ever suffered by the Roman army,"[152] the battle at Beth Horon.

> (2.547) Now while the Judeans applied less pressure in the open spaces, once they [the Romans] had become crowded together into narrow spaces and the descent, those [Judaeans] who had gone ahead were blocking them from the exit route, whereas others were pushing those at the rear down into the ravine, and the whole horde, having strung themselves out above the neck of the road, kept coating the column with projectiles. (548) And there, with the infantry being completely stumped as to how to come to their own aid, the predicament was yet more precarious for the cavalrymen. For they were not able to proceed in order down the road while being bombarded, and the ascent up to the enemy was not horse-friendly. (549) This way and that were crags and ravines, into which they fell and were obliterated. One had neither a place for escape nor a plan for defense, but in utter helplessness they were reduced to wailing and lamentation in their despair . . .[153]

---

[151] So Jonathan Goldstein, *II Maccabees*, vol. 41A, Anchor Yale Bible Commentaries (New Haven: Doubleday, 1983), 402–3; Goldstein, *I Maccabees*, 40–1.

[152] In Jodi Magness, *Masada: From Jewish Revolt to Modern Myth* (Princeton: Princeton University Press, 2019), 144.

[153] In case the Greek of 2.549 is of interest: τὸ δὲ ἐπὶ θάτερα κρημνοὶ καὶ φάραγγες, εἰς οὓς ἀποσφαλέντες κατεφθείροντο, καὶ οὔτε φυγῆς τις τόπον οὔτε ἀμύνης εἶχεν ἐπίνοιαν, ἀλλ᾽ ὑπ᾽ ἀμηχανίας ἐπ᾽ οἰμωγὴν ἐτράποντο καὶ τοὺς ἐν ἀπογνώσεσιν ὀδυρμούς. There are no close textual parallels to the Apocalypse of the Birds (nor would I expect there to be!), though "crags and ravines into which they fell (κρημνοὶ καὶ φάραγγες, εἰς οὓς ἀποσφαλέντες)" is a decent analogue to "falling into shadow." Text from Benedikt Niese, *Flavii Iosephi Opera* (Berolini: Apud Weidmannos, 1887).

At this point, night falls, and Cestius Gallus uses the cover of darkness to sneak some (though not all) of his soldiers out of the topographic death-trap created by his fateful attempt to move his forces via an escape-route covered by Judaean archers holding the high ground. At the end of things, Josephus reports 5,300 infantry and 480 cavalry killed. So ended the series of events that would go down in history (or, at least, in Josephus' own account) as "the calamity of Cestius" (ἡ Κεστίου συμφορά) at JW 2.556.

The so-called calamity of Cestius is an excellent candidate for the rout of 1 En 90.15, not only because of its chronological location after the flight from Jerusalem, and the fact that it is a stark defeat of Jewish adversaries just when we are looking for a defeat, but also because of the ways the battle might shed light on what it means for the ravens to "fall into shadow." I find it intriguing, though not convincing independent of the other considerations, that Josephus' narrative of the account has so much to do with the ways that this defeat was made possible by the topography of Beth Horon, by the crags and ravines into which Josephus claims the Romans fell to their deaths.[154] Many soldiers, quite literally, fell into darkness.

But ultimately, if we strictly follow the order of the words-in-order, 1 En 90.15 teaches us to look for a withdrawal followed by a massive defeat. And the failed siege of Jerusalem and Battle of Beth Horon provide exactly that, in rapid succession – as Mordecai Gichon sums up "the calamity of Cestius": "the retreat degenerated into a rout."[155]

Experiences of 66 CE: the Apocalypse of the Birds between optimism and regret

The proposed setting of 66 CE, and the Battle of Beth Horon in particular, presents an especially tantalizing climax for the Apocalypse of the Birds.

First, "the calamity of Cestius" was so calamitous for the Romans, not just because of his ignominious defeat, but because one of the legions (presumably Legio XII Fulminata) lost its aquila, or eagle standard, to the Judaean forces. In the account of Suetonius, in *Life of Vespasian* 4.5:

> There had spread over all the Orient an old and established belief, that it was fated at that time for men coming from Judaea to rule the world. This prediction, referring to the emperor of Rome, as afterwards appeared

---

[154] The topography of Beth Horon today doesn't exactly support Josephus' portrait of an epic, "alpine" landscape. Bar-Kochva and Gichon work to defend the accuracy of Josephus' account by shifting the scene of battle slightly, where Mason is happy to say that Josephus merely dramatized the scenery for narrative effect. See Bar-Kochva, "Šēron and Cestius Gallus," 18–19; Gichon, "Gallus's Campaign," 58–9; Mason, "Nero's War I," 300–1.

[155] In Gichon, "Gallus's Campaign," 57.

from the event, the people of Judaea took to themselves; accordingly they revolted and after killing their governor, they routed the consular ruler of Syria as well, when he came to the rescue, and took one of his eagles.[156]

Losing an eagle standard to a scuffle in a provincial revolt was a thoroughly disgraceful affair for a Roman legion.[157] As Graeme Ward puts it, "the history of Legion XII Fulminata of Rome was nothing for its soldiers to boast about in the mid-first century CE."[158] But to the Judaean victors, it would be a portentous symbolic victory. Josephus' reflections in his *Life*, written largely after his *War*, emphasize the importance of this particular event in fueling support for the Revolt:

[Cestius] came indeed, and engaged in battle, but he was defeated when many of the men with him fell. And this misstep of Cestius became a misfortune for our entire nation, for those who had devoted themselves to the war were even more excited by this and, having defeated the Romans, hoped to the end (*Life* 24).[159]

Say we imagine the Apocalypse of the Birds to take shape in the heady times after this unexpected triumph, having robbed the Roman forces of their eagle, and with the last-narrated event being, perhaps, the Battle of Beth Horon. Perhaps we have, in this historical moment, something of the spark that animates not only the optimism of the Enochic account, but also the curious literary investment in the symbolic device of birds, instead of beasts, and eagles most specifically. I have already noted that the Roman eagles were the most important among the rest, with the other birds assigned as secondary considerations. I have also noted ways in which Romans and eagles paired neatly together in Jewish and Christian literature of the period; so there is no lack of precedent for the pairing in the Apocalypse of the Birds. But if we are convinced of historical identifications culminating in the victory at Beth Horon, we might reflect on how symbols made materially manifest and implicated in historical events (such as the aquila wrested from Roman hands) might prompt, encourage, or develop literary encapsulations of these same symbols. Perhaps

---

[156] Translation from Suetonius, *Lives of the Caesars*, trans. J. C. Rolfe, vol. 2, Loeb Classical Library 38 (Cambridge, MA: Harvard University Press, 1914).

[157] Note that Josephus doesn't mention the loss of the eagle in his account. Remembering his statement later in book 3 that the eagle standards represent "whoever may be their adversaries, an omen of victory," perhaps it was sufficiently embarrassing as to warrant exclusion in the tale woven for his Flavian audience.

[158] Graeme A. Ward, "'By Any Other Name': Disgrace, Defeat, and the Loss of Legionary History," in *Brill's Companion to Military Defeat in Ancient Mediterranean Society*, ed. Jessica H. Clark and Brian Turner (Leiden: Brill, 2018), 284.

[159] Translation from Steve Mason, *Life of Josephus* (Boston: Brill, 2003).

the imagined Roman eagles of the Apocalypse of the Birds were created in a time when a quite-real Roman eagle had been taken. The Apocalypse of the Birds, if we understand it as having taken shape in these historical climes, is not just resistance literature, relying more or less arbitrarily on contemporarily relevant symbols, but a nose-thumbing parody, building its world with literary equivalents to material blocks stolen from its enemies.

Either way, concluding the way it does, the Apocalypse of the Birds is an optimistic work. Remember that 1 En 90.15 is the final verse which narrates already-completed history, and everything thereafter belongs to the still-to-come eschaton. History thus draws to a close with a fabulous, divinely engineered victory. We will soon read the normal (for apocalypses) litany of judgments and punishments needed to right all the extant wrongs, but the last identifiable historical event is that of a shocking and Lord of the Sheep-supported victory. This is not always how we imagine apocalyptic literature to be most suitably fostered. It is much more common to posit chaos, crisis, or catastrophe as compositional sparks.[160] (And there are certainly no shortage of social,cultural, and political complaints in the Apocalypse of the Birds!) But if we take the device of *ex eventu* prophecy seriously as a method by which we establish probable provenance, and we are satisfied that we can track the references in the Apocalypse of the Birds up until the early years of the Jewish Revolt, then we are forced to recognize that history, as we know it, ends on a high note. This supports a slightly different imagination of what might trigger the composition of apocalyptic literature, proposed by Bernard McGinn:

> It is not so much crisis in itself, as any form of challenge to the established understanding of history, that creates the situation in which apocalyptic forms and symbols, either inherited or newly minted, may be invoked. These challenges may be positive as well as negative, unexpected strokes of good fortune as well as terrible disasters.[161]

My conclusions here work in concert with McGinn's observations and speak against the ways that apocalyptic has been twinned so closely with the perception of social and cultural tides turning against its intended audience.

Note that this optimistic framework was apparently shared by other participants in the events of 66 CE. So, although the eschaton did not materialize as

---

[160] So, in the influential phrasing of Adela Yarbro Collins, "apocalyptic literature is often defined as literature evoked by a crisis." In the case of Revelation, she modifies this to include *perception* of crisis, not just what historians gauge to represent crisis-level deprivations and oppressions. See Adela Yarbro Collins, *Crisis and Catharsis: The Power of the Apocalypse* (Philadelphia: Westminster Press, 1984), 85.

[161] Bernard McGinn, *Visions of the End: Apocalyptic Traditions in the Middle Ages* (New York: Columbia University Press, 1979), 31.

the Apocalypse of the Birds predicted, the conviction that the tenor of Jewish history had absolutely and fundamentally changed with the victories of 66 CE was shared by other observers of the Jewish Revolt. We have both numismatic and documentary evidence that Jews in the half-decade after 66 (before its tragic ultimate outcomes were fully realized) understood the Revolt to open up a new chronological era, by which coins and documents could be dated. Seven documents from the caves in Wadi Murabba'at, carbon-dated with 95% probability to a date within a range that includes the First Jewish Revolt,[162] are dated according to formula ranging from "year three of the freedom of Jerusalem," to "year two of the redemption of Israel in Jerusalem."[163] The last, dating from 71 CE, simply states, "year six."[164]

Similarly, the thousand-plus coins that we have dating to the Jewish Revolt date themselves from 66 forwards.[165] We have coins bearing dates stretching from Years 1–5. Some bear slogans similar to our documents, like "for the freedom of Zion" (לגאלת ציון), or "Jerusalem the holy" (ירושלים הקדושה) as on this coin (Figure 6.8) dated to year 3.

---

[162] And, most crucially, excludes the Bar Kokhba revolt. Said differently, given the reliance of the document upon what appears to be revolutionary-styled dating (year X of the freedom of Jerusalem, etc.), with the Bar Kokhba revolt eliminated, this makes the hypothesis that the documents within the stated range (91 BCE–78 CE) most probably belong to the era of the First Jewish Revolt quite strong. See Hanan Eshel, Magen Broshi, and Timothy A. J. Jull, "Four Murabba'at Papyri and the Alleged Capture of Jerusalem by Bar Kokhba," in *Law in the Documents of the Judaean Desert*, ed. Ranon Katzoff and David Schaps (Leiden: Brill, 2005), 45–50.

[163] Proposing and building on a Revolt-era dating, see Hanan Eshel, "Documents of the First Jewish Revolt from the Judean Desert," in *The First Jewish Revolt: Archaeology, History, and Ideology*, ed. Andrea M. Berlin and J. Andrew Overman (London: Routledge, 2002), 157–63. The texts in question were originally published by Józef T. Milik, "Textes Hébreux et Araméens," in *Les Grottes de Murabba'at*, ed. Pierre Benoit, Roland de Vaux, and Józef T. Milik, Discoveries in the Judaean Desert 2 (Oxford: Clarendon Press, 1961), 67–205.

[164] Note that this last dates to 71 CE. To explain the short formulation, Eshel summarizes Yadin's conclusions "they could not write 'Year 6 to the Redemption of Israel' or "Year 6 to the Freedom of Jerusalem," because Judaea was already under Roman rule and the Temple had been destroyed. Therefore, they simply wrote "Year 6." The motivations proposed here both explain the cessation of the use of this chronological reckoning, while also reinforcing the optimism inherent in its very existence, fueled by the turning of the tide spotted in the events of 66.

[165] For some recent studies of the this enormous cache of numismatic data, see I. Goldstein and J. P. Fontanille, "A New Study of the Coins of the First Jewish Revolt against Rome, 66–70 CE," *American Numismatic Association Journal* 1, no. 2 (2006): 9–32; Robert Deutsch, "Coinage of the First Jewish Revolt Against Rome: Iconography, Minting Authority, Metallurgy," in *The Jewish Revolt against Rome: Interdisciplinary Perspectives*, ed. Mladen Popović (Leiden: Brill, 2011), 361–72; Donald Tzvi Ariel, "Identifying the Mints, Minters, and Meanings of the First Jewish Revolt Coins," in *The Jewish Revolt against Rome: Interdisciplinary Perspectives*, ed. Mladen Popović (Leiden: Brill, 2011), 373–98.

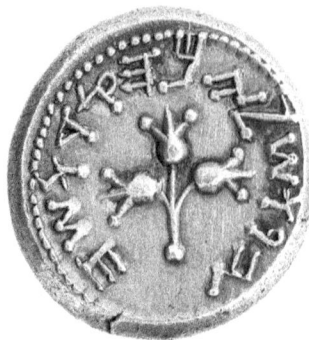

Figure 6.8 "Jerusalem the Holy," Silver Shekel, Jerusalem, "Year 3," American Numismatic Society

The understanding that 66 broke open the bounds of time to make way for a new era was not only the apocalyptically tinged conviction of the Apocalypse of the Birds as I have proposed here, but was shared by Jews responsible for the scribing and deposition of these documents in Wadi Murabba'at, and the minting and circulation of the coinage of the Revolt. Although 66 CE looks like the beginning of the end (of the Second Temple period) to modern scholars, to Jews it might have seemed the start of something new and unprecedented within living memory – an independent, autonomous state. The Apocalypse of the Birds would be, then, a vestige of the shock and optimism engendered by this surprising series of events.

The Apocalypse of the Birds, and new directions in the study of the Jewish Revolt

If we grant that the Apocalypse of the Birds finds a comfortable compositional home in the early Jewish Revolt, there are significant conclusions for scholars of the Revolt.

First, if the Apocalypse of the Birds is a chronicle of the Jewish Revolt, it is fascinating to consider the inverted and contrary perspective it brings out, over and against that of Josephus. The Apocalypse of the Birds might allow us to reposition Josephus on the spectrum of Jewish responses and reactions to the Revolt. To use the symbolism of the Apocalypse of the Birds, Enoch would be on the side of the rams, and would castigate Josephus for being on the side of the blind sheep (or, at least, was by the time he wrote in Flavian Rome). Many scholars are concerned by the singularity of Josephus' retrospective, since he has thrown his lot so heavily in with his Flavian sponsors, and his account is entirely suffused with regret (real, or performed) over his and his fellow Jews' actions. There is a certain amount of inevitability that emerges from Josephus' account – likely intentionally done, on his part – as he laments that the Revolt was doomed to fail, and gives voice to characters who admit as much in his carefully crafted narrative. The Apocalypse of the Birds grants no such thing, and casts those who do as "exceedingly blinded and deaf" sheep. It is a fundamentally optimistic work, convinced that something new and exciting is breaking into space and time. It is the literary echo of the coins minted and documents scribed in the immediate aftermath of 66 CE.

Second, Martin Goodman and James McLaren have lamented the ways that the moniker "Jewish Revolt" unintentionally replicates a pro-Roman and after-the-fact perspective.[166] They argue that this is a poor descriptor of how the events of 66–70 must have felt to Jews on the ground. Josephus' downcast and fatalist pessimism does not help us reclaim this perspective. But the Apocalypse of the Birds might provide just the kind of evidence they are looking for – of Jews thrilled at the rapidly actualizing prospect of a successful "revolution," rather than with looming dread as the inevitable losers of a failed "revolt."

Third, the Apocalypse of the Birds would represent concrete evidence for messianic and apocalyptic ideologies long-suspected to be related to the outbreak and outcomes of the Revolt, among some portion of the pro-revolutionary contingent of Judaea. But how significant would this population have been? There may be a gap between what we surmise about the worldview of the Apocalypse of the Birds, and how the work claims its contemporaries interpreted current events. The text does not necessarily demonstrate what Tessa Rajak calls "revolutionaries motivated in their militancy by a conviction that they were welcoming the Messiah or ushering in the End of Time."[167] In some ways, the Apocalypse of the Birds indicates that the motivations of the armed conflicts' participants had everything to do with social and political outrage, especially with the injustice visited by the violent excesses of the shepherds and birds. The work reveals to its own audience an apocalyptic framing in which this smaller conflict is nestled, but this may have been a small (and elite!) audience indeed. If this is, indeed, an account of the early years of the Jewish Revolt, it could be one executed at a certain intellectual (or physical!) distance from the events in question. Nevertheless, the addition of an apocalyptic source for the study of the Revolt should redirect the study of its religious dimensions in future years. As Rajak has noted, "For apart from the bronze revolt coins ... there is no direct expression outside Josephus of the ideology of revolt."[168] The Apocalypse of the Birds would change that.

---

[166] McLaren and Goodman, "The Importance of Perspective."
[167] In Tessa Rajak, "Jewish Millenarian Expectations," in *The First Jewish Revolt: Archaeology, History, and Ideology*, ed. Andrea M. Berlin and J. Andrew Overman (London: Routledge, 2002), 182.
[168] Rajak, 177.

Moreover, the Apocalypse of the Birds could even provide a ready candidate for the ambiguous oracle that purportedly sparked Jews to revolution, as later reported by Tacitus, Suetonius, and Josephus. So, Josephus complains that:

> What more than all else incited them to the war was an ambiguous oracle, likewise found in their sacred scriptures, to the effect that at that time one from their country would become ruler of the world. This they understood to mean someone of their own race, and many of their wise men went astray in their interpretation of it. The oracle, however, in reality signified the sovereignty of Vespasian, who was proclaimed Emperor on Jewish soil (War 6.312).[169]

Tacitus, similarly, reports that, "The majority firmly believed that their ancient priestly writings contained the prophecy that this was the very time when the East should grow strong and that men starting from Judaea should possess the world. This mysterious prophecy had in reality pointed to Vespasian and Titus (Histories 5.13)."[170] And, as noted above, Suetonius asserts that, "there had spread over all the Orient an old and established belief, that it was fated at that time for men coming from Judaea to rule the world. This prediction, referring to the emperor of Rome, as afterwards appeared from the event, the people of Judaea took to themselves (Life of Vespasian 4.5)."[171] The three historians agree that there was an ambiguous prophecy connecting current events, Judaea, and a figure who would rise to dominant political rule. Scholars have had a difficult time pinning down the referent of this prophecy, not least because the trio aver Jews mistakenly interpreted the prophecy as referring to a Jewish leader on the imperial throne, where those in-the-know recognized that it truly refers to a Roman emperor. With this caveat, scholars have been hard-pressed to find an identification among extant Jewish literature, as few provide a time-sensitive prophecy of a figure with powerful political ambitions from Judaea, that could also refer to a non-Jewish ruler.[172]

The Apocalypse of the Birds, however, features the arrival of a figure who might fit the bill. Here I am not referring to the rams, whom I have identified with Jewish military leaders of the early Revolt, but the great-horned bull introduced near the end of the work in 1 En 90.37. The identity of this animal as a bull, not a sheep, implies a return to the patriarchal, pre-Israel age, and away

---

[169] Flavius Josephus, *The Jewish War: Volume III*, Loeb Classical Library 210 (Cambridge, MA: Harvard University Press, 1928), 269.
[170] Tacitus, *Histories*, 199.
[171] Suetonius, *Lives of the Caesars*.
[172] On the history of scholarship on possible identifications, see Anthony J. Tomasino, "Oracles of Insurrection: The Prophetic Catalyst of the Great Revolt," *The Journal of Jewish Studies* 59, no. 1 (2008): 86. See also Christopher Begg and Paul Spilsbury, *Judean Antiquities Books 8–10* (Leiden: Brill, 2005), 313–14.

from the ovine particularity characterizing the descendants of Israel. As such, it would be reasonable to interpret the individual as a Jew, or non-Jew, depending on one's perspective. Moreover, it is noted that the bull has big horns, a symbol of military prowess, and it is prophesied that "all the wild animals and all the birds of heaven were afraid of it, and entreated it continually," a clear statement of political dominion. If this reading were accepted, it would not only solve a long-standing scholarly debate on the oracle in question, but connect the Apocalypse of the Birds quite directly with the outbreak of the Revolt. Of course, even if the Apocalypse of the Birds is to be identified with the ambiguous oracle given significant airtime by Josephus (and Tacitus and Suetonius), we should remember that Josephus' apologetic political project is well-served by outfitting the rabble with rabble-rousing material. Moreover, we should remember once more that the composition and reading of apocalyptic literature, as literacy more generally, was an elite phenomenon. The Apocalypse of the Birds, then, may not be an accurate portrait of what (to quote Tacitus) "the majority firmly believed."

These are some of the many avenues of research emerging from the preliminary study of the Apocalypse of the Birds as a remnant of the Revolt, and I have no doubt more will arise as study continues.

Conclusions: the Apocalypse of the Birds, the Jewish Revolt, and the end of time

In my reading, the Apocalypse of the Birds narrates the history of Israel from the destruction of the First Temple, and ends its historical narration on the precipice of a conflict that it predicted would result in the replacement of

Table 6.6 The Apocalypse of the Birds: A First-Century Reading

Verses	Summary	My Reading
89.65–72a	First Period: Twelve Shepherds	Babylonian Period
89.72b–90.1	Second period: Twenty-Three Shepherds	Persian–Hellenistic Period
90.2–5	Third Period: Twenty-Three Shepherds	Roman Period
90.4	Attacks of Dogs, Eagles, Ibises	Massacres of 66 CE
90.6–7	Resistance of Lambs, Apathy of Sheep	Early Judean Resistance
90.8–11	Attacks of Ravens, Rise of Rams and Great-Horned Sheep	Cestius Gallus's Campaign
90.12–15	Intervention of Lord of the Sheep on Ram's Behalf	Rebuffed Siege of Jerusalem, Victory at Beth Horon
90.16–19	Battle at End of Seventy Shepherds' Reign	Beginning of Eschaton
90.28–9	Removal of Old Jerusalem, Replacement with New Jerusalem	*Terminus Ante Quem* 70 CE?

the Second Temple and the arrival of a final judgement. In the text, immediate regional victories seem to herald a soon-to-arrive universal victory. This implied turning point also marked the end of a horrible, oppressive period of angelic guardianship, whose structured chronology is imagined to reset with the inbreaking of the eschaton. I have proposed that one possible set of matches for the events taking place at this imagined turning point can be found in the early days of the Jewish Revolt.

Given the ubiquity of the Maccabean-era hypothesis in scholarship on the Animal Apocalypse, it is worth highlighting what I perceive to be the comparative advantages of my new scheme situating this work in the climes of the first century CE, over and against the consensus opinion.

Our earliest manuscript of the Apocalypse of the Birds comes to us from fourteenth-century Ethiopia, not second-century BCE Judaea. This does not mean that the work belongs to fourteenth-century Ethiopia, but it does mean that every step backwards in time and outside of Ethiopia must be defended, and not assumed. It does not go without saying that the Apocalypse of the Birds belongs in the Maccabean period, and we must therefore search for additional evidence by which to establish the existence of the work outside of medieval Ethiopia.

The earliest readership for the work for which we have evidence is Barnabas, and perhaps the Testaments of the Twelve Patriarchs. If we feel comfortable importing the *text* of the Apocalypse of the Birds to sites where we suspect the *work* was being read, which is a large though not unreasonable assumption, then we have evidence that the Apocalypse of the Birds existed by no later than the second century CE. With this date established, we begin our quest for a more secure provenance from the second-century Mediterranean basin, rather than fourteenth-century Ethiopia.

The conflict, battles, and victories of the sheep of 1 En 90.6–15 are sufficiently flexible that, read in isolation, they could conceivably be matched to either a Maccabean or Roman context. Similarly, the chronology of the seventy shepherds could conceivably be adjusted to accommodate either a Maccabean- or Roman-era end-date. Progressive exposition of these verses within a Maccabean framework can be found in multiple places (perhaps most prominently, Charles, Tiller, Nickelsburg, and Olson). I have offered my own progressive exposition within a Roman framework here.

Table 6.7 The Apocalypse of the Birds: A Comparison of Approaches

Verses	Summary	Tiller	My Reading
89.65–72a	First Period: Twelve Shepherds	Babylonian Period	Babylonian Period
89.72b–90.1	Second period: Twenty-Three Shepherds	Persian Period	Persian–Hellenistic Period

Verses	Summary	Tiller	My Reading
90.2–5	Third Period: Twenty-Three Shepherds	Ptolemaic Period	Roman Period
90.4	Attacks of Dogs, Eagles, Ibises	Unknown "conflicts during the Ptolemaic period between Judah and the Semitic inhabitants of the coastal plain."[a]	Massacres of 66 CE
90.6–7	Resistance of Lambs, Apathy of Sheep	Seleucid Period & Rise of Hasidim/Maskilim	Early Judean Resistance
90.8–11	Attacks of Ravens, Rise of Rams and Great-Horned Sheep	"Persecutions associated with the Hellenization of Judah under Jason and Menelaus,"[b] 175 BCE and onwards.	Cestius Gallus's Campaign
90.12–15	Intervention of Lord of the Sheep on Ram's Behalf	"Unsuccessful Syrian campaigns against Judas under Apollonius and Seron"[c]	Rebuffed Siege of Jerusalem, Victory at Beth Horon
90.16–19	Battle at End of Seventy Shepherds' Reign	Beginning of Eschaton	Beginning of Eschaton

[a] Tiller, *Commentary*, 347.
[b] Tiller, *Commentary*, 352.
[c] Tiller, *Commentary*, 357.

But here are the specific advantages offered by my proposal that I consider to represent independently convincing evidence speaking in favor of a Roman provenance, especially given the weakness of the Maccabean-era hypothesis at these particular points:

1. In the Maccabean-era hypothesis, the second period is strictly understood as the Persian period. I noted, however, that the Persians are nowhere represented in the text. I therefore proposed wider horizons of interpretation, which include both Persian- and Hellenistic-era events.
2. In the Maccabean-era hypothesis, the eagles are contextually identified with the initial Macedonian expansion. There are no parallel Jewish or Christian texts which equate eagles with Alexander. Against this, my proposal that the eagles represent the Romans finds clear support in 4 Ezra, Josephus, and Matthew, not to mention non-Jewish/Christian Roman materials.
3. In the Maccabean-era hypothesis, the eagles which purportedly represent the Macedonians continue to be potent forces in later chapters of world history, even after scholars tracking a progression of history within the text would grant that Alexander's empire had collapsed and given way to

successor states. Various scholarly solutions proposed (that later instantiations of the "eagles" refer to Macedonian mercenaries, or that the eagles mean two different things at different points of the text) fail insofar as they require us to sacrifice the key narrative device of the work (one species for every people group). Conversely, my identification of the eagles as the Romans explains the qualifier that they "led" the other birds, allows for a consistent symbolism throughout and explains the eagles' continued existence, even as a more proximate antagonist (ravens) gains prominence in the estimation of the story.

4. The Maccabean-era hypothesis has a difficult time identifying the dogs at 1 En 90.4, as there is little evidence for a group calling themselves Philistines, nor independent evidence for any historical conflict between Jews and Hellenistic-era "Philistines." Meanwhile, my identification of the dogs as non-Jewish residents of Judeo-Syria is supported by a parallel "nicknaming" of this group as "dogs" in the Synoptic tradition, as well as a demonstrable (and bloody) historical conflict between these groups in the Roman period.

5. The Maccabean-era hypothesis does not explain the shift to birds of prey. I have suggested that the strength of the Roman=eagle symbol, perhaps bolstered by the shocking acquisition of the Twelfth Legion's *aquila* in the Battle of Beth Horon, might have sparked the shift to avian symbolism.

With these specific advantages in view, alongside my progressive exposition of the historical sections of the Apocalypse of the Birds within a first-century Judaean context, I hope to have shifted the balance of probability away from an earlier Maccabean provenance, towards a slightly later (but closer to our earliest readers) milieu. I have argued that the *terminus post quem* for the Apocalypse of the Birds should be moved up by about two centuries – to 66 CE. In my exposition, the Apocalypse of the Birds is a Roman-era work, and a narrative of the events of the early Jewish Revolt.

I have cautioned that the attainment of a new *terminus post quem* for a historical apocalypse does not immediately provide us with a *terminus ante quem*. I think it is certainly possible that this work was written all of a piece, quite early in the Revolt. Indeed, there is a certain satisfaction to regarding it as another expression of the expectant optimism that produced some of the numismatic and documentary evidence of the Revolt surveyed above. Still, I also acknowledge that we have not yet arrived at a robust methodology by which we might conceptualize the end of the development of apocalyptic works. How, for instance, do we draw the line between an event not known and an event not mentioned? I think it clear that the Apocalypse of the Birds's horizons open onto the Jewish Revolt. But it is not as yet clear to me when, in subsequent decades, these horizons might have closed. This is a line of inquiry that remains open to future study and scholarship.

Appendix: why not the Bar Kokhba Revolt?

I have noted above the flexibility of the Apocalypse of the Birds's historical account – it has been previously interpreted as a summation of the events of the Maccabean Revolt, though I propose that a better interpretation is to view it as a summation of the early events of the First Jewish Revolt. The reader might be curious whether the Bar Kokhba revolt would also represent a good candidate. Many of the key events of the Bar Kokhba revolt could find echo in the Apocalypse of the Birds: conflict with the Romans (cf. 1 En 90.2), regional violence in Egypt and Syria in the run-up to the Revolt (cf. 1 En 90.4), the rise of a resistance movement (cf. 1 En 90.6–7), the ascent of a key military leader (cf. 1 En 90.9) and at least some military victories (cf. 1 En 90.12–15). Indeed, as we have seen, Gustav Volkmar suggested as much.[173] But there is a strong case to be made against this identification.

First and foremost, I have proposed that the Apocalypse of the Birds is cited by Barnabas, and Barnabas is generally dated to the period before, and not including, the Bar Kokhba revolt. A minority position states that Barnabas might be roughly contemporary to the Bar Kokhba revolt, but I know of no scholarship that argues Barnabas greatly postdates the Bar Kokhba revolt. So, if the Apocalypse of the Birds is a source for the pre-Bar Kokhba Barnabas, we would need to postulate that it was written largely before 132 CE as well.

Second, Barnabas and the (more ambiguously dated, but still likely second century) Testaments of the Twelve Patriarchs read the Apocalypse of the Birds as if it were a prophecy of 70 CE and the destruction of the Temple. Though the interpretation of our earliest readers is not the only possible explanation, it is interesting that multiple independent works read the Apocalypse of the Birds as a witness to the events of the first century CE.

Third, to engage the only (to my knowledge) extant version of the thesis, Volkmar's correlation of the Apocalypse of the Birds to the Bar Kokhba revolt is extremely flawed.[174] His proposal that the seventy shepherds are pagan rulers that

---

[173] See Volkmar, "Beiträge zur Erklärung; Volkmar, "Über die katholischen Briefe"; Volkmar, *Eine Neu-Testamentliche Entdeckung.*

[174] His work was not well received, though it was much engaged. R. H. Charles complains, "A.D. 132 [was] a year which has exercised a strange fascination over him and has been fatal to his reputation as a critic ... his views have received more attention than they deserved through the rejoinders of Hilgenfeld, Dillmann, Langen, Sieffert, Gebhardt, Drummond, and Stanton." In Charles, *Enoch or, 1 Enoch*, xxxiv. His contemporary David Friedrich Strauss called him a "ludicrous little owl," as translated in Anne Vig Skoven, "Mark as allegorical rewriting of Paul: Gustav Volkmar's understanding of the gospel of Mark," in *Mark and Paul: Comparative Essays Part II. For and Against Pauline Influence on Mark*, ed. Eve-Marie Becker, Troels Engberg-Pedersen, and Mogens Müller, Arbeiten zur Geschichte des antiken Judentums und des Urchristentums 8 (Berlin: De Gruyter, 2014), 13–27.

rule over ten years apiece is purely speculative and also inconsistently applied in his work: he will sometimes stretch or compress periods to coalesce with his scheme. (For instance, he has a very difficult time with the Roman emperors whose reigns were of quite disparate lengths.)[175] Many of the readings that he needs to maximally match the Enochic text to Jewish history are quite strained: he proposes that the dogs of 90.4 represent the Hasmoneans *and* Herodians (just one verse after 90.3, which he views as a coded encapsulation of the Maccabean Revolt), that the *dabela* of 90.9 is the same as the messianic figure at 90.37–8 and that the ravens are first the Seleucids and then a Roman legion (albeit one from Syria). Volkmar's contemporary critics found the fatal flaw of his work to be his failure to account for 70 CE:

> it is unlikely in the highest degree that . . . while the early destruction of Jerusalem and the temple is expressly recorded, the still recent and more appalling one under Titus should be passed over in total silence, and the reader be allowed to suppose that the second temple was to be removed by supernatural agency after the judgment had taken place. This latter circumstance [e.g. this last critique of Volkmar] alone may well be deemed conclusive.[176]

I have been circumspect about the extent to which historical disclosure is expected in historical apocalyptic and tried not to transform the absence of a clear reference to the events of 70 CE into a firm *terminus ante quem*. That said, Volkmar's contemporaries found the postulate that a writer of a historically interested work in 132 CE would not only skip over 70 CE, but also place the removal of the Second Temple in the eschatological future, to be counterfactual beyond belief. Volkmar claims that the destruction of the Temple would have been of no interest to the Apocalypse of the Birds because the Temple was deemed impure from its reconstruction, but it *is* nevertheless accounted for explicitly in the text – rebuilt at 89.73–4, and replaced with an eschatological temple at 90.28–9.

Fourth, and finally, although our sources on the revolt may not be as clear as we would like, scholars agree that key motivators for the Bar Kokhba revolt

---

[175] Note the English summation given by a contemporary, Vincent Stanton: "He is brought to this date alike by two methods of reckoning; first by taking each of the times of the seventy shepherds at 'ten years and somewhat over,' and again by taking a time as exactly ten years, but regarding seventy as equivalent to seventy-two, which he is pleased to call 'the great-seventy' or in another place 'the high seventy.'" In Vincent Henry Stanton, *The Jewish and the Christian Messiah: A Study in the Earliest History*. (Edinburgh: T&T Clark, 1886), 89.

[176] James Drummond, *The Jewish Messiah, a Critical History of the Messianic Idea among the Jews from the Rise of the Maccabees to the Closing of the Talmud* (London: Longmans, Green and Co., 1877), 47–8.

would include one or more of the following: Hadrian's foundation of Aelia Capitolina, the prohibition of circumcision and the failure of a promised attempt to rebuild the Temple.[177] To my mind, these events are nowhere to be found in the text of the Apocalypse of the Birds.

Ultimately, I find the Bar Kokhba Revolt to be a less plausible setting than the First Jewish Revolt, though the universally negative reception of Volkmar's admittedly problematic work might have prematurely dismissed a Bar Kokhba hypothesis without granting it a fair hearing. For instance, the death blow in many of his contemporaries' appraisals of his work is the non-mention of the Temple's destruction. I too find this to be a telling omission, but I also think it possible that the field (myself included) over-expects the disclosure of 70 CE in literature of the period. That said, my own work which demonstrates that the Apocalypse of the Birds was a source for Barnabas and was read by early interpreters as a narration of the first century CE, could provide new and stronger grounds on which to counter his proposal.

---

[177] These are the three reigning options cited in Peter Schäfer, ed., *The Bar Kokhba War Reconsidered: New Perspectives on the Second Jewish Revolt against Rome* (Tübingen: Mohr Siebeck, 2003), XI.

CHAPTER 7

On Animal Apocalypses in the First Century and Beyond

At the start of this project, I provided a summary of the Animal Apocalypse as it has been handled in previous scholarship: as a product of the Maccabean Revolt. I can now provide my own summary, this time focusing on the Apocalypse of the Birds's function within the tumultuous and complex historical and literary world of first-century Roman Judaea.

As the first century CE progressed, an already fraught relationship between province and empire deteriorated. Various Jews acting in opposition to the Roman Empire (including Jesus of Nazareth) experienced some degree of local popularity but little military success. Then, for reasons still largely opaque to modern historians, what had previously been isolated and quickly extinguished sparks of resistance caught flame in 66 CE. Surprising ancient and modern observers alike, a Judaean resistance force rebuffed a Roman siege of Jerusalem and achieved a decisive rout of the retreating legion. According to Suetonius, it walked away from this stunning victory with no less a trophy than the legion's aquila, or eagle standard. This historical matrix is the first horizon in which I situate the emergence of the Apocalypse of the Birds.

Meanwhile, a work that I have labeled the Vision of the Beasts was in circulation among Jews. The Vision of the Beasts as it has come down to us is heavily invested in the idea of natural conflict. By this I mean, first, the idea of a kind of inevitability of struggle; any ancient people practiced in animal husbandry knows that sheep will always be beset by predators. But, second, this presumption of natural conflict is predicated upon an understanding of the world as inherently segmented into different and irreconcilable groupings. There are many ways to tell a story of Israelite history, but the Vision of the Beasts's particular symbolism ensures that the Israelites are envisioned as fundamentally vulnerable to and separable from other groups of people. Since we likely do not have the full version of the Vision of the Beasts as it once circulated, it is not clear to what end this imaging of the precarious position of the Israelites in history was originally pursued. But one way to transform and complete the story of the history of Israel is found in a first-century composition enacted as a revision of and addendum to the Vision of the Beasts: the Apocalypse of the Birds.

It is at this fusion of horizons – the escalating friction between province and empire, and the literary invitation presented by the natural conflict narrated in the Vision of the Beasts – that I understand the Apocalypse of the Birds to have emerged. Perhaps we can be even more specific. I have previously suggested that the Judaeans' capture of the Twelfth Legion's eagle standard might have provided a particularly direct bridge from contemporary conflict to literary animalistic allegorization thereof. The specific and shocking conquest of an eagle might have sparked observers to develop literature that envisioned the foibles of human emperors by way of the avian kingdom, this time culminating in a stunning reversal of fortunes.

The Apocalypse of the Birds, as an addendum to the Vision of the Beasts, places the conflicts in which it was embroiled within a lineage that stretches back through Israelite history to the very beginning of time. What was taking place with the Roman, Syrian, and Egyptian forces is situated as the culmination of a bloody and difficult history, albeit one always overseen by the Lord of the Sheep (God). The blindness condemned in a contemporary context is the continuation of centuries of apostasy. The horned rams that rise to lead the lambs are the heirs to previous rams, Saul, David, and Solomon. And the transformation of the sheep into white bulls at the very end of familiar history marks the re-emergence of a species that has not roamed the earth since the days of Jacob. In these and other ways, the Apocalypse of the Birds self-situates as the conclusion to the portrait of history drawn in the Vision of the Beasts.

But the Apocalypse of the Birds also charts out new territory. God is newly distant, as the seventy shepherds are inserted in the chain of command between the Lord and the sheep. A new breed of enemies has come to harass the sheep, in the form of birds swarming from the heavens. And time is running out; the device of the seventy shepherds establishes a quickly approaching end of the age. And so, even as the Apocalypse of the Birds emulates the animalistic style of the Vision of the Beasts, it tells a new story informed by its own contemporary stressors.

The Apocalypse of the Birds at 1 En. 90.1–19 allegorizes events explored in detail in the last chapter: the increasing oppression of the sheep undertaken by the birds, and the subsequent emergence of lambs and rams who fight back. Under the leadership of a ram with a great horn, the rams achieve a surprising and total victory. It is not entirely clear where history ends and the eschaton begins, but the birds (and beasts, now reappearing in the chaotic last moments) are thoroughly defeated.

Beginning at 1 En 90.20, the Apocalypse of the Birds puts the "apocalypse" in Animal Apocalypse. We have not previously discussed this work's account of the eschaton in detail, largely because it offers little independent help in matters of dating and textual history. When other factors point us towards the first century CE though, we might note that this account of the end of time sounds very much like the accounts of works dated to around the same time, especially Revelation, 4 Ezra, and 2 Baruch. Though these intertextual parallels demonstrate a certain amount of literary confluence, I will not imply any direct relationship or dependency. Occasionally, these non-Enochic works participate in small but different ways in the animalistic discourse that gets its fullest expression in the Apocalypse of the Birds. For example, Revelation consistently uses the image or title of "Lamb" to denote Jesus (e.g. Rev 21.22–6).[1] Though some uses of this expression in Revelation show little parallel to the Enochic work, other passages in Revelation, in which the Lamb is anthropomorphized and acting in a military capacity (Rev 6.16, 17.14), have recalled the Animal Apocalypse to previous scholars.[2] Revelation also situates carrion birds in the run-up to the eschaton (Rev 19.17–18). We have already explored 4 Ezra's eagle vision above at length. In addition to this, 4 Ezra 5.6 predicts a chaotic time when "the wild beasts shall roam beyond their haunts," and at 5.18 asks that "you [God] may not forsake us, like a shepherd who leaves his flock in the power of savage wolves." To my mind, these echoes demonstrate the presence of animalistic language in the soup of first-century apocalyptic from which Revelation and 4 Ezra would draw, rather than any immediate historical connection.[3] As we move through the rest of the Apocalypse of the Birds, I will track these motifs to demonstrate further contemporary consonances.

In the Apocalypse of the Birds's apocalypse, a throne is constructed upon which the Lord of the Sheep sits in judgment (cf. the great white throne of Rev 20.11, or the seat of judgment 4 Ezra 7.33). This judgment takes place by means of the unsealing of books that chronicle the misdeeds of the shepherds and the excesses of punishment they visited upon their sheep during their respective reigns (cf. the books of life and of the dead in Rev 20.12; the books of sins and sinners of 2 Bar 24.1). The shepherds and a selection of blind sheep

---

[1] The connection between Revelation and the Animal apocalypse is even a bit closer in Ethiopic, as the Gəʿəz for ἀρνίον in Revelation is not lamb (ማሕሰእ, maḥasəʾə) but sheep (በጔ, bägəʿ). See Josef Hofmann, *Die äthiopische Übersetzung der Johannes-Apokalypse*, Corpus Scriptorum Christianorum Orientalium 281 (Leuven: Secrétariat du CorpusSCO, 1967).

[2] See the review of Revelation scholarship's search for a "militaristic ram tradition in early Judaism" and treatment of the Animal Apocalypse in Loren L. Johns, *The Lamb Christology of the Apocalypse of John: An Investigation into Its Origins and Rhetorical Force* (Tübingen: Mohr Siebeck, 2003), 76–80, 88–96.

[3] I borrow the metaphor of soup from a 1947 lecture given by J. R. R. Tolkien. When speaking about a genre he called "fairy stories," he imagined a constantly cooking "Pot of Soup ... Cauldron of Story" from which stories are drawn and to which they subsequently add. Recently republished as J. R. R. Tolkien, "On Fairy-Stories," in *The Monsters and the Critics: And Other Essays*, ed. Christopher Tolkien (Croydon: HarperCollins, 2006), 109–62.

are judged and found guilty. So too are the stars, or fallen angels, for their ancient transgressions (cf. the punishment of Satan at Rev. 20.1–3). All the transgressors are thrown into a deep and fiery abyss, apparently located to the south of Jerusalem (cf. the lake of fire of Rev. 20.14–15, or the pit of torment of 4 Ezra 7.36). At this point, the house (Jerusalem, likely including the Temple) is removed.[4] The house is replaced with a new and larger house, in which the Lord of the Sheep is resident once more (cf. the New Jerusalem of Rev 21.1–2, 4 Ezra 10.25–7 and 2 Bar 4.2–3). It seems that the Apocalypse of the Birds imagines the Temple to be rebuilt as some part of the new house, rather than explicitly clarifying that the Temple will become superfluous in the new age (cf. Rev 21.22), though this is ambiguous.

The exact chronology of the account is somewhat difficult to ascertain, as 1 En 90.31 seems to enact a flashback to a time before the final judgment, though what follows in 1 En 90.31–8 presupposes the arrival of the new house which took place textually earlier (and therefore chronologically later?) at 1 En 90.28–9. But, allowing for some creative liberties with the nature and function of time in the imagined era of its closure, the Apocalypse of the Birds reflects upon the community of the eschaton. The new house is filled with white sheep, with thick and pure wool (cf. the white-clothed armies of heaven of Rev 19.14, the great multitude from every nation wearing white of Rev 7.9, and the white-clothed people of 4 Ezra 2.34). These pure sheep are joined by the wild animals and birds of heaven. In the Apocalypse of the Birds, the respective fates of the sheep and beasts/birds are not always clearly differentiated. At some points, it seems as though the wild animals and birds of heaven are allowed only a kind of subservient existence, waiting upon both the sheep in the house (1 En 90.30) and a white bull who is born among the sheep (1 En 90.37). At others, the birds and beasts are gathered in the house alongside the sheep, to the Lord's great joy (1 En 90.33), and with the sheep undergo the final great eschatological transformation of all into bulls (1 En 90.38). If we equate the white bull of 1 En 90.37 with the horned *nägär* of 1 En 90.38, which I discussed at length in Chapter 5, this final transformation is overseen by a figure who is a manifestation of the *logos*, horned as an heir to David, and the first of the renewed species of bulls.

At this juncture in particular, we can note that the Apocalypse of the Birds might spark many avenues of future research into the history and literature of the first century CE. I can offer a few (very brief) forays into the implications of my work for the study of this controversial period.

---

[4] The possible parallels we might assemble here very much depend on whether 90.28 is taken as a clear account of the destruction of Jerusalem (in which case cf. the narration of the same in 4 Ezra 10.19, 2 Bar 6.6–8, 32 and 80.2–6, as well as Apoc. Ab 27.3–7, Sib. Or 1.387–400, 4.115–16 and 5.397–402), or an ambiguous account of something like it (cf. Rev 11.1–2, Mark 13.1–2, Matt 24.1–2, Luke 21.5–6).

First, I have suggested that my work on the Apocalypse of the Birds bears significant importance for those interested in the method by which we date ancient works and works belonging to the early centuries CE in particular. This work, along with Daniel, is one of the few bona-fide historical apocalypses on which the method of dating in accordance with *vaticinium ex eventu* is trained, at least when it comes to ancient Judaism and Christianity.[5] But I have argued it contains only ambiguous references to what is presumably the most mentionable event of the Jewish and/or Christian common era – the destruction of the Temple in 70 CE – according to which many works belonging to, for example, the New Testament are dated.[6] If the methodology falters in this case, why do we expect it to generate dates about which we might be confident elsewhere?

Second, my re-dating of the Apocalypse of the Birds could bear substantial conclusions for Pauline studies, and especially the pursuit of Paul's thought within Judaism. The distinctive universalism of 1 En 90.37–8, in which all species are transformed into white bulls under the apparent supervision of the *nägär*, has played an important role in scholarship on the contested and changing role of Gentiles in Jesus-following communities, especially in assessing the thought of Paul.[7] The universalist eschatology of 90.37–8 is said to be "without parallel in pre-Christian Jewish literature," "surprising," and

---

[5] Note the positive evaluation of the Animal Apocalypse in the critical overview of *post facto* dating offered by Erho: e.g. "The most weight must be placed upon detailed 'prophetical' historical digressions (e.g. Dan. 8; 11; 1 En. 89–90) whose end unequivocally supports the affixation of a terminus a quo." In Erho, "Internal Dating Methodologies," 86.

[6] The importance of 70 CE for the dating of the New Testament can also be quickly demonstrated with reference to a negative formulation: the controversial but much-engaged work of John A. T. Robinson which redates the entirety of the New Testament to pre-70 CE, on the grounds that this event is never explicitly mentioned (or at least, not mentioned as explicitly as he would like). Although his conclusions have not been well received, the very existence and impact of his argument admirably demonstrates the extent to which 70 CE has been and continues to be appealed to in the dating of first-century works like the New Testament. See John A. T. Robinson, *Redating the New Testament* (London: S.C.M. Press, 1976). For a contemporary's attempt to use Robinson's work to reflect on the history of scholarship on dating the New Testament, see E. Earle Ellis, "Dating the New Testament★," *New Testament Studies* 26, no. 4 (July 1980): 487–502.

[7] For instance: four scholars working on Paul, Terence Donaldson, Amy Genevieve Dibley, Kathy Ehrensperger, and Matthew Thiessen, are interested in the possibility that the "they all" of 90.38 refers only to the immediate antecedent, being the beasts and birds of 90.37, and that the Gentiles are the only animals that transform into white bulls. The sheep, or Jews, simply remain white sheep, and the Gentiles are thus set up as the true heirs to the (ostensibly superior) Abrahamic lineage. This could evidence a stripe of Judaism that anticipates a new Pauline or radical new Pauline vision of the respective roles of Jews and Gentiles, and the role of "Gentiles qua Gentiles,", to borrow one scholar's phrase. Ultimately, this re-reading is built on what is, at best, a mild ambiguity in the Gəʿəz, and it is not conclusive on its own. See Donaldson,

contain "striking" similarities to Paul in three recent commentaries on the Animal Apocalypse.[8] In previous scholarship, this passage has provided crucial background by which a Pauline foreground might be established. In his reconstruction of Jewish antecedents to Paul's radical interest in Gentile soteriology, E. P. Sanders treats 1 En 90 and 1 En 108, another piece missing from Qumran, as two pieces of a "small handful of explicit references to the possibility of salvation of Gentiles in Palestinian Jewish literature."[9] Without 1 En 90, Paul's thought would look all the more idiosyncratic and perhaps even contrarian. The pursuit of Paul within Judaism, which is a stated goal of New Perspectivists like Sanders, and Radical New Perspectivists like John Gager, could be complicated a bit if this Jewish work is removed from Paul's contemporary milieu.[10] If the Apocalypse of the Birds is to be dated in the decades after Paul, then perhaps we need to think about the Apocalypse of the Birds as an (indirect) legacy of Paul, rather than the other way around.

Such a discussion brings into stark relief a larger methodological concern: that the dating of Second Temple works may be motivated by desire for background for the New Testament.[11] Although the search for intellectual precedent often goes hand in hand with hypotheses of chronological precedence, I wonder whether relative dating is not, in fact, a dubious quest to begin with. Does it actually matter which work came first, or is the chronological framing just a way of enshrining "background" and "foreground" as if such choices were a consequence of historical sequence, and not the interests of

---

Judaism and the Gentiles, 111–17; Amy Genevive Dibley, "Abraham's Uncircumcised Children: The Enochic Precedent for Paul's Paradoxical Claim in Galatians 3:29" (PhD diss., UC Berkeley, 2013), 98–9, https://escholarship.org/uc/item/2qs60947; Kathy Ehrensperger, "The Pauline Εκκλεσια and Images of Community in Enoch Traditions," in *Paul the Jew: Rereading the Apostle as a Figure of Second Temple Judaism*, ed. Gabriele Boccaccini and Carlos Segovia (Minneapolis: Fortress Press, 2016), 183–216; Thiessen, "Paul, the Animal Apocalypse," 70–1.

[8] Tiller, *Commentary*, 20; Olson, *A New Reading*, 242; George W. E. Nickelsburg, *1 Enoch 1*, 407.

[9] See E. P. Sanders, *Paul and Palestinian Judaism: A Comparison of Patterns of Religion* (Minneapolis: Fortress Press, 1977), 35.

[10] For an encapsulation of the question of Paul within Judaism, see the recent collection of articles (many engaging the legacy of Sanders' work on Paul) in the 2018 issue of the aptly named *Journal of the Jesus Movement in its Jewish Setting*. For John Gager's work on Paul, see John G. Gager, *Reinventing Paul* (Oxford: Oxford University Press, 2000).

[11] This question is asked by Michael Stone and Ted Erho about the pursuit of a pre-synoptic gospels date for the Book of Parables. As Stone puts it, "perhaps few would zealously attempt to reach chronological precision with such meager evidence had the title not occurred in the Gospels." In Michael E. Stone, "Enoch's Date in Limbo: Or: Some Considerations on David Suter's Analysis of the Book of Parables," in *Enoch and the Messiah Son of Man*, ed. Gabriele Boccaccini (Grand Rapids, MI: Eerdmans, 2007), 445; Erho, "Historical-Allusional Dating," 510–11. Note also the framing of the questions in Charlesworth's recent volume on the Parables: "who influenced whom?" (p. x), and "Does the Parables of Enoch Antedate Jesus?" (p. xvi), in Charlesworth and Bock, *Parables of Enoch*.

the scholar? I thereby understand the redating of the Apocalypse of the Birds to a few decades past Paul to open up new directions in Pauline studies, not only insofar as the field does or does not make use of the text of the Animal Apocalypse, but in encouraging further reflection on how to think about Paul (and many other works belonging to the New Testament) between context and reception. It has mattered, to scholars, "when" certain Jewish works are placed around the life of Paul, whether before (context) or after (reception). The operative function that each of those respective classifications is doing deserves further study.

Third, the Apocalypse of the Birds demonstrates the limits of our ability to use the pseudepigrapha to enact binary categorizations of phenomena belonging to Judaism and Christianity respectively, especially with reference to the contentious use of Christological references as a criterion for Christian provenance. We can take the arrival of the *nägär* of 1 En 90.38, discussed above in Chapter 5, as a case study. The history of scholarship evidences a sense of dissonance and tension between what we expect of a purportedly Jewish text, and the curiously Christian language we are greeted with instead, and the lexeme "word (*nägär*)" was accordingly emended to "lamb" or "ram." The text here resembles the kind of Christological passage that would traditionally have triggered philologists to excise the text as a "later gloss," but falls just short. Similarly, I have noted that 1 En 90.38 comes close to certain phrases in the Gospel of John. These two criteria – a Christological reference, or a reference to the New Testament – are the usual ways of identifying Christian intervention in Jewish texts, or Christian composition more generally. In the case of the Testaments of the Twelve Patriarchs, for instance, editors sometimes excise references to Jesus and New Testament references in order to restore a Jewish version.[12] These thresholds have been inoperative in the history of the editing of the Animal Apocalypse, since the typical means of managing such dissonance has been conjectural emendation of the tricky term *nägär*. Part of this history of editing has to do with the previous consensus dating of the work to the second century BCE, making Christian composition an impossibility. If the Apocalypse of the Birds dates to the first century CE, as I have argued, it could very well have been written by followers of Jesus. But my point is not that Christian composition is obvious. I think it clear that the Apocalypse of the Birds was composed by Jews, though it is not clear whether our composers

---

[12] The explicit Jesus-references in the Testaments of the Twelve Patriarchs have, in many ways, conditioned the reflexes by which we conceptualize phases of Christian transmission. So, in Michael Knibb's discussion of the transmission of Enoch by Christians, in which he is more open than most to substantial Christian intervention, he says with reference to the Parables that "it is very hard to explain the absence of any explicit Christological references in the Parables if they really are Christian, and here the contrast with the Christian Testaments of the Twelve Patriarchs is very instructive." See Knibb, "Christian Adoption," 71.

were also Jesus followers or not. My point here is that our rubrics of what would be Jewish (and not Christian) and what would be Christian (and not Jewish) are either insufficiently sensitive to effectively guide our interpretation of the text, or misguided in their optimism that such a sorting of phenomena is possible.

In this respect, the Apocalypse of the Birds deserves to be studied alongside those texts in which the textual veneer of Christianity is thin indeed: works with firmly Christian reception histories (as my analysis in Chapter 5 indicates was the case for the Apocalypse of the Birds) but without the Jesus or Christ references that are often taken to be a hallmark of Christian textual creation. I am thinking in particular of the Shepherd of Hermas, 6 Ezra, the Epistle of James, and the Apocalypse of Adam, which feature minimal or no references to Jesus, but whose reception histories allow them to be studied under the heading of Christianity.[13] The ambiguous and boundary-treading case of the Apocalypse of the Birds forces us to ask whether "Jews who were also Christians" would write differently than "Jews who were not also Christians," when describing a

---

[13] The Epistle of James features what Dale Allison calls "unexpected silences" on Jesus (who is mentioned only in brief asides at 1.1 and 2.1). Allison notes that Jülicher called this work "the least Christian book in the New Testament." See Dale C. Allison, "The Jewish Setting of the Epistle of James," *In Die Skriflig* 49, no. 1 (2015): 1–9; A. Jülicher, *Einleitung in Das Neue Testament* (Tübingen: J.C.B. Mohr, 1931), 209.

The Shepherd of Hermas famously never mentions Jesus, nor Christ (though refers often to "God's son") nor does it quote any work belonging to the New Testament. It nevertheless proved to be immensely popular among early Christian readers. One wonders how we might classify it if that had not proved to be the case. On its contentious "christology," see discussion and literature cited in Carolyn Osiek, *Shepherd of Hermas: A Commentary*, Hermeneia – A Critical and Historical Commentary on the Bible (Minneapolis: Fortress Press, 1999), 34–6.

The Apocalypse of Adam is the only work from Nag Hammadi included among Charlesworth's *Old Testament Pseudepigrapha*, as it is deemed by its translator, MacRae, to be "independent of Christian influence," in George MacRae, "The Apocalypse of Adam," in Charlesworth, *The Old Testament Pseudepigrapha*, 1:708. Others find the allusions to Christianity and the New Testament to be "numerous," "transparent," and "rather obvious," as stated in Edwin M. Yamauchi, *Pre-Christian Gnosticism: A Survey of the Proposed Evidences*, 2nd ed. (Grand Rapids, MI: Baker Book House, 1983), 110. Even without weighing in on the contested NT allusions, the question here, as above, is how to classify texts that do not explicitly refer to Jesus among Judaism and Christianity.

6 Ezra also lacks references to Jesus. It has been described by Theodore Bergren as Christian, though John Marshall has recently objected that it should instead be read as a Jewish work of Asia Minor. James Davila aptly summarizes Bergren's position, and its immediate problem: "6 Ezra is a Christian work, even though no explicitly Christian ideas appear in it." See Bergren, "Sixth Ezra"; John W. Marshall, "6 Ezra and Apocalyptic Judaism in Asia Minor," in *Beyond the Gnostic Gospels: Studies Building on the Work of Elaine Pagels*, ed. Eduard Iricinschi et al. (Tübingen: Mohr Siebeck, 2009), 427–45; James Davila, "The Book of 6 Ezra (2 Esdras 15–16) – Old Testament Pseudepigrapha," 2007, https://otp.wp.st-andrews.ac.uk/abstracts-lectures/the-book-of-6-ezra-2-esdras-15-16

messianic figure, and even more specifically, how.[14] Annette Yoshiko Reed has described the category "Jewish-Christian," as "a heuristic irritant . . . push[ing] us to think out and beyond some of the systems and practices of classification that we most take for granted."[15] I think the end of the Apocalypse of the Birds encapsulates what can be so usefully irritating about phenomena studied under the heading of Jewish-Christianity: it forces us to recognize just how little we know about how and whether Jewish or Christian identities interacted with textual production and transmission in the early centuries CE.

The full exploration of many or any of these avenues will have to wait for a future project, one that I hope to take up in due time. As it is, I understand the Apocalypse of the Birds to be an impactful addition to our library of first-century Jewish (and Jewish-Christian?) literature.

What is the animal apocalypse?

For now, in pursuit as we are of Animal Apocalypses of Enoch, we would do well to linger on the closing lines.

> (39) And I was asleep in the middle of them; and I woke up and saw everything. (40) And this is the vision which I saw while I was asleep, and I woke up and blessed the Lord of righteousness and ascribed glory to him. (41) But after this I wept bitterly, and my tears did not stop until I could not endure it; when I looked, they ran down on account of that which I saw, for everything will come to pass and be fulfilled; and all the deeds of men in their order were shown to me. (42) That night I remembered my first dream, and because of it I wept and was disturbed, because I had seen that vision.

These verses are often treated as if they were added by a redactor of the larger Book of Dreams (1 En 83–90) – someone who inherited an Animal Apocalypse and brought it together with the earlier Flood Vision (1 En 83–4).[16] I agree that

---

[14] My categories are borrowed from Martha Himmelfarb, "3 Baruch Revisited: Jewish or Christian Composition, and Why It Matters," *Zeitschrift für antikes Christentum/Journal of Ancient Christianity* 20, no. 1 (2016): 53.

[15] Annette Yoshiko Reed, *Jewish-Christianity*, XXI.

[16] It is possible verses 39–41 are to be separated from 42 and assigned to the Apocalypse of the Birds, where only 42 is to be assigned to a later redactor. It is also possible that 39–42 belong to the compositional moment that produced the Apocalypse of the Birds, and that moment was also responsible for the combination of the Flood Vision, Vision of the Beasts, and Apocalypse of the Birds into the super-entity called the Book of Dreams (1 En 83–90). I am ultimately agnostic on this issue, and it does not impact my argument below about the importance of 90.42 in particular as enshrining the unity of the Animal Apocalypse as it would be received.

this makes good sense, especially since 83.2 sets up what is to follow as two visions (ካልእት ራእይት, *kälə'etä ra'əyatä*), the second of which takes place "before I took a wife," a qualification also stated as the framing device at the start of the Animal Apocalypse in Gəʿəz: "Before I took your mother Edna" (85.3).

I find it fascinating that the Animal Apocalypse is explicitly treated and numbered as one entity. It is one vision; when added to the Flood Vision, the visions number two. I think it basically impossible to date 1 En 90.39–42 and establish whether their composition predates the composition of the Apocalypse of the Birds (so, perhaps the two visions are the Flood Vision and Vision of the Beasts!). But as they are extant in Gəʿəz, at the end of a progression comprising 1 En 85–90, they represent a crucial moment in the reception history of the Animal Apocalypse, in which the works that I have traced to two (at least) compositional moments are received as a single entity. This reception is not necessarily discordant with what we have surmised about the composition of animal apocalypses. I suggested above that the Apocalypse of the Birds likely functioned as something like an addendum to the Vision of the Beasts, so that whenever the Apocalypse of the Birds emerged, so too did something like the narrative progression we find in 1 En 85–90. I imagine that the composers of the Apocalypse of the Birds would be quite pleased to learn that their work extending an Animal Apocalypse into their own times was so (well) received. I take not only 1 En 90.42, but also the centuries of scholarship that have pursued the Vision of the Beasts and Apocalypse of the Birds as a single work, to be a testament to these scribes' tremendous literary achievement.

At this point, it may seem I have taken apart the Animal Apocalypse and left it in pieces. What was once the Animal Apocalypse is now the Vision of the Beasts and the Apocalypse of the Birds, and perhaps there is a feeling that this kind of textual surgery leaves us with less than we started with. Scholars have voiced this lament with reference to source criticism of the Hebrew Bible and even 1 Enoch.[17] But I do not feel the Animal Apocalypse is gone at all. Instead, I think it quite vibrant.

---

[17] With reference to the Hebrew Bible, a powerful critical voice has been Robert Alter, who contrasts a "literary" reading with source criticism. Concerning Genesis, he remarks, "I am deeply convinced that conventional biblical scholarship has been trigger-happy in using the arsenal of text-critical categories, proclaiming contradiction wherever there is the slightest internal tension in the text, seeing every repetition as evidence of a duplication of sources, everywhere tuning into the static of transmission, not to the complex music of the redacted story." In Robert Alter, *Genesis* (New York: W.W. Norton, 1998), xlii–xliii. With reference to 1 Enoch, Annette Yoshiko Reed notes, "excavative interests have perhaps distracted from the task of explaining how the integration of multiple traditions about the fallen angels contributes to the meaning of the apocalypse as a whole ... they tacitly dismiss the redacted product as a muddled combination and conflation of originally coherent 'legends.'" In Annette Yoshiko Reed, *Fallen Angels and the History of Judaism and Christianity: The Reception of Enochic Literature* (New York: Cambridge University Press, 2005), 26.

In chapter one, I introduced John Bryant's conception of a work as energy, with the attendant suggestion that the power of literature is to be found in change, movement, and variance.[18] It strikes me that the source critic's instincts towards deconstruction can, in some cases, provide the multiplicities needed to witness creativity in motion. As Bryant puts it, "texts, when taken together, give us a vivid material impression of the flow of creativity."[19] Source criticism, as I have here performed with reference to the Animal Apocalypse, transforms what was once a single "text" into "texts," providing us with the multiple data points needed to perceive change and movement. We have, as Lied and Lundhaug put it, "snapshots of evolving traditions."[20]

So I have not replaced the Animal Apocalypse with the Vision of the Beasts and Apocalypse of the Birds – it is not gone. Instead, the Vision of the Beasts and Apocalypse of the Birds are Animal Apocalypses. By this I do not mean the re-imposition of expectations from Gəʿəz on our earlier materials, as 1 En 85–90, the entity called the Animal Apocalypse in previous scholarship, post-dated the initial writing of these two works. Rather, I want to use the concept of a work – whatever modern scholars have invested in the title (that modern scholars invented) Animal Apocalypse – to delineate a set of literary horizons within which multiple people read and wrote and redacted and more in a lively conversation stretching across centuries.[21] To quote Bryant once more, "fluid-text analysis constructs meaning out of the evolutionary 'spaces' between historically

---

[18] This is not the only definition of work that has been operative in this study. I noted that the boundaries of a work in the study of 1 Enoch, and ancient literature more generally, are often controlled by modern scholars' estimations of likely sites of composition. I followed this to an extent throughout my study – the Apocalypse of the Birds is a work identifiable from the Vision of the Beasts because it seems to have been written at a different time. But I see no problem using multiple definitions of what is obviously a quite elusive concept to tease out the implications of my work. Indeed, to do source criticism in the age of material philology, one would need to be comfortable code-switching a bit and using both.
[19] Bryant, *The Fluid Text*, 6.
[20] Lied and Lundhaug, *Snapshots of Evolving Traditions*.
[21] The model I am describing now is deeply indebted to, though not identical with, new directions in scholarship reflecting on pseudepigraphy as an open discourse tied to a founding figure, and the efflorescence of literature that can flow from that generative conception. On which, see especially Hindy Najman, *Seconding Sinai: The Development of Mosaic Discourse in Second Temple Judaism* (Leiden: Brill, 2003); Eva Mroczek, *The Literary Imagination in Jewish Antiquity* (Oxford: Oxford University Press, 2016); Irene Peirano, *The Rhetoric of the Roman Fake: Latin Pseudepigrapha in Context* (New York: Cambridge University Press, 2012). One small wrinkle in placing the Animal Apocalypses within these theoretical models is that the Apocalypse of the Birds, though preserving a first-person narrative style, engages the personage of Enoch barely at all, in stark contrast to the development of other works like the Book of the Watchers, or Book of Parables, whose textual development may be more intertwined with the reception history of the figure of Enoch. For one exploration of how the figure of Enoch might have influenced the transmission history of 1 Enoch see Elena Dugan, "Enochic Biography and the Manuscript History of 1 Enoch: The Codex Panopolitanus Book of the Watchers," *Journal of Biblical Literature* 140, no. 1 (2021): 113–38.

sequenced inscriptions."²² My study has created new space – specifically, a space between the earlier Vision of the Beasts, and the later Apocalypse of the Birds. It represents a first step in the study of what this space represents, facilitating a new understanding of how the Animal Apocalypse(s) moved through antiquity.

I understand my contribution to demonstrate the potential that source criticism has for new or material philology more generally. Source criticism can be pursued within the framework of a rather traditional philology. But, viewed differently, its method contains the seeds of significant dissent from a classical philological model. The reality that what works may be broken into sources, which means that they came together in stages, fundamentally effaces any hypothetical boundary between composition and transmission (or "original" and variant). Even if traditional source-critical projects chose to place an artificial boundary after which creativity purportedly stops and the process of transmission (and accumulation of variants) begins – like a purported moment of "publication" – this is a secondary, and separable, choice. In identifying multiple discrete stages of development, source critics identify that very "space between historically sequenced inscriptions" and can uniquely enable an exploration of energetic works in antiquity.

All that said, source criticism is not the only pathway by which scholars might witness the vivacious and dynamic lives of ancient works. Source criticism can be a crucial tool in the case of works with minimal documentation, or documentation in only a single tradition, such as the Animal Apocalypses. There are other works, however, where our documentation has more readily enabled the study and development of language for textual change. Study of the complex worlds of Heikhalot literature, in particular, provides helpful language to describe the ongoing movement of the Animal Apocalypses. Peter Schäfer introduces a conceptual pair: microform, "an independently transmitted redactional unit," and macroform, "a superimposed entirety." These are quite similar to the concepts of work (similar to macroform) and subsidiary work (similar to microform) which I introduced in Chapter 1 – a distinction helpful in distinguishing different entities to which to fit our documents, and enabling our spotting the absence of the Apocalypse of the Birds from Qumran. But with that line of argumentation complete, it is time to think with Schäfer's more complex terminology about the implications of my project.

Schäfer's crucial contribution in this regard is demonstrating that the boundary between microform and macroform is fundamentally porous, and certain entities can function as one or the other in different material contexts.²³ Ra'anan Boustan notes that, in Heikhalot literature, textual stability cannot be sought at the beginning (an Ur-text) or end (a "finally redacted form") of the transmissional

---

²² Bryant, "Witness and Access," 19.
²³ In English, see Peter Schäfer, *The Hidden and Manifest God: Some Major Themes in Early Jewish Mysticism* (Albany: State University of New York Press, 1992), 6n14.

process – change, rather than fixity, is the true constant of the Heikhalot tradition.[24] My proposed transmissional history of the Animal Apocalypse(s) should be differentiated somewhat from the complicated Heikhalot tradition(s). As noted above, scholars generally assume the genre of historical apocalyptic to impart a greater degree of textual stability over time. But the particular contribution of the categories of microform and macroform is in its creation of flexible and malleable distinctions within the larger category of "work" that are sensitive to both material attestation and scholarly source criticism.[25]

The microform/macroform pair emphasize both the contingency of any given classification and its participation in a web of relations stretching beyond any given document. The Vision of the Beasts is both microform (an identifiable subsection of the Animal Apocalypse), and macroform (I have argued that it is the entirety of the "Animal Apocalypse" as we know it at Qumran). The Apocalypse of the Birds is both microform (also an identifiable subsection of the Animal Apocalypse), and macroform (a unified composition which I sought to explain at length in this study).[26] 1 En 85–90, the entity previously called the Animal Apocalypse, is both microform (an independently transmitted section of both the Book of Dreams and the larger Ethiopic work known as 1 Enoch), and macroform (an entirety on its own, as treated by many scholars). I have suggested that 1 En 85–90 might also fruitfully be viewed another way: as what Schäfer calls an "superordinate macroform" (*übergeordneten Makroform*), in which two macroforms (the Vision of the Beasts and Apocalypse of the Birds) are combined into another macroform still.[27] The very same textual progressions can be variously classified as microforms or macroforms, depending on the era, region, and documents of which we ask the question.

Ultimately, the Animal Apocalypse, as I understand it, encompasses all of these entities, and does not reduce to any particular one. One trajectory of development is attested in Ethiopic Enoch 85–90, in which the Vision of the

---

[24] Boustan, "Heikhalot Literature," 139.
[25] Note that Schäfer uses "macroform" to replace the term "work" ("I employ the term macroform for a superimposed literary unit, instead of the term writing or work", in Schäfer, *The Hidden and Manifest God*, 6n14.). But my definition of work stated in Chapter 1 ("Works are conceptual constructs that readers agree have enough in common with each other, and enough not-in-common with other entities, to be separated into their own category"), borrowed from Liv Lied, encompasses both microform and macroform. I do not view this tweaking of terminology to be a critique of his language, but rather an attempt to keep things as terminologically consistent as possible in my own project.
[26] The fact that we cannot document its independent circulation, and my hypothesis that it represents an addendum to the Vision of the Beasts, may seem to complicate this classification a bit. But macroform is used by Schäfer to refer to a superimposed literary unit, and the internal structure of the Apocalypse of the Birds does recommend itself under that classification.
[27] Peter Schäfer, *Hekhalot-Studien*, Texte und Studien zum antiken Judentum 19 (Tübingen: Mohr Siebeck, 1988), 200. It is possible this superordinate macroform was the production of the composers of the Apocalypse of the Birds, as proposed above.

Beasts is "completed" by the Apocalypse of the Birds. If we were to ask for the Animal Apocalypse in Ethiopian codices, 1 En 85–90 is the textual progression that would be returned. Another trajectory is attested in four manuscripts at Qumran, in which the Vision of the Beasts circulates alone. If we were to ask for the Animal Apocalypse in second century BCE Judaea, 1 En 85.1–89.59 is the textual progression that might have been returned. But all of our versions – documented or hypothesized – can be fruitfully brought together for study under the heading of a work that scholars call the Animal Apocalypse, in which Jews and perhaps Christians conversed with their scribal ancestors about the meaning of history and the nature of the eschaton, with the unique assistance of a beastly menagerie.

The Animal Apocalypse, continued: on a "Little Animal Apocalypse"

According to the model I have constructed in this study, the Animal Apocalypse (like many other ancient works) was a lively and inviting literary seedling that later scribes could transplant, cultivate, and grow in their own soil. A particular feature of the Animal Apocalypse that was imparted to the tradition by the Vision of the Beasts is its tantalizing encapsulation of all of history in zoomorphic allegory, beginning from the very beginning. The Vision of the Beasts presented a ready vehicle for historiographic thinking, and I have argued, it was developed in just such a manner by the composers of the Apocalypse of the Birds, who shifted the historical horizons in order to include the difficult and exciting events of their own present day. Were there no more examples, one might object that I am unfairly extrapolating a general rule about the irresistibility of the Animal Apocalypse from the specific activity of one historical moment. But I believe I can demonstrate that the story of the work, the Animal Apocalypse, extends beyond the Apocalypse of the Birds.

The Armenian version of the Testament of Joseph, from the Armenian Testaments of the Twelve Patriarchs, has been variously dated between the fifth and tenth centuries.[28] In chapter 19, a redactor turns a dream vision attributed to Joseph into an animal apocalypse:[29]

> (2) I saw twelve stags which were pasturing and of them, nine were scattered but three were saved. And on the following day they too were

---

[28] On the date of the Armenian translation see Michael E. Stone, *An Editio Minor of the Armenian Version of the Testaments of the Twelve Patriarchs*, Hebrew University Armenian Studies 11 (Leuven: Peeters, 2012), 10–13.

[29] I agree with most scholars that the Armenian represents a secondary version of this passage. This was not always the consensus. The majority of Charles' manuscripts for his 1908 edition

scattered. (3) And I saw that the three stags became three lambs and they cried out to the Lord and he brought them forth out of darkness into light and he brought them to a green and watered place. (4) And there they cried out to the Lord until the nine stags were gathered to them and they became like twelve sheep and after a little they increased and became many flocks. (5) After this I saw, and behold, twelve bulls which were suckling the one cow which, through the vast amount of her milk, was making a sea. And the twelve flocks and the innumerable sheep were drinking from it. (6) And the horns of the fourth bull were elevated up to the heavens and became like a wall for the flocks and another horn flowered between the horns. (7) And I saw a calf which circled it twelve times and became an aide to the bulls altogether. (8) And I saw among the horns a virgin who had a many-colored garment and from her a lamb went forth. And from its right side all wild beasts and creeping things attacked and the lamb overcame them and destroyed them. (9) And the bulls and the cow and the three horns were glad because of it and rejoiced with it. (10) This must take place in its time.[30]

The earlier Greek version only included material corresponding to verses 2 and 8–10, leaving a gaping historical window. Apparently, the Greek version is reticent to narrate anything between the collapse of the twelve tribes and the advent of Christ.[31] If we can surmise from the parallels between the Greek

were Armenian, and he states with reference to this chapter that "we are obliged to trust ourselves wholly to the Armenian version" even though he deems it "unsatisfactory" in Charles, *Testaments*, 190. Since Charles' day, more Greek manuscripts were discovered, and the priority of the Greek version has been accordingly more broadly established and documented. By the time of Hollander and de Jonge's magisterial commentary, the passage is regarded as "secondary," and they do not translate or comment upon it, in de Jonge and Hollander, *Testaments* (1985), 407. In agreement that 19.3–7 is to be regarded as secondary, see Kugler, *Testaments*, 83; Jürgen Becker, *Untersuchungen zur Entstehungsgeschichte der Testamente der zwölf Patriarchen*, Arbeiten zur Geschichte des antiken Judentums und des Urchristentums 8 (Leiden: Brill, 1970), 60–8. See, however, the recent review of scholarship and interest in reclaiming the Armenian version of this passage as potentially quite early in Vered Hillel, *The Testaments of the Twelve Patriarchs: Structure, Source, and Composition* (Lewiston, NY: Edwin Mellen Press, 2013), 200–23.

[30] Translation from Stone, *Editio Minor*. I have also consulted his earlier translation, in Michael E. Stone, *The Armenian Version of the Testament of Joseph: Introduction, Critical Edition, and Translation*, Texts and Translations 6 (Missoula, MT: Scholars Press for the Society of Biblical Literature, 1975), 53–7. See also the Greek and Armenian translations compared in Kee, "Testaments," 824; Charles, *Testaments*, 190–3.

[31] The Greek version: "Listen, my children, also to the visions that I saw. Twelve deer were feeding and the nine were scattered and dispersed over the earth; likewise also the three. And I saw that from Judah a virgin was born, wearing a linen garment, and from her a lamb without spot came forth, and on its left side (it was) as a lion. And all the beasts rushed against it, and the lamb overcame them and destroyed them to be trodden under foot. And the angels and men and the whole earth rejoiced at him. And these things will happen in their season in the last days." Translation from de Jonge and Hollander, *Testaments* (1985).

Testament of Joseph and Revelation that the vision of the virgin and lamb is narrating an eschatological war,³² the historical gap grows wider still – little is covered between the decline of the twelve tribes and the eschaton.

This "gap" presented a blank canvas to a later scribe. As Jürgen Becker puts it, "precisely because there was no post-exilic era, A[rmenian] filled the gap with v. 3–7."³³ I suggest that someone was confronted with an animalistic apocalypse and a historiographical vacuum. Both features recalled the distinctive contributions of the Animal Apocalypse, such that a new composition was inspired.³⁴ The literary direction of the textual transformation can be quickly ascertained with a telling example from the parallel material: the concluding statement in Greek "the angels and men and the whole earth rejoiced at him," receives an animal allegorical treatment in Armenian, becoming "the bulls and the cow and the three horns were glad because of it and rejoiced with it." I do not think Armenian T. Jos 19.3–10 directly quotes any text corresponding to the Animal Apocalypse.³⁵ Still, I think it shows no small degree of knowledge of the Animal Apocalyptic tradition: first, as I demonstrated above, because the Animal Apocalypse was known in Greek to some contributors to the Testaments; second, the use of animal symbolism to tell an allegorical history

---

³² I take the Greek version of this passage to present many parallels with Revelation. E.g. for a woman clad in linen, see Rev 19.9; for the birth of Christ to a woman, see Rev 12.1–6; for Christ as lamb, see Rev 5.6; for Christ as lion, see Rev 5.5; for a battle between beasts and lamb, see Rev 17.14; for the rejoicing of angels, see Rev 19.1ff. Accordingly, much scholarship on this passage has been undertaken by scholars interested in contextualizing the lamb symbolism in Revelation, especially with reference to 19.8. See Joachim Jeremias, "Das Lamm, das aus der Jungfrau hervorging (Test Jos 19, 8)," *Zeitschrift für die neutestamentliche Wissenschaft und die Kunde der älteren Kirche* 57, no. 3–4 (1966): 216–19; Klaus Koch, "Das Lamm, das Agypten vernichtet," *Zeitschrift für die neutestamentliche Wissenschaft und die Kunde der älteren Kirche* 57, no. 1–2 (1966): 79–93; B. Murmelstein, "Das Lamm in Test Jos 19:8," *Zeitschrift für die neutestamentliche Wissenschaft und die Kunde der älteren Kirche* 58, no. 3–4 (1967): 273–9; J. C. O'Neill, "The Lamb of God in the Testaments of the Twelve Patriarchs," *Journal for the Study of the New Testament* 1, no. 2 (March 1979): 2–30; Johns, *Lamb Christology*, 80–7.

³³ "Eben weil die nachexilische Zeit fehlte, füllte A die Lücke mit V. 3–7," in Becker, *Untersuchungen*, 63.

³⁴ 1 Enoch did not circulate in Armenian, to our knowledge, which suggests that the Armenian version here is a witness to textual development that took place during Greek transmission of the Testaments (as is generally assumed about the Armenian). I will nevertheless refer to it as "the Armenian," as that is the language in which it is extant.

³⁵ Part of the difficulty in establishing a relationship is that the "Little Animal Apocalypse" does not, to my eye, present many direct textual links to the Animal Apocalypse of Enoch – which is to say, its words-in-order do not match very closely. Were we to pursue the reception history of the *text* of the Animal Apocalypse (as I did in Chapter 5), this passage would not strictly qualify (and, indeed, I did not treat it there). This narrow pursuit of parallels on the level of text is the heart of the conflict between Charles, who proposed TJos 19 was a reference to the Animal Apocalypse, and Tiller, who said the "correspondence" was not close enough, in Charles, *Enoch or, 1 Enoch*, 216; Tiller, *Commentary*, 387.

of groups of Jewish protagonists is an idiosyncratic shared feature.[36] I take this passage to represent a new vessel into which the distinctive features of the Animal Apocalypse overflowed.[37] I propose that this passage represents another compositional moment in horizons opened up by the Animal Apocalypse, one that was not collated in the Gəʿəz version. I cannot resist calling it the "Little Animal Apocalypse."[38]

Few scholars, to my knowledge, have hazarded guesses as to the referents of this curious animal allegory.[39] It is very difficult to reconcile with post-exilic Jewish history as we know it. Becker correlates verse 2 with the Assyrian and Babylonian conquests, but then laments: "otherwise, this text is anything but understandable."[40] It is possible that a better match could be found if the historical window is expanded into the common era to cover events belonging to early Christianity, though proposing and defending a specific solution goes outside the framework of this project.[41]

---

[36] One objection might be the circulation of other works using theriomorphic symbolism, like Daniel. But while animal symbolism is used in Daniel, animals symbolize antagonists (Alexander, Antiochus). Furthermore, the animal allegorization is incomplete: in Daniel 7 and 8, beasts confront *people*.

[37] For some more specific parallels: the split of the twelve tribes into a nine-and-three division in Armenian T. Jos 19.2 might be compared to the grouping of three sheep returning from exile at 1 En 89.72 and the rejoicing of the bulls and cow and three horns of T. Jos 19.9 is reminiscent of the Lord of the Sheep rejoicing in 1 En 90.33 and 38.

[38] On analogy with the so-called "Little Apocalypse" embedded in the synoptic gospels.

[39] One attempt came from Charles, who proposed the progression symbolizes the rise of the Maccabees, on analogy with his Maccabean reading of the Animal Apocalypse and his second century BCE dating of the Testaments broadly speaking. But even bracketing that I differ from Charles on the provenance of these two works, his interpretative framework leads to many forced readings and leaves much unsolved. For instance, Charles is stumped by the proposal that the twelve tribes are reunited in verse 2, suggesting "the writer seems to pass from the sphere of history to prediction," a problem which remains unaddressed as the twelve reappear at verse 4. Charles, *Testaments*, 191–2.

Another recent hypothesis is advanced by Vered Hillel, who believes the text to break into two separate visions. In her view, one vision comprises 19.2–4 and tells of the dispersion and redemption of the twelve tribes, and another comprises 19.5–8 which is a prophecy of eschatological restoration featuring Judah (bull), Levi (calf), Jesus (lamb), Mary (virgin), and God (cow). But I find the subdivision of the unit into two pieces to be an unnecessary intervention, as the cited grounds are that the use of visionary transitional clauses like "behold" or "again I saw" landmark the transition to different conceptual units, which is not borne out in the study of other apocalyptic texts. This subdivision is crucial to her interpretation of the allegorical referents as it allows the timeline to be reset after 19.2–4, which clearly narrates something like the exile, so that pre-exilic figures like Judah and David might be identified in verses 5 and 6. See Hillel, *Testaments*, 200–23.

[40] "Auch sonst ist dieser Text alles andere als verstandlich." From Becker, *Untersuchungen*, 62.

[41] A Christian-referent line of inquiry might have been largely precluded because scholars who read the Testaments as Christian compositions are generally much influenced by de Jonge and Hollander who, as previously mentioned, considered this passage to be a later

The Little Animal Apocalypse represents another instance in which the creatures of the Animal Apocalypse were set free to roam in the historical climes of a writer's own choosing. This is the model by which I explained the development and emergence of the Apocalypse of the Birds in the first century CE. The function of the two textual productions – the Little Animal Apocalypse and the Apocalypse of the Birds – proves to be quite different. The Apocalypse of the Birds continues and updates the Vision of the Beasts. The Little Animal Apocalypse changes course from the textual progression of the work that seems to have inspired it and fills in the blanks of a brief visionary account.

Even with so many open questions, the Little Animal Apocalypse helps us speak with greater precision about the contribution of the Apocalypse of the Birds to the Animal Apocalyptic tradition. Both are animal apocalypses designed to fill a historical gap, conjuring creatures to tell a story of how a community got from "then" to "now." The Little Animal Apocalypse illustrates an ancient scribe's idea that world history ought to be covered in an animal apocalypse, while the Apocalypse of the Birds speaks to a scribal instinct that the Animal Apocalypse ought to cover all of world history.

and secondary addition and therefore excluded it from their edition and commentary. But, for an attempt: I think it possible that the reunion of the twelve deer (v. 3–4) and their transformation into sheep (v. 4) that so stumped Charles could represent the collection of the twelve disciples. The twelve sheep seem to become twelve bulls between verse 4 and verse 5. Perhaps the transformation of sheep to bulls at 1 En 90.37–8 is running in the background, and we are to restore the temporal turning point gleaned from Enoch (which equates this transformation with the advent of a messiah, representing Jesus to the writers of the Testaments) at this juncture. If so, it is possible that the transformation from sheep to bull was held to be something like "conversion" to apostleship of Christianity. The detail in verse 5 that the twelve bulls were drinking from a sea of milk is curious – milk never appears in the Animal Apocalypse. Milk was, however, a powerful and controversial symbol used by writers from Paul (1 Cor 3.1–3) to Augustine to reflect on the nature and formation of Christian identity. The flowing of milk from a female cow might prove analogous to the early Christian imaging of this milk as flowing from mothers, and "Mother Church" in particular (see Augustine, Ennarat. Ps 130.11). Perhaps the four bulls of verse 6 refer to four disciples remembered as making up the inner circle of the twelve. The names imagined to belong to Jesus' inner-circle change depending on which ancient authority or work is asked the question. But at least in the canonical gospels, Peter is always included. Simon called Peter, famously acclaimed in Matthew as the rock on which Jesus claimed he would build his church, could easily represent the fourth bull who rose to prominence and becomes "a wall for the flocks" (Stone) or a "rampart for the herds" (Kee) in verse 6. I confess to being unsure who or what the calf of verse 7 might represent. As noted above, I understand the line between remembered history and anticipated eschaton to be crossed with verse 8, with the narration of the adorned virgin and the victory of the lamb over the armies of beasts. So interpreted, Joseph's dream in Armenian is a potted history stretching from the Israelite exiles under Assyria and Babylonia, through the life of Jesus and formation of communities of disciples, culminating in the inbreaking of the eschaton.

Bryant's energetic works take on lives of their own. Some of those lives can be placed (or place themselves) in a direct genealogical line from one to another. As I have argued, the Apocalypse of the Birds positions itself as heir and successor to the Vision of the Beasts. Others are distant but identifiable relations, as I think the Little Animal Apocalypse of the Testaments represents a kind of distant cousin to the materials preserved in 1 Enoch. The closeness of the textual conversation does matter, if only to scholars. I would not say, for instance, that the Little Animal Apocalypse should be classified under the same "work" heading as the Animal Apocalypse, as I have tried to hint in my assignment of another name. But just as the Vision of the Beasts overflowed its bounds, inspiring the Apocalypse of the Birds, so too did the Animal Apocalypse(s) of Enoch overflow into ancient Mediterranean literary cultures, generating (directly or indirectly) the Little Animal Apocalypse.

Conclusion: time, text, and the Animal Apocalypse

> "I feel that it is more interesting, and also in its way more difficult, to consider what [stories] are, what they have become for us, and what values the long alchemic processes of time have produced in them."
>
> J. R. R. Tolkien

This study has not clarified the earliest origins of the Animal Apocalypse. I do not know to whom or when or where we are to attribute the curious idea that the history of the children of Abraham and Jacob should be told with the aid of flocks, herds, packs and swarms. Nor have I offered any direct guidance on a final Animal Apocalypse at which we can look today, as found in codices containing scriptures of the Ethiopian Orthodox Church. Instead, I have addressed myself to the chaotic, cloudy environs of the first century CE through which I believe the Animal Apocalypse to have wound. This project does not tell the story of an original nor a final Animal Apocalypse, but instead tries to think about some of the very many lost copies that must have existed along the way. I worry not about the start, or finish, but the invisible middle.

I have argued that the Gəʿəz Animal Apocalypse (1 En 85–90) encloses two compositional moments. One of those moments took place in response to the bloody but (to the composers) thrilling events of the first century CE. I think the Apocalypse of the Birds provides a snapshot of the heady early days of the Revolt, when future victory against the Romans felt assured. It did not, however, prove a prescient predictor of future events, as victory belonged to the Romans in the end. This was not the first, nor was it the last, apocalypse to get things wrong. But it is an instructive case all the same.

It is possible that this work lived on because of a mismatch between the events it was written to portray and the events later readers thought it encapsulated. Barnabas and the Testaments seem to have taken the Apocalypse of the Birds as a prophecy of victory of a kind, though certainly not of the victory of the Judaeans over the Romans. An Ethiopian commentary tradition known as the *Andəmta* reads Jesus as the ram of 90.9 and identifies the remainder of the work as a prophecy of subsequent Christian history.

Readers and writers perceived the Animal Apocalypse to be a fundamentally flexible and malleable entity. This might be a curious conclusion given the way that the work might present itself: as a strict, rule-following historical apocalypse that assiduously martials the relevant events of world history into a totalizing scheme. But the Vision of the Beasts was apparently interrupted and redirected by the scribes of the Apocalypse of the Birds, who needed it to march elsewhere. The Apocalypse of the Birds was read as if it explained the downfall of Judaea, when it may actually have been written with every confidence that such a defeat would never take place.

The story of the Animal Apocalypse is located at the crossroads between inheritance and invention. I take it to remind us of the ways that the line between original and copy can be blurred. But most of all, because of its curiously historiographic orientation, it also provides an unusually direct encapsulation of what Tolkien calls the "long alchemic processes of time," as seen by different eyes from different centuries. All texts travel through time. But not all texts tell us the times through which they travel, as does the Animal Apocalypse.

Appendix: An Annotated Apocalypse of the Birds (1 Enoch 89.59–90.42)

Adapted from Michael Knibb's translation of MS Rylands 23, with suggested identifications

Introducing the Apocalypse of the Birds

(59) And he called seventy shepherds and cast off those sheep that they might pasture them; and he said to the shepherds and to their companions: "Each one of you from now on is to pasture the sheep, and do whatever I command you. (60) And I will hand (them) over to you duly numbered and will tell you which of them are to be destroyed, and destroy them." And he handed those sheep over to them (61) And he called another and said to him: "Observe and see everything that the shepherds do against these sheep, for they will destroy from among them more than I have commanded them. (62) And write down all the excess and destruction which is wrought by the shepherds, how many they destroy at my command, and how many they destroy of their own volition; write down against each shepherd individually all that he destroys. (63) And read out before me exactly how many they destroy of their own volition, and how many are handed over to them for destruction, that this may be a testimony for me against them, that I may know all the deeds of the shepherds, in order to hand them over (for destruction), and may see what they do, whether they abide by my command which I have commanded them, or not. (64) But they must not know (this), and you must not show (this) to them, nor reprove them, but (only) write down against each individual in his time all that the shepherds destroy and bring it all up to me."

Period 1: the Babylonians, and the fall of Jerusalem

(65) And I looked until those shepherds pastured at their time, and they began to kill and to destroy more than they were commanded, and they gave those sheep into the hands of the lions. (66) And the lions and the tigers devoured and swallowed up the majority of those sheep, and the wild-boars devoured with them; and they burnt down that tower and demolished that house. (67) And I was extremely sad about the tower, because that house of the sheep had been demolished; and after that I was unable to see whether those sheep went into that house. (68) And the shepherds and their companions handed those sheep over to all the animals that they might devour them; each one of them at his time received an exact number, and (of) each one of them after the other there was written in a book how many of them he destroyed. (69) And each one killed and destroyed more than was prescribed, and I began to weep and to moan very much because of those sheep.

This passage forms a doublet with the Vision of the Beasts's destruction of Jerusalem (1 En 89.54-8): see Chapter 2.

The records of the shepherds

(70) And likewise in the vision I saw that one who wrote, how every day he wrote down each one which was destroyed by those shepherds, and (how) he brought up and presented and showed the whole book to the Lord of the sheep, everything that they had done, and all that each one of them had made away with, and all that they had handed over to destruction. (71) And the book was read out before the Lord of the sheep, and he took the book in his hand, and read it, and sealed it, and put it down.

Period 2: return from exile

(72) And after this I saw how the shepherds pastured for twelve hours, and behold, three of those sheep

returned and arrived and came and began to build up all that had fallen down from that house; but the wild-boars hindered them so that they could not. (73) And they began again to build, as before, and they raised up that tower, and it was called the high tower; and they began again to place a table before the tower, but all the bread on it (was) unclean and was not pure. (74) And besides all (this) the eyes of these sheep were blinded so that they could not see, and their shepherds likewise; and they handed yet more of them over to their shepherds for destruction, and they trampled upon the sheep with their feet and devoured them. (75) But the Lord of the sheep remained still until all the sheep were scattered abroad and had mixed with them, and they did not save them from the hand of the animals. (76) And that one who wrote the book brought it up, and showed it, and read (it) out in the houses of the Lord of the sheep; and he entreated him on behalf of them, and petitioned him as he showed him all the deeds of their shepherds, and testified before him against all the shepherds. (77) And he took the book, and put it down by him, and went out.

1 En. 89.72-3 narrate the return from exile under the Persians. 74-5 narrate Hellenistic-era events (cf. Daniel 7-8). See Chapter 6.

Period 3: the arrival of the birds

(90.1) I And I looked until the time that thirty-seven shepherds had pastured (the sheep) in the same way, and, each individually, they all completed their time like the first ones; and others received them into their hands to pasture them at their time, each shepherd at his own time. (2) And after this I saw in the vision all the birds of heaven coming: the eagles, and the vultures, and the ibises, and the ravens; but the eagles led all the birds; and they began to devour those sheep, and to peck out their eyes, and to devour their flesh. (3) And the sheep cried out because their flesh was devoured by the birds, and I cried out and lamented in my sleep on account of that shepherd who pastured the sheep. (4) And I looked until those sheep were devoured by the dogs

The Birds: Eagles (Romans, ch.6), Vultures (?), Ibises (Egyptian legions, ch.5), Ravens (Syrian legions, ch.6).

90.4: violent events in Egypt, S. Levant (dogs: non-Jewish residents of Judaea/Syria), and Jerusalem in 66 ce.

and by the eagles and by the ibises, and they left on them neither flesh nor skin nor sinew until only their bones remained; and their bones fell upon the ground, and the sheep became few. (5) And I looked until the time that twenty-three shepherds had pastured (the sheep); and they completed, each in his time, fifty-eight times.

Period 4: the revolt of the rams

(6) And small lambs were born from those white sheep, and they began to open their eyes, and to see, and to cry to the sheep. (7) But the sheep did not cry to them and did not listen to what they said to them, but were extremely deaf, and their eyes were extremely and excessively blinded. (8) And I saw in the vision how the ravens flew upon those lambs, and took one of those lambs, and dashed the sheep in pieces and devoured them. (9) And I looked until horns came up on those lambs, but the ravens cast their horns down; and I looked until a big horn grew on one of those sheep, and their eyes were opened. (10) And it looked at them, and their eyes were opened, and it cried to the sheep, and the rams saw it, and they all ran to it.

(11) And besides all this those eagles and vultures and ravens and ibises were still continually tearing the sheep in pieces and flying upon them and devouring them; and the sheep were silent, but the rams lamented and cried out. (12) And those ravens battled and fought with it, and wished to make away with its horn, but they did not prevail against it. (13) And I looked at them until the shepherds and the eagles and those vultures and ibises came and cried to the ravens that they should dash the horn of that ram in pieces; and they fought and battled with it, and it fought with them and cried out that its help might come to it. (14) And I looked until that man who wrote down the names of the shepherds and brought (them) up before the Lord of the sheep came, and he helped that ram and showed it everything, (namely,

Great horn: a leader of the First Jewish Revolt. The onslaught of the ravens: the campaign of 66 ce led by Cestius Gallus.

Cestius Gallus' failed siege of Jerusalem, heavy losses at Beth Horon, loss of XII Legion's aquila.

that) its help was coming down. (15) And I looked until that Lord of the sheep came to them in anger, and all those who saw him fled, and they all fell into the shadow before him.

(16) All the eagles and vultures and ravens and ibises gathered together and brought with them all the wild sheep, and they all came together and helped one another in order to dash that horn of the ram in pieces. (17) And I looked at that man who wrote the book at the command of the Lord until he opened that book of the destruction which those twelve last shepherds had wrought, and he showed before the Lord of the sheep that they had destroyed even more than (those) before them. (18) And I looked until the Lord of the sheep came to them and took in his hand the staff of his anger and struck the earth; and the earth was split, and all the animals and the birds of heaven fell from those sheep and sank in the earth, and it closed over them. (19) And I looked until a big sword was given to the sheep, and the sheep went out against all the wild animals to kill them, and all the animals and the birds of heaven fled before them.

Eschatological final battle

The last judgment

(20) And I looked until a throne was set up in the pleasant land, and the Lord of the sheep sat on it; and they took all the sealed books and opened those books before the Lord of the sheep. (21) And the Lord called those men, the seven first white ones, and commanded (them) to bring before him the first star which went before those stars whose private parts (were) like the private parts of horses and they brought them all before him. (22) And he said to that man who wrote before him, who was one of the seven white ones – he said to him: "Take those seventy shepherds to whom I handed over the sheep, and who, on their own authority, took and killed more than I commanded them." (23) And behold, I saw them all bound, and they all stood

before him. (24) And the judgement was held first on the stars, and they were judged and found guilty; and they went to the place of damnation, and were thrown into a deep (place), full of fire, burning and full of pillars of fire. (25) And those seventy shepherds were judged and found guilty, and they also were thrown into that abyss of fire. (26) And I saw at that time how a similar abyss was opened in the middle of the earth which was full of fire, and they brought those blind sheep, and they were all judged and found guilty and thrown into that abyss of fire, and they burned; and that abyss was on the south of that house. (27) And I saw those sheep burning, and their bones were burning.

The end of old Jerusalem, the coming of new Jerusalem

(28) And I stood up to look until he rolled up that old house, and they removed all the pillars, and all the beams and ornaments of that house were rolled up with it; and they removed it and put it in a place in the south of the land. (29) And I looked until the Lord of the sheep brought a new house, larger and higher than that first one, and he set it up on the site of the first one which had been rolled up; and all its pillars (were) new, and its ornaments (were) new and larger than (those of) the first one, the old one which he had removed. And the Lord of the sheep (was) in the middle of it. (30) And I saw all the sheep which were left, and all the animals on the earth and all the birds of heaven falling down and worshipping those sheep, and entreating them and obeying them in every command.

Reference to destruction of Temple in 70 CE? So read in Barn/T. 12 Patr (ch. 5), unlikely reading in text itself (ch. 6)

Flashback: the arrival of a messiah, transformation of gentiles

(31) And after this those three who were dressed in white and had taken hold of me by my hand, the

ones who had brought me up at first – they, with the hand of that ram also holding me, took me up and put me down in the middle of those sheep before the judgement was held. (32) And those sheep were all white, and their wool thick and pure. (33) And all those which had been destroyed and scattered and all the wild animals and all the birds of heaven gathered together in that house, and the Lord of the sheep rejoiced very much because they were all good and had returned to his house. (34) And I looked until they laid down that sword which had been given to the sheep, and they brought it back into his house, and it was sealed before the Lord; and all the sheep were enclosed in that house, but it did not hold them. (35) And the eyes of all of them were opened, and they saw well, and there was not one among them that did not see. (36) And I saw that that house was large and broad and exceptionally full.

(37) And I saw how a white bull was born, and its horns (were) big, and all the wild animals and all the birds of heaven were afraid of it and entreated it continually. (38) And I looked until all their species were transformed, and they all became white bulls; and the first one among them was the Word and the Word was a great animal and had big black horns on its head. And the Lord of the sheep rejoiced over them and over all the bulls.

On the flashback apparently enacted here, see the discussion in parallel with T. Benj 9 in ch. 5.

This passage may be read Christologically in Barn/T. 12 Patr (ch. 5). The possibility of an earlier non-Christian referent is uncertain (ch. 6).

Conclusion to dream visions

(39) And I was asleep in the middle of them; and I woke up and saw everything. (40) And this is the vision which I saw while I was asleep, and I woke up and blessed the Lord of righteousness and ascribed glory to him. (41) But after this I wept bitterly, and my tears did not stop until I could not endure it; when I looked, they ran down on account of that which I saw, for everything will come to pass and be fulfilled; and all the deeds of men in their order were shown to me. (42) That night I remembered my first dream, and because of it I wept and was disturbed, because I had seen that vision.

These verses unify multiple dream visions of Enoch into one. They may belong to the Apocalypse of the Birds or a later redactor (ch. 7).

Bibliography

Aalen, Sverre. "St Luke's Gospel and the Last Chapters of I Enoch." *New Testament Studies* 13, no. 1 (1966): 1–13.
Adler, William. "The Apocalyptic Survey of History Adapted by Christians: Daniel's Prophecy of 70 Weeks." In *The Jewish Apocalyptic Heritage in Early Christianity*, edited by James C. VanderKam and William Adler, 201–38. Leiden: Brill, 1996.
Alexander, Paul J. "Medieval Apocalypses as Historical Sources." *The American Historical Review* 73, no. 4 (1968): 997–1018.
Allison, Dale C. "The Jewish Setting of the Epistle of James." *In Die Skriflig* 49, no. 1 (2015): 1–9.
Allison, Dale C., and W. D. Davies. *A Critical and Exegetical Commentary on the Gospel According to Saint Matthew XIX–XXVII*. Vol. 3. International Critical Commentary on the Holy Scriptures of the Old and New Testaments. Edinburgh: T&T Clark, 1988.
Alter, Robert. *Genesis*. New York: W.W. Norton, 1998.
Ambrose, Shannon O. "The Codicology and Palaeography of London, BL, Royal 5 E. XIII and Its Abridgement of the Collectio Canonum Hibernensis." *Codices Manuscripti & Impressi*, no. 54 (2006): 1–26.
———. "The De Vindictis Magnis Magnorum Peccatorum: A New Hiberno-Latin Witness to the Book of Kings." *Eolas: The Journal of the American Society of Irish Medieval Studies* 5 (2011): 44–60.
Archer, Gleason L., trans. *Jerome's Commentary on Daniel*. Grand Rapids, MI: Baker Book House, 1958.
Ariel, Donald Tzvi. "Identifying the Mints, Minters, and Meanings of the First Jewish Revolt Coins." In *The Jewish Revolt against Rome: Interdisciplinary Perspectives*, edited by Mladen Popović, 373–98. Leiden: Brill, 2011.
Ariel, Donald Tzvi, and Jean-Philippe Fontanille. *The Coins of Herod: A Modern Analysis and Die Classification*. Leiden: Brill, 2011.
Asale, Bruk Ayele. *1 Enoch as Christian Scripture: A Study in the Reception and Appropriation of 1 Enoch in Jude and the Ethiopian Orthodox Tewahǝdo Canon*. Eugene, OR: Pickwick Publications, 2020.
Assefa, Daniel. "5.5.1: Enoch: The Book of Dreams: Greek." In *Textual History of the Bible*, edited by Armin Lange. Vol. 2. Brill, 2020. https://doi.org/10.1163/2452-4107_thb_COM_0205050200
———. *L'apocalypse des animaux (1 Hen 85–90): une propagande militaire? : approches narrative, historico-critique, perspectives théologiques*. Leiden: Brill, 2007.

———. "The Enigmatic End of the Animal Apocalypse in Light of Traditional Ethiopian Commentary." In *Proceedings of the XVth International Conference of Ethopian Studies Hamburg 2003*, edited by Siegbert Uhlig, 1:552–60. Wiesbaden: Harrassowitz Verlag, 2012.

Aune, David E. *Revelation 17–22*. Grand Rapids, MI: Zondervan, 2017.

Baden, Joel S. *The Composition of the Pentateuch: Renewing the Documentary Hypothesis*. New Haven: Yale University Press, 2012.

Bagnoud, Marie. "P. Gen. Inv. 187: Un Texte Apocalyptique Apocryphe Inedit." *Museum Helveticum* 73, no. 2 (2016): 129–53.

Bagnoud, Marie, and Kelley Coblentz Bautch. "5.7.5: Enoch: The Book of the Watchers: An Otherworldly Journey of an Unknown Figure (P.Gen. Inv. 187)." In *Textual History of the Bible*, edited by Armin Lange. Vol. 2. Brill, 2020. https://doi.org/10.1163/2452-4107_thb_COM_0205070500

Bar-Kochva, B. "Sēron and Cestius Gallus at Beith Horon." *Palestine Exploration Quarterly* 108, no. 1 (January 1976): 13–21.

Barnard, Leslie W. "The 'Epistle of Barnabas' and Its Contemporary Setting." *ANRW* II.27.1 (1993): 159–207.

Bautch, Kelley Coblentz. "5.1.1 Textual History of 1 Enoch." In *Textual History of the Bible*, edited by Armin Lange. Brill, February 19, 2020.

Becker, Jürgen. *Untersuchungen zur Entstehungsgeschichte der Testamente der zwölf Patriarchen*. Arbeiten zur Geschichte des antiken Judentums und des Urchristentums 8. Leiden: Brill, 1970.

Bedenbender, Andreas. *Der Gott der Welt tritt auf den Sinai: Entstehung, Entwicklung und Funktionsweise der frühjüdischen Apokalyptik*. Berlin: Institut Kirche und Judentum, 2000.

Begg, Christopher, and Paul Spilsbury. *Judean Antiquities Books 8–10*. Leiden: Brill, 2005.

Bergren, Theodore A. "Sixth Ezra." In *Old Testament Pseudepigrapha: More Noncanonical Scriptures*, edited by Richard Bauckham, James R. Davila, and Alexander Panayotov, 1:483–97. Grand Rapids, MI: Eerdmans, 2013.

Berlin, Andrea M. "Identity Politics in Early Roman Galilee." In *The Jewish Revolt against Rome: Interdisciplinary Perspectives*, edited by Mladen Popović, 69–107. Leiden: Brill, 2011.

———. "Romanization and Anti-Romanization in Pre-Revolt Galilee." In *The First Jewish Revolt: Archaeology, History and Ideology*, edited by Andrea M. Berlin and J. Andrew Overman, 57–73. London: Routledge, 2003.

Bernstein, Moshe J. "Pesher Habakkuk." In *Encyclopedia of the Dead Sea Scrolls*, edited by Lawrence H. Schiffman and James C. VanderKam, 2:647–51. New York: Oxford University Press, 2000.

Beyer, Klaus. *Die aramäischen Texte vom Toten Meer*. Gottingen: Vandenhoeck & Ruprecht, 1984.

Bhayro, Siam. *The Shemihazah and Asael narrative of 1 Enoch 6–11: Introduction, Text, Translation and Commentary with Reference to Ancient Near Eastern and Biblical Antecedents*. Alter Orient und Altes Testament 322. Münster: Ugarit-Verlag, 2005.

Birenboim, Hannan. "The Halakhic Status of Jerusalem According to 4QMMT, '1 Enoch', and Tannaitic Literature (Heb.)." *Meghillot: Studies in the Dead Sea Scrolls* 7 (2009) 3–17.

Bishop, M. C. "Legio V Alaudae and the Crested Lark." *Journal of Roman Military Equipment Studies* 1 (1990): 161–4.

Black, Matthew. *Apocalypsis Henochi Graece*. Leiden: Brill, 1970.

———. *The Book of Enoch or I Enoch: A New English Edition*. Leiden: Brill, 1985.

———. "The 'Two Witnesses' of Rev. 11: 3f. in Jewish and Christian Apocalyptic Tradition." *Donum Gentilicium: New Testament Studies in Honour of David Daube*, 1978, 227–37.

Boccaccini, Gabriele. *Beyond the Essene Hypothesis: The Parting of the Ways between Qumran and Enochic Judaism*. Grand Rapids, MI: Eerdmans, 1998.

———, ed. *Enoch and the Messiah Son of Man: Revisiting the Book of Parables*. Grand Rapids, MI: Eerdmans, 2007.

———. "Response to George Nickelsburg: The Epistle of Enoch and the Qumran Literature." In *George W. E. Nickelsburg in Perspective: An Ongoing Dialogue of Learning*, edited by Jacob Neusner and Alan J. Avery-Peck, 1:123–33. Leiden: Brill, 2003.

Bock, Darrell L. "Dating the Parables of Enoch: A Forschungsbericht." In *Parables of Enoch: A Paradigm Shift*, edited by James H. Charlesworth and Darrell L. Bock, 58–113. London: Bloomsbury, 2012.

Bond, Helen K. "New Currents in Josephus Research." *Currents in Research: Biblical Studies* 8, no. 1 (2000): 162–90.

Bonner, Campbell. *The Last Chapters of Enoch in Greek*. London: Christophers, 1937.

Bouriant, Urbain. "Fragments du texte grec du livre d'Henoch et de quelques écrits attribués à Saint Pierre." In *Memoires publies par les membres de la Mission archeologique ecrits attribues a Saint Pierre*, 93–147. Paris: Libraire de la Societe asiatique, 1892.

Boustan, Ra'anan S. "The Study of Heikhalot Literature: Between Mystical Experience and Textual Artifact." *Currents in Biblical Research* 6, no. 1 (2007): 130–60.

Breed, Brennan W. *Nomadic Text: A Theory of Biblical Reception History*. Bloomington: Indiana University Press, 2014.

Brinkman, John A. *A Political History of Post-Kassite Babylonia: 1158–722 B.C.* Rome: Pontificum Inst. Biblicum, 1968.

Brooke, George J. "The Kittim in the Qumran Pesharim." In *Images of Empire*, edited by Loveday Alexander, 135–59. Sheffield: Sheffield Academic Press, 1991.

Brunk, Gregory G. "A Hoard from Syria Countermarked by the Roman Legions." *Museum Notes (American Numismatic Society)* 25 (1980): 63–76.

Bryant, David. *Cosmos, Chaos and the Kosher Mentality*. Sheffield: Sheffield Academic Press, 1995.

Bryant, John. *The Fluid Text: A Theory of Revision and Editing for Book and Screen*. Editorial Theory and Literary Criticism. Ann Arbor: University of Michigan Press, 2002.

———. "Witness and Access: The Uses of the Fluid Text." *Textual Cultures*, 2007, 16–42.

Burton, Antoinette. "Thinking beyond the Boundaries: Empire, Feminism and the Domains of History." *Social History* 26, no. 1 (January 1, 2001): 60–71.

Caquot, André. "1 Hénoch." In *La Bible. Écrits Intertestamentaires.*, edited by André Dupont-Sommer and Marc Philonenko, 464–525. Paris, 1987.

Cardinal, Pierre. "L'Apocalypse des animaux aux sources de la Grande révolte juive." Paper presented at the Graduate Enoch Seminar, Montreal, QC, May 20, 2014.

Carr, David McLain. *The Formation of the Hebrew Bible: A New Reconstruction*. New York: Oxford University Press, 2011.

Carter, Warren. "Are There Imperial Texts in the Class? Intertextual Eagles and Matthean Eschatology as 'Lights out' Time for Imperial Rome (Matthew 24:27–31)." *Journal of Biblical Literature* 122, no. 3 (2003): 467–87.

Cavallo, Guglielmo, and Herwig Maehler. *Greek Bookhands of the Early Byzantine Period*, AD 300–800. JSTOR, 1987. http://www.jstor.org/stable/pdf/43646221.pdf

Cerquiglini, Bernard. *In Praise of the Variant: A Critical History of Philology*. Translated by Betsy Wing. Baltimore: Johns Hopkins University Press, 1999.

Chae, Young S. *Jesus as the Eschatological Davidic Shepherd: Studies in the Old Testament, Second Temple Judaism, and in the Gospel of Matthew*. Tübingen: Mohr Siebeck, 2006.

Charles, R. H. *The Testaments of the Twelve Patriarchs*. London: Adam and Charles Black, 1908.

———. *The Book of Enoch or, 1 Enoch: Translated from the Editor's Ethiopic Text*. Oxford: Clarendon Press, 1912.

———. *The Book of Enoch Translated from Professor Dillmann's Ethiopic Text*. Oxford: Clarendon Press, 1893.

———. *The Ethiopic Version of the Book of Enoch*. Oxford: Clarendon Press, 1906.
———. *A Critical and Exegetical Commentary on the Revelation of St. John*. Vol. 2. Edinburgh: T&T Clark, 1920.
Charlesworth, James H. "A Rare Consensus Among Enoch Specialists." *Henoch* 24 (2002): 225–34.
Charlesworth, James H., and Darrell L. Bock, eds. *Parables of Enoch: A Paradigm Shift*. London: Bloomsbury, 2012.
Chartier, Roger, and Peter Stallybrass. "What Is a Book?" In *The Cambridge Companion to Textual Scholarship*, edited by Neil Fraistat and Julia Flanders, 188–204. Cambridge: Cambridge University Press, 2013.
Chesnutt, Randall D. "Oxyrhynchus Papyrus 2069 and the Compositional History of 1 Enoch." *Journal of Biblical Literature* 129, no. 3 (2010): 485–505.
Clines, David J. A. "New Directions in Pooh Studies: Überlieferungs-Und Religionsgeschichtliche Studien Zum Pu-Buch." In *On the Way to the Postmodern. Old Testament Essays, 1967–1998*, vol. 2, 830–9. Journal for the Study of the Old Testament Supplement 293. Sheffield: Sheffield Academic, 1998.
Cohen, Shaye J. D. *Josephus in Galilee and Rome: His Vita and Development as a Historian*. Leiden: Brill, 1979.
Cohn, Naftali S. *The Memory of the Temple and the Making of the Rabbis*. Philadelphia: University of Pennsylvania Press, 2013.
Collins, Adela Yarbro. *Crisis and Catharsis: The Power of the Apocalypse*. Philadelphia: Westminster Press, 1984.
———. *Mark: A Commentary*. Hermeneia – A Critical and Historical Commentary on the Bible. Minneapolis: Fortress Press, 2007.
———. *The Combat Myth in the Book of Revelation*. Missoula, MT: Scholars Press for Harvard Theological Review, 1976.
Collins, John J. *Daniel: A Commentary on the Book of Daniel*. Edited by Frank Moore Cross. Minneapolis: Fortress Press, 1993.
———. "Sibylline Oracles." In *The Old Testament Pseudepigrapha*, edited by James Charlesworth, 1:317–473. London: Darton, Longman & Todd, 1983.
———. *The Apocalyptic Imagination: An Introduction to Jewish Apocalyptic Literature*. 3rd ed. Grand Rapids, MI: Eerdmans, 2016.
———. "The Place of the Fourth Sibyl in the Development of the Jewish Sibyllina." *Journal of Jewish Studies* 25 (1974): 365–80.
———. *The Scepter and the Star: Messianism in Light of the Dead Sea Scrolls*. 2nd ed. Grand Rapids, MI: Eerdmans, 2010.
Collman, Ryan D. "Beware the Dogs! The Phallic Epithet in Phil 3.2." *New Testament Studies* 67, no. 1 (January 2021): 105–20.
Cook, Michael. "Eschatology and the Dating of Traditions." *Princeton Papers in Near Eastern Studies* 1 (1992): 23–47.
Coulston, J. C., and M. C. Bishop. *Roman Military Equipment: From the Punic Wars to the Fall of Rome*. 2nd ed. Oxford: Oxbow, 2006.
Cowley, Roger W. "Old Testament Introduction in the Andəmta Commentary Tradition." *Journal of Ethiopian Studies* 12, no. 1 (1974): 133–75.
———. *The Traditional Interpretation of the Apocalypse of St. John in the Ethiopian Orthodox Church*. University of Cambridge Oriental Publications 33. New York: Cambridge University Press, 1983.
Crawford, Sidnie White and Cecilia Wassen, eds. *The Dead Sea Scrolls at Qumran and the Concept of a Library*. Studies on the Texts of the Desert of Judah 116. Boston: Brill, 2016.
D'Amato, Raffaele, and Graham Sumner. *Arms and Armour of the Imperial Roman Soldier from Marius to Commodus, 112 BC–AD 192*. London: Frontline Books, 2010.

---. "The Book of 6 Ezra (2 Esdras 15–16) – Old Testament Pseudepigrapha," 2007. https://otp.wp.st-andrews.ac.uk/abstracts-lectures/the-book-of-6-ezra-2-esdras-15-16/

Davila, James R. *The Provenance of the Pseudepigrapha: Jewish, Christian, or Other?* Leiden: Brill, 2005.

Davis, Kipp. "The Social Milieu of 4QJera (4Q70) in a Second Temple Jewish Manuscript Culture: Fragments, Manuscripts, Variance, and Meaning." In *The Dead Sea Scrolls and the Study of the Humanities*, edited by Pieter Hartog, Alison Schofield, and Samuel I. Thomas, 53–76. Studies on the Texts of the Desert of Judah 125. Leiden: Brill, 2018.

---. "'There and Back Again': Reconstruction and Reconciliation of the War Text 4QMilḥamaa (4Q491a–c)." In *The War Scroll, Violence, War and Peace in the Dead Sea Scrolls and Related Literature: Essays in Honour of Martin G. Abegg on the Occasion of His 65th Birthday*, edited by Kipp Davis, Kyung S. Baek, Peter W. Flint, and Dorothy Peters, 125–46. Studies on the Texts of the Desert of Judah 115. Leiden: Brill, 2016.

DeSilva, David A. "The Testaments of the Twelve Patriarchs as Witnesses to Pre-Christian Judaism: A Re-Assessment." *Journal for the Study of the Pseudepigrapha* 23, no. 1 (September 1, 2013): 21–68.

Deutsch, Robert. "Coinage of the First Jewish Revolt Against Rome: Iconography, Minting Authority, Metallurgy." In *The Jewish Revolt against Rome: Interdisciplinary Perspectives*, edited by Mladen Popović, 361–72. Leiden: Brill, 2011.

Dibley, Amy Genevive. "Abraham's Uncircumcised Children: The Enochic Precedent for Paul's Paradoxical Claim in Galatians 3:29." PhD diss., UC Berkeley, 2013. https://escholarship.org/uc/item/2qs60947

Dillmann, August. *Das Buch Henoch*. Leipzig: Fr. Chr. Wilh. Vogel, 1853.

---. *Lexicon linguae aethiopicae cum indice latino*. Leipzig: Weigel, 1865.

Dimant, Devorah. "1 Enoch 6–11: A Fragment of a Parabiblical Work." *Journal of Jewish Studies* 53, no. 2 (2002): 223–37.

---. "Ideology and History in the Animal Apocalypse (1 Enoch 85–90)." In *From Enoch to Tobit: Collected Studies in Ancient Jewish Literature*, 91–119. Tübingen: Mohr Siebeck, 2017.

---. "Jerusalem and the Temple in the Animal Apocalypse (1 Enoch 85–90) in Light of the Qumran Community Worldview." In *From Enoch to Tobit: Collected Studies in Ancient Jewish Literature*, 119–39. Tübingen: Mohr Siebeck, 2017.

---. "New Light from Qumran on the Jewish Pseudepigrapha – 4Q390." In *The Madrid Qumran Congress: Proceedings of the International Congress on the Dead Sea Scrolls, Madrid 18–21 March, 1991*, edited by Julio Trebolle Barrera and Luis Vegas Montaner, 405–48. Leiden: Brill, 1992.

---. "The Biography of Enoch and the Books of Enoch." In *From Enoch to Tobit: Collected Studies in Ancient Jewish Literature*, 59–73. Tübingen: Mohr Siebeck, 2017.

---. "The Seventy Weeks Chronology (Dan 9, 24–27) in the Light of New Qumranic Texts." In *The Book of Daniel in the Light of New Findings*. Bibliotheca Ephemeridum Theologicarum Lovaniensium. Leuven: Peeters, 1993, 187–210.

DiTommaso, Lorenzo. *The Book of Daniel and the Apocryphal Daniel Literature*. Leiden: Brill, 2005.

---. "Dating the Eagle Vision of 4 Ezra: A New Look at an Old Theory." *Journal for the Study of the Pseudepigrapha* 10, no. 20 (October 1999): 3–38.

Donadoni, Sergio. "Un Frammento Della Versione Copta Del «Libro Di Enoch»." *Acta Orientalia* 25 (1960): 197–202.

Donaldson, Terence L. *Judaism and the Gentiles: Jewish Patterns of Universalism (to 135 CE)*. Waco, TX: Baylor University Press, 2007.

Drawnel, Henryk. "5.5.2: Enoch: The Book of Dreams: Aramaic." Edited by Kelley Coblentz Bautch and Archibald Wright. In *Textual History of the Bible*, edited by Armin Lange. Brill, 2020. https://doi.org/10.1163/2452-4107_thb_COM_0205050200

———. *Qumran Cave 4: The Aramaic Books of Enoch*. Oxford: Oxford University Press, 2019.

———. *The Aramaic Astronomical Book (4Q208–4Q211) from Qumran: Text, Translation, and Commentary*. Oxford; New York: Oxford University Press, 2011.

Driscoll, Matthew J. "The Words on the Page: Thoughts on Philology, Old and New." In *Creating the Medieval Saga: Versions, Variability, and Editorial Interpretations of Old Norse Saga Literature*, edited by Judy Quinn and Emily Lethbridge, 85–102. Odense: University Press of Southern Denmark, 2010.

Drummond, James. *The Jewish Messiah, a Critical History of the Messianic Idea among the Jews from the Rise of the Maccabees to the Closing of the Talmud*. London: Longmans, Green and Co., 1877.

Dugan, Elena. "Enochic Biography and the Manuscript History of 1 Enoch: The Codex Panopolitanus Book of the Watchers." *Journal of Biblical Literature* 140, no. 1 (2021): 113–38.

Ehrensperger, Kathy. "The Pauline Ἐκκλεσια and Images of Community in Enoch Traditions." In *Paul the Jew: Rereading the Apostle as a Figure of Second Temple Judaism*, edited by Gabriele Boccaccini and Carlos Segovia, 183–216. Minneapolis: Fortress Press, 2016.

Ehrman, Bart D. *The Apostolic Fathers, Volume II: Epistle of Barnabas. Papias and Quadratus. Epistle to Diognetus. The Shepherd of Hermas*. Loeb Classical Library 25. Cambridge, MA: Harvard University Press, 2003.

Ellis, E. Earle. "Dating the New Testament★." *New Testament Studies* 26, no. 4 (July 1980): 487–502.

Erho, Ted M. "Historical-Allusional Dating and the Similitudes of Enoch." *Journal of Biblical Literature* 130, no. 3 (2011): 493–511.

———. "Internal Dating Methodologies and the Problem Posed by the Similitudes of Enoch." *Journal for the Study of the Pseudepigrapha* 20, no. 2 (2010): 83–103.

Erho, Ted M., and Loren T. Stuckenbruck. "A Manuscript History of Ethiopic Enoch." *Journal for the Study of the Pseudepigrapha* 23, no. 2 (2013): 87–133.

———. "The Gəʿəz Manuscript Tradition and the Study of 1 Enoch: Problems and Prospects." Paper presented at the 10th Enoch Seminar: Enoch and Enochic Traditions in the Early Modern Period: A Reception History from the 15th to the end of the 19th Centuries. Florence, Italy, 2019.

Eshel, Esther, and Hanan Eshel. "New Fragments from Qumran:, 4Q226, 8QGen, and XQpapEnoch." *Dead Sea Discoveries* 12, no. 2 (2005): 134–57.

Eshel, Hanan. "Documents of the First Jewish Revolt from the Judean Desert." In *The First Jewish Revolt: Archaeology, History, and Ideology*, edited by Andrea M. Berlin and J. Andrew Overman, 157–63. London: Routledge, 2002.

———. "The Two Historical Layers of Pesher Habakkuk." In *Northern Lights on the Dead Sea Scrolls: Proceedings of the Nordic Qumran Network 2003–2006*, edited by Anders Klostergaard Petersen, Torleif Elgvin, Cecilia Wassen, Hanne von Weissenberg, and Mikael Winninge, 107–17. Studies on the Texts of the Desert of Judah 80. Leiden: Brill, 2009.

Eshel, Hanan, Magen Broshi, and Timothy A. J. Jull. "Four Murabbaʿat Papyri and the Alleged Capture of Jerusalem by Bar Kokhba." In *Law in the Documents of the Judaean Desert*, edited by Ranon Katzoff and David Schaps, 45–50. Leiden: Brill, 2005.

Fine, Steven. *Art and Judaism in the Greco-Roman World: Toward a New Jewish Archaeology*. Cambridge: Cambridge University Press, 2005.

Flemming, Johannes Paul Gotthilf. *Das Buch Henoch: äthiopischer Text*. Leipzig: J. C. Hinrichs, 1902.

Flusser, David. "Jerusalem in the Second Temple Literature." In *Judaism of the Second Temple Period: The Jewish Sages and Their Literature*, translated by Azzan Yadin, 44–75. Grand Rapids, MI: Eerdmans, 2009.

Foucault, Michel. *The Order of Things: An Archaeology of the Human Sciences*. New York: Pantheon Books, 1971.

Frankfurter, David. "Beyond 'Jewish-Christianity': Continuing Religious Sub-Cultures of the Second and Third Centuries and Their Documents." In *The Ways That Never Parted: Jews and Christians in Late Antiquity and the Early Middle Ages*, edited by Adam H. Becker and Annette Yoshiko Reed, 131–43. Minneapolis: Fortress Press, 2007.

———. *Elijah in Upper Egypt: The Apocalypse of Elijah and Early Egyptian Christianity.* Studies in Antiquity and Christianity. Minneapolis: Fortress Press, 1993.

Frisch, Alexandria. "Matthew 24:28: 'Wherever the Body Is, There the Eagles Will Be Gathered Together' and the Death of the Roman Empire." In *The Gospels in First-Century Judaea*, edited by R. Steven Notley and Jeffrey P. García, 58–75. Leiden: Brill, 2016.

Fröhlich, Ida. "The Symbolical Language of the Animal Apocalypse ('1 Enoch' 85–90)." *Revue de Qumrân* 14, no. 4 (1990): 629–36.

Fuks, Gideon. "Some Remarks on Simon Bar Giora." *Scripta Classica Israelica* 8–9 (1988): 106–19.

Gager, John G. *Reinventing Paul.* Oxford: Oxford University Press, 2000.

García Martínez, Florentino. *Qumran and Apocalyptic: Studies on the Aramaic Texts from Qumran.* Leiden: Brill, 1992.

Gaston, Lloyd. *No Stone on Another: Studies in the Significance of the Fall of Jerusalem in the Synoptic Gospels.* Novum Testamentum, Supplements 23. Leiden: Brill Archive, 1970.

Gichon, Mordechai. "Cestius Gallus's Campaign in Judaea." *Palestine Exploration Quarterly* 113, no. 1 (January 1981): 39–62.

Gil, Moshe. "The Ethiopic Book of Enoch Reconsidered." In *Related Worlds: Studies in Jewish and Arab Ancient and Early Medieval History*. Aldershot, Hampshire; Burlington, VT: Ashgate, 2004.

Gildemeister, J. "Ein Fragment des griechischen Henoch." *Zeitschrift der Deutschen Morgenländischen Gesellschaft* 9, no. 2 (1855): 621–4.

Gitlbauer, Michael. *Die Ueberreste griechischer Tachygraphie im Codex Vaticanus Graecus 1809.* Wien, 1878.

Goldstein, I., and J. P. Fontanille. "A New Study of the Coins of the First Jewish Revolt against Rome, 66–70 CE." *American Numismatic Association Journal* 1, no. 2 (2006): 9–32.

Goldstein, Jonathan. *I Maccabees.* Anchor Yale Bible Commentaries 41. Garden City, NY: Doubleday, 1976.

———. "How the Authors of 1 and 2 Maccabees Treated the 'Messianic' Promises." *Judaisms and Their Messiahs at the Turn of the Christian Era*, 1987, 69–96.

———. *II Maccabees.* Anchor Yale Bible Commentaries 41A. Doubleday, 1983.

Gonzalez, Hervé. "Zechariah 9–14 and the Continuation of Zechariah during the Ptolemaic Period." *The Journal of Hebrew Scriptures* 13 (January 1, 2013).

Goodman, Martin. "Current Scholarship on the First Revolt." In *The First Jewish Revolt: Archaeology, History and Ideology*, edited by Andrea M. Berlin and J. Andrew Overman, 15–24. London: Routledge, 2003.

———. *The Ruling Class of Judaea: The Origins of the Jewish Revolt against Rome A.D. 66–70.* Cambridge: Cambridge University Press, 1987.

Gore-Jones, Lydia. "Animals, Humans, Angels and God: Animal Symbolism in the Historiography of the 'Animal Apocalypse' of 1 Enoch." *Journal for the Study of the Pseudepigrapha* 24, no. 4 (2015): 268–87.

Green, Stefan. "'The Temple of God and Crises in Isaiah 65–66 and 1 Enoch.'" In *Studies in Isaiah: History, Theology and Reception*, edited by Tommy Wasserman, Greger Andersson, and David Willgren, 47–66. Library of Hebrew Bible/Old Testament Studies 654. London: Bloomsbury T&T Clark, 2017.

Greenfield, Jonas C., and Michael E. Stone. "Enochic Pentateuch and the Date of the Similitudes." *Harvard Theological Review* 70, no. 1–2 (1977): 51–65.

Greet, Benjamin James Robert. "The Roman Eagle: A Symbol and Its Evolution." PhD diss., University of Leeds, 2015. http://etheses.whiterose.ac.uk/12543/

Gzella, Holger. *A Cultural History of Aramaic: From the Beginnings to the Advent of Islam*. Leiden; Boston: Brill, 2015.

Hachlili, Rachel. *Ancient Jewish Art and Archaeology in the Land of Israel*. New York: Brill, 1988.

Hamidovič, David. "1 Enoch 17 in the Papyrus Geneva 187." In *Apocryphal and Esoteric Sources in the Development of Christianity and Judaism. The Eastern Mediterranean, the Near East, and Beyond.*, edited by Igor Dorfmann-Lazarev, 437–49. Texts and Studies in Eastern Christianity 21. Leiden: Brill, 2021.

Hammond, Wayne G. *J. R. R. Tolkien: A Descriptive Bibliography*. Winchester Bibliographies of 20th Century Writers. Newcastle, Delaware: Oak Knoll Books, 1993.

Harrington, Hannah. "Intermarriage in Qumran Texts: The Legacy of Ezra-Nehemiah." In *Mixed Marriages: Intermarriage and Group Identity in the Second Temple Period*, edited by Christian Frevel, 251–80. New York: T&T Clark, 2011.

Hempel, Charlotte. "Sources and Redaction in the Dead Sea Scrolls: The Growth of Ancient Texts." In *Rediscovering the Dead Sea Scrolls: An Assessment of Old and New Approaches and Methods*, edited by Maxine Grossman, 162–81. Grand Rapids, MI: Eerdmans, 2010.

Hengel, Martin. *Judaism and Hellenism: Studies in Their Encounter in Palestine during the Early Hellenistic Period*. London: SCM Press, 1974.

Henze, Matthias. "Enoch's Dream Visions and the Visions of Daniel Reexamined." In *Enoch and Qumran Origins: New Light on a Forgotten Connection*, edited by Gabriele Boccaccini, 17–22. Grand Rapids, MI: Eerdmans, 2005.

Hillel, Vered. *The Testaments of the Twelve Patriarchs: Structure, Source, and Composition*. Lewiston, NY: Edwin Mellen Press, 2013.

Himmelfarb, Martha. "3 Baruch Revisited: Jewish or Christian Composition, and Why It Matters." *Zeitschrift für antikes Christentum/Journal of Ancient Christianity* 20, no. 1 (2016): 41–62.

———. "Levi, Pineas, and the Problem of Intermarriage at the Time of the Maccabean Revolt." In *Between Temple and Torah: Essays on Priests, Scribes, and Visionaries in the Second Temple Period and Beyond*, 25–47. Tübingen: Mohr Siebeck, 2013.

———. "Levi, Phinehas, and the Problem of Intermarriage at the Time of the Maccabean Revolt." *Jewish Studies Quarterly* 6, no. 1 (1999): 1–24.

———. "R. Moses the Preacher and the Testaments of the Twelve Patriarchs." *AJS Review* 9, no. 1 (1984): 55–78.

———. *The Apocalypse: A Brief History*. Blackwell Brief Histories of Religion. Malden, MA: Wiley-Blackwell, 2010.

von Hofmann, Johann Christian Konrad. *Der Schriftbeweis: Ein theologischer Versuch*. Vol. 1. Nördlingen: Beck'schen Buchhandlung, 1857.

Hofmann, Josef. *Die äthiopische Übersetzung der Johannes-Apokalypse*. Corpus Scriptorum Christianorum Orientalium 281. Leuven: Secrétariat du CorpusSCO, 1967.

Hogan, Karina Martin. "The Watchers Traditions in the Book of the Watchers and the Animal Apocalypse." In *The Watchers in Jewish and Christian Traditions*, edited by Angela Kim Harkins, Kelley Coblentz Bautch, and John C. Endres, 107–20. Minneapolis: Fortress Press, 2014.

———. *Theologies in Conflict in 4 Ezra: Wisdom, Debate, and Apocalyptic Solution*. Leiden: Brill, 2008.

Howgego, C. J. "The XII Fulminata: Countermarks, Emblems and Movements under Trajan or Hadrian." In *Armies and Frontiers in Roman and Byzantine Anatolia*, edited by Stephen Mitchell, 41–6. Oxford: B.A.R., 1983.

Hunt, Arthur S., and Bernard Pyne Grenfell. *The Oxyrhynchus Papyri. Part XVII*. London: Egypt Exploration Fund, 1927.

Hvalvik, Reidar. "The Struggle for Scripture and Covenant: The Purpose of the Epistle of Barnabas and Jewish-Christian Competition in the Second Century." PhD diss., Det teologiske menighetsfakultet, 1994.

Isaac, E. "1 Enoch: A New Translation and Introduction." In *The Old Testament Pseudepigrapha*, edited by James H. Charlesworth, 1:5–89. London: Darton, Longman & Todd, 1983.

James, Montague Rhodes. *Apocrypha Anecdota*. Cambridge: Cambridge University Press, 1893.

Jeremias, Joachim. "Das Lamm, das aus der Jungfrau hervorging (Test Jos 19, 8)." *Zeitschrift für die neutestamentliche Wissenschaft und die Kunde der älteren Kirche* 57, no. 3–4 (1966): 216–19.

Jewett, Robert. *Romans: A Commentary*. Edited by Eldon Jay Epp. Hermeneia – A Critical and Historical Commentary on the Bible. Minneapolis: Fortress, 2007.

Johns, Loren L. *The Lamb Christology of the Apocalypse of John: An Investigation into Its Origins and Rhetorical Force*. Tübingen: Mohr Siebeck, 2003.

Jokiranta, Jutta. "What Is 'Serekh Ha-Yahad (S)'? Thinking about Ancient Manuscripts as Information Processing." In *Sibyls, Scriptures, and Scrolls: John Collins at Seventy*, edited by Joel Baden, Hindy Najman, and Eibert Tigchelaar, 611–35. Leiden: Brill, 2017.

de Jonge, Marinus. "The Main Issues in the Study of the Testaments of the Twelve Patriarchs*." *New Testament Studies* 26, no. 4 (July 1980): 508–24.

———. *Pseudepigrapha of the Old Testament as Part of Christian Literature: The Case of the Testaments of the Twelve Patriarchs and the Greek Life of Adam and Eve*. Leiden: Brill, 2003.

de Jonge, Marinus, and H. W. Hollander. *The Testaments of the Twelve Patriarchs: A Commentary*. Leiden: Brill, 1985.

———. *The Testaments of the Twelve Patriarchs: A Critical Edition of the Greek Text*. Leiden: Brill, 1978.

Josephus, Flavius. *The Jewish War: Volume II*. Translated by Henry St. John Thackeray. Loeb Classical Library 487. Cambridge, MA: Harvard University Press, 1927.

———. *The Jewish War: Volume III*. Translated by Henry St. John Thackeray. Loeb Classical Library 210. Cambridge, MA: Harvard University Press, 1928.

Jülicher, A. *Einleitung in Das Neue Testament*. Tübingen: J. C .B. Mohr, 1931.

Justnes, Årstein. "4Q Apocryphon of Daniel AR (4Q246) and the Book of Daniel." In *The Seleucid and Hasmonean Periods and the Apocalyptic Worldview*, edited by Lester L. Grabbe, Gabriele Boccaccini, and Jason M. Zurawski, 183–93. London: Bloomsbury T&T Clark, 2016.

Justnes, Årstein, and Torleif Elgvin. "A Private Part of Enoch: A Forged Fragment of 1 Enoch 8:4–9:3." In *Wisdom Poured Out Like Water: Studies on Jewish and Christian Antiquity in Honor of Gabriele Boccaccini*, 195–203. Deuterocanonical and Cognate Literature Studies 38. Berlin: De Gruyter, 2018.

Kasher, Aryeh. *The Jews in Hellenistic and Roman Egypt: The Struggle for Equal Rights*. Tübingen: J.C.B. Mohr, 1985.

Keddie, G. Anthony. "Iudaea Capta vs. Mother Zion: The Flavian Discourse on Judaeans and Its Delegitimation in 4 Ezra." *Journal for the Study of Judaism* 49, no. 4–5 (November 2018): 498–550.

Kee, Howard Clark. "Testaments of the Twelve Patriarchs." In *The Old Testament Pseudepigrapha*, edited by James H. Charlesworth, 1:775–828. London: Darton, Longman & Todd, 1983.

Kenyon, Frederic G. *Fasciculus 8: Enoch and Melito. The Chester Beatty Biblical Papyri Descriptions and Texts of Twelve Manuscripts On Papyrus of the Greek Bible*. London: Walker, 1941.

Kister, Menahem. "Barnabas 12:1; 4:3 AND 4Q Second Ezekiel." *Revue Biblique* 97, no. 1 (1990): 63–7.

———. "Concerning the History of the Essenes / לתולדות כת האיסיים." *Tarbiz* 56, no. 1 (1986), 1–18.

Klein, Ralph W. *1 Chronicles: A Commentary*. Edited by Thomas Krüger. Hermeneia – A Critical and Historical Commentary on the Bible. Minneapolis: Fortress Press, 2007.

Knibb, Michael A. "Christian Adoption and Transmission of Jewish Pseudepigrapha: The Case of 1 Enoch." In *Essays on the Book of Enoch and Other Early Jewish Texts and Traditions*, 56–77. Leiden: Brill, 2009.

———. "The Book Of Enoch Or Books Of Enoch? The Textual Evidence For 1 Enoch." In *The Early Enoch Literature*, edited by Gabriele Boccaccini and John J. Collins, 21–40. Supplements to the Journal for the Study of Judaism 121. Leiden: Brill, 2007.

———. *The Ethiopic Book of Enoch: A New Edition in the Light of the Aramaic Dead Sea Fragments*. 2 vols. Oxford: Clarendon Press, 1978.

———. "The Exile in the Literature of the Intertestamental Period." *The Heythrop Journal* 17, no. 3 (1976): 253–72.

———. "The Text-Critical Value of the Quotations from 1 Enoch in Ethiopic Writings." In *Interpreting Translation: Studies on the LXX and Ezechiel in Honour of Johan Lust, Louvain*, edited by Florentino García Martínez and M. Vervenne, 225–35. BETL 192. Leuven: Leuven University Press; Peeters, 2005.

Koch, Klaus. "Das Lamm, das Agypten vernichtet." *Zeitschrift für die neutestamentliche Wissenschaft und die Kunde der älteren Kirche* 57, no. 1–2 (1966): 79–93.

———. *Vor der Wende der Zeiten: Beiträge zur apokalyptischen Literatur*. Neukirchen-Vluyn, Germany: Neukirchener, 1996.

Koenen, L. "A Supplementary Note on the Date of the Oracle of the Potter." *Zeitschrift für Papyrologie und Epigraphik* 54 (1984): 9–13.

Koester, Craig R. *Revelation: A New Translation with Introduction and Commentary*. Anchor Yale Bible 38A. New Haven: Yale University Press, 2014.

Kosmin, Paul J. *Time and Its Adversaries in the Seleucid Empire*. Cambridge: Harvard University Press, 2019.

Kraft, András. "The Last Roman Emperor 'Topos' in the Byzantine Apocalyptic Tradition." *Byzantion* 82, no. 2 (2012): 213–57.

Kraft, Robert A. "The Epistle of Barnabas: Its Quotations and Their Sources: A Thesis." PhD diss., Harvard University, 1961.

———. *Barnabas and the Didache*. Vol 3 of *The Apostolic Fathers: A New Translation and Commentary*. New York: Nelson, 1965.

———. "Enoch and Written Authorities in Testaments of the Twelve Patriarchs." In *Exploring the Scripturesque: Jewish Texts and Their Christian Contexts*, 163–72. JSJSup 137. Leiden: Brill, 2009.

———. *Exploring the Scripturesque: Jewish Texts and Their Christian Contexts*. Leiden; Boston: Brill, 2009.

———. "The Pseudepigrapha and Christianity, Revisited: Setting the Stage and Framing Some Central Questions." In *Exploring the Scripturesque: Jewish Texts and Their Christian Contexts*, 35–61. Leiden; Boston: Brill, 2009.

Kraus, T. J. "7Q5 – Status Quaestionis And Fundamental Remarks To Qualify The Discussion Of The Papyrus Fragment." In *Ad Fontes: Original Manuscripts and Their Significance for Studying Early Christianity*, 231–59. Leiden: Brill, 2007.

Kugler, Robert. *Testaments of the Twelve Patriarchs*. Sheffield: Bloomsbury Publishing, 2001.

Kulik, Alexander, Gabriele Boccaccini, Lorenzo DiTommaso, David Hamidovič, and Michael E. Stone, eds. *A Guide to Early Jewish Texts and Traditions in Christian Transmission. A Guide to Early Jewish Texts and Traditions in Christian Transmission*. Oxford: Oxford University Press, 2019.

Laato, Antti. "The Chronology in the Animal Apocalypse of 1 Enoch 85–90." *Journal for the Study of the Pseudepigrapha* 26, no. 1 (2016): 3–19.

Lake, Kirsopp. *The Apostolic Fathers*. Vol. 2. London: Heinemann, 1912.

Lange, Armin. "Your Daughters Do Not Give to Their Sons and Their Daughters Do Not Take for Your Sons (Ezra 9,12): Intermarriage in Ezra 9–10 and in the Pre-Maccabean Dead Sea Scrolls." *Biblische Notizen* 137, no. 1 (2008): 17–39.

Langlois, Michaël. "Les Manuscrits de La Mer Morte à l'aune de La Philologie Matérielle." *Revue d'Histoire et de Philosophie Religieuses* 95, no. 1 (2015): 3–31.

Langlois, Michael, Kipp Davis, Ira Rabin, Ines Feldman, Myriam Krutzsch, Hasia Rimon, Årstein Justnes, and Torleif Elgvin. "Nine Dubious 'Dead Sea Scrolls' Fragments from the Twenty-First Century." *Dead Sea Discoveries* 24, no. 2 (2017): 189–228.

Larson, Erik W. "The Translation of Enoch: From Aramaic into Greek." PhD diss., New York University, 1995.

Laurence, Richard. *The Book of Enoch, the Prophet*. Oxford: JH Parker, 1838.

Lawlor, Hugh J. "Early Citations from the Book of Enoch." *The Journal of Philology* 25, no. 50 (1897): 164–225.

Lee, Ralph. "The Ethiopic 'Andəmta' Commentary on Ethiopic Enoch 2 (1 Enoch 6–9)." *Journal for the Study of the Pseudepigrapha* 23, no. 3 (March2014): 179–200.

Levine, Amy-Jill. *The Social and Ethnic Dimensions of Matthean Social History*. Studies in the Bible and Early Christianity 14. Lewiston, NY: Edwin Mellen Press, 1988.

Lied, Liv Ingeborg. "Media Culture, New Philology, and the Pseudepigrapha: A Note on Method." Paper presented at the SBL Annual Meeting, Chicago, 2012. https://www.academia.edu/4131828/Lied_Media_Culture_New_Philology_and_the_Pseudepigrapha_SBL_2012

———. "Text–Work–Manuscript: What Is an 'Old Testament Pseudepigraphon'?" *Journal for the Study of the Pseudepigrapha* 25, no. 2 (2015): 150–65.

Lied, Liv Ingeborg, and Hugo Lundhaug, eds. *Snapshots of Evolving Traditions: Jewish and Christian Manuscript Culture, Textual Fluidity, and New Philology*. Texte und Untersuchungen zur Geschichte der altchristlichen Literatur 175. Boston: De Gruyter, 2017.

Lied, Liv Ingeborg, and Loren T. Stuckenbruck. "Pseudepigrapha and Their Manuscripts." In *The Old Testament Pseudepigrapha*, edited by Liv Ingeborg Lied and Matthias Henze, 203–30. Fifty Years of the Pseudepigrapha Section at the SBL. Atlanta: SBL Press, 2019.

Lilla, Salvatore. *Il Testo tachigrafico del "De Divinis nominibus", Vat. gr. 1809*. Vatican City: Biblioteca apostolica vaticana, 1970.

Lin, Yii-Jan. *The Erotic Life of Manuscripts: New Testament Textual Criticism and the Biological Sciences*. New York: Oxford University Press, 2016.

Lindars, Barnabas. "A Bull, a Lamb and a Word: I Enoch XC. 38." *New Testament Studies* 22, no. 04 (1976): 483–6.

Loader, William R. G. *Enoch, Levi, and Jubilees on Sexuality: Attitudes towards Sexuality in the Early Enoch Literature, the Aramaic Levi Document, and the Book of Jubilees*. Grand Rapids, MI: Eerdmans, 2007.

Longenecker, Bruce W. "Revelation 19,10: One Verse in Search of an Author." *Zeitschrift für die Neutestamentliche Wissenschaft und die Kunde der Älteren Kirche; Berlin* 91, no. 3 (January 1, 2000): 230–7.

Lücke, Friedrich. *Versuch einer vollständigen Einleitung in die Offenbarung des Johannes: oder allgemeine Untersuchungen über die apokalyptische Litteratur überhaupt und die Apokalypse des Johannes insbesondere*. Bonn: Weber., 1852.

Luz, Ulrich. *Matthew 1–7: A Commentary*. Edited by James E Crouch and Helmut Koester. Hermeneia – A Critical and Historical Commentary on the Bible. Minneapolis: Fortress Press, 2007.

Macaskill, Grant. "Matthew and the Parables of Enoch." In *Parables of Enoch: A Paradigm Shift*, edited by Darrell L. Bock and James Charlesworth, 218–30. London: Bloomsbury T&T Clark, 2013.

Machiela, Daniel A. *The Dead Sea Genesis Apocryphon: A New Text and Translation with Introduction and Special Treatment of Columns 13–17*. Leiden: Brill, 2009.

MacRae, George. "The Apocalypse of Adam." In *The Old Testament Pseudepigrapha*, edited by James H. Charlesworth, 1:707–20. London: Darton, Longman & Todd, 1983.

Magness, Jodi. *Masada: From Jewish Revolt to Modern Myth*. Princeton: Princeton University Press, 2019.

Marcus, Joel. *Mark 8–16: A New Translation with Introduction and Commentary*. New Haven: Yale University Press, 2009.

———. "The Testaments of the Twelve Patriarchs and the Didascalia Apostolorum: A Common Jewish Christian Milieu?" *The Journal of Theological Studies* 61, no. 2 (October 2010): 596–626.

Marshall, John W. "6 Ezra and Apocalyptic Judaism in Asia Minor." In *Beyond the Gnostic Gospels: Studies Building on the Work of Elaine Pagels*, edited by Eduard Iricinschi, Lance Jenott, Nicola Denzey Lewis, and Philippa Townsend, 427–45. Tübingen: Mohr Siebeck, 2009.

Mason, Steve. *Flavius Josephus: Translation and Commentary. 1B: Judean War 2*. Leiden: Brill, 2008.

———. *Life of Josephus*. Boston: Brill, 2003.

———. "Nero's War I: The Blunder of Cestius Gallus." In *A History of the Jewish War: AD 66–74*, 281–334. Cambridge: Cambridge University Press, 2016.

———. "What Is History? Using Josephus for the Judaean-Roman War." In *The Jewish Revolt Against Rome: Interdiscplinary Perspectives*, edited by Steve Mason and Mladen Popovic, 155–240. Leiden: Brill, 2011.

———. "Why Did They Do It?: Antecedents, Circumstances, and 'Causes' of the Revolt." In *A History of the Jewish War: AD 66–74*, 199–280. Cambridge: Cambridge University Press, 2016.

Mastnjak, Nathan. *Before the Scrolls: A Material Approach to Israel's Prophetic Library*. Oxford: Oxford University Press, forthcoming.

Mathewson, Dave. *A New Heaven and a New Earth: The Meaning and Function of the Old Testament in Revelation 21.1–22.5*. London: Bloomsbury Publishing, 2003.

McGann, Jerome J. *A Critique of Modern Textual Criticism*. Chicago: University of Chicago Press Chicago, 1983.

McGinn, Bernard. *Visions of the End: Apocalyptic Traditions in the Middle Ages*. New York: Columbia University Press, 1979.

McLaren, James. "Going to War against Rome: The Motivation of the Jewish Rebels." In *The Jewish Revolt against Rome: Interdisciplinary Perspectives*, edited by Mladen Popović, 129–54. Leiden: Brill, 2011.

McLaren, James, and Martin Goodman. "The Importance of Perspective: The Jewish-Roman Conflict of 66–70 CE as a Revolution." In *Revolt and Resistance in the Ancient Classical World and the Near East*, edited by John J. Collins and J. G. Manning, 203–18. Leiden: Brill, 2016.

Meshel, Naphtali S. *The "Grammar" of Sacrifice: A Generativist Study of the Israelite Sacrificial System in the Priestly Writings with the Grammar of [Sigma]*. Oxford: Oxford University Press, 2014.

Meshorer, Ya'akov. *Ancient Jewish Coinage*. Vol. 2. Dix Hills, NY: Amphora Books, 1982.

———. "The Coins of Masada." In *Masada: The Yigael Yadin Excavations, 1963–1965: Final Reports*, 71–128. Jerusalem: Israel Exploration Society, 1989.

Metso, Sarianna, and James M. Tucker. "The Changing Landscape of Editing Ancient Jewish Texts." In *Reading the Bible in Ancient Traditions and Modern Editions: Studies in Textual and Reception History in Memory of Peter W. Flint*, edited by Andrew B. Perrin, Kyung S. Baek, and Daniel K. Falk, 269–88. Atlanta: SBL Press, 2017.

Meyers, Eric M. "Sepphoris: City of Peace." In *The First Jewish Revolt: Archaeology, History and Ideology*, edited by Andrea M. Berlin and J. Andrew Overman, 110–20. London: Routledge, 2003.

Michel, Otto. "Studien Zu Josephus: Simon Bar Giora." *New Testament Studies* 14, no. 3 (April 1968): 402–8.

Milik, Józef T. "Fragments Grecs Du Livre d'Hénoch (P. Oxy. XVII 2069)." *Chronique d'Egypte* 46, no. 92 (1971): 321–43.

———. *Ten Years of Discovery in the Wilderness of Judaea*. Studies in Biblical Theology 26. Naperville, IL: Alec R. Allenson Inc., 1959.

———. "Textes Hébreux et Araméens." In *Les Grottes de Murabba'at*, edited by Pierre Benoit, Roland de Vaux, and Józef T. Milik, 67–205. Discoveries in the Judaean Desert 2. Oxford: Clarendon Press, 1961.

———. *The Books of Enoch: Aramaic Fragments of Qumran Cave 4*. Oxford: Clarendon Press, 1976.

Milikowsky, Chaim. *Seder 'olam: mahadurah mada'it, perush u-mavo*. Jerusalem: Yad Yitshak Ben-Tsevi: Keren ha-Rav David Mosheh ye-'Amalyah Rozen, 2013.

———. "Seder Olam: A Rabbinic Chronography." PhD diss., Yale University, 1981.

Milstein, Sara J. *Tracking the Master Scribe: Revision through Introduction in Biblical and Mesopotamian Literature*. New York: Oxford University Press, 2016.

Modrzejewski, Joseph. *The Jews of Egypt: From Rameses II to Emperor Hadrian*. Princeton: Princeton University Press, 1995.

Momigliano, Arnaldo. "Ciò Che Flavio Giuseppe Non Vide." In *Settimo Contributo Alla Storia Degli Studi Classici e Del Mondo Antico*, 305–17. Rome: Edizioni di Storia e Letteratura, 1984.

———. "What Josephus Did Not See." In *On Pagans, Jews, and Christians*, 108–19. Middletown: Wesleyan University Press, 1987.

Monger, Matthew P. "4Q216: A New Material Analysis." *Semitica* 60 (2018): 309–33.

———. "4Q216 and the State of Jubilees at Qumran." *Revue de Qumran*, no. 4 (2014): 595–612.

———. "4Q216: Rethinking Jubilees in the First Century BCE." PhD diss., MF Norwegian School of Theology, 2018. https://mfopen.mf.no/mf-xmlui/handle/11250/2491963

———. "The Development of Jubilees 1 in the Late Second Temple Period." *Journal for the Study of the Pseudepigrapha* 27, no. 2 (2017): 83–112.

———. "The Many Forms of Jubilees: A Reassessment of the Manuscript Evidence from Qumran and the Lines of Transmission of the Parts and Whole of Jubilees." *Revue de Qumran* 30, no. 2 (2018): 191–211.

Mroczek, Eva. *The Literary Imagination in Jewish Antiquity*. Oxford: Oxford University Press, 2016.

Müller, Karlheinz. *Studien zur frühjüdischen Apokalyptik*. Stuttgart: Verlag Katholisches Bibelwerk, 1991.

Muraoka, T. *A Greek-Hebrew/Aramaic Two-Way Index to the Septuagint*. Paris: Peeters, 2010.

Murmelstein, B. "Das Lamm in Test Jos 19:8." *Zeitschrift für die neutestamentliche Wissenschaft und die Kunde der älteren Kirche* 58, no. 3–4 (1967): 273–9.

Muro, Ernest A. "The Greek Fragments of Enoch From Qumran Cave 7 ('7Q4, 7Q8, & 7Q12=7QEn Gr= Enoch' 103.3–4, 7–8)." *Revue de Qumrân* 18, no. 2 (1997): 307–12.

Nahkola, Aulikki. *Double narratives in the Old Testament: the foundations of method in biblical criticism*. Beihefte zur Zeitschrift für die alttestamentliche Wissenschaft 273. New York: Walter de Gruyter, 2001.

Najman, Hindy. *Seconding Sinai: The Development of Mosaic Discourse in Second Temple Judaism*. Leiden: Brill, 2003.

Najman, Hindy, and Eibert Tigchelaar. "Unity after Fragmentation." *Revue de Qumran* 26, no. 4 (2014): 495–500.

Nati, James. *Textual Criticism and the Ontology of Literature in Early Judaism: An Analysis of the Serekh Ha-Yahad*. Supplements to the Journal for the Study of Judaism 198. Leiden: Brill, 2021.

———. "The Rolling Corpus: Materiality and Pluriformity at Qumran, with Special Consideration of the Serekh Ha-Yaḥad." *Dead Sea Discoveries* 27, no. 2 (2020): 161–201.

Nebe, G. Wilhelm. "'7Q4' – Möglichkeit und Grenze einer Identifikation." *Revue de Qumrân* 13, no. 1/4 (1988): 629–33.

Neujahr, Matthew. *Predicting the Past in the Ancient Near East: Mantic Historiography in Ancient Mesopotamia, Judah, and the Mediterranean World*. Brown Judaic Studies 354. Providence, RI: Brown Judaic Studies, 2012.

———. "When Darius Defeated Alexander: Composition and Redaction in the Dynastic Prophecy." *Journal of Near Eastern Studies* 64, no. 2 (2005): 101–7.

Neusner, Jacob. "Map without Territory: Mishnah's System of Sacrifice and Sanctuary." *History of Religions* 19, no. 2 (1979): 103–27.

Newman, Hillel I. "Dating Sefer Zerubavel: Dehistoricizing and Rehistoricizing a Jewish Apocalypse of Late Antiquity." *Adamantius* 19 (2013): 324–36.

Newsom, Carol A. "Enoch 83–90: The Historical Resume as Biblical Exegesis." Unpublished paper presented at Harvard University Seminar, Harvard, 1975.

———. "The Development of 1 Enoch 6–19: Cosmology and Judgment." *The Catholic Biblical Quarterly* 42, no. 3 (1980): 310–29.

Nichols, Stephen G. "Introduction: Philology in a Manuscript Culture." *Speculum* 65, no. 1 (1990): 1–10.

———. "Why Material Philology? Some Thoughts." *Zeitschrift Für Deutsche Philologie* 116, no. 13 (1997): 12.

Nickelsburg, George W. E. *1 Enoch 1*. Edited by Klaus Baltzer. Hermeneia – A Critical and Historical Commentary on the Bible. Minneapolis, : Fortress Press, 2012.

———. "Apocalyptic and Myth in 1 Enoch 6–11." *Journal of Biblical Literature* 96, no. 3 (1977), 383–405.

———. "Response to Gabrielle Boccaccini." In *George W. E. Nickelsburg in Perspective: An Ongoing Dialogue of Learning*, edited by Jacob Neusner and Alan J. Avery-Peck, 1:133–8. Leiden: Brill, 2003.

———. "The Epistle of Enoch and the Qumran Literature." In *George W. E. Nickelsburg in Perspective: An Ongoing Dialogue of Learning*, edited by Jacob Neusner and Alan J. Avery-Peck, 1:105–22. Leiden: Brill, 2003.

———. "Riches, the Rich, and God's Judgment in 1 Enoch 92–105 and the Gospel According to Luke." *New Testament Studies* 25, no. 3 (1979): 324–44.

———. "The Greek Fragments of '1 Enoch' From Qumran Cave 7: An Unproven Identification." *Revue de Qumrân* 21, no. 4 (2004): 631–4.

Nickelsburg, George W. E. and James C. VanderKam. *1 Enoch: The Hermeneia Translation*. Minneapolis: Fortress Press, 2004.

Niese, Benedikt. *Flavii Iosephi Opera*. Berolini: Apud Weidmannos, 1887.

Nikiprowetsky, Valentin. "Reflexions sur quelques problemes du quatrième et du cinquième livre des Oracles Sibyllins." *Hebrew Union College Annual* 43 (1972): 29–76.

Nir, Rivka. "'And Behold, Lambs Were Born of Those White Sheep' (1 Enoch 90:6) The Color White and Eschatological Expectation in the Animal Apocalypse." *Henoch* 35 (2013): 50–69.

Nongbri, Brent. *God's Library: The Archaeology of the Earliest Christian Manuscripts*. New Haven: Yale University Press, 2018.

Novenson, Matthew V. *The Grammar of Messianism: An Ancient Jewish Political Idiom and Its Users*. New York: Oxford University Press, 2019.

O'Callaghan, José. "¿Papiros neotestamentarios en la Cueva 7 de Qumrān?" *Biblica* 53, no. 1 (1972): 91–100.

Olson, Daniel C. *A New Reading of the Animal Apocalypse of 1 Enoch "All Nations Shall Be Blessed."* Studia in Veteris Testamenti Pseudepigrapha 24. Danvers, MA: Brill, 2013.

O'Neill, J. C. "The Lamb of God in the Testaments of the Twelve Patriarchs." *Journal for the Study of the New Testament* 1, no. 2 (March 1979): 2–30.

Osiek, Carolyn. *Shepherd of Hermas: A Commentary*. Hermeneia – A Critical and Historical Commentary on the Bible. Minneapolis: Fortress Press, 1999.

Paget, James Carleton. *The Epistle of Barnabas: Outlook and Background*. Tübingen: Mohr-Siebeck, 1994.

Pakkala, Juha, Baas ter Haar Romeny, and Reinhard Müller. *Evidence of Editing: Growth and Change of Texts in the Hebrew Bible*. Resources for Biblical Study 75. Atlanta: SBL Press, 2014.

Parker, David C. *The Living Text of the Gospels*. Cambridge: Cambridge University Press, 1997.

Pat-El, Na'ama, and Aren Wilson-Wright. "Features of Archaic Biblical Hebrew and the Linguistic Dating Debate." *Hebrew Studies* 54, no. 1 (2013): 387–410.

Pedersen, Johannes. "Zur erklärung der eschatologischen Visionen Henochs." *Islamica* 2 (1926): 416–29.

Peirano, Irene. *The Rhetoric of the Roman Fake: Latin Pseudepigrapha in Context*. New York: Cambridge University Press, 2012.

Peltonen, Kai. "A Jigsaw without a Model? The Date of Chronicles." In *Did Moses Speak Attic?: Jewish Historiography and Scripture in the Hellenistic Period*, edited by Lester L. Grabbe, 225–72. London: Bloomsbury Publishing, 2001.

Perrin, Andrew B. "Dream Visions (1 Enoch 83–84)." In *T&T Clark Encyclopedia of Second Temple Judaism*, edited by Loren T. Stuckenbruck and Daniel Gurtner, 175–6. London: Bloomsbury Publishing, 2020.

Person, R. F., and R. C. Rezetko. "Introduction: The Importance of Empirical Models to Assess the Efficacy of Source and Redaction Criticism." In *Empirical Models Challenging Biblical Criticism*, edited by R. F. Person and R. C. Rezetko. Atlanta: SBL Press, 2016.

Petitmengin, Pierre. "La Compilation 'De Uindictis Magnis Magnorum Peccatorum' Exemples d'anthropophagie Tirés Des Sièges de Jérusalem et de Samarie." In *Philologia Sacra. Biblische Und Patristische Studien Für Hermann J. Frede Und Walter Thiele Zu Ihrem Siebzigsten Geburtstag. Band II: Apokryphen, Kirchenväter, Verschiedenes*, edited by Roger Gryson, Hermann Josef Frede, and Walter Thiele, 622–38. Freiburg, 1993.

Philippi, Ferdinand. *Das Buch Henoch: sein Zeitalter und sein Verhältniss zum Judasbriefe: ein Beitrag zur neutestamentlichen Isagogik: nebst einem Anhange über Judä V. 9 und dis Mosesprophetie*. Stuttgart: S.G. Liesching, 1868.

Portier-Young, Anathea. *Apocalypse Against Empire: Theologies of Resistance in Early Judaism*. Wm. B. Eerdmans Publishing, 2011.

Prigent, Pierre. "Introduction." In *Épître de Barnabé*, 9–66. Paris: Éditions du Cerf, 1971.

Puech, Émile. "Sept fragments grecs de la 'Lettre D'Hénoch' ('1 Hén' 100, 103 et 105) dans la Grotte 7 de Qumrân (= '7QHéngr')." *Revue de Qumrân* 18, no. 2 (1997): 313–23.

Rajak, Tessa. "Jewish Millenarian Expectations." In *The First Jewish Revolt: Archaeology, History, and Ideology*, edited by Andrea M. Berlin and J. Andrew Overman, 164–88. London: Routledge, 2002.

———. "Cio Che Flavio Giuseppe Vide: Josephus and the Essenes." In *Josephus and the History of the Greco-Roman Period*, 141–60. Leiden: Brill, 1994.

———. "Friends, Romans, Subjects: Agrippa II's Speech in Josephus' Jewish War." In *Jewish Dialogue with Greece and Rome: Studies in Cultural and Social Interaction*. Leiden: Brill, 2000.

Rappaport, Uriel. "Jewish-Pagan Relations and the Revolt against Rome in 66–70 CE." *Jerusalem Cathedra* 1 (1981): 81–95.

Ratzon, Eshbal. "The First Jewish Astronomers: Lunar Theory and Reconstruction of a Dead Sea Scroll." *Science in Context* 30 (June 1, 2017): 113–39.
Redmond, Sheila A. "The Date and Provenance of the Fourth Sibylline Oracle." Master's thesis, University of Ottawa, 1985.
———. "The Date of the Fourth Sibylline Oracle." *Second Century: A Journal of Early Christian Studies* 7, no. 3 (Fall 1989–1990): 129–50.
Reed, Annette Yoshiko. *Demons, Angels, and Writing in Ancient Judaism*. Cambridge: Cambridge University Press, 2020.
———. *Fallen Angels and the History of Judaism and Christianity: The Reception of Enochic Literature*. New York: Cambridge University Press, 2005.
———. *Jewish-Christianity and the history of Judaism: collected essays*. Texte und Studien zum antiken Judentum 171. Tübingen: Mohr Siebeck, 2018.
———. "The Textual Identity, Literary History, and Social Setting of 1 Enoch." *Archiv Für Religionsgeschichte* 5, no. 1 (2003): 279–96.
Reese, Günter. *Die Geschichte Israels in der Auffassung des frühen Judentums: Eine Untersuchung der Tiervision und der Zehnwochenapokalypse des äthiopischen Henochbuches, der Geschichtsdarstellung der Assumptio Mosis und der des 4Esrabuches*. SBAB. Berlin: Philo, 1999.
Reeves, John C. "An Enochic Citation in Barnabas 4:3 and the Oracles of Hystaspes." *Pursuing the Text: Studies in Honor of Ben Zion Wacholder on the Occasion of His Seventieth Birthday*. Sheffield: Sheffield Academic Press, 1992, 260–77.
Reeves, John, and Annette Yoshiko Reed. *Enoch from Antiquity to the Middle Ages. Vol. 1. Sources from Judaism, Christianity, and Islam*. Kettering: Oxford University Press, 2017.
Regev, Eyal. "The Ram and Qumran: The Eschatological Character of the Ram in the Animal Apocalypse (1 En. 90: 10–13)." In *Apocalyptic Thinking in Early Judaism: Engaging with John Collins' The Apocalyptic Imagination*, edited by Sidnie White Crawford and Cecilia Wassen, 181. Supplements to the Journal for the Study of Judaism 182. Leiden: Brill, 2018.
Reicke, Bo. "Official and Pietistic Elements of Jewish Apocalypticism." *Journal of Biblical Literature* 79, no. 2 (1960): 137–50.
Reid, Stephen Breck. *Enoch and Daniel: A Form Critical and Sociological Study of the Historical Apocalypses*. BIBAL Monograph Series 2. Berkeley, CA: BIBAL Press, 1989.
Rezetko, Robert, and Ian Young. "Currents in the Historical Linguistics and Linguistic Dating of the Hebrew Bible: Report on the State of Research as Reflected in Recent Major Publications." *HIPHIL Novum* 5, no. 1 (July 2, 2019): 3–95.
Richey, Madadh, David S. Vanderhooft, and Oded Lipschits. "Two Private Babylonian Period Stamp Impressions from Ramat Rahel." *Maarav* 23, no. 2 (2019): 289–306.
Ringe, Sharon. "A Gentile Woman's Story, Revisited." In *A Feminist Companion to Mark*, edited by Amy-Jill Levine, 79–100. Sheffield: Sheffield Academic Press, 2001.
Robinson, H. Russell. *The Armour of Imperial Rome*. New York: Scribner, 1975.
Robinson, John A. T. *Redating the New Testament*. London: S.C.M. Press, 1976.
Rofé, Alexander. "Not Exile but Annihilation for Zedekiah's People: The Purport of Jeremiah 52 in the Septuagint." In *VIII Congress of the International Organization for Septuagint and Cognate Studies, Paris 1992*, edited by Leonard Greenspoon and O. Munnich, 165–70. Atlanta: Scholars Press, 1995.
Rogers, Guy MacLean. *For the Freedom of Zion: The Great Revolt of Jews Against Romans 66–74 CE*. New Haven: Yale University Press, 2022.
Rosenstiehl, Jean Marc. *L'Apocalypse d'Élie: Introduction, Traduction et Notes*. Paris: Paul Geuthner, 1972.
Rothschild, Clare K. "Ethiopianising the Devil: Ὁ Μέλας in Barnabas 4." *New Testament Studies* 65, no. 2 (April 2019): 223–45.

Sanders, E. P. *Paul and Palestinian Judaism: A Comparison of Patterns of Religion*. Minneapolis: Fortress Press, 1977.
Schäfer, Peter. *Hekhalot-Studien*. Texte und Studien zum antiken Judentum 19. Tübingen: Mohr Siebeck, 1988.
———. "Research into Rabbinic Literature: An Attempt to Define the Status Quaestionis." *Journal of Jewish Studies* 37, no. 2 (1986): 139–52.
———, ed. *The Bar Kokhba War Reconsidered: New Perspectives on the Second Jewish Revolt against Rome*. Tübingen: Mohr Siebeck, 2003.
———. *The Hidden and Manifest God: Some Major Themes in Early Jewish Mysticism*. Albany: State University of New York Press, 1992.
Schodde, George Henry. *The Book of Enoch: Translated from the Ethiopic, with Introduction and Notes, by . . . G.H. Schodde, Etc.* Andover, MA: W. F. Draper, 1882.
Schultz, Brian. "Not Greeks but Romans: Changing Expectations for the Eschatological War in the War Texts from Qumran." In *The Jewish Revolt against Rome: Interdisciplinary Perspectives*, edited by Mladen Popović, 107–28. Leiden: Brill, 2011.
Schürer, Emil. "Das Buch Henoch." In *Lehrbuch Der Neutestamentlichen Zeitgeschichte*, 521–35. Leipzig: J.C. Hinrichs, 1874.
———. "The Book of Enoch." In *A History of the Jewish People in the Time of Jesus Christ*, translated by Peter Christie, 3.2:59–73. New York: Charles Scribner's Sons, 1891.
Schwartz, Daniel R. "On Some Papyri and Josephus' Sources and Chronology for the Persian Period," *Journal for the Study of Judaism in the Persian, Hellenistic, and Roman Period* 21, no. 2 (1990): 175-199.
———. "Introduction: Was 70 CE a Watershed in Jewish History? Three Stages of Modern Scholarship, and a Renewed Effort." In *Was 70 CE a Watershed in Jewish History?: On Jews and Judaism Before and after the Destruction of the Second Temple*, edited by Daniel R. Schwartz and Zeev Weiss, 1–19. Leiden: Brill, 2012.
Schwartz, Seth. *Josephus and Judaean Politics*. Columbia Studies in the Classical Tradition 18. New York: Brill, 1990.
Shukster, Martin B., and Peter Richardson. "Temple and Bet Ha-Midrash in the Epistle of Barnabas." In *Anti-Judaism in Early Christianity. Volume 2. Separation and Polemic*, edited by Stephen G. Wilson, Peter Richardson, and David M. Granskou, 17–32. Waterloo: Wilfred Laurier University Press, 1986.
Shuttleworth Kraus, Christina. "From Exempla to Exemplar? Writing History around the Emperor in Imperial Rome." In *Flavius Josephus and Flavian Rome*, edited by Jonathan Edmondson, Steve Mason, and James Rives, 181–200. Oxford: Oxford University Press, 2005.
Sims, David C. "Matthew 22.13 a and 1 Enoch 10.4 a: A Case of Literary Dependence?" *Journal for the Study of the New Testament* 15, no. 47 (1992): 3–19.
Sirat, Colette. "Les manuscrits en caractères hébraïques: réalités d'hier et historie d'aujourd'hui." *Scrittura e Civiltà*, no. 10 (1986): 239–88.
———. "Les rouleaux bibliques de Qumrân au Moyen Âge: du Livre au Sefer Tora, de l'oreille à l'œil." *Comptes rendus des séances de l'Académie des Inscriptions et Belles-Lettres* 135, no. 2 (1991): 415–32.
Skoven, Anne Vig. "Mark as allegorical rewriting of Paul: Gustav Volkmar's understanding of the gospel of Mark." In *Mark and Paul: Comparative Essays Part II. For and Against Pauline Influence on Mark*, edited by Eve-Marie Becker, Troels Engberg-Pedersen, and Mogens Müller, 13–27. Arbeiten zur Geschichte des antiken Judentums und des Urchristentums 8. Berlin: De Gruyter, 2014.
Smallwood, E. Mary. *The Jews Under Roman Rule: From Pompey to Diocletian: A Study in Political Relations*. Leiden: Brill, 2001.

Sommer, Benjamin D. "Dating Pentateuchal Texts and the Perils of Pseudo-Historicism." In *The Pentateuch: International Perspectives on Current Research*, edited by Thomas B. Dozeman, Konrad Schmid, and Baruch J. Schwartz, 85–108. Forschungen Zum Alten Testament 78. Tübingen: Mohr Siebeck, 2011.

Spottorno, Maria Victoria. "Can Methodological Limits Be Set in the Debate on the Identification of 7Q5?" *Dead Sea Discoveries* 6, no. 1 (1999): 66–77.

Stanton, Vincent Henry. *The Jewish and the Christian Messiah: A Study in the Earliest History*. Edinburgh: T&T Clark, 1886.

Stern, Menahem. "The Relations between Judea and Rome during the Rule of John Hyrcanus / יוחנן הורקנוס בימי ורומא יהודה בין היחסים על." *Zion* 26, no. 1 (1961): 1–22.

Stewart Lester, Olivia. *Prophetic Rivalry, Gender, and Economics: A Study in Revelation and Sibylline Oracles 4–5*. Wissenschaftliche Untersuchungen zum Neuen Testament 2nd ser, vol. 466. Tübingen: Mohr Siebeck, 2018.

———. "The Four Kingdoms Motif and Sibylline Temporality in Sibylline Oracles 4." In *Four Kingdom Motifs before and beyond the Book of Daniel*, edited by Andrew B. Perrin and Loren T. Stuckenbruck, 121–41. Themes in Biblical Narrative 28. Brill, 2020.

Stoffregen-Pedersen, Kirsten, and Tedros Abraha. "Andəmta." In *Encyclopaedia Aethiopica*, edited by Siegbert Uhlig and Alessandro Baussi, 1:258–9. Wiesbaden: Harrassowitz Verlag, 2003.

Stone, Michael E. "The Book of Enoch and Judaism in the Third Century B.C.E." *The Catholic Biblical Quarterly* 40, no. 4 (1978): 479–92.

———. *An Editio Minor of the Armenian Version of the Testaments of the Twelve Patriarchs*. Hebrew University Armenian Studies 11. Leuven: Peeters, 2012.

———. *Apocrypha, Pseudepigrapha and Armenian Studies: Collected Papers*. 2 vols. Orientalia Lovaniensia Analecta 144–5. Dudley, MA: Peeters, 2006.

———. "Enoch's Date in Limbo: Or: Some Considerations on David Suter's Analysis of the Book of Parables." In *Enoch and the Messiah Son of Man*, edited by Gabriele Boccaccini, 444–9. Grand Rapids, MI: Eerdmans, 2007.

———. *Fourth Ezra: A Commentary on the Book of Fourth Ezra*. Hermeneia – A Critical and Historical Commentary on the Bible. Minneapolis: Fortress Press, 1990.

———. *The Armenian Version of the Testament of Joseph: Introduction, Critical Edition, and Translation*. Texts and Translations 6. Missoula, MT: Scholars Press for the Society of Biblical Literature, 1975.

———. "The Genealogy of Bilhah." *Dead Sea Discoveries* 3, no. 1 (January 1, 1996): 20–36.

Stone, Michael E., and Matthias Henze. *4 Ezra and 2 Baruch: Translations, Introductions, and Notes*. Minneapolis: Fortress, 2013.

Stuckenbruck, Loren T. "'Reading the Present' in the Animal Apocalypse (1 Enoch 85–90)." In *Reading the Present in the Qumran Library: The Perception of the Contemporary by Means of Scriptural Interpretations*, edited by Kristen De Troyer and Armin Lange, 91–103. Atlanta: SBL Press, 2005.

———. "The Book of Enoch: Its Reception in Second Temple Jewish and in Christian Tradition." *Early Christianity* 4 (2013): 7–40.

———. *1 Enoch 91–108*. Berlin: De Gruyter, 2007.

———. "The Early Traditions Related To 1 Enoch From The Dead Sea Scrolls: An Overview And Assessment." In *The Early Enoch Literature*, edited by Gabriele Boccaccini and John J. Collins, 41–64. Supplements to the Journal for the Study of Judaism 121. Leiden: Brill, 2007.

Suetonius. *Lives of the Caesars*. Translated by J. C. Rolfe. Vol. 2. Loeb Classical Library 38. Cambridge, MA: Harvard University Press, 1914.

Suter, David W. "Fallen Angel, Fallen Priest: The Problem of Family Purity in 1 Enoch 6–16." *Hebrew Union College Annual* 50 (1979): 115–35.

Szkołut, Paweł. "The Eagle as a Symbol of Divine Presence and Protection in Ancient Jewish Art." *Studia Judaica (Krakow)* 5 (2002): 1–11.
Tacitus. *Histories: Books 4–5. Annals: Books 1–3*. Translated by Clifford H. Moore and John Jackson. Loeb Classical Library 249. Cambridge, MA: Harvard University Press, 1931.
Tanselle, George Thomas. *A Rationale of Textual Criticism*. Philadelphia: University of Pennsylvania Press, 1992.
Teeter, Andrew, and William A. Tooman. "Standards of (In) Coherence in Ancient Jewish Literature." *Hebrew Bible and Ancient Israel* 9, no. 2 (2020): 94–129.
Thiessen, Matthew. "Paul, the Animal Apocalypse, and Abraham's Gentile Seed." In *The Ways That Often Parted: Essays in Honor of Joel Marcus*, edited by Lori Baron, Jill Hicks-Keeton, and Matthew Thiessen, 65–79. Atlanta: SBL Press, 2018.
Tigchelaar, Eibert. "Constructing, Deconstructing and Reconstructing Fragmentary Manuscripts: Illustrated by a Study of 4Q184 (4QWiles of the Wicked Woman)." In *Rediscovering the Dead Sea Scrolls: An Assessment of Old and New Approaches and Methods*, edited by Maxine Grossman, 26–47. Grand Rapids, MI: Eerdmans, 2010.
———. "The Qumran 'Jubilees' Manuscripts as Evidence for the Literary Growth of the Book." *Revue de Qumran* 26, no. 4 (2014): 579–94.
———. "Working with Few Data: The Relation between 4Q285 and 11Q14." *Dead Sea Discoveries* 7, no. 1 (2000): 49–56.
Tigchelaar, E.J.C, and Florentino García Martínez. "4QAstronomical Enoch." In *Qumran Cave 4 XVI: Miscellanea, Part I*, 95–172. Discoveries in the Judaean Desert. Oxford: Clarendon Press, 2000.
Tiller, Patrick A. *A Commentary on the Animal Apocalypse of I Enoch*. Atlanta: Scholars Press, 1993.
Tite, Philip L. "Textual and Redactional Aspects of the Book of Dreams (1 Enoch 83–90)." *Biblical Theology Bulletin* 31, no. 3 (2001): 106–20.
Tolkien, J. R. R. "On Fairy-Stories." In *The Monsters and the Critics: And Other Essays*, edited by Christopher Tolkien, 109–62. Croydon: HarperCollins, 2006.
Tomasino, Anthony J. "Oracles of Insurrection: The Prophetic Catalyst of the Great Revolt." *The Journal of Jewish Studies* 59, no. 1 (2008): 86–111.
Torrey, Charles C. "Alexander Jannaeus and the Archangel Michael." *Vetus Testamentum* 4, no. 2 (1954): 208–11.
Trachsler, Richard. "How to Do Things with Manuscripts: From Humanist Practice to Recent Textual Criticism." *Textual Cultures*, 2006, 5–28.
Trebolle Barrera, Julio. "4Q49: 4QJudges a." In *Discoveries in the Judaean desert. Qumran cave 4, IX: Deuteronomy, Joshua, Judges, Kings XIV*, edited by Eugene Ulrich and Frank Moore Cross, 161–4. Oxford: Clarendon Press, 1995.
Uhlig, Siegbert. *Das äthiopische Henochbuch*. Gütersloh: Gütersloher Verlagshaus, 1984.
Ulrich, Eugene. *The Dead Sea Scrolls and the Developmental Composition of the Bible*. Supplements to Vetus Testamentum 169. Boston: Brill, 2015.
Van Henten, Jan Willem. "Ruler or God? The Demolition of Herod's Eagle." In *The New Testament and Early Christian Literature in Greco-Roman Context: Studies in Honor of David A. Aune*, edited by John Fotopolous, 257–87. Leiden: Brill, 2010.
Van Minnen, Peter. "The Greek Apocalypse of Peter." In *The Apocalypse of Peter*, edited by J. N. Bremmer and I. Czachesz, Studies on Early Christian Apocrypha 7, 15–39. Leuven: Peeters, 2003.
VanderKam, James C. *1 Enoch 2: A Commentary on the Book of 1 Enoch: Chapters 37–82*. Hermeneia – A Critical and Historical Commentary on the Bible. Minneapolis: Fortress Press, 2012.
———. *Enoch and the Growth of an Apocalyptic Tradition*. Catholic Biblical Quarterly Monograph Series. Washington, DC: Catholic Biblical Association of America, 1984.

———. "Open and Closed Eyes in the Animal Apocalypse (1 Enoch 85–90)." In *The Idea of Biblical Interpretation: Essays in Honor of James L. Kugel*, edited by Hindy Najman and Judith Newman, 279–92. Leiden: Brill, 2004.

Verheyden, Joseph. "Evidence of 1 Enoch 10:4 in Matthew 22:13?" In *Flores Florentino: Dead Sea Scrolls and Other Early Jewish Studies in Honour of Florentino García Martínez*, edited by Anthony Hilhorst, Émile Puech, and Eibert Tigchelaar, 449–66. Leiden: Brill, 2007.

Volkmar, Gustav. "Beiträge zur Erklärung des Buches Henoch: nach dem äthiopischen Text." *Zeitschrift der Deutschen Morgenländischen Gesellschaft* 14, no. 1/2 (1860): 87–296.

———. *Eine Neu-Testamentliche Entdeckung und deren Bestreitung: oder, die Geschichts-Vision des Buches Henoch im Zusammenhang*. Zurich: Kiesling, 1862.

———. "Über die katholischen Briefe und Henoch." *Zeitschrift für wissenschaftliche Theologie* 4 (1861): 422–36.

Walbank, F. W., and Christian Habicht, eds. *Polybius: The Histories, Books 5–8*. Translated by W. R. Paton. Vol. 3. Loeb Classical Library 138. Cambridge, MA: Harvard University Press, 2011.

Walck, Leslie W. *The Son of Man in the Parables of Enoch and in Matthew*. Jewish and Christian Texts in Contexts and Related Studies 9. London: T&T Clark, 2011.

Ward, Graeme A. "'By Any Other Name': Disgrace, Defeat, and the Loss of Legionary History." In *Brill's Companion to Military Defeat in Ancient Mediterranean Society*, edited by Jessica H. Clark and Brian Turner, 284–308. Leiden: Brill, 2018.

Wechsler, Michael G., ed. *Evangelium Iohannis Aethiopicum*. Corpus scriptorum Christianorum Orientalium 617. Leuven: Peeters, 2005.

Werman, Cana. "Epochs and End-Time: The 490-Year Scheme in Second Temple Literature." *Dead Sea Discoveries* 13, no. 2 (2006): 229–55.

Wiedemann, T. E. J. "Tiberius to Nero." In *The Augustan Empire, 43 BC–AD 69*, edited by Alan K. Bowman, Edward Champlin, and Andrew Lintott, 198–255. The Cambridge Ancient History 10. 2nd ed. Cambridge: Cambridge University Press, 1996.

Wilker, Julia. "'God Is with Italy Now' Pro-Roman Jews and the Jewish Revolt." In *Jewish Identity and Politics between the Maccabees and Bar Kokhba*, edited by Benedikt Eckhardt, 157–87. Leiden: Brill, 2012.

———. "Josephus, the Herodians, and the Jewish War." In *The Jewish Revolt against Rome*, edited by Mladen Popović, 271–89. Leiden: Brill, 2011.

Williamson, H. G. M. "The Historical Value of Josephus' 'Jewish Antiquities' XI.297–301." *The Journal of Theological Studies* 28, no. 1 (1977): 49–66.

Yamauchi, Edwin M. *Pre-Christian Gnosticism: A Survey of the Proposed Evidences*. 2nd ed. Grand Rapids, MI: Baker Book House, 1983.

Zahn, Molly M. *Genres of Rewriting in Second Temple Judaism: Scribal Composition and Transmission*. Cambridge: Cambridge University Press, 2020.

Index

1 Enoch
   Aramaic, 48–9
   five books, 9–10, 17
   New Testament, 33–4, 96, 126, 162, 220
   19th-century proposals for date, 96–8
   subsidiary works and attestation in manuscripts, 11–28

2 Baruch
   destruction of Jerusalem, 174–6
   parallels with Apocalypse of the Birds, 218–19

4 Ezra
   dating, 160
   eagles, 163–4
   parallels with Apocalypse of the Birds, 218–19
   twelve wings, 101, 160–1

Animal Apocalypse (1 Enoch 85–90)
   Codex Vaticanus Graecus, 27, 40, 47, 49, 62, 77, 105
   double narration of destruction of Jerusalem, 41, 55–60, 76
   Hasmonean hypothesis, 96
   P. Oxy 2069, 26–7, 31, 40, 136
   Qumran manuscripts, 68–72
   seventy–shepherd schema, 51–2
   terminological differences, 61–3
   textual stability, 49–51

Apocalypse of the Birds (1 Enoch 89.59–90.42)
   absence from Qumran, 68–72
   chronology, 98–102
   comparison of Maccabean and Roman hypotheses, 210–12
   destruction of Jerusalem, 174–6, 219
   'dogs' as non-Jewish neighbors, 181–2
   eagles as Macedonians, 157
   eagles as Rome, 146, 156–70
   house symbolism, 45, 111, 171–3, 177, 219, 241
   in first-century context, 216–20
   knowledge of 70 CE, 170–8
   Maccabean hypothesis, 92–3
   messianic figure, 123–9, 222–3
   optimism, 204
   original language, 62, 73
   parallels with Daniel, 150–2
   Persian and Hellenistic period, 147–53
   religious reformer hypothesis, 93–4
   source of bird symbolism, 167–9
   universalism, 78, 124

Astronomical Book (1 Enoch 72–82)
   Aramaic and Ethiopic versions, 16
   date, 88–9
   title, 9–10

Bar Kokhba Revolt
   as setting for Apocalypse of the Birds, 213–15
   dating of Epistle of Barnabas, 107
   Volkmar's dating of 1 Enoch 97, 100, 167

Book of Dreams (1 Enoch 83–90)
   attestation of subsidiary works, 26–8, 136
   Flood Vision (1 En 83–84), 28, 34, 39, 224–5

Book of Jubilees
  Non-reader of the Apocalypse of the Birds, 135–8
  unified composition or anthology, 10
  Qumran fragments and compositional history, 28–2, 72
Book of Parables (1 Enoch 37–71)
  absence from Qumran, 16, 28
  date, 221
  New Testament, 33, 96, 172
  possible Christian authorship, 35–6, 97
  title, 9–10
Book of the Watchers (1 Enoch 1–36)
  attestation of subsidiary works, 17–23
  date, 85–7
  title, 9–10

dabela (ram)
  Apocalypse of the Birds, 194–6
  Coptic Apocalypse of Elijah, 137
  Daniel, 151
Daniel
  chronology, 44, 100–1, 148, 154–5
  parallels with Apocalypse of the Birds, 150–2
dating
  compression of the Persian period in ancient Jewish historiography, 153–6
  with reference to destruction of Jerusalem, 143
  methodology of historical-allusional dating, 16, 37, 50, 107, 139–45, 221
  vaticinium ex eventu, 50, 140–1, 161, 220
dogs as non-Jewish neighbors, 179–82, 184, 212

Egypt
  Alexandrian massacre of 66 CE, 183, 197
  ibises, 167–8, 182–6, 196–7, 238
Epistle of Barnabas, 106–9
  Alexandrian provenance, 107
  destruction of Jerusalem, 111
  as reader of Enoch, 108–9
Epistle of Enoch (1 Enoch 91–108)
  attestation of subsidiary works, 23–6
  missing subsidiary works and New Testament, 32–4
  subsidiary works, 18–20
  title, 9–10
Ethiopian contexts for Enoch
  Andəmta, 95, 125, 127, 137
  Ethiopian Orthodox Church, 6, 31
  manuscript tradition, 2, 48

First Jewish Revolt
  Alexandrian massacre, 183
  apocalypticism, 207
  avian sacrifice (66 CE), 169
  Battle of Beth Horon, 185, 201–3, 212, 239
  campaign of Cestius Gallus, 187–8, 191–2, 197–9, 201
  Gessius Florus, 183
  leaders, 195–6
  Legio XII Fulminata, 187, 202
  messianic and apocalyptic thought, 207
  optimism after 66 CE, 205
  origins of resistance, 186–91
  Pro-Roman Jews, 185, 189–90
  ravens as legionary forces, 191–4
  Roman loss of eagle standard, 202–4
  Simon Bar Giora, 188, 195–6
  Syrian legionary coalition, 188, 191, 199
  urban turmoil in Syria, 182–3

Gospel of Mark
  dating, 143, 176, 178
  dogs and Canaanite woman, 181–2
  endings, 73
Gospel of Matthew
  dogs and Syrophoenician woman, 181–2
  eagles, 161–2
  relationship with 1 Enoch, 162
Gospel of John
  parallel phrasing with the Apocalypse of the Birds, 127

Heikhalot literature, 32, 227–8, 245

Jewish-Christianity, 114, 223–4
Jewish texts in Christian transmission, 4, 30–6, 221–3
Josephus
  perspective contrary to Apocalypse of the Birds, 206–7

referent of ambiguous oracle (War 6.312), 208–9
reliability of account of First Jewish Revolt, 179
Romans and eagles, 164–5

"Little Animal Apocalypse", 15, 229, 231–4

New Jerusalem
  Apocalypse of the Birds, 170–4, 219
  Revelation, 173–4, 219
  Testaments of the Twelve Patriarchs, 116–17
New Philology
  source criticism, 226–8
  work, text, document, 4–8, 39–40

Paul, 15, 124, 213, 220–2
pseudepigrapha, Christological readings, 35, 95, 122–9, 222–3

Revelation
  dating, 178
  function of apocalyptic literature, 204
  parallels with Apocalypse of the Birds, 110, 218–19
  parallels with the Little Animal Apocalypse, 231
  presence of Temple in New Jerusalem, 173–4
  repetition and composition, 64–5

Seder Olam Rabbah, 154–5
Seleucid Empire
  Fourth-period antagonists in Apocalypse of the Birds, 92, 101, 157–8
  Third-period antagonists in Apocalypse of the Birds, 150–3
Sibylline Oracles, 30, 74–5, 219
source criticism
  apocalyptic literature, 64–6
  coherence, 6–7, 10, 65–6
  New Philology, 226–8
  pseudepigrapha, 41
  updating endings, 73–5

Testaments of the Twelve Patriarchs
  Armenian Testament of Joseph, 229–33
  common elements in passages attributed to Enoch, 115–18
  dating, 114–15
  destruction of Jerusalem, 116–18
  Testament of Benjamin, 115–22, 129–30
  Testament of Levi, 115–20, 130–2
Tolkien, J. R. R., 5–7, 218, 234–5

Vision of the Beasts (1 Enoch 85.1–89.58)
  Aramaic, 87–8
  Chronicles, 89–90
  dating, 83–90
  Qumran manuscripts, 68–72

EU representative:
Easy Access System Europe
Mustamäe tee 50, 10621 Tallinn, Estonia
Gpsr.requests@easproject.com

www.ingramcontent.com/pod-product-compliance
Lightning Source LLC
Chambersburg PA
CBHW050213240426
43671CB00013B/2314